Writing Liverpool

WRITING LIVERPOOL
Essays and Interviews

Edited by
MICHAEL MURPHY
and
DERYN REES-JONES

Liverpool University Press

First published 2007 by
Liverpool University Press
4 Cambridge Street
Liverpool L69 7ZU

British Library Cataloguing-in-Publication data
A British Library CIP record is available

ISBN 978-1-84631-073-7 cased
978-1-84631-074-4 limp

Typeset in Bembo by XL Publishing Services Ltd, Tiverton
Printed and bound in the European Union by Bell and Bain Ltd, Glasgow

Contents

Acknowledgements

The editors would like to thank Anthony Cond, commissioning editor at Liverpool University Press, for his support and encouragement; the advisers consulted by the Press for their helpful comments and suggestions; Paul Leahy for all his many kindnesses, not least of which was the use of *Greythorn* in Mayo; Gladys and Terry Murphy and Angela and David Rees-Jones for childcare; and Simon and Jenny Craske for their friendship.

The editors are grateful to Alan Bleasdale, Terence Davies, Linda Grant, Roger McGough, Willy Russell and Levi Tafari for the generosity and openness they brought to being interviewed.

An earlier version of Chapter 2 appered in Patrick J. Quinn (ed.), *Recharting the Thirties* (Susquehanna University Press, 1996). A version of Chapter 1 first appeared on the website of the Centre for Political Song, Glasgow Caledonian University (www.caledonian.ac.uk/politicalsong).

It was a great honour and a privilege to be involved in editing this book. For making it an enormous pleasure, we would like to thank all our contributors.

List of Contributors

Chris Ackerley is Professor and former Head of Department at Otago University, New Zealand. His speciality is annotation. He is co-author of the recent Grove Press and Faber *Companion to Samuel Beckett*, and has published widely on Malcolm Lowry. His *Companion to Under the Volcano* (1984), the standard commentary, is complemented by a recent website devoted to Lowry's masterpiece.

Peter Barry is Professor of English, University of Wales, Aberystwyth, and reviews and poetry editor for *English* (the journal of the English Association). His books include *Contemporary British Poetry and the City* (2000), *Beginning Theory* (2nd edition 2002), *English in Practice* (2003), *Poetry Wars* (2006) and *Literature in Contexts* (2007).

John Bennett is Senior Lecturer in Drama and Theatre Studies at Liverpool Hope University. He researches in the field of Contemporary Popular Theatre, and has published a comparative analysis of the work of John Godber's Hull Truck Theatre Company (*Studies in Theatre and Performance*, 26.3). His next project is a book examining regional influences on playwrights such as Godber and Willy Russell.

Helen Carr is Emeritus Professor of English and was Pro-Warden (Academic) at Goldsmiths, University of London. Her publications include *Inventing the American Primitive* and *Jean Rhys*, and she is a co-editor of *Women: A Cultural Review*. She grew up in Liverpool, where her father taught Semitic Languages at the University of Liverpool.

Sandra Courtman teaches literature and creative writing at the

University of Sheffield. Her doctorate was on West Indian women's writing of the 1960s and 1970s. She has published research on working-class and migrant writing of the 1970s and a multi-disciplinary collection, *Beyond the Blood, the Beach and the Banana: New Perspectives in Caribbean Studies* (2004).

Ralph Crane is Professor of English and Head of the School of English, Journalism and European Languages at the University of Tasmania, Australia. He has published widely on Anglo-Indian (Raj) fiction, Indian English fiction, and J.G. Farrell. His work on Farrell includes two books: *Troubled Pleasures: The Fiction of J.G. Farrell* (with Jennifer Livett) and *J.G. Farrell: The Critical Grip* (editor). He is currently preparing a scholarly edition of A.E.W. Mason's *The Broken Road* for Oxford University Press India as part of a larger 'Raj Recovery Project'.

Paul du Noyer left Liverpool for the London School of Economics, then wrote for the *NME*, edited *Q Magazine*, founded *Mojo*, helped invent *Heat*, and is now Contributing Editor of *The Word*. His books include *We All Shine On: Stories behind John Lennon's Songs* (1997), and *Liverpool: Wondrous Place – Music from the Cavern to the Coral* (new edition 2004), the definitive history of his home town's music scene.

Julia Hallam teaches film and television at the University of Liverpool; her publications include numerous articles on television drama and a monograph, *Lynda La Plante* (Manchester University Press, 2005). She is a contributing editor to *Critical Studies in Television* and principal researcher on the AHRC-funded 'City in Film' project.

Michael Murphy teaches English Literature at Nottingham Trent University. He is the author of two collections of poetry, and his poems appear in *The New Irish Poets*, ed. Selina Guinness (2004). His critical books include *Poetry and Exile* (2004) and *James Joyce* (2004). A monograph on Marcel Proust, *Proust and America*, is published by Liverpool University Press (2007).

Terry Phillips is Dean of Arts and Humanities at Liverpool Hope University. She has published several articles on women's writing, and has additional research interests in First World War writing and Irish Literature, on both of which she has also published.

Joseph Pridmore completed his PhD, 'Fiction and Subversion in the 1930s', at Nottingham Trent University in 2005. He has been published in *The European English Messenger, Critical Survey* and *The Penniless Press*, and is co-editor of *Textual Variations: The Impact of Textual Issues on Literary Studies* (University of Leicester, 2006).

Deryn Rees-Jones teaches English at the University of Liverpool. Her *Consorting with Angels* and *Modern Women Poets: An Anthology* were published by Bloodaxe in 2005. She is the author of three collections of poetry, most recently *Quiver*, a murder mystery set in Liverpool that explores the nature of creativity.

Andy Sawyer is the librarian of the Science Fiction Foundation Collection at the University of Liverpool Library, and Course Director of the MA in Science Fiction Studies offered by the School of English. He is also Reviews Editor of *Foundation: The International Review of Science Fiction* and has published numerous essays and articles on science fiction and fantasy.

Philip Smith is a filmmaker whose work has been shown by UK, European and American broadcasters, and includes the BAFTA and Royal Television Society award winning series *This Is Modern Art* (Channel 4). He has recently directed drama-documentaries for C4, BBC and ITV as well as the film *Superfly*, which traced the history of a century of genetics. *Superfly* won a Royal Television Society award in 2003. His earlier work includes five years as a producer on BBC 2's innovative arts and media programme *The Late Show,* during which time he occasionally reviewed writing on film and television for the *Times Literary Supplement*.

Stan Smith holds the Research Chair in Literary Studies at Nottingham Trent University. His recent books include *The Cambridge Companion to W.H. Auden* (editor, 2004), *Irish Poetry and the Construction of Modern Identity* (2005), *Globalisation and Its Discontents* (editor, 2006). His study of *Contemporary Poetry and Displacement* is published by Liverpool University Press (2007).

George Szirtes has published thirteen collections of poetry, including *The Slant Door* (Secker, 1979), which won the Geoffrey Faber Memorial Prize, *Metro* (1998), *The Budapest File* (Bloodaxe, 2000), *An English*

Apocalypse (Bloodaxe, 2001), and most recently *REEL* (Bloodaxe, 2004) for which he was awarded the T.S. Eliot Prize. His *Collected Poems* will be published by Bloodaxe in 2008.

Dave Ward is co-founder of the Windows Project, co-ordinating writing workshops in educational and community venues throughout Merseyside and the north-west. His publications include *Jambo* (Impact Books), *Candy and Jazzz* (Oxford University Press), *The Tree of Dreams* (HarperCollins) and *Tracts* (Headland). In 2006 he undertook tours to universities and schools in Singapore, Hong Kong and Harbin, northern China.

Patrick Williams is Professor of Cultural Studies at Nottingham Trent University. His publications include *Ngugi wa Thiong'o* (author); *Introduction to Post-Colonial Theory* (co-author); *Edward Said* (editor); and *Colonial Discourse and Post-Colonial Theory: A Reader* (co-editor).

For our neighbours

Introduction:
Sounding Liverpool

Michael Murphy and Deryn Rees-Jones

In the year that the city celebrates its 800th birthday, followed in 2008 by its designation as 'European Capital of Culture', the question is not whether there needs to be a book that examines the history and identity of literature from Liverpool but why that book should choose to concentrate on writing from the last eighty years. The latter is easier to address. Though notable writers such as William Roscoe (1753–1881), Felicia Hemans (1793–1835) and Arthur Clough (1819–61) were born in Liverpool, the city was from the late seventeenth to the early twentieth century more associated with trade than art. The origins of this reputation make for uncomfortable reading. In 1699, the same year as its first slave ship, the *Liverpool Merchant*, set sail for Africa, where it picked up a 'cargo' of 220 Africans who were later 'deposited' in Barbados, Liverpool was afforded parish status by an Act of Parliament. Significantly, one of the movers behind the separation of Liverpool from the parish of Walton-on-the-Hilll, Sir Thomas Johnson, one of the part-owners of the *Liverpool Merchant*, became known in his own lifetime as 'the founder of modern Liverpool'. The slave trade was to provide the financial impetus that allowed the city not only to cement its position within Britain but to grow in international influence and prestige. By the close of the eighteenth century, Liverpool controlled over 41 per cent of European and 80 per cent of Britain's slave commerce. By the start of the nineteenth century, 40 per cent of the world's trade was passing through Liverpool's docks.

What we think of as a distinctive literary voice only began to emerge in the 1930s – at precisely the time when the city experienced a sudden and rapid decline in economic fortune. It is impossible to imagine that when the *Industrial Survey* of 1932 forecast 'a vast problem of unem-

1

ployment will weigh on Merseyside for many years',[1] it envisaged this continuing into the next millennium. The facts tell a story of their own: a 44 per cent decline in population between 1951 and 2001; the award in 1993 of 'Objective 1' status funding in recognition that the area's per capita gross domestic product was less than 75 per cent of the European Union average;[2] and the fact that in 2005, in five Liverpool constituencies, 40 per cent or more of children were living in a family on benefit.[3] The year 2008, then, marks a key moment in deciding whether the downward trajectory embarked upon in the thirties will continue or instead provide an impetus that allows the city to re-emerge as a thriving twenty-first-century city.

Writing Liverpool is intended to mark the beginning of what promises to be a new period in the history of the city and its environs. We have chosen to focus on the more recent past in order to pose the question, 'What has Liverpool writing been?' More importantly, we hope to contribute to the debate as to what it might and should become. In so doing, we have taken certain liberties in deciding which authors fall under the banner of 'Liverpool Writers'. From Malcolm Lowry and Adrian Henri (Birkenhead) to J.G. Farrell (who, aged four when war broke out 1939, left the city for the safety of Southport, never to return), James Hanley (Dublin) and Beryl Bainbridge (Formby), a number of the writers discussed here were either born or grew up in what we might call 'Greater Liverpool'. As such they should be considered (if neither unequivocally or unproblematically) part of a 'Liver-school' – writers who, in their literary preoccupations, reflect and, more importantly, define qualities that have come to be recognized as essentially *Liverpudlian*.

The soubriquet is important, summoning up as it does an image immediately recognizable. What is interesting, however, are the many

---

1 See John Belchem (ed.), 'Introduction: Celebrating Liverpool', in *Liverpool 800: Culture, Character and History* (Liverpool: Liverpool University Press, 2006), p. 38. The editors would like to acknowledge the immense debt they owe to the work of John Belchem, Jenny Kermode, Jane Longmore, Colin G. Pooley, Graeme J. Milne, Donald M. MacRaild and Jon Murden, whose *Liverpool 800* has proved a fascinating guide to Liverpool past and present and an invaluable resource in editing our own book.

2 For a detailed history of Liverpool's economic development, see Chris Couch, *City of Challenge and Change: Urban Planning and Regeneration* (London: Ashgate, 2003).

3 See the 'End Child Poverty' campaign website at http://www.ecpc.org.uk/index.php?id=39. Accessed 18 January 2007.

contradictions this designation of regional identity implicitly holds: by turns the Liverpudlian is hard-working and work-shy; hard-faced and sentimental; doggedly independent yet insecure; salt-of-the-earth but always on the make; good for a laugh and quick to take offence; cosmo-politan yet inward looking and parochial. Like Liverpudlian, 'Scouser', too, conjures a number of recognizable figures: from the iconic mop-tops of the 1960s to Harry Enfield's curly-haired, moustachioed and tracksuit-wearing 'scally' ('Calm down! Calm down!'; 'You fightin'?', 'You askin'?') of the early 1990s. The shift from the one to the other is telling. In contrast to the city being viewed in terms of an anarchic opti-mism which reflected the wider affluence of the sixties (years which, as Stan Smith comments in his essay on Brian Patten, are best seen as an intermission between periods of economic decline), the full effect of Thatcherism and mass unemployment meant that male, white working-class writers, keen to address political issues, began to grab the nation's attention with depictions of Liverpool. Two examples serve to illustrate the differences in representing the city and the difficulties it was expe-riencing. *Letter to Brezhnev* (1985), a bittersweet romantic comedy written by Frank Clarke, dealt with the paucity of working-class aspi-rations, especially women's, at the height of the Cold War, through the relationship between a Liverpool girl and a Soviet sailor. The success of a writer such as Alan Bleasdale in capturing the *Zeitgeist*, on the other hand, was markedly different, as evidenced by how quickly the char-acter of 'Yozzer' Hughes was turned back on the city and used to either demonize or parody it. Such stereotyping has, because of the mass audi-ence of television, become a prominent part of how the rest of the UK has been encouraged to view Liverpool. The result was a city in danger of becoming fatally stereotyped. Nowhere is this better exemplified than in Channel 4's flagship soap opera *Brookside* (1982–2003), which moved from being a programme capable of re-defining the soap as a medium that could tackle gritty, hard-edged social issues (and in the process establish as household names a generation of actors, directors and writers) to one bereft of identity and reliant on increasingly melodra-matic storylines.

It is one of the aims of this book to challenge this process of stereo-typing – not in order to ignore it but rather to clear a space for future writers to reinvent the city and its people in ways that are compelled by the pressures of the current moment rather than overwhelmed by the past. Great art, we know, arises in times of transition rather than stability. Nor need such transitions be from good to bad. It would take self-deception of truly Panglossian proportions to sustain the argument that for Merseyside the events of the last century have provided the best of all possible outcomes in the best of all possible worlds. Yet the writers represented in this book have taken a city in crisis and fashioned from its threatened survival poems, novels, film and drama which not only have sustained and nourished that identity but given it a dynamic human presence. Equally important are the ways in which writers have refused to settle for the easy clichés with which the wider city has sometimes felt more comfortable. In these terms no one spoke out more forcibly than the writer and seaman George Garrett, who, as Joseph Pridmore recounts, warned in 1921 that the unemployed should not swallow the lie that foreign workers were to blame for 'stealing' jobs: 'All workers are slaves to the capitalists no matter what their race, colour or creed is, and there is more slavery under British Imperialism and the Union Jack than under any other flag ... There people are only trying what we should be doing, breaking the bonds of their serfdom.' Garrett's words, which continue to resonate in the New Europe of the twenty-first century, find an echo in the remarkable novels of J.G. Farrell, who, as Ralph Crane says, used the comic and the grotesque to chart the decline of empire and the emergence of once-colonized voices into the mainstream of literature in English.

Farrell's later residence in Dublin from the age of twelve, and his return to Ireland before his untimely death by drowning in Bantry Bay in 1979, has frequently led to his being classified an Irish writer. Certainly the popular elision of Liverpool and Ireland has had an enormous influence, not least in terms of developments in the city's relationship with the rest of mainland Britain. A memorial in the grounds of St Luke's Church on Leece Street stands as a record that between 1849 and 1852 some 1,241,410 Irish immigrants arrived in the city, and that from Liverpool they dispersed to locations around the world. Despite the help they received within the city, some 7,000 died of malnutrition in one year alone.[4] Heavy as such attrition was, the census of 1851 records that one quarter of the city's population was Irish-born. This did much to turn Liverpool into a pariah as far as the rest of the country was concerned, and can be said to have alienated the city from

---

4 There is also a memorial on the gates to Clarence Dock. Unveiled in 2000, the plaque carries an inscription in Gaelic and English that reads: 'Through these gates passed most of the 1,300,000 Irish migrants who fled from the Great Famine and "took the ship" to Liverpool in the years 1845–52.'

aspects of itself. The presence of so many Catholic Irish immigrants fuelled sectarian divisions and contributed to continued Tory electoral dominance. Neither was it a short-lived phenomenon. J.B. Priestly reported from Liverpool in the early thirties that the Irish had turned parts of Liverpool into a 'slum, or, finding a slum, have promptly settled down to out-slum it'. 'I imagine,' he added, 'Liverpool would be glad to be rid of them now.'[5] One of the triumphs of the rise of Liverpudlianism and Scouse has been the way in which Liverpool's Irish population has risen above the kind of vicious and racist stereotyping that blighted Anglo-Irish relations for the best part of a century. We might, though, see some lasting impression of late-nineteenth and early twentieth-century caricatures of the Irish as heavy-drinking, feckless and unintelligible as persisting in 'popular' depictions of the Scouser.

Successive waves of Irish immigration had a lasting effect on writing from the city. Roger McGough, for example, discusses in the interview with him included here, the importance of his Irish-Catholic heritage. Garston-born Heidi Thomas, in the popular BBC drama *Lilies* (2007), draws extensively on the experiences in the 1920s of her working-class grandmother and aunts. What *Lilies* testifies to, moreover, is the fact that 'Irishness' was far from being a stable identity. While the father in the family is Irish Protestant, the mother is Catholic. As a result the daughters are raised Catholic, while the boys are expected to follow the father and become loyal Ulstermen. Such tensions divided families and communities across the city for long decades, and have only recently been fully acknowledged and addressed.[6] Less attention, however, has been afforded other Celtic influences and attendant divisions within the city. As John Belchem and Donald M. MacRaild have pointed out, in comparison to the difficulties encountered by the city's Irish population, the Welsh enjoyed a much more comfortable connection with a city frequently adopted as the 'Capital of Wales', while the Scots, many of whom, in contrast to Irish settlers, were skilled workers, joined with Liverpool's indigenous population in adopting a 'censorious attitude to

5   J. Belchem and D.M. MacRaild, 'Cosmopolitan Liverpool', in John Belchem (ed.), *Liverpool 800: Culture, Character and History* (Liverpool: Liverpool University Press, 2006), p. 382.

6   The establishing in 2003 of the city's first annual Irish Festival would until recently have been unimaginable. For details of previous festival programmes, and news of future events, see http://www.liverpoolirishfestival.com

the Irish'.[7] Alongside the city's Irish connections, other Celtic influences have continued to reverberate. John McGrath, as will be discussed in more detail below, uniquely joined his Liverpool-Irish upbringing with a political and artistic commitment to Scotland; while Niall Griffiths's novel *Wreckage*, in ways reminiscent of James Hanley's Furys chronicle, establishes rural Wales as opposed to urban Liverpool as a place of escape and nurture.

A further international influence must be considered. Almost everywhere we look in these essays and interviews, the United States is an unavoidable presence. Unlike the Irish, Welsh or Scots, however, Americans visiting the city rarely stayed for long. Though it was 'the first "note" of Europe' to meet American visitors, many like Strether in Henry James's *The Ambassadors* (1903) chose to move on quickly to Chester rather than stay for 'a "look round" at the beauties of Liverpool'.[8] In part this may have been because the city had little that was new to offer, the 'showy waterfront', Graeme J. Milne says, 'being rooted in its transatlantic perspective. By the 1890s, to be American was to be modern, and Liverpool made much of its association'.[9] Those who had stayed gave further indications as to why those who followed did not. Nathaniel Hawthorne, American consul across the Mersey in Birkenhead's Washington Buildings, begins his reminiscences by bemoaning how, in 'a stifled and dusky chamber' he 'spent wearily four good years of my existence'. His task was to look after the flotsam and jetsam of the city's visitors, 'principally Americans, but including almost every other nationality, especially the distressed and downfallen ones'.[10] Again, the example of George Garrett is instructive. A member of the most famous of all American labour movements, the Industrial Workers of the World ('Wobblies'), Garrett brought with him from New York and Chicago not only political but aesthetic means of resistance. It was to become an unmistakable strain in writing from Liverpool. We can go further and say that more than any other external influence – even taking into consideration Ireland – it was that of the United States which made possible a number of distinctive trends in writing from the city, providing a means of liberating the imagination of men and women who

---

7 Belchem, *Liverpool 800*, p. 353.

8 Henry James, *The Ambassadors* (London: Penguin, 1986), pp, 55, 56.

9 Graeme J. Milne, 'Maritime Liverpool', in Belchem, *Liverpool 800*, p. 278.

10 Nathaniel Hawthorne, *Our Old Home: A Series of English Sketches* (1863, 1883), full online text available at http://www.eldritchpress.org/nh/ooh.html#consular. Accessed 21 January, 2007.

might otherwise have struggled to find artistic role models. Terence Davies recalls the euphoria of seeing *Singin' in the Rain* for the first time; discovering, aged fourteen, a collection of stories by the Rhode Island-born H.P. Lovecraft in a Liverpool sweetshop made Ramsey Campbell want to be a writer; the 'Liverpool Poets' – McGough, Henri and Patten – were influenced by American pop art;[11] Alan Bleasdale's mother introduced him to the detective fiction of Hammett and Chandler; the popularity of American rock and soul songs in the early sixties meant that John Lennon and Paul McCartney became songwriters to make up for the shortage of material available for local bands to cover; and American poets as otherwise diverse as William Carlos Williams, Elizabeth Bishop, Lawrence Ferlinghetti, the Beats, Allen Ginsberg, and more recently Michael Donaghy have proved decisive in forming the voices of successive waves of poets from the city. It is also important to note how this American presence cuts across forms and genres. Paul du Noyer describes the easy availability of American records through the Liverpool docks accustomed the locals to jazz, blues and country music; Andy Sawyer notes a considerable overlap between science fiction and popular music enthusiasts; and Terence Davies, famous for his cinematic portraits of the city in the forties and fifties, has gone on to make two film adaptations of novels by American writers, Edith Wharton and John Kennedy Toole. Similarly, the series of 'events' and readings organized by Adrian Henri in the early sixties were clearly influenced by the New York 'happenings' of the same period. Henri juxtaposed poetry, painting and taped music – 'bits of modern jazz and rock and roll' – so as to 'deliberately ... erode the divisions between the arts'.[12] The importance of these interdisciplinary 'events' cannot be overestimated. For while the most famous event was the Albert Hall 'Poetry Incarnation' on 11 June 1965, when an audience of 7,000 people witnessed and participated in performances by young British and American poets, still it was Henri who had the vision and the energy to introduce the 'happening' to Britain.

---

11 Henri first came to prominence as a painter rather than poet. In this there is a comparison with the poet Henry Graham, with whom Henri exhibited in 1959. Graham, has published six collections of poems, most recently *Kafka in Liverpool* (2002). He is also one of the poetry editors of *Ambit*, which in 1999 published a special Liverpool issue.

12 Frank Milner, Introduction to *Adrian Henri: Paintings 1953–1998* (Liverpool: Bluecoat Press, 2000), p. 18.

The relationship between Liverpool and the United States led to the city's becoming known not just as the second city of the British Empire but also as 'America in England'.[13] Such an appellation was not unproblematic. For while Liverpool has much reason to be grateful to America, the shadow of British involvement in the slave trade, shamefully unmarked until 1999, when the city council issued a formal apology for Liverpool's involvement in the traffic of human souls, is inextricably part of the history of economic and cultural 'exchanges' between North America, the West Indies, West Africa and Liverpool. It is an inheritance dwelt on by Jamie McKendrick when he writes,

> a thousand leg-irons fixed to their quarterdecks,
> those boats were christened with bright abstract names:
> *Integrity, Providence, Friendship, Liberty*.[14]

In the same year as the city publicly acknowledged this part of its history, Sandra Courtman visited the Phoenix Adult Education Centre in Liverpool 8 to meet with the founding members of Scotland Road Writers. Having heard that the writers' group had forged an alliance between activists and black migrants who joined Scotland Road in the early 1970s, she was interested in exploring how, in a city with a reputation for social division, recent black arrivals to Liverpool joined with descendants of Irish immigrants to create a forum for creative expression. As Courtman points out, 2000 also saw the publication of Carribean-born Caryl Phillips's *The Atlantic Sound*, which details Phillips's often painful journeys within the Atlantic slave trade 'triangle'. In his book Phillips describes a morning spent strolling through Liverpool visiting cafés and landmark buildings before he realizes: 'I have not encountered a single black person. Where on earth is Liverpool's black population?'[15] Incidents such as the racially motivated murder in July 2005 of the student Anthony Walker strongly suggest that social and cultural integration remains an urgent issue that the city has yet to find a way of resolving.

Exchanges between America and Britain occupy Linda Grant in her

13 Nik Cohn, *Awopbopaloobop Alopbamboom: The Golden Age of Rock* (London: Paladin, 1969), p. 148.

14 Jamie McKendrick, 'Inheritance', in *The Kiosk on the Brink* (Oxford: Oxford University Press, 1993), p. 56.

15 Caryl Phillips, *The Atlantic Sound* (London: Faber & Faber, 2000), p. 85.

Orange Prize-winning novel *Still Here* (2002), in which she weaves together the narratives of Alix Rebick, the daughter of Jewish refugees who fled to the city during the Second World War, and Joseph Shields, a Chicago-born architect commissioned to design and build a landmark 'art hotel' in Liverpool. Shields's commitment to the city's future, despite his being harassed and hindered by local gangsters and thugs, comes about when he discovers the real-life building that stands at 16 Cook Street. Designed by Peter Ellis, the building, Shields says, 'is a honeycomb of plate-glass oriel windows held together by a skeleton frame of stone designed to look like cast iron, and these windows give back to the street the reflection of a building next to it, a hive of windows reflecting another hive'.[16]

Shields is dumbstruck that such a building could have made its appearance in Liverpool in the middle of the nineteenth century, and concludes that Ellis must have taken the design from somewhere: 'Probably Chicago ... because that's where Modernism started.' The hypothesized truth, however, tells another story:

> When I start looking things up I find out that, no, Ellis didn't copy from Chicago, Chicago copied him. The precursor of American Modernism was someone called Root and it turns out that during the Civil War his parents sent him to England to escape the hardship at home and all that time was spent in Liverpool. This kid stands on Cook Street and watches Ellis's building being put up. He goes back to Chicago after the war and always in his mind is a crazy glassed-in spiral staircase he's seen in Liverpool.[17]

It's an inspiring vision of Liverpool's (admittedly unwitting) contribution to architectural modernism. Yet Grant's novel is ambivalent about the city's desire to embrace the modern let alone modernism. The Jews who fled Eastern and Central Europe during the previous two centuries and settled in Liverpool did not, like the American architect Root, always have the city in mind as a point of origin. They thought they were bound for America, but they were instead put ashore at Liverpool's Pier Head. Mistaking the seafront for New York, by the time they realized they had been tricked, it was too late. Many hoped one day to complete the journey, while others like Alix recognize that they

---

16 Linda Grant, *Still Here* (London: Little, Brown, 2002), p. 82.
17 Grant, *Still Here*, p. 84.

have settled for a place 'on the most westerly margins of the continent of Europe, so nearly there, so nearly America'.[18]

As well as immigrants from Eastern Europe, Liverpool was from the mid-nineteenth century a port of embarkation for Irish immigrants also seeking a new life in the New World. Lack of funds meant that many were unable to complete the journey and so stayed. Among them were some American citizens who, Hawthorne describes,

> deliberately spend all [their] resources in an aesthetic peregrination of Europe. Often their funds held out just long enough to bring them to the doors of my Consulate. Among these stray Americans I remember one ragged, patient old man, who soberly affirmed that he had been wandering about England more than a quarter of a century, doing his utmost to get home, but never rich enough to pay his passage.[19]

Even for those able to afford passage, arrival in the New World wasn't guaranteed. The failure to reach America is the subject of Beryl Bainbridge's *Every Man for Himself* – here figured in the doomed first sailing of the *Titanic*, which, though built in Belfast and launched in Southampton, was registered in Liverpool.

As recently as 1907 (exactly 700 years after being granted its first charter), the city was being likened to a frontier town that had more in common with the American West than mainland Britain: 'Its people are people who have been precipitately gathered together from north, from south, from overseas by a sudden impetuous call. Its houses are houses, not merely of recent birth, but pioneer houses planted instantly upon what, so brief a while ago, was unflawed meadowland and marsh.'[20]

Liverpool's unsettled and unsettling position is not uncommon for city-ports. What does seem particular is that the city has consistently reminded those who settled here, or simply passed through on the way somewhere else, of other cities. To previous generations, the dream of

18 Grant, *Still Here*, p. 18.
19 Hawthorne, *Our Old Home*, http://www.eldritchpress.org/nh/ooh.html#consular. Accessed 21 January 2007.
20 Walter Dixon Scott, *Liverpool 1907* (1907, reprinted 1979) cited in John Belchem, *Merseypride: Essays in Liverpool Exceptionalism* (Liverpool: Liverpool University Press, 2006), p. 42. Liverpool is similarly likened to a 'frontier town in the wild west' by Paul McCartney in Barry Miles, *Paul McCartney: Many Years from Now* (London: Secker & Warburg, 1997), p. 11.

rivalling London and becoming a 'second metropolis' conjured earlier epochs: the city was a 'modern Tyre' or a 'Florence of the north'.[21] Moreover, Liverpool was regarded as essentially alien to the rest of the country: it was 'the mecca of all British jetsam';[22] while the riverfront, Nikolaus Pevsner noted in 1969, 'might indeed stand at Durban or Hong Kong just as naturally as at Liverpool'.[23] For Jamie McKendrick, a poet born in Liverpool in 1955, this 'composite history of different peoples, invasions and occupations' allowed him to draw a comparison between Liverpool and the Neapolitan riviera, one which left him with 'the comforting but haunted feeling of being back home again'.[24] In one poem, 'Landing', he takes an imaginary flight in time and space, suspended above the city in 'a bucket strapped below / a vast balloon like an eyeball':

> clattering northwards past the gunboats
> and the crowds on the quayside waving flags [...]
> I saw the India Buildings and the Pier Head
>
> . . . .
>
> I could taste iron in the air, and naphthalene.
> Either the rocks were bleeding or the horizon
> was on fire. *This is the stain of Empire*[.][25]

Even the idea of homecoming proves disorientating.

The sense of Liverpool as a place not quite identifiable, whether Jung's dreamed city or Hanley's fictionalized Gelton, a locus that remains both haunted by its history and haunting in its presence, is perhaps due to the way in which it becomes a projection of all that remains undealt with in the continuing negotiation of what it means to be English. We might cautiously wonder whether Liverpool's positioning as geographical and economic 'other' has seen it become a harbinger of all that Englishness cannot contain within itself, both literally and metaphorically. Following the late Edward Said's classification

---

21 See Belchem, *Merseypride*, pp. 37–38.

22 Pat O'Mara, *The Autobiography of a Liverpool Irish Slummy* (1934), cited in Belchem, *Merseypride*, p. 40.

23 Cited in Joseph Sharples, *Liverpool: Pevsner Architectural Guides* (New Haven and London: Yale University Press, 2004), p. 67.

24 Peter Robinson (ed.), *Liverpool Accents: Seven Poets and a City* (Liverpool: Liverpool University Press, 1996), p. 91.

25 Robinson, *Liverpool Accents*, pp. 102–03.

of the relations between Orient and Occident in his seminal work *Orientalism*, it can be argued that Liverpool and the Liverpudlian, rather than being, in Said's terms, a 'fantasy' are 'a created body of theory and practice in which, for many generations, there has been a considerable material investment'.[26] Such projections are nowhere more vividly imagined than in Emily Brontë's *Wuthering Heights*, in which the child Heathcliffe, 'dark almost as if it came from the devil', is discovered by Old Mr Earnshaw 'in the streets of Liverpool where he picked it up and inquired for its owner – Not a soul knew to whom it belonged.'[27] Heathcliffe's racial otherness is not a matter of dispute. He is repeatedly referred to as a 'gypsy'; Mr Linton recognizes him as 'that strange acquisition my late neighbour made in his journey to Liverpool – a little Lascar, or an American or Spanish castaway'; and the servant Nelly comments that Heathcliffe's father might have been the 'Emperor of China' and his mother 'an Indian queen'.[28] In effect, his exoticism functions as a necessary cipher for everything that unsettled the precarious stability of mid-nineteenth-century Victorian England.

If in the twentieth century Liverpool learned to cultivate this 'otherness', becoming in the process defiantly 'elsewhere' – what Ralph Crane calls 'a liminal position … a transitional place, looking out over the Irish Sea and the Atlantic Ocean while turning its back on the rest of the country' – it has nevertheless been at the cost of marginalizing those writers who do not easily fit the accepted norms of writing from the city. Helen Carr, for example, in looking to understand the lack of critical attention afforded Beryl Bainbridge, suggests that the term 'Liverpool diaspora' be given consideration: 'After all, there's increasing discussion of Scottish writing in terms of postcolonialism, so why not Liverpool? And Bainbridge is undoubtedly a writer of the Liverpool diaspora, but so far that's not been a critical category.' Bainbridge would be far from alone in benefiting from such a category. Indeed it is a central element in the essays and interviews that follow just how many writers from Merseyside have felt an urgent compulsion to leave. The reasons for this have been many: George Garrett was appalled by both Liverpool's sectarian divisions and the brutality with which the city council

---

26 Edward Said, 'From Orientalism', in Patrick Williams and Laura Chrisman (eds), *Colonial Discourse and Post-Colonial Theory: A Reader* (London: Longman, 1994), p. 133.

27 Emily Brontë, *Wuthering Heights* (1847) (London: Penguin, 1965), p. 77.

28 Brontë, *Wuthering Heights*, pp. 91, 98.

and central government (under the aegis of the then Home Secretary, Winston Churchill) connived to treat striking Liverpool transport workers in 1911; Malcolm Lowry hit not only the bottle but the high seas; Terence Davies left to escape the kind of spiritual and sexual slow death so harrowingly depicted in his film *Madonna and Child*; Lynda La Plante looked to London and the States for examples of what Philip Smith calls 'metropolitan female achievement which may, in part, be read as a flight from the world of the "feckless" male Scouser'; and of the Liverpool poets, although Roger McGough remained in the city until his forties, only Adrian Henri, born in Birkenhead, was to stay.[29]

Given all this, it is little wonder that the docks and shipping have remained such an important focus of the city's imagination: from the stories of Garrett, Hanley and Lowry set on board merchant ships during the First World War (or in Lowry's case, Q-boats or 'Mystery Ships' which, as Chris Ackerley explains, were gunboats disguised as merchantmen to tempt submarines to the surface by a show of apparent surrender) to the Second World War setting of Nicholas Monsarrat's *The Cruel Sea* (1951) and *The Ship That Died of Shame* (1959), plus his collection of ocean-going stories, *H.M.S. Marlborough Will Enter Harbour* (1949). Helen Carr describes how Beryl Bainbridge's father, who had briefly been to sea, would recall the busy docks and over-flowing warehouses of the early twentieth century. This no doubt influenced the young Bainbridge, whose *The Birthday Boys* (1994) is a fictionalized account of Scott's 1910–12 expedition to the Antarctic, while *Every Man for Himself* (1996), dealing as it does with the *Titanic*, has been likened to a 'Ship of Fools, humanity in microcosm sailing toward the destruction that will be World War I'.[30] Terence Davies's *The Long Day Closes*

29 We should not underestimate the number of writers whose relationship with the city was permanently disrupted by being evacuated during the Second World War. The playwright Peter Schaffer, for example, born into a Jewish family in Liverpool in 1926, no doubt speaks for many when he describes the difficulty of returning to a home that had become unrecognizable: 'We were evacuated, and I spent my childhood thereafter in many places, many towns in England. I think we moved about eight times during the war ... Prior to that my childhood was spent very uneventfully in the city of Liverpool, which I doubt if I would recognize anymore; it was heavily bombed during the war, and it's been completely rebuilt, no doubt in the usual hideous manner that cities in England are... It was a happy childhood.' http://www.ingecenter.org/interviews/PeterShaffertext.htm#Fantasies_of_ playwriting_. Accessed 5 February 2007.

30 http://www.bookpage.com/9611bp/fiction/everymanforhimself.html. Accessed 17 January 2007.

(1992) contains a remarkable scene where Bud, accompanied on the soundtrack by Kathleen Ferrier singing 'Blow the wind southerly, southerly, southerly', day-dreams at his school desk of 'the Liverpool skyline … a huge sailing ship … sail[ing] in slow motion through huge, heavy seas, wind and rain'. A close-up of Bud shows him with 'wind and rain on his face and hair. He gasps as he tries to keep gazing at the ship.'[31] The scene suggests that the glory days of Liverpool shipping, as perhaps typified by Liverpool-born Cyril Abraham's long-running BBC TV drama *The Onedin Line* (1971–80), already belonged more to the realms of imagination and folksong than current economic reality.[32] Such a generational shift can be observed in the poetry of Matt Simpson (b. 1936) and Paul Farley (b. 1965). While Simpson writes about the city through a movingly wrought 'dialogue' with his merchant seaman father, a relationship which, as Peter Barry says, 'is also about the fraught relationship between the old Liverpool of ships, docks, and warehouses and the new city of culture, entertainment, and education', Farley (who left Liverpool to study Fine Art at Chelsea), focuses in his poem 'The Landing Stage' not on ocean-going ships, but on the Mersey ferry. That the poem is addressed to a relative suffering from Alzheimer's (a disease about which Linda Grant has written in *Remind Me Who I Am, Again*) suggests that the lines of communication between the generations – and the kinds of Liverpool that each generation might have inhabited – are friable.

Given that Liverpool is as much a place of departure as arrival, it is ironic that those writers who do leave are often heavily criticized. Nowhere is this more evident than in the case of the Beatles, who, as both Paul du Noyer and Willy Russell comment, were for a long period anathema to the city's sense of identity. Such problems are only compounded if writers who have left Liverpool continue to be strong advocates of the city, the usual criticism being that they are either being sentimental about a place they no longer care to live in or are 'coasting' on the city's new-found hip-ness. The truth might be better summarized as, what do they know of Liverpool who only Liverpool know? Such at least has been the trajectory of Willy Russell's plays, where

---

31 Terence Davies, *A Modest Pageant: Six Screenplays with an Introduction* (London: Faber & Faber, 1992), p. 144.

32 Though *The Onedin Line* sparked a series of some six novels, they were not written by Abrahams. He did, however, publish *The Blazing Ocean* (1979), set like Monsarrat's novels during the Second World War.

various characters' journeys of self-exploration necessitate leaving Liverpool; or the families in novels as otherwise different as Hanley's *Furys* chronicle or Grace Jolliffe's debut novel, *Piggy Monk Square* (Tindall Street Press, 2005) that leave respectively for Wales and Ireland. In Jollife's case the reasons for departure are vivid and pressing, the novel being set during the years running up to the Toxteth riots of 1981. But as Terry Phillips comments in relation to Lyn Andrews's *The Leaving of Liverpool* (1994), such notions of escape are built on ambiguity: that Liverpool is both 'special' and yet doomed, a place the novel celebrates but which its central character is fated to abandon.

An interesting case in this respect is the playwright John McGrath (1935–2002). He was born in Birkenhead of Irish parents, but the family moved at the outbreak of war to Mold in North Wales. After studying at Oxford and subsequently qualifying as a teacher, McGrath was invited by George Devine to work and write for London's Royal Court theatre. In the early sixties McGrath began writing for the BBC, co-creating the Liverpool-set *Z-Cars* (1962–78) with Troy Kennedy Martin. He returned to Liverpool as writer-in-residence at the Everyman Theatre in 1970 at a pivotal time in its development as one of the country's most important repertory companies. While at the Everyman he helped establish the Scottish company 7:84, the name of which refers to the startling fact that 84 per cent of the wealth in Britain was owned by just 7 per cent of the population. McGrath continued to re-invent himself, through both his political commitment and his writerly experimentation in locations that were not 'home'.

Comedy of various sorts has been a dominant strain in Liverpool writing by both men and women. Carla Lane's TV series *The Liver Birds*, which ran between 1969 and 1979, explored the comedy of two women living as flatmates in 1970s' Liverpool and exploited the difference in class between characters originally played by Pauline Collins and Polly James. Lane subsequently charted the lives of more affluent women in *Butterflies* (1978–82), *Solo* (1981) and *The Mistress* (1985), before moving back to Liverpool with the popular series *Bread* which ran from 1986 to 1991. While Lane's revision of the sitcom was less hard hitting than, say, Jimmy McGovern's writing for *Brookside*, it's worth noting the extent to which explorations of gender dominate the writing of near contemporaries Bleasdale and Russell: Bleasdale through his interest in vulnerable and damaged masculinity, and Willy Russell in his exploration of the position of women in stage plays and films, such as *Educating Rita* (1981) and *Shirley Valentine* (1988). Similar concerns underpin

Adrian Henri's use of the dramatic monologue, which can in turn be seen in the adoption of 'female' voices in the poetry of Roger McGough and Glyn Wright, whose first book, *Could Have Been Funny* (1995), was shortlisted for the T.S. Eliot prize.[33] Wright's dramatic monologues are by turns comic and painful. They provide a form that allows him to draw sharp and realistic portraits ('Mrs Mop', a blank-verse sonnet, concludes with an army wife standing on a dockside 'always waving / into the long bitter winter night') while also providing an opportunity to revel in puns and other verbal associations that reveal him to be an astute and sympathetic reader of contemporary mores. 'A Woman of Letters', for example, elides literary love ('Scarlett O'Hara lost three husbands, / which like they say is very careless') with a more mundane if secure reality:

> I put the condom in the glass ashtray
> and then he slips it under the pillow.
> The only problem with French letters is,
> if you don't pay attention you get them inside out.
> Madame Bovary's head is stuffed with romantic nonsense
> but if you ask me Flaubert was one miserable bugger'[34]

With its privileging of oral forms working hand in hand with a desire to write and speak as 'other', the dramatic monologue presents itself as an exemplary Liverpudlian genre. In this Wright can be seen as following in a tradition initiated by *The Mersey Sound*, which, Stan Smith says, spoke in a voice that mixed 'irreverent proletarian-chic' with an

---

33 Spike, a press founded by Dave Ward and committed to publishing new poetry and prose from the city, has been remarkably successful in helping to establish poets like Wright and later Jean Sprackland on the national scene. Sprackland's *Tattoos for Mother's Day* (1997) was shortlisted for the Forward Prize for Best First Collection, and in 2004 she was chosen as a Next Generation Poet. Like a number of other poets from the city, Wright and Sprackland were involved in both the Dead Good Poets Society (http://www.deadgoodpoetssociety.co.uk/) and worked as writers in schools under the aegis of the Windows Project (http://www.windowsproject. demon.co.uk/wpinfa.htm). See 'Dead Good Poets, Dead Good Poetry' by Carol Baldock and 'The Windows Project' by Dave Ward in *Gladsongs and Gatherings*. Wade's collection of essays also includes 'Open Floor!' by David Bateman which provides information on Merseyside's other small presses and the performance poetry scene.

34 Glyn Wright, *Could Have Been Funny* (Liverpool: Spike, 1995), pp. 55, 60.

awareness of 'fragility and transience'. What Smith says about Brian Patten's poetry being 'shadowed by the tone of elegy' is equally true of Wright, as it is of Simpson and Farley.

Another way in which the city has re-negotiated its relationship with English *sang-froid* is the streak of surrealism that informs a good deal of the work of the city's writers and artists. This is exemplified in Adrian Henri's series of paintings depicting Jarry's Ubu wandering round Liverpool (one of which, painted in 1968, the year of *les événements* in Paris, is reproduced as the cover to this book), or long-time Liverpool resident Robert Sheppard's *Thelma*, a poetic re-writing of Breton's surrealist novel *Nadja*. In part this may arise from the nature of the city itself, a jumble of influences and ghostly echoes that reminds us of Breton's description of surrealism in his manifesto of 1924:

> a monologue consequently unencumbered by the slightest inhibition and which was, as closely as possible, akin to *spoken thought*. It had seemed to me, and still does – the way in which the phrase about the man cut in two had come to me is an indication of it – that the speed of thought is no greater than the speed of speech, and that thought does not necessarily defy language, nor even the fast-moving pen.

If this ability to function as the nation's unconscious, to shape-shift and adopt the voice of otherness is a strong characteristic of recent generations of Liverpool writers, it is often premised on the dichotomization of gender as represented in the city's humour: male belligerence countered by an endlessly stoical female resilience; Liverpool as the 'female' other to the nation's imperial masculinity. John Belchem refers to Liverpudlian humour as wit

> accentuated by such devices as circumlocution, an Irish-like preference for the long-winded picturesque and aphoristic phrase; 'diddymisation', a seemingly contradictory liking for shortforms and pet names formed by adding a 'y' to the first syllable … and the comic malapropism, verbal 'near-misses' known locally as Malapudlianisms or Merseypropisms.[35]

Little wonder, then, that Frank Cottrell Boyce, a writer whose work for film and television has steadfastly seemed not to engage with the city

35 Belchem, *Merseypride*, p. 53.

(apart from his involvement early in his career in the Brookside spin-off *Damon and Debbie*), should have been drawn to adapting that most circumlocutory of novels, Lawrence Sterne's *Tristram Shandy*. His *A Cock and Bull Story* (2005) marks the end of what has been an extraordinary working relationship between Boyce and the director Michael Winterbottom. The relationship has been distinguished by an eclecticism that is little short of protean: from the sci-fi of *Code 46* (2003) to *24 Hour Party People* (2002) depicting the rise and fall of Manchester's Factory Records; from the brutal realism of *Welcome to Sarajevo* (1997) to *The Claim* (2000), a 'Western' loosely based on Thomas Hardy's *The Mayor of Casterbridge*.

Like Boyce's adoption of a wide variety of cinematic forms and genres, humour is a way of challenging authority. It seeks to disorient, as described here by a young sailor in McKendrick's 'Sky Nails':

> That first day, to break me in,
> my hardened comrades
> sent me scampering …
>
> . . . .
> for a bag of sky nails
>
> . . . .
> that will nail anything
> to nothing
> and make it stay.[36]

If we accept that Liverpudlian identity is premised on a comic response to deprivation and despair, it is worth asking to what extent such characteristics are further determined not only by gender but nationality and ethnicity. What Belchem calls the city's Irish-like tendencies in speech are themselves, as with humour, symptomatic of the exertion of English colonial power over a 'feminized' (i.e. illogical) Irish language and culture. If the Irish are funny, as the Liverpudlian is funny, that funny-ness is also an uncanniness, or as Helen Carr reminds us in her essay on Bainbridge, part of the 'unhomeliness' of Liverpool's identity.

Something of this characterizes the poetry of Peter Reading. Born in

36 McKendrick, *Kiosk on the Brink*, p. 20. The poem clearly holds a talismanic significance for McKendrick, who used it as the title of his selected poems published by Faber & Faber in 1997.

the city in 1946, Reading studied Fine Art at the Liverpool College of Art, where he later lectured in History of Fine Art before, aged twenty-four, moving to Shropshire where he worked at an agricultural feedmill. Laurie Smith has described how Reading's earliest work (he has to date published twenty-six collections of poems) was characterized by a lack of 'sentimentality, warmth or (though reviewers searched anxiously for it) much humour'.[37] On the face of things, then, Reading would seem to be the antithesis of what is generally understood by Liverpudlian. Yet in many ways his poems, littered as they are with the shards of what appears to be an abandoned civilization, can be read as charting the disintegration of not only the fabric of the city but the nation as a whole. This he describes in 'Neighbourhood Watch', a satire addressed to those who find beggars 'offensive to the sensibility' and indebted to the Scots of Robert Burns's 'Address of Beelzebub':

> The hallions are more than an aesthetic
> displeasure, they represent the end of us;
> the hallions are hammering at the door;
> the neighbourhood is going to the dogs.
> [But more than electoral bluster is required
> to arrest the momentum of this gathering maelstrom.][38]

The 'hallions' (rascals) are the new barbarians. Theirs is a voice that comes sweeping in from the bleak estates and new towns of the fifties and sixties, built as Reading says '"to encourage / a sense of culture and pride / in those who will live there"'.[39] What arises instead, as the epigraph to *Work in Regress* says, is a belief (if that isn't too strong a word to use in relation to Reading's poetry) that 'Desperate Circumstances demand disparate measures'. Such disparities mean that Reading's poetry is a textual ferment where tabloid headlines, scientific reports, love letters, graffiti, typographical experiments, the metres of ancient Greek and Latin poetry, and a recognizably Scouse idiom become not so much interwoven as violently juxtaposed. And violence is central to Reading's

37 Laurie Smith, 'Posthumous Poems: Laurie Smith Reviews *Marfan* by Peter Reading (Bloodaxe) and *Reading Peter Reading* by Isobel Martin (Bloodaxe)'. http://www.magmapoetry.com/poem.php?article_id=124. Accessed 31 January 2007
38 Peter Reading, *Faunal* (Newcastle upon Tyne: Bloodaxe, 2002), p. 13.
39 Peter Reading, 'Three', in *Work in Regress* (Newcastle upon Tyne: Bloodaxe, 1997), p. 11.

aesthetic. From his rendering of a homicidal Odysseus intent on revenge ('Plying a keen-edged blade, they sawed his nose and ears off, / carved off his genitals, tossed them aside as meat for the mongrels. / Finally, hacking his hands and his feet off, their fury was sated')[40] to geo-politics ('Their warfare is occasioned by the lack / of jealous-guarded pitiful resources. // Frontiers reflect past acts of butchery'),[41] Reading is in no doubt that *all* culture, 'high' and 'low', is underwritten by aggression. In '15th February' from *Diplopic* (1983), for example, he writes in the voice of a man who, having 'tried to put in what I really felt. / ... / I really felt it – what I tried to put', vents his post-Valentine *triste* with an act of revenge that retells Ovid through Jack Nicholson in *The Shining*:

> The heart was scarlet satin, sort of stuffed.
> I sort of felt it was me own heart, like.
> . . . .
> I sort of stuffed and tore her sort of scarlet.
> I stuffed her, like, and felt her sort of satin.
> I sort of felt she'd tore out all me stuffing.
> . . . .
> I tore her satin felt her stuffed her scarlet
> tore out her heart stuff scarred her Satan har
> . . . .
> felt stiff scarf tight tore scarlet heart her scare
> her scare stare stabbed heart scarlet feel torn mur[42]

What we are witness to here is a rage different from Odysseus' only in that it is described in a language that becomes steadily numbed to horror. The fluid, camera-like movement of 'Homerics' (in which we 'cut' from one act of brutality to the next) is here atrophied. There is no escape from the repetition of words that become meaningless in the re-telling. Ironically language becomes a series of cells ('heart', 'scarlet', 'satin') which offer no closure.

While it would be crass to see this in any way as being funny, there is something of the Grand Guignol about Reading's writing that touches on the often difficult distinction between horror and humour. Anfield-born Alexei Sayle, perhaps unsurprisingly for someone who grew up

40 Peter Reading, 'Homerics', *Last Poems* (London: Chatto & Windus, 1994), p. 9.
41 Reading, 'Anthropological', in *Faunal*, p. 18.
42 Peter Reading, *Collected Poems: 1970–1984* (Newcastle upon Tyne: Bloodaxe, 1995), p. 225.

with Jewish working-class parents who were members of the Communist Party, seems to have taken to heart Marx's maxim that history repeats itself, first as tragedy, then as farce. His debut collection of short stories, *Barcelona Plates* (2000), offers a mercilessly comic version of contemporary Britain full of indiscriminate, cartoon-like violence: Barnaby, who, jilted by his long-term girlfriend for being boring, wreaks murderous havoc in the back alleys of London and the roads of Paris alike; the locals of a quiet English market town who, on Saturday nights after the pubs have shut, ritually engage in hand-to-hand fighting with the police ('The urge to combat seeped up through the ground in these parts along with the radon gas and the coppers had no will or desire to resist'); or two dwarf actors who carry 'American Gerbers, tiny versions of their rubber-handled survivor knives ... sharp and lethal, shockingly to scale', and who leave a theatre director with the backs of his trousers covered in 'loads of tiny slashes in them below the knee'. Then there is the Scouse ex-soldier, now in his seventies, who kills a mugger with 'the Tokarev army pistol that I'd taken off of the body of a dead Chinese officer in Korea all them years ago'. Feeling rejuvenated after the incident – 'The aches and pains of years had slid off me, was that what it took?' – he travels from Liverpool to London and starts a new life as a contract killer. It's a career for which his early experiences in Liverpool as much as the Korean war have prepared him:

> I've always drunk in the same pub since I was a lad: The Jester, corner of Netherfield Road and Everton Valley ... It was always an ugly pub and it was always a rough pub ... As if annoyed with its name, it was also a fucking miserable pub. The violence in there though was like out of one of them books about the history of warfare ... The fists and feet era was what you might call the pre-Columban period, since it was the coming of the drugs that speeded it all up. The kids started using knives and clubs and stuck to them for a fair while ... But you can't stand in the way of progress ... If a shooter is hanging up in the armoury of any modern police force in the world, then it's also hanging about in The Jester.[43]

The 'deadliness' of Liverpool humour – which in so many ways can be seen as a sublimated and aggressive defence mechanism – has been replaced in recent fiction from the city by a more direct and literal

---

43 Alexei Sayle, 'The Minister for Death', in *Barcelona Plates* (London: Hodder & Stoughton, 2000), pp. 58–59.

engagement with violence and cruelty. So in Neil Griffiths's most recent novels, *Kelly + Victor* (2002) and *Wreckage* (2005), there is a direct correlation between the themes of self-abasement and abuse and the city's history of poverty, exploitation and the slave trade. Middle-class characters are 'southern' and 'soft'. In *Kelly + Victor* the satirized pronouncements of Natasha, an unstable university lecturer who sees 'all forms of deviance, including sexual ones' as 'a valid protest against … the normalizing absolutes of mainstream culture' are held up as inauthentic because they do not emanate from a direct experience of prostitution: 'She may have the words to sum it up, like, but what the fuck does she really know about it? Vicky's the one in men's houses. Vicky's the one doin it, livin it.'[44]

The central character of *Kelly + Victor*, Kelly, allows herself to take part in an act of sadomasochistic prostitution not only because she wants the cash but because the punter is male, white, fat and middle-class, lives in Heswall and owns a framed Manchester United shirt signed by Eric Cantona. Griffiths' depiction of disaffected youth may teeter at times on the edge of caricature, but the violence felt by Kelly, and her dismay at being stuck in a shop with no prospect of advancement remains a powerful indictment of the city's failure to hold on to the working-class values of community and solidarity. In one representative passage, Kelly, like the Louis Aragon of *Le paysan de Paris* wandering through the Passages of Paris, walks through the January sales:

> Ther tuttin an snarlin an dartin into shops, jumpin queues, elbowin each other out of the way. It's manic and oppressive. Everything's for sale; the Gap, River Island, Body Shop, Schuh; everythin can be bought. Billboards an posters advertising not things, not products, but a sense of community, belonging, self-respect, which is a fuckin laugh considerin the desperate fevered mass trampling over each other to purchase such things. It's one great big fuckin mess. New fuckin millennium an sod all's changed. In fact, in some ways it's got worse … [45]

Later in the novel, she staggers in a drugged stupor through the city, reflecting on her own role as torturer, justifying her sadism as a need to escape 'this moronic fuckin driftin through alleyways that lead nowhere.

44 Niall Griffiths, *Kelly + Victor* (2002) (London: Vintage, 2003), p. 215.
45 Griffiths, *Kelly + Victor*, p. 244.

This fuckin timid capitulation, this fuckin accepted puppetry.'[46] Her own role as an inflictor of torture and suffering is directly juxtaposed with the history of the slave trade and the city's commercial success in the late nineteenth century: 'So many fuckin slaves dyin to feed that growth'. She goes on:

> Thee were demons, a fuckin disgrace to humanity an we christen parts of our cities in ther names, honur them, fuckin revere them. An all because they made fuckloads of money … God fuckin help me. Someone show me what to do.[47]

In *Wreckage*, meanwhile, a series of dramatic monologues (reminiscent of Breton's 'monologue … unencumbered by the slightest inhibition and … akin to *spoken thought'*) are brought together to give the history of the protagonists, which again is positioned as part of a wider collective emotional history of a city 'which has never neglected its genesis in sludge and which found itself the focus for the wrath of obsessed rulers'. It is a description that forms part of a three-page history of the city, interrupting the dramatic monologues and telling of a place 'built on and sunk in sumps of blood'.[48]

Two elements bind the work of younger novelists such as Griffiths, Walsh and Kevin Sampson: an explicit and unfictionalized version of the city's geography; and the use of 'Scouse' as a mediator of their protagonists' experiences. A former music journalist for the *NME, The Face* and *Sounds*, Sampson's first novel, *Awaydays* (1998), emerged from the flurry of new writing that owed a clear debt to Irving Welsh's *Trainspotting*. As with Walsh's *Brass*, there is a determination to appear 'authentic':

> In *Awaydays* and *Outlaws* I used the slang – not to excess, though. It's important to get the rhythm of the streets if you're writing about the streets. For what regards the characters [*sic*], well, we're not really supposed to sympathise with any of them. I've tried to give a glimpse of their lives and show the way they see themselves, but none of them is especially endearing.[49]

46 Griffiths, *Kelly + Victor*, p. 331.
47 Griffiths, *Kelly + Victor*, pp. 331–32.
48 Niall Griffiths, *Wreckage* (2005) (London: Vintage, 2006), p. 69.
49 Interview with Anna Battista, http://www.erasingclouds.com/08ap.html, accessed 29 December 2006

The use of Scouse can be seen as a linguistic marker which dramatizes what John Belchem refers to as a kind of 'self-referential otherness'.
These novels declare themselves unashamedly part of the modern city,
and at the same time rooted in an historical continuum. Yet it is only
relatively recently that Scouse has been recognized as a dialect at all. A
'late flower', as it is called in *The Story of English*,[50] the Survey of English
Dialect, a study conducted between 1950 and 1961, made no mention
of the Scouse accent. The holding up of Scouse as a badge of Liverpool
authenticity therefore demands that we ask wider questions about the
connection between location and language, and whether the direct
equation between Liverpool and 'Scouseness' holds true. It is certainly
the case that for many of the city's poets – Elaine Feinstein, A.S.J. Tessi-
mond, Grevel Lindop, Jamie McKendrick, and Peter Robinson, for
example – and with the exception of Matt Simpson and Glyn Wright
– neither the Liverpool accent nor the kinds of usage we find in contemporary novels has proved to be a distinguishing feature. This is not to
say that the city's geography hasn't played a crucial role. More often
than not its importance is as a metaphor for emotional states. As Simpson
writes in the title poem of his first collection:

> I am making these arrangements into meaning
> to re-inhabit after twenty years some places of
> myself – backyards full of ships and cranes,
> of hard-knock talk, and death …[51]

While the grain of the voice of those characters who make up
Wright's universe is central to his tragi-comic narratives of ordinary
Liverpool lives, the 'Bit Part Players' as one poem calls them, for
Simpson the Liverpool accent is more problematic, forcing him to
'recognise a sort of linguistic schizophrenia, the tension between two
kinds of language in my make-up'. He continues:

One was a BBC-inflected voice deriving from school, cinema,
church; the other was the voice (or voices) of my working-class background, loving voices speaking of betrayal – the ghosts of all those

---

50 Robert McCrum, William Cran and Robert McNeil, *The Story of English: New and
   Revised Edition* (London: Faber & Faber, 1992), p. 205.
51 Matt Simpson, *Making Arrangements* (Newcastle upon Tyne: Bloodaxe, 1982), p. 50.

seafarers who were saying I had not taken the family direction of on-board and away to sea.[52]

Something similar is commented on by Terence Davies, who talks of having 'lost' his Liverpool accent, not through any deliberate desire to disguise himself, but because 'When I listened [to the radio] I must have heard someone speaking in a particular way that I thought was beautiful and just started imitating it.' This, of course, was before the Beatles (a distinguishing feature of whom was that they didn't adopt fake American accents as did so many other acts) or the plays of the 'Angry Young Men' with their revolutionary use of regional accents. Simpson and Davies are both aware that to declare oneself a writer in Liverpool is to risk censure, misunderstanding, hostility or ridicule. While other cities celebrate the writer as a dissident voice, such dissent in Liverpool is often regarded as a betrayal of class and family. To write is to 'get above yourself'; it's to break rank, think yourself better than you are. It is to become one of Them instead of Us. The experience of Levi Tafari is instructive:

In places like the Czech Republic or Germany where they take literature seriously – people see you in a different light. They see you as more than just someone who puts words together in rhymes. They also see you as a counsellor. I find in the Middle East, when I've worked there, they also see you as a spiritual person like a shaman, someone who deals with spiritual matters or who has a 'third eye'. It's not just an occupation, they see it as part of your life, both social and cultural.

What emerges in *Writing Liverpool* is a portrait (or soundscape) of a city that holds a very particular place in the popular imagination. Nevertheless, if writing from Liverpool is to continue to matter it will need to re-invent itself in ways that at present appear as indistinct and fragile as the city's budding transformation from a place that is a shadow of its nineteenth-century self to a city that has ambitions to command the attention of Europe and the wider world. That this will happen is far from guaranteed. The unarguable and much-needed benefits to be gained from economic and urban renewal and regeneration may not best suit the creation of art that is distinctive in anything like the ways

52 Robinson, *Liverpool Accents*, p. 166.

in which the writing of the past eighty years has been. More than any other city in the UK (Belfast may prove the nearest comparison, though there, too, if for patently different reasons, the future is anything but secure), Liverpool has gained uniquely from the deprivations resulting from cycles of boom and bust. Much now depends on how individuals and groups respond to the challenge of remaining independent in a city that has a designated Independent Quarter, or how many poets and painters can afford the rent for a garret in the Bohemian Quarter. Much, too, will depend on how the city squares its famous anti-authoritarian impulses with the necessary fiscal prudence demanded by Big Business and central government alike. Famed for its community spirit, Liverpool nevertheless has a history of social disharmony rooted in religion, race and class. The year 2008 may offer an opportunity for the city to pull together; it may equally put previous fractures under renewed strain. Will Capital of Culture mean the same in Walton in the city's economically deprived north as it does in leafy, media friendly Woolton?[53]

Many justifiably fear that the ongoing process of regeneration, or 'gentrification', will rip the heart from the city and leave it with little more than a string of high-fashion retail chains and coffee shops. Among them is the novelist Helen Walsh, who was born in Warrington in 1977 and left for Barcelona at the age of sixteen, where she worked as a 'fixer' in the red-light district. She returned to study in Liverpool, eventually working with socially deprived teenagers in the north of the city. In an interview with Michael Williams, she reflects precisely on this sense of dismay at the change currently taking place. Walsh's view that what is replacing the 'old' Liverpool is a newness that is somehow inauthentic is reflected in the character of Millie, the female protagonist of *Brass* (2004), her provocative and hard-hitting debut novel. For Walsh, Millie (like many of the central female characters in the very different work of Helen Forrester) becomes representative of Liverpool itself: 'She applies that whole principle of pleasure being an inalienable right. And the whole thing of consumer culture, she applies that to sex. I think she

---

53 Historically a Labour stronghold, Walton nevertheless has a history of returning MPs who have proved thorns in the side of the Labour Party in both office and opposition. The redoubtable Eric Heffer was MP from 1964 to 1991, followed by Peter Kilfoyle, who resigned from his post in the Ministry of Defence in 1999, claiming the Blair Government had abandoned its voters in traditional Labour seats. Woolton, meanwhile, which marks the city's eastern boundary and only became a part of Liverpool in 1913, enjoys a reputation for designer boutiques and makeovers from the television chef, Gordon Ramsay.

even says, "The most precious of all interactions can be reduced to a new top from Morgan."[54]

Walsh's interest in the work of the French philosopher Michel Foucault (her undergraduate dissertation focused on queer theory, masculinities and pornography) sees her detailing Millie's Sadean sexual extremes, particularly her use of female prostitutes and her rape of a teenage woman. The extent to which this behaviour is being explored as a means of figuring capitalism's destructive effect on femininity (and the city) is, however, unclear:

> I'm much more at ease with the realigning of the city's skyline now, I'm even pleased for Liverpool – I want things to work out for my city, I do, but at the same time I still feel sad when I see the new buildings and new faces – pasting new life on the veins of the old city. The red light district where *Brass* is set for example is no longer a working red light district. It was so poetic, so incredibly beautiful back in the late nineties – you'd see working girls tottering along the cobbled streets in their heels and now they've been pushed back to the ugly, depressed flats of North Liverpool. *Brass* land is now a hotbed of trendy designer restaurants and hotels.[55]

Many would want to challenge the view that there is anything essentially 'poetic' about the sex trade, arguing instead that such sentimentality is unlikely to form part of the experience of women forced into prostitution by drug dependency and poverty. Nevertheless, this nostalgia for the changing face of the city typifies a current unease and is all the more notable here given Walsh's youth.

What enables Liverpool to emerge from the scare quotes of the tabloids (local as well as national) is the fact that it has long existed as a locus not of despair but aspiration. Liverpool exists as a projection of the migrant hope that tomorrow will be better than today, the place we are building better than the wreckage or slums we have left behind. It has proved a refuge and an inspiration, and its generosity of spirit was nowhere more recently captured than in the welcome success of Tony Green's play *The Kindness of Strangers*, premiered at the Everyman

---

54 Interview with Michael Williams, 2004 http://www.bbc.co.uk/dna/collective/ A2499799
55 http://www.plastikmaedchen.net/stories/1263/

Theatre in October 2004. The play ambitiously juxtaposes life among the city's asylum seekers with a narrative that encompasses a prostitute who is also a single parent, a young Irish agoraphobic preyed on by an unscrupulous landlord, and Cliff, an extravagant drag queen. Accompanied by a rousing soundtrack of Beatles numbers, Gemma Bodinetz's production managed to strike a balance between a particular Liverpool sensibility and sentimentality with an unashamed attempt at producing the kind of ideas-driven, state-of-the-nation drama too long absent from the Everyman stage. With further commissions from home-grown writers – *Fly* by Katie Douglas and *Urban Legend* by Laurence Wilson in 2004, *Electric Hills* by Michael McLean and Stephen Sharkey's *The May Queen* in 2007 – the indication is that the Everyman's commitment to fostering new writing talent may initiate a new golden age in the history of the theatre.

The changes now set in motion are undoubtedly exciting, and where they will lead should not be prescribed or predetermined. One thing only is certain: that the city would be advised to continue to provide a safe harbour to the twenty-first-century versions of those English, Irish, Welsh, Scots, Chinese, West Indian, African, Somali, American, Jewish, Norwegian, Polish and German residents who made the city what it has been, and who should in turn be allowed their say in the place it dreams of becoming. To do so, it may be that Liverpool has to re-negotiate some aspects of itself. For while there is no doubt that the reasons behind the increased usage of the term 'Liverpudlian' from the early 1950s reflected a genuine desire to assert the city's cultural independence in the aftermath of the Second World War and the Festival of Britain in 1951– what Belchem calls 'Liverpudlian adaptability in the face of adversity'[56] – there is now a different challenge: to free Liverpool from the kind of monoculture that Liverpudlianism is in danger of becoming. That the word only established itself in the latter half of the twentieth century counters the argument that Liverpudlianism stands for an 'authentic' Liverpool any more than the term 'Liverpolitanism' which it replaced. If Liverpolitanism failed it was because it proved unable to establish a distinctive identity that embraced the city's divergent ethnic and 'racial' influences. Some similar charge might now be brought against Liverpudlianism. The time may be right for a new Mersey sound, one that has the confidence to cast itself adrift on the tide and re-discover itself elsewhere.

56 Belchem, *Liverpool 800*, p. 43.

1

George Garrett, Merseyside Labour and the Influence of the United States

Joseph Pridmore

Despite being the author of stories praised for their 'distinctiveness' and Conradian intensity',[1] the name George Garrett seldom appears in accounts of British writers from the 1930s.[2] His reputation at the time, particularly among influential figures on the Left, was altogether more significant. Sylvia Townsend Warner believed him to be a writer with a 'serious outlook upon mankind',[3] while John Lehmann, in a characteristically wide-ranging study of new European writing in 1940, praised his 'robust' approach to detailing 'events in the day to day struggle in which he himself took an active part'.[4] Of course the 'struggle' for Garrett meant balancing the necessity of supporting a family with the no less pressing need to write. The demands of the former, as with so many writers from a working-class environment, allied to the difficulty Garrett had finding work after the Second World War because of his being blacklisted as a 'Communist', meant that writing had more and more to take a back seat. Which isn't to say that Garrett hadn't always to find other outlets for continuing the struggle. As Jerry Dawson, who first met Garrett in 1937, writes:

> In the late thirties G.G. played a big part in the establishment of Merseyside Unity Theatre (or Left Theatre as it was called then). He

1 Adrian Wright, *John Lehmann: A Pagan Adventure* (London: Duckworth, 1998), p. 94.
2 The exceptions are Andy Croft's invaluable *Red Letter Days: British Fiction in the 1930s* (1990) and Valentine Cunningham's *British Writers of the Thirties* (1989).
3 Sylvia Townsend Warner, 'Underlying Morality', *Left Review*, July 1937, p. 367.
4 John Lehmann, *New Writing in Europe* (London: Pelican, 1940), pp. 83–84.

had some experience in America with the Princetown Group, and in England he had already taken the leading part in a Merseyside production of [Eugene] O'Neill's *The Hairy Ape*. His first parts in Unity were what might have been expected. He played Agate Keller in *Waiting for Lefty* and Driscoll in *Bury the Dead*[5] – and it is unlikely that they were ever played better anywhere, for all George's experience, not only in this country, but even more in the Wobbly movement in the USA went into them. In these years, too, it was not only G.G.'s ability as an actor that was invaluable to such a theatre group but even more what he was as a man. Many of us learned much more about the meaning of socialism from our contact with him than we did from the Left Book Club choices, *Left Review* or *New Writing*.[6]

Garrett's commitment was forged by a childhood that left him exposed to two of the most damaging forces plaguing Merseyside at that time: endemic poverty and the tension caused by sectarian divisions. Born in 1896 at Seacombe on Wirral, his mother came from a family of Irish Republicans while his father, a confectioner who later took work as a stevedore on the docks, was a member of the Loyal Orange Lodge.[7] From these unpromising beginnings grew a man who became one of the most prominent and respected campaigners for working-class rights in Liverpool and beyond. An active participant and organizer in the National Unemployed Workers' Movement, the Seaman's Vigilance Committee and, as Dawson says, the Unity Theatre network, Garrett was close friends with the MP Bessie Braddock, knew and worked with a host of other famous left-wing protesters and agitators, and was there in person for such public upheavals as the bloodbath that concluded the 1911 Liverpool transport workers' strike, the 1921 'storming of the Walker Art Gallery', the national unemployment marches on London that ran from 1922 to 1936, and the seamen's strikes of 1966. According to an interview that I conducted with one

5 *Waiting for Lefty* (1935) was written by Philadelphia-born Clifford Odets; *Bury the Dead* (1936) by New York-born Irwin Shaw.

6 Quoted in Michael Murphy, 'George Garrett and the Collective Memory of War', *Socialist History 20: Contested Legacies* (2001), pp. 56–57. Dawson was later to edit a valuable if not always textually accurate collection of Garrett's stories, *Out of Liverpool* (1982), as well as Garrett's *Liverpool 1921–1922* (1980).

7 Michael Murphy (ed.), 'Introduction', in *The Collected George Garrett* (Nottingham: Trent Editions, 1999), p. ix.

of his sons in 2002, when Garrett appeared at what was to prove his last rally he not only organized a whip-round for the guest speaker, but despite his advanced years and ill health (he died of throat cancer shortly after addressing the rally) contributed his own bus fare and walked several miles home.

Such commitment was commented on by George Orwell, who met Garrett in February 1936 when he helped Orwell with the research he was then conducting for *The Road to Wigan Pier*. Orwell writes that he was 'very greatly impressed by Garrett',[8] but the feeling was not reciprocated. Like many working-class writers of the thirties, Garrett found Orwell insincere and regarded his interest in proletarian lifestyles as detached or even voyeuristic. Orwell, for his part, misidentifies Garrett as a communist in his notes. In actual fact, Garrett openly denounced the self-serving Leninist philosophy that the proletarian 'masses' needed Comintern leadership to effect social change, and was himself a dedicated syndicalist, believing that the potential for change lay in the working class organizing themselves. In this, Garrett displays some accord with the thoughts of his friend Jack Braddock (husband to Bessie), who announced after a trip to the Soviet Union, 'The poor working-class stiffs are getting it in the neck,' and ripped up his Communist Party membership card.[9] Garrett in interview with Millie Toole likened communism to the Catholic faith of his mother that he himself abandoned, saying, 'Another sort of Pope was in the offing. I had already dumped one off my back; there was no point in humping a second.'[10]

Orwell's description of Garrett is nonetheless useful in that it remains the lengthiest contemporary account we have of a writer who is all but forgotten today. Garret produced only a small quantity of works: 'Living in about two rooms on the dole with a wife (who, I gather, objects to his writing) and a number of kids, he finds it impossible to settle to any long work and can only do short stories.'[11] Indeed, just ten of these short stories, along with two pieces of reportage and a handful of articles, were published in his lifetime, although since his death some further unpub-

---

8 George Orwell, 'The Road to Wigan Pier Diary', in Ian Angus and Sonia Orwell (eds), *George Orwell, the Collected Essays, Journalism and Letters*, vol. 1, *An Age Like This, 1920–1940* (London: Secker & Warburg, 1968), p. 187.

9 Millie Toole, *Mrs. Bessie Braddock MP: A Biography* (London: Robert Hale Ltd., 1957), p. 92.

10 Toole, *Mrs Bessie Braddock*, p. 92.

11 Orwell, *Road to Wigan Pier Diary*, pp. 187–88.

lished works have come to light.[12] Furthermore, though Garrett briefly found popularity as a writer in the 1930s, this was compromised by tensions arising with the end of the Second World War and the beginning of the Cold War. Growing paranoia surrounding the threat posed by communist Russia, led to a sharp decline in the success of western proletarian writers such as Garrett, who had voiced their support of left-wing politics during the thirties. This fall from grace affected many of Garrett's contemporaries, and authors such as James Hanley, Jack Hilton and Jim Phelan are still neglected and under-researched figures in most current overviews of British writing from between the wars. Unlike Hanley and Phelan, seafaring writers both, Garrett was not a novelist. As Paul Lester has said, 'His reputation must rest on a small, impressive body of short stories, a form denied the novel's prestige ... Hence an unrepresentativeness and bias in the literary canon.'[13]

The study of Garrett's work is rewarding, not least for what it reveals about left-wing politics, labour history on Merseyside, the stylistics of resistance writing, and tactics for overcoming the implicit class hierarchies that lie within conventional literary forms. Most significant to this chapter, though, is the fact that Garrett's work also contains fascinating details concerning the interaction between British and American left-wing organizations during the 1920s and 30s. This was an immensely lively time for socialist movements on both sides of the Atlantic, and I'd like to look in particular at the various ways in which Garrett's life and writing were influenced by one of the most famous of all American labour movements: the Industrial Workers of the World.

12 Some of these unpublished works later appeared in the *Collected George Garrett* and Jerry Dawson's earlier collection, *Out of Liverpool: Stories of Land and Sea* (Liverpool: Merseyside Writers, 1982). Many of his works exist only in manuscript form to this day. Among them is the highly significant play *Flowers and Candles,* written in New York in 1925. What's fascinating about *Flowers* is that Garrett produced an English version of the play as well as an American one, keeping the same essential story but changing certain details of dialect and character origins to provide appropriate local flavour ('Candies' becomes 'chocolates,' 'Mom' becomes 'Mam,' Manuel, a Filipino immigrant worker, becomes Charlie, an Afro-Caribbean, and so on), thereby making his drama accessible to theatregoers on both sides of the Atlantic. The Nottingham Trent University's Raymond Williams Centre for Recovery Research holds a number of Garrett's manuscript and draft texts, and Alan O'Toole's unpublished monograph, *George Garrett: Seaman, Syndicalist and Writer.*

13 Paul Lester, review of *The Collected George Garrett, London Magazine* (June/July 2000), p. 134.

Garrett joined the 'Wobblies', as IWW members were nicknamed, around 1918. It was not his first visit to America: in 1913 he stowed away on a tramp steamer bound for Buenos Aires and spent several years travelling 'hobo-style' in South America; and after returning to sea as a ship's stoker, he made several visits to the United States. This was not an uncommon practice, for Liverpool's status as a thriving port ideally situated for trade between Britain and the United States made for a lively (and often illegal) traffic between the two countries, with ocean-going ships providing passage for both immigrant workers and stowaways. As a result not only material goods but political ideas were freely exchanged across the Atlantic, and Bob Holton for one has written that this interplay was at its most stimulating in the 1920s. Little wonder, then, that Liverpool fast became a centre for new conceptions of labour, socialism and protest arriving from the States.

Orwell makes brief mention of the colourful life Garrett led during his time in America, noting how he 'worked in an illicit brewery in Chicago during prohibition, saw various hold-ups, saw Battling Siki immediately after he had been shot in a street brawl, etc. etc.'[14] Orwell also correctly observes that none of this distracted Garrett from what he could learn about socialist politics in the United States, and how he might apply these lessons to the struggle back in Britain. On returning to Liverpool, Garrett joined the Merseyside branch of the IWW, set up by Jack Braddock and his brother Wilf during the First World War, and which provided a refuge for American Wobblies fleeing persecution at home and sent funds to help members facing trial in the United States. Liverpool was simultaneously playing an almost identical role for the rebels closer to home in Ireland; and Garrett, no doubt affected by his mother's influence and experience, would surely have been among those who helped transport both finances and refugees during his sea crossings.[15] From all this arose the creative impact that IWW politics and writing made upon much British working-class literature.

The IWW was founded in 1905 and still exists today. Key Wobblies who played an active role in beginning the organization were Daniel de Leon, Eugene V. Debs, Lucy and Albert Parsons and 'Big' Bill Haywood, a former cowboy who had already experienced militant

14 Orwell, 'Road to Wigan Pier Diary', p. 187.
15 Bob Holton, 'Syndicalism and Labour on Merseyside 1906–14', in Harold Hikins, (ed.), *Building the Union: Studies on the Growth of the Workers' Movement, Merseyside* (Liverpool: Toulouse Press, 1973), pp. 126–27.

industrial action as part of the Western Federation of Miners.[16] Philip Sheldon Foner writes that the Wobblies' primary goal was to establish 'one big union', which would bring together all workers, 'regardless of skill, sex, colour or nationality'.[17] This union would operate through a series of strikes and passive demonstrations, which were to culminate in the abolition of the capitalist wage system and introduce a new order in which the workers would run industries themselves.

The idea of a union free of all boundaries and distinctions was a bold one, given that racial and social prejudice in America had hindered previous attempts to create similar collectives. However, the Wobblies quickly generated a huge following among poorly paid workers who suffered under the wage system, particularly those from other countries who were either unemployed or being exploited in menial jobs. Indeed, much of the Wobblies' early success as a political movement may be due to the fact that they welcomed people of all races and nationalities at a time when America was deluged with migrant workers from across Europe and the world.

The IWW's principles could not have been more appealing to Garrett, partly because its syndicalist stance mirrored his own politics, but also because he was a lifetime advocate of equality, tolerance and acceptance, sometimes displaying attitudes that were considerably ahead of his time. Take, for example, the following segment from a speech made by Garrett at a Liverpool unemployment demonstration in 1921:

> Fellow workers, it is all very well criticizing the alien as one of your speakers has been doing, and telling you that he is the cause of your unemployment. It is not so. The present rotten system is the cause ... All workers are slaves to the capitalists no matter what their race, colour or creed is, and there is more slavery under British Imperialism and the Union Jack than under any other flag ... You Britishers, you some-times give me a pain. I don't tell people I'm a Britisher. I had no choice in being where I was when I was born. How many of you have the guts of the Indians who are following Ghandi [*sic*] in India today, or following Michael Collins in Ireland? There people are only trying what we should be doing, breaking the bonds of their serfdom.[18]

16 Philip Sheldon Foner, *The Case of Joe Hill* (New York: New World Paperbacks, 1965), pp. 9–10.
17 Foner, *Joe Hill*, p. 10.
18 The speech was made on the 12 September 1921, and Garrett's words were noted by one of the CID Special Branch members monitoring the demonstration at the

The IWW achieved its widest popularity and highest membership figures in the years leading up to 1914. By 1918 the movement was already a shadow of its former self, having suffered ruthless suppression and numerous witch-hunts during the war years. More about this later; for the moment, suffice to say that by the time Garrett joined the Wobblies, their glory days were over. Furthermore, the IWW member who had the greatest individual influence on Garrett's works was already dead. This was the most famous and best-remembered Wobbly of all: songwriter and lyricist Joe Hill.

Born Joel Emmanuel Hägglund in 1879, he changed his name first to Joseph Hillstrom and then to Joe Hill after moving to America from his native Sweden in 1902.[19] In 1910 he joined the Wobblies, after working for seven years in a variety of menial jobs, and also experiencing periods of unemployment and vagrancy, as Garrett and countless other immigrants to the United States had done.[20] During his time as a member of the IWW, Joe Hill produced some of America's most famous protest songs, including 'Casey Jones the Union Scab', 'There Is Power in a Union', 'We Will Sing One Song' and 'The Rebel Girl' (dedicated to Elizabeth Gurley Flynn, an IWW member with whom Hill had a light romantic attachment, and also with an affectionate nod to a ten-year-old named Katie Phar who wrote to Hill while he was in prison). Even today those who have not heard of Joe Hill will probably have used, at least a few times, a phrase that he coined. It may surprise some to learn that the expression 'pie in the sky' comes from Hill's song 'The Preacher and the Slave', and originally meant a hollow, palpable promise intended to keep the masses content but which provided no material comfort in the real world. It is surely best expressed in the first verse and chorus of the song in which it originally appeared:

> Long-haired preachers come out every night,
> Try to tell you what's wrong and what's right,
> But when asked about something to eat,
> They will answer with voices so sweet:

time. Michael Murphy, in his introduction to *Collected George Garrett*, p. xxv, reproduces Garrett's words in full.

19 Dean Nolan and Fred Thompson, *Joe Hill: IWW Songwriter* (Sheffield: Pirate Press, n.d.), p. 2.

20 Foner, *Joe Hill*, p. 9.

CHORUS
You will eat (you will eat) by and by,
In that glorious land in the sky (way up high).
Work and pray, live on hay,
You'll get pie in the sky when you die (that's a lie).[21]

Joe Hill was arrested on 13 January 1914 for the murder of ex-police officer John Morrison and his seventeen-year-old son Alving.[22] Whether Hill actually committed the crime, or whether the arrest was a frame-up intended to eliminate a man who was by that time viewed by many as a dangerous radical and rebel-rouser, has been the subject of much spirited debate in the decades since. His trial was lengthy and extremely involved (Patrick Renshaw remarks that only the Sacco and Vanzetti affair of the 1920s has rivalled it for sheer complexity), but the final verdict came in as guilty and Hill was executed by firing squad on 18 November 1915.[23] His last words, wired to IWW leader 'Big' Bill Haywood, were: 'Don't waste time in mourning. Organize!'[24]

Although Garrett never met Joe Hill, we know that he was a great fan of his works and that he owned at least one edition of *Songs of the Workers*, or *The Little Red Songbook*.[25] This text, first released around 1912 and updated and reissued periodically, published songs by Joe Hill and other IWW activists with the intention of 'fanning the flames of discontent'. Garrett was forced to leave America in 1920 after a crackdown on illegal immigrants by the US authorities, and soon afterwards he began producing protest songs himself in Liverpool, taking his cue from Hill and those other Wobbly lyricists he had encountered.

Michael Murphy has suggested a link between Garrett's lyrical works and the songs of Joe Hill.[26] I would like to make this link clear by exam-

---

21 All Joe Hill songs in this paper are transcribed from the 1954 Folkways Record Album *The Songs of Joe Hill, Sung by Joe Glazer with Guitar.*
22 Foner, *Joe Hill*, p. 2.
23 Patrick Renshaw, *The Wobblies: The Story of Syndicalism in the United States* (London: Eyre & Spottiswode, 1967), p. 194.
24 Renshaw, *The Wobblies*, p. 203.
25 Jerry Dawson, 'Introduction', in George Garrett, *Liverpool 1921–1922* (Liverpool: Merseyside Unity Theatre, 1980), p. ii.
26 Murphy, *Collected George Garrett*, p. xii.

ining the two surviving musical numbers by Garrett, 'Marching On!' and 'Seamen Awake'. The former was one of Garrett's first published works, and was sold as a broadsheet to raise funds for the Liverpool contingent of the 1922 national march on London. This was the first of six such marches that took place between that year and 1936, and Garrett organized the marchers from the Merseyside region along with a Boer War veteran friend named McMahon (upon whom the character 'Old Soldier McMahon' in Garrett's 1935 short story 'The Redcap' is based). 'Marching On!' is set to the tune of an English transport workers' strike song titled 'Hold the Fort', and the segments from both songs reproduced below illustrate the similarities:

'Hold the Fort', verses 2–3	*'Marching On!', verses 2–3*
Look, my comrades, see the Union	Onwards, comrades, organize,
Banners waving high.	Burst the ruthless chain.
Reinforcements now appearing,	Solidarity shall prove
Victory is nigh.	Our quest is not in vain.
See our numbers still increasing,	Too long we've starved in silence grim
Hear the bugle blow.	And watched the parasite
By our union we shall triumph	Waste in luxury the wealth
Over every foe.[27]	Produced by Labour's might.[28]

The practice among political radicals of setting new words to existing tunes was commonplace long before Garrett, Joe Hill or the Wobblies, and dates back to at least the eighteenth century.[29] Hill and the other IWW songwriters were contributing to an existing tradition by reworking hymns and popular music, and turning their lyrics into parodies of the original words. Garrett's protest songs are part of this tradition, and demonstrate an awareness of popular common themes in their lyrics. If we compare 'Marching On!' with Hill's 'Workers of the World Awaken!', the similarities are striking:

27 Anonymous, 'Hold the Fort', in *Out of Work*, 1.53 (1922), p. 4.
28 Garrett, *Liverpool 1921–1922*, p. iv.
29 Charles Hobday, 'Two Sansculotte Poets: John Freeth and Joseph Mather', in John Lucas (ed.), *Writing and Radicalism* (Harlow: Longman, 1996), p. 62.

'Marching On!', verses 2–3	'Workers of the World Awaken!', verse 1
Onwards, comrades, organize,	Workers of the world, awaken!
Burst the ruthless chain.	Break your chains, demand your rights.
Solidarity shall prove	All the wealth you make is taken
Our quest is not in vain.	By exploiting parasites.
Too long we've starved in silence grim	Shall you kneel in deep submission
And watched the parasite	From your cradles to your graves?
Waste in luxury the wealth	Is the height of your ambition
Produced by Labour's might.	To be good and willing slaves?

Similarly, parts of Garrett's song 'Seamen Awake', which was probably written around the same time as 'Marching On!', strongly recall Hill's 'There Is Power in a Union'. The common ground here is Percy Bysshe Shelley's poem 'The Mask of Anarchy', written in 1819. The poem, a response to the Peterloo Massacre, calls upon the revolutionary language emerging from France at the time, and was hugely popular among radicals of the nineteenth and twentieth centuries for its exhortations to the working class to rise against the capitalist system that exploited them. Many motifs popular in twenties' and thirties' protest songs, such as the breaking of chains, the right to be more than a simple wage-slave and the plutocrat wasting his wealth in comfort, first appeared in Shelley's polemic, and have been seized upon by countless proletarian songwriters since. Among the most influential stanzas are the following:

> Rise like lions after slumber
> In unvanquishable number,
> Shake your chains to Earth like dew,
> Which in sleep had fallen on you –
> Ye are many – they are few – [...]
>
> 'Tis to work and have such pay
> As just keeps life from day to day
> In your limbs, as in a cell,
> For the tyrants' use to dwell ...
>
> 'Tis to hunger for such diet
> As the rich man in his riot

> Casts to the fat dogs that lie
> Surfeiting beneath his eye ...[30]

So great was Shelley's popularity among working-class socialists and radicals that Joe Hill and Garrett would both have heard of him and been influenced by his works. We can see from this that Garrett's songs, while most immediately inspired by Joe Hill and the other IWW lyricists he would have come across in his copy of *The Little Red Songbook,* were also a part of radical and popular traditions that both he and Hill can be said to belong to. But it's not just in his protest songs that Garrett's experiences with the Wobblies emerge and are made use of. His heftier works of literature, in particular one piece of reportage, tie Garrett's life, politics and writing most closely to the IWW.

Liverpool 1921–1922, Garrett's longest surviving work and the last to be published in his lifetime, recalls classic IWW writing in two ways. Firstly, its author uses the established Wobbly technique of disguising real-life figures as social types. Garrett himself features as a two different characters, 'The Young Seaman' and 'The Syndicalist'; and many other important figures from 1920s left-wing Liverpool appear under such aliases as 'The Old Police Striker' (Robert Tisseyman), 'The Deportee from America' (Jack Meehan), 'The Man in the Stetson' (Jack Braddock) and 'The Woman Organiser' (Mary 'Ma' Bamber, mother of Bessie Braddock).[31]

Liverpool 1921–1922 is also reminiscent of Wobbly writing in that it deals with many of the same issues, problems and ambiguities that the IWW had faced, and which Garrett had encountered during his time with them. By 1921 Garrett was back on Merseyside, still unemployed, and an active member of the National Unemployed Workers' Movement (NUWM). This organization was founded by Wal Hannington in 1921, and was in many ways similar to the Wobblies in that it set out to be a nationwide union and was founded on principles of non-violent protest, tolerance and passive demonstration. Its goal, to provide the British proletariat with 'work or full maintenance', recalls the Wobblies' quest to better the lives of the poorly treated working class.[32] The

---

30 Percy Bysshe Shelley, 'The Mask of Anarchy' (1819), in *Poems and Prose: Percy Bysshe Shelley* (London: Everyman, 1995), pp. 154–55.

31 A full list of Garrett's character-types and the real people they represent is provided on the title page of *Liverpool 1921–1922*.

32 Tony Lane, 'Some Merseyside Militants of the 1930s', in Hikins, *Building the Union,* p. 156.

NUWM was also similar to the IWW in that it faced many of the same types of opposition from the government and local authorities.

All this can be keenly felt in *The First Hunger March*. First published in John Lehmann's *New Writing* in 1937, Garrett's first-hand account of the Liverpool branch of the 1922 Hunger March was singled out for praise by Townsend Warner in terms that would appear to be mutually irreconcilable but can be seen as anticipating an important strand of Liverpool writing from J.G. Farrell to Alan Bleasdale. An 'account of men in earnest and a practical joke', the narrative tells of how the marchers, not unlike the 'happenings' and 'events' in the United States and Britain of the late fifties through to the mid-sixties, put on a mock burial of a tin of 'bully' (corned) beef. As Murphy has said, the scene is 'part mummer's play, part agit-prop'[33] and it provides yet another self-portrait of Garrett, who this time appears (no doubt reflecting his antagonism towards religious faith of any denomination) with a 'blubbery priest's face'. Such relatively gentle mockery of the Church is as nothing to the scorn reserved for the way in which the military has historically exploited the working class:

> 'Friends,' he began with an ecclesiastical drawl. 'We are gathered here to pay a last tribute to our dearly departed comrade, B.B. The greatness of our empire is in no mean measure due to him. He served on all fronts in the last war. A very good soldier, he saw service in the Boer War. He was always at hand, and could be rushed anywhere in an emergency. We are mindful of the praise lavished on prominent generals … but with all due respects to them, our late comrade B.B. was the real backbone of the British army.'[34]

Replete, again as Murphy comments, with all the trapping of imperial majesty – flags, firing squad, military and religious costume, kettle drums, marching, and the Bible[35] – theatre is being used to expose (and to ridicule) the ideology of power. Such a fusion of the theatrical and the anti-war is hardly surprising given, as Jerry Dawson wrote, Garrett's performances in Irwin Shaw's powerful and provocative anti-war play,

33 Murphy, 'George Garrett', p. 67.
34 Garrett is also, of course, drawing our attention to the close ties that exist constitutionally between the Church and armed forces in Britain.
35 Murphy, 'George Garrett', p. 68.

Bury the Dead, in which soldiers from the Great War rise from the grave to address the audience.

Garrett's disguised/fictionalized appearance in these pieces also sheds an interesting light on another defining aspect of his writing. For though Garrett was known as a writer of short stories to people such as Lehmann and Orwell, what neither could have guessed (though Orwell did later find out) was that he also published in *Adelphi* between June 1934 and November 1935 four stories under the pseudonym of 'Matt Low'.[36] Indeed, almost half Garrett's stories were to appear under the assumed name. Given the ultimately cataclysmic divisions of the thirties, such an appellation was clearly more *nom de guerre* than *nom de plume*. And as Murphy is no doubt right to suggest, the need 'to translate himself, to create an alter ego ... may owe something to Garrett's notoriety as a political militant'.[37] Thus we see a genuine fear of discovery (and it is worth pointing out that Garrett was 'an illegal alien' throughout his stay in America) underpinning his assumption of a Wobblies-inspired aesthetic.

The Wobblies opposed America's entry into the First World War 1917. They were immediately accused of encouraging anti-war attitudes, of resisting American involvement in the conflict, and of sabotage and other subversive acts.[38] On such charges many members were arrested, jailed or even, as in the case of influential member Frank Little, lynched. It was also put about that the movement was in receipt of gold from the the Kaiser in order to carry out its misdeeds, which led Senator Henry F. Ashurst to suggest that the letters IWW stood for 'Imperial Wilhelm's Warriors'.[39] This allegation would have been particularly badly received in Liverpool, which had a large German population descended from settlers who arrived in the mid- to late nineteenth century. After the sinking of the *Lusitania* in May 1915, violent anti-German riots broke out in the city and around 150 German residents were sent to Scotland to be interned.[40] Garrett writes in *Liverpool 1921–1922* that the NUWM faced exactly these types of unfounded prejudice and institutionalized suppression in the early twenties. This is seen most

---

36 From the French *matelot*, meaning a sailor.
37 Murphy, 'George Garrett', p. 68.
38 Jim Burns, 'Rebel Voices', *The Penniless Press*, 16 (Autumn 2002), p. 25.
39 Renshaw, *The Wobblies*, p. 218.
40 For more on this, see John Belchem and Donald M. MacRaid's essay 'Cosmopolitan Liverpool', in John Belchem (ed.), *Liverpool 800: Culture, Character and History* (Liverpool: Liverpool University Press, 2006), pp. 364–67.

vividly in the segment that deals with the so-called 'storming of the Walker Art Gallery' on 12 September 1921. On that day, Garrett and several hundred other members of the NUWM were batoned down by troops during a non-violent protest at Liverpool's Walker Art Gallery, and many were arrested, tried and accused of receiving funds from Communist Russia.[41] There's a striking similarity between this chapter in the NUWM's history and the ordeal of the Wobblies in wartime America, and in drawing this parallel Garrett becomes able to engage with many key IWW debates in *Liverpool 1921–1922*. At the forefront of these is the issue of non-violent protest and whether it has any value in a world where the struggle for working-class rights seems to be ruthlessly crushed time and time again by uncaring authority. This debate was eternally troubling for Garrett and the Wobblies, and sadly it is not easily resolved.

Liverpool 1921–1922 remains a vital document to anyone interested in the writings of the IWW, or who wants to see the ways in which creative interaction occurred between Wobblies in Britain and the United States. Though he belonged to many different left-wing movements, Garrett's political self was perhaps shaped most of all by the first radical organization he ever encountered. Garrett's loyalty to the ethos of the Wobblies is evident in his protest songs and throughout his writings. *Liverpool 1921–1922* and *The First Hunger March* amply display the personal politics that made him an exemplary IWW member and which commanded the respect and admiration of those who knew him personally and who read his stories. He saw people as essentially the same, superficially diverse but motivated by common needs and afflicted by similar problems. He believed that the world's workers could rise up in one big union, and put their differences aside for the mutual goal of bettering the lot of the poor and underprivileged. This was the goal that motivated his existence, and gave life to his writing.

---

41 Garrett was among the NUWM protestors brought to trial after the debacle, and was accused by the prosecuting lawyer of receiving gold from a government body. Garrett immediately pleaded guilty to this. The lawyer, astonished by his willing confession, asked him to tell him which government was funding him. Garrett replied: 'The British Government. I'm on the dole' (Murphy, *Collected George Garrett*, p. 211).

2

'No Struggle but the Home':
James Hanley's *The Furys*

Patrick Williams

James Hanley was born in Dublin in 1901, though his family moved to Liverpool when he was very young. Like many of his early fictional characters (including various members of the Fury family), Hanley left home in his teens (in his case before he was fourteen), and joined the merchant navy despite the not very encouraging model of his father's experiences in that area. During the First World War he served on troopships in the Mediterranean, then, using an assumed name, joined the Canadian army and fought in France with the Thirteenth Battalion. After the war, Hanley returned to Liverpool and his parents' home and spent the next ten years working on the railways, reading voraciously, writing and having his writing rejected by a variety of publishers. After his first book, *Drift*, was accepted in 1929, Hanley left both Liverpool and the railways, and moved to the Welsh village where he spent much of the remainder of his life producing a steady, sometimes remarkable, quantity of work, principally novels, but also, particularly in later years, short stories and plays. With the determination and application which characterized his entire career, he continued writing into his eighties. James Hanley died in 1985.

Few twentieth-century writers can have suffered a more contradictory fate than James Hanley: on the one hand, consistently praised by reviewers in lavish, if not extravagant terms, and on the other, consistently ignored by that academic section of the literary establishment whose kind attention guarantees a proper posterity. As Edward Stokes notes, Hanley has been compared, usually favourably, with (among many others) Beckett, Conrad, Dickens, Faulkner, Hardy, Joyce, Lawrence, Melville, Pinter, Dylan Thomas, Balzac, Maupassant, Zola,

Dostoyevsky, Kafka and Strindberg.[1] At the same time, critics have been unable to find a place for Hanley among the 'serious' contemporary writers that such a formidable list of comparisons would seem to demand. Whether this contradictory fate owes anything to the contradictory nature of Hanley's writing is clearly a matter of debate. Without pretending to resolve such issues, the present chapter will examine some of the contradictions in one of Hanley's most important novels from a particularly productive decade.

Published in 1935, *The Furys* was the first part of what over the next two decades was to become a sequence of five novels charting the lives of the Furys, a Liverpool-Irish family.[2] The novel can be read as simultaneously typical of Hanley's early work and as a series of departures from whatever norms he had established in his writing, and poses a range of questions for the critic. *The Furys* appeared in the middle of a decade which saw important changes both in the forms of Hanley's writing and in its success. In the twenties, in common with other aspiring working-class authors, Hanley had written short stories, but, perhaps as a result of his 'difficult' style, had had even less success than many contemporaries in finding a publisher. Consequently, his earliest writings were privately printed. In the thirties, however, apart from the collection *Men in Darkness* (1931), which could be seen as a continuation of his work of the twenties, his output consisted principally of novels, though it also included a sociological study of working-class Welsh children[3] and an autobiographical 'excursion',[4] while the range of publishers involved in the production of his writings included respected firms such as Methuen, Chatto and Bodley Head. The growing success could, on the one hand, be attributed to a proper recognition of Hanley's talent, but it could also be seen as significantly linked to the patronage of him by literary and establishment figures such as John Lehmann and Nancy Cunard. While this type of patronage was not uncommon, and Hanley along with other working-class writers was published in such magazines as *Criterion* and *New Writing*, it does nevertheless create the potential for producing further contradictions at the level of class location and affiliation, the tension, as Carole Snee says, 'between a working class person who writes

1 See Edward Stokes, *The Novels of James Hanley* (Melbourne: F.W. Cheshire, 1964).
2 *The Furys* was followed by *The Secret Journey* (1936), *Our Time Is Gone* (1940), *Winter Song* (1950) and *An End and a Beginning* (1958).
3 James Hanley, *Grey Children* (London: Methuen, 1937).
4 James Hanley, *Broken Water* (London: Chatto & Windus, 1937).

in order to explore his world, and a person from the working class who seeks to become an "Author" with all that that implies of the dominant literary culture'.[5]

However such tensions might manifest themselves, a disavowal of working-class origins or of working-class life as the subject matter for his novels was not among them. Throughout a writing career which lasted over half a century, Hanley continued to use the conditions of the working class – at home in the cities, or, most famously, on board ship – as material for his stories. This dual source of narratives – at home or abroad, at rest or in motion, concerned with place or with forms of displacement – is how the German writer and Marxist aesthetician, Walter Benjamin, also writing in the thirties, categorized the two funda-mental forms of storytelling: 'If one wants to picture these two groups through their archaic representatives, one is embodied in the resident tiller of the soil, and the other in the trading seaman. Indeed, each sphere of life has, as it were, produced its own tribe of storytellers.' Although these may be in some senses analytically and historically separable, as Benjamin goes on to point out, 'The actual extension of the realm of storytelling in its full historical breadth is inconceivable without the most intimate interpenetration of these two archaic types.'[6] Ken Worpole, in 'Expressionism and Working Class Fiction',[7] one of the most useful articles on the subject, extends Benjamin's model to twentieth-century working-class writing.

The Furys is representative of the movement of Hanley's novels in the thirties in bringing together the two loci of narration. Whereas earlier works like *Boy* (1931) or *Captain Bottell* (1933) had concentrated on life on board ship, and later ones like *Stoker Bush* (1935) alternated between ship and shore, *The Furys* is set entirely on land, though ships remain an important dimension – past, present and future – of the life of the Fury family. If *The Furys* is slightly unusual among Hanley's novels of the period in being set entirely on shore, then it is even more so to the extent that it includes some militant working-class action, in the shape of a strike

---

5 Carole Snee, 'Working Class Literature or Proletarian Writing?', in Jon Clark, Margot Heinemann, David Margolies and Carole Snee, *Culture and Crisis in Britain in the 30s* (London: Lawrence & Wishart, 1979), p. 181.

6 Walter Benjamin, 'The Storyteller', in *Illuminations* (London: Fontana, 1973), pp. 84–85.

7 Ken Worpole, 'Expressionism and Working Class Fiction', *New Left Review*, 130 (1981), reprinted in *Dockers and Detectives* (London: Verso, 1983), pp. 77–93.

which paralyses Gelton[8] (Hanley's fictionalized Liverpool) for several weeks. This location on land has a number of consequences in the novel. One is that the book focuses on a family and its problems. Indeed, as the first part of a five-volume family saga, it is without parallel in working-class writing, with the exception of Lewis Grassic Gibbon's *A Scots Quair*[9] and perhaps Alan Sillitoe's projected but incomplete chronicle of the Seaton family begun in *Saturday Night and Sunday Morning* (1958). Only the early films of Terence Davies offer a comparison. This 'return to the family' on Hanley's part might seem no more than a proper return to what many regarded as the appropriate focus for working-class fiction. As Worpole remarks, 'Family life, then, was portrayed as the natural cell of the working class community, and the permanent continuity of place and employment were the buttresses needed to ensure that family life continued as it should.'[10] While such an image is by no means completely divorced from reality, it was the case, as Worpole acknowledges, that for some sections of the working class stability and continuity were categorically not the norm. For each group, the needs of capitalism for a static or a fluid workforce (or even for no workforce at all in certain circumstances), rather than any characteristic or dynamic of the community itself, determine whether the lived experience is one of place and continuity or transience and displacement. (These could of course be experienced in different ways, as, for instance, when people aimed for continuity of employment by following the same job from place to place, or, perhaps a more common option, where by choosing to remain in one place people were forced to move from one job to another.)

Although the family is the focus of *The Furys*, it is a fragmented family, divided against itself at every level, where even those members who are still living together are variously alienated from one another. Even Denny Fury, the father and perhaps the most human character, feels this: 'Family. His family. Christ! It made him laugh. Bloody fool he was ever leaving the *Cardine*. Yes, he thought, a bunch of strangers. Their father. It made him laugh.'[11] The novel follows a period of crisis in the family,

8 'Gelt' was a slang term for 'money'. See Eric Partridge, *Dictionary of Slang and Unconventional English*, vol. 1, 5th edn (London: Routledge & Kegan Paul, 1961), p. 320.

9 Gibbon's *A Scots Quair* consists of *Sunset Song* (1932), *Cloud Howe* (1933) and *Grey Granite* (1934). It is a first-person narrative of a Scottish woman's painful transition from farm to city life in the years before and after the First World War.

10 Worpole, *Dockers and Detectives*, p. 78.

11 James Hanley, *The Furys* (1935) (Harmondsworth: Penguin, 1985), pp. 50–51. Hereafter *Furys*.

(which happens to coincide with the period of the strike). The youngest son Peter returns home unexpectedly from his Catholic college in Ireland, expelled, as we learn later, for immorality. This is a particular blow to his mother, Fanny, who has not only invested all her hopes and aspirations in him, but also rather more money in the shape of college fees than other family members considered reasonable, and it is resentment over the preferential treatment given to Peter which is one of the divisive factors in family relations. The alienation of the family members from one another is a mirror of relations in society at large – in a classically Marxist way, though this is certainly not the perspective Hanley is using. Personal contact appears limited, superficial or undesired; neighbours are interfering, workmates tedious. Exaggerated, even callous, individualism is counselled and practised, but then, in one of the novel's many disconcerting shifts, is (seemingly) undermined by the extraordinary and unlooked-for generosity shown by Joe Kilkey, the son-in-law whom Fanny has previously despised and shunned.

Sudden shifts also occur frequently in the characters' assessments of one another, which can make reading an unsettling process. To her husband, Fanny can be stubborn, domineering, over-emotional, unpredictable, even 'a devil', 'driven by an almost insane ambition', but then suddenly she can be 'a brick', worth ten of her sister, and far too good a person to be treated in the way that Peter is currently behaving towards her. Perhaps the most extreme example of such a *volte face* occurs in Peter's strange, almost hallucinatory, encounter with the bizarre Professor Titmouse, which ends with Peter's violent rejection of the latter's sexual advances. Thereafter, Peter feels disgusted, nauseated at the memory of this 'madman', but in a sentence or two this has changed to '"Poor man!", said Peter, "he said he was lonely. Poor man!"' (*Furys*, p. 250). One effect of such shifts is no doubt to discourage any secure reader position with regard to the character being assessed, and, in addition, to the character doing the assessing. Such a lack of readerly certainty finds a correlate in the world of the novel, where nothing, it seems, can be relied on, and certainly not people. For Fanny, this is powerfully demonstrated by the person she had placed her hopes on, her favourite son Peter, who progressively crushes her, firstly by his departure from the seminary, secondly by the revelation that he was expelled for immoral behaviour, and finally by the disclosure, on the last page of the novel, of his affair with his sister-in-law.

Questions of place and displacement may be subject to less disconcerting shifts, but are nevertheless not the site of any stable signification.

Place, not surprisingly, connotes roots and security: before the onset of complete senility, old Mr Mangan, Fanny's father, frequently expresses the desire to return to Ireland; for Denny, in spite of all the upheavals, 'There was something splendid about the word "home", there was something to look forward to ...' (*Furys*, p. 207). At the same time, it can be stagnation or entrapment: Denny, for example, (contradictorily, unsurprisingly) feels stifled on land and longs to go back to sea: 'Once he had been a seaman. Now he felt he was nothing. He was unused to living ashore; a street was only another sort of monstrous stone cage, behind the brick bars of which the human monkeys chattered incessantly' (*Furys*, p. 49). For the Fury family, their years in Hatfields seem a period of stagnation and missed opportunities rather than of stability or security. Conversely, displacement can be seen negatively: Mr Mangan forced to leave home by his father during a period of famine; both Fanny and Denny forced to come to England to look for work; the family dispersed and disunited. It can also have its appealing aspects, however, in the freedoms offered by a life in the merchant navy, for instance, which claims so many members of the Fury family.

It is the depiction of, and attitudes towards, work (including the merchant service) and the working class which form the most important area of representation in the novel. The detailed description of work (especially the manual labour of the working class) does not often appear in mainstream literature. In *The Political Unconscious*, Fredric Jameson notes what he calls the 'aestheticising strategy' by which the fact of work is transformed in literature into something 'derealised', hence more acceptable and consumable. In Joseph Conrad's *Lord Jim* (1900), for instance, which Jameson discusses, labour issues as a distant rhythmic noise from somewhere deep inside the ship. In *The Furys*, a possible parallel would be the work in the bone yard which issues as an all-pervading smell (though it is perhaps difficult to see this breath-stopping stench as 'aesthetic'). The novel does, however, contain an important representation of work, when Peter observes the railway gangs at work at night. Apart from showing the actual processes of work, the passage is important because it also emphasizes the difficult conditions of work, its extreme dangers (one man is almost killed as Peter watches), and the fact that such unremitting and unseen work is the basis for the continuation of ordinary daytime existence. It is, however, the last description of work, since the chapter ends with the news that the strike has begun.

If work is rather conspicuous by its absence, it nevertheless functions as a kind of 'absent cause', determining the actions, the presence or absences of characters, organizing their lives, and to that extent, arguably ever-present. Paradoxically, its double absence during the strike only seems to make it more obsessively present in people's thoughts and conversations. The strike has been mentioned – if scarcely discussed – prior to its starting. The general attitude in the Fury household appears to be to ignore it until it happens. Here again, we meet the apparently unmotivated swings of opinion mentioned earlier. Denny, for example, rejects the strike: 'Strike. Confound the damn strike. It would come now' (*Furys*, p. 78), but soon after comes to say, '"There's going to be a real strike. No half-hearted affair. They want us to support the miners. Poor bastards! They always do it dirty on the miners"' (*Furys*, p. 106). People such as Fanny's sister Brigid see the strike purely in terms of how it inconveniences them personally, while others like George Postleth-waite feel it is an infringement of their individual rights which far outweighs any potential collective gain: '"Rights! What rights? Seems everybody's gassing about rights. What about other people's rights, Fury? What with all these rights that's been fought for and lost, and fought for and lost again, seems to me there's precious little rights left"' (*Furys*, p. 183). For Fanny, the strike is a series of obstacles which stand in the way of her getting on with what is important to her – the day-to-day struggle to survive, and for many others, the strike is no more than a novel, temporary, and curious backdrop to their daily lives. Even the fact that it lasts for several weeks only serves to make it seem somehow normal, a quasi-fact of life.

The ideological implications of this downgrading of the importance of the strike can perhaps be gauged by contrast with the weight which a strike can carry in literature:

> Indeed, a curious sub-form of realism, the proletarian novel demon-strates what happens when the representational apparatus is confronted by that supreme event, the strike as figure for social revo-lution, which calls social 'being' and the social totality itself into question, thereby undermining that totality's basic preconditions: whence the scandal of this form, which fails where it succeeds and succeeds where it fails, thereby evading categories of literary evalua-tion inherited from 'great realism'.[12]

12 Fredric Jameson, *The Political Unconscious* (London: Methuen, 1981), p. 193.

In *The Furys*, however, there is absolutely no question of the strike acting as a figure for revolution or the undermining of the social totality.

The downgrading of the strike is paralleled by the nature of the representation of political action and political activists. The character apparently most committed to the working-class struggle is Fanny and Denny's eldest son, Desmond, but he is revealed as both self-seeking and contemptuous of the people on whose behalf he is organizing:

> '[I'm] going to walk out of this stinking muck-heap, and on some-body's back too. Doesn't matter whose ...'
> 'Well,' said Peter, 'that's honest. Is that why you joined the Labour Party?' 'Yes,' he said. '... Do you think those people are interested in bettering themselves, in improving their conditions? No sir! ... Let the bastards vegetate, let them lie in their own muck. They're not interested.' (*Furys*, p. 277)

Other working-class organizers are shown to have similarly insulting attitudes; for Desmond, however, the strike is principally an opportunity for advancement, and one which he is determined not to let slip. Though the ruling class is ultimately the enemy for Desmond, there is no sense of his being motivated by the sort of mean-spirited desire to overthrow them simply because they are the ruling class which is held to characterize working-class leaders (and indeed in later volumes in the Fury saga he seems actively to prefer the idea of joining the rulers rather than beating them). While this is perhaps a change from the standard middle-class explanation of working-class political action as motivated by *ressentiment*,[13] it is scarcely a great improvement.

Although the attitudes of Desmond and his comrades may seem crudely contemptuous, there is no alternative or more positive image of mass action, or of the mass of the people to be found in the book. Professor Titmouse may be politically very distant from Desmond, but his view of the crowd gathered to protest against earlier police brutality is at least as negative: '"Come," said the professor. "Stand up and look into the seething abyss. Behold those who have risen from ten thousand stinking mattresses, who have emerged from their rat-holes. Look at them! Bury your nose in that stinking heap"' (*Furys*, p. 247). Significantly, both Professor Titmouse and the labour leader who comes to

13 See Jameson, *The Political Unconscious*, chap. 4.

address the mass meeting regard crowds as 'headless monsters', and their rapid degeneration from orderly meeting to rampaging mob would seem to bear out that assessment. There remains the suspicion, however, that it is behaviour rather than politics which counts: we are told of the mass meeting, 'It was not authority that was being questioned by the crowd, but the manners of authority' (*Furys*, p. 197) – a question, then, not so much of politics as of *politesse*.

This whole area does appear to have been a continuing problem for Hanley. Worpole comments on an earlier book:

> Socialist politics enter the novel only briefly, represented by the least convincing of any of the characters in *Drift*. The socialists are portrayed as middle and upper class aesthetes who lounge about in each other's flats listening to Beethoven and talking about Tolstoy and modern sculpture. Such a portrait was clearly a deliberate misrepresentation by Hanley[.][14]

The upper-class aesthetes may have gone from *The Furys* (leaving Professor Titmouse as a distant, surreal echo), but arguably the misrepresentation of working-class politics in Liverpool remains as strong. The possible explanation for this type of attitude, that the early thirties was a period of disenchantment with working-class politics after the failure of the General Strike, is not available in this case, since activism, and strikes, continued.

If work stops or disappears from view in the novel, if the working-class struggle is accorded little importance, there is still one place where work continues, and that is the home. Revealingly, this is also the only context in which the word 'struggle' actually occurs in the book, used on a number of occasions by Fanny, and as such warrants the inversion of the title of Edward Upward's novel *No Home but the Struggle* – written in the 1930s but not published until the seventies – in the title of this chapter. This ideological shift to the private sphere is no doubt justified in the text's terms, since, despite Worpole's assertion – 'Once again, this family, or "workers' dynasty" as Soviet critics have come to call this kind of novel, is centred round the whims and wishes of the father, Denny Fury'[15] – it is Fanny, not Denny, who is the centre of what

14 Worpole, *Dockers and Detectives*, p. 81.
15 Worpole, *Dockers and Detectives*, p. 83.

happens in the family (as well as being the character whose behaviour merits the term 'whim'). This is not simply a 'realist' shift of focus or emphasis as a result of the absence of 'proper' work outside the home, but owes more to a revaluing in various ways of the domestic, the female and the personal in the novel, at the expense of the public, male and collective dimensions. *The Furys* is a more female-centred text than Hanley's earlier works, with women featuring as central, and generally autonomous, characters. Not that female autonomy is necessarily seen as a good thing: in some ways, the most autonomous (because least constrained by accepted norms of proper behaviour for women) is Sheila, Desmond's wife, who refuses both domestic role and domestic location. The fact that she goes for a walk or sits on the seashore alone is at best a puzzle and at worst a scandal for family and neighbours. This appearance of being out of control is most warranted by her sexual behaviour: she is willing to start an affair with her young brother-in-law Peter, and there is a suggestion that she may be a part-time prostitute. Significantly, however, the impetus for the affair comes not so much from her as from Peter. Although this maintains an interest in the problems of adolescent sexuality visible in some of Hanley's earlier works, it shifts the emphasis from the adolescent as sexual prey – graphically enacted in *Boy* – to the adolescent as sexual predator. Like his predecessor Joe in *Drift*, Peter has been involved with a prostitute (the reason for his expulsion from the seminary), but his decision to start an affair with his sister-in-law does seem much more predatory. Worpole comments:

> Sexuality is 'an abyss of desire' which is likely to consume and devour. It stands in opposition to the declared values of proper family life and therefore can only be found away from the community in the twilight world of those who have rejected (or have been rejected by) the puritan certainties of those working class communities where religion is a much more powerful ingredient of consciousness than are the material exigencies of class.[16]

On the face of it, sex with your sister-in-law might seem anything but 'outside the community', but the contradiction may be more apparent than real. Sheila is a Protestant, and in marrying her Desmond has put

16 Worpole, *Dockers and Detectives*, p. 81.

himself on the margins of, if not completely outside, certain forms of community: he is ostracized by his family; he does not go to church, but he is still part of the working, and politically active, segments of the community, insofar as any sense of community can survive in Hanley's world of fragmented families, antagonistic neighbours, alienated and self-seeking individuals.

The contradictions examined so far at the level of content and ideology are also present at the level of genre and style, as the novel shifts between detailed realism and non-realist modes, including allegory and what we might call hyper-realism. The latter is most strongly present in such scenes as Peter and Professor Titmouse's visit to the gathering in the square, which has a Joycean 'Nighttown' feel to it, but also occurs in the daydreams, visions and strange mental states experienced by a number of characters. This stylistic variation has troubled critics' attempts to locate Hanley: early commentators tended to see him as a realist; Stokes reads him as both realist (of sorts) and naturalist; Worpole argues for him as an expressionist.

Those allegorical elements which critics have noted are most visible in the move away from geographical and historical specificity. For instance, although the strike in *The Furys* is a major one, there is no attempt to locate it historically, and virtually no internal evidence on which to base an informed guess. Consequently, commentators make of it what they will: the Penguin reprint makes the obvious assumption, and decides that it is the General Strike of 1926; Stokes says that it is 'the railway strike of 1911' and/or 'the 1912 transport strike'; Worpole puts it a decade later: '[Peter] witnesses the large demonstrations of the Liverpool unemployed and their brutal suppression by the police (described at length by George Garrett in *Liverpool 1921–1922* and later by Jim Phelan in *Ten-a-Penny-People*).'[17] The politics of allegory are contradictory: on the one hand, the lack of specificity has historically been claimed as a necessary precaution against adverse reaction, including censorship or suppression of the text; on the other hand, that same lack of specificity has been attacked, by black and Third World critics, for example, as a refusal to engage directly with contemporary political and social problems – an accusation which might with some justice be levelled at Hanley.

There is, however, another reading of allegory which would make

17 Worpole, *Dockers and Detectives*, p. 84.

its use here appear more appropriate. For Walter Benjamin, modernity is characterized by discontinuity, fragmentation and shock, and his description of allegory is of a mode particularly suited to the contemporary world and our experience of it. Allegory for Benjamin is a mode of fragments, 'the privileged mode of our own life in time, a clumsy deciphering of meaning from moment to moment, the painful attempt to restore a continuity to heterogeneous disconnected instants'.[18] These, plus Benjamin's paradoxical notion of progress as catastrophe, typify life under contemporary capitalism as experienced by Hanley's characters. In this, the home – imagined as a fictionalized Liverpool – usually seen as a place of safety and certainty, is, no less than the world outside, the site of the crucial struggle to make meaning, to make the connections that matter.

18 Fredric Jameson, *Marxism and Form* (Princeton: Princeton University Press, 1971), p. 72.

3

Paradise Street Blues:
Malcolm Lowry's Liverpool

Chris Ackerley

In deference to Malcolm Lowry's masterpiece, *Under the Volcano*, biographers and scholars often begin at the end, with his death. Lowry's end did not quite complete the circle of its beginning; equally, most of his projected work remained incomplete, a voyage that never ended. Lowry was born and raised in Cheshire, but most of his erratic schooling was in Cambridge, and after an acrimonious break with his family he did not return to the Liverpool area. Rather, he married an American woman, Jan Gabrial, in France; followed her to New York and Los Angeles; and took her to Mexico (1936–37), where the drinks were cheaper and his allowance went further. The marriage did not survive the Mexican inferno, but after escaping to Los Angeles Lowry met Margerie Bonner, his second wife, and settled in Vancouver for the happiest and most productive decade of his otherwise shambolic life.

The success of *Under the Volcano* (1947) relieved some of Lowry's financial and artistic worries, and after much travelling the Lowrys in 1956 settled in the small Sussex village of Ripe. Although Margerie made brief contact with the Lowry family, Malcolm did not, and when visiting the Lake Country, he avoided Liverpool and Cheshire. His death by misadventure on the night of 26 June 1957 (after swallowing a bottle of sodium amytal sleeping tablets) may or may not have been tacitly abetted by his wife, whose accounts were contradictory, but it generated a last jest that Lowry would have appreciated. Douglas Day, Lowry's early biographer, traces the events of that fraught evening: Margerie upset; a row ensuing; Lowry buying a bottle of gin; a botched last supper; a further row over the volume of a BBC Stravinsky concert; Margerie trying to take away the gin; Malcolm attacking her; Margerie taking refuge with Mrs Mason next door; and her resolution when she woke up the next morning to get 'poor Malcolm' a cup of tea, then go up to Liverpool to see if she could get control of part of the estate to hold over him when he had such attacks. Day's first chapter concludes by telling how Margerie climbed up to the bedroom and found Malcolm on the floor beside the smashed gin bottle: 'Without hesitating, Margerie ran back to Mrs. Mason's. "Oh, Winnie," she cried, "he's gone!" "Where, Liverpool?" asked Mrs. Mason. "No, he's dead." And so he was.'[1]

Clarence Malcolm Lowry, the subject of this dark comedy, was born at midnight on 28 July 1909 at 'Warren Crest', North Drive, New Brighton, the fourth of four sons of Arthur Osborne and Evelyn Boden Lowry. Muriel Bradbrook, born in the same town and in the same year, describes the house as being on a high sandstone ridge, overlooking several golf courses, light-houses, sand-dunes and market gardens; an elegant residence with a view of the sea.[2] The house is no longer there, Wallasey having suffered heavy bomb damage during the Second World War and the site redeveloped. Lowry liked to recall that he was born close to Rock Ferry where Nathaniel Hawthorne was US Consul to Liverpool, and 'where Herman Melville had announced to Hawthorne his determination to be annihilated'.[3] The family soon moved to 'Inglewood', in Caldy, on the other side of the Wirral, on the Dee estuary south of Hoylake. Bradbrook comments:

> To stand at the site of either of Lowry's homes is to look westwards over a wide scene of great beauty and variety. Behind, and eastward, across the Mersey estuary, lies the port of Liverpool, which for Lowry came to symbolise hell; before, the expanse of the Bay. Green levels behind the dunes stretch towards the Clwyd range; the sunsets are of extraordinary brilliance. This was Lowry's first Eden.[4]

Bradbrook affirms that the 'topography of Leasowe lighthouse, the sunken remains of the primeval forest in the early golfing scenes of *Under the Volcano* are all faithful'.[5] She acknowledges the lighthouse and the

1 Douglas Day, *Malcolm Lowry: A Biography* (London: Oxford University Press, 1974), p. 49.
2 Muriel Bradbrook, *Malcolm Lowry: His Art and Early Life: A Study in Transformation*. (Cambridge: Cambridge University Press, 1974), p. 29.
3 Gordon Bowker, *Pursued by Furies: A Life of Malcolm Lowry* (London: St Martin's Press, 1997), p. 7.
4 Bradbrook, *Malcolm Lowry*, p. 30.
5 Bradbrook, *Malcolm Lowry*, p. 30.

forest as 'powerful elements' in the novel, but insists that 'the landscape is literally precise' and should not be interpreted as if it were a cabbalistic setting. Bowker confirms Lowry's exact description: 'the broad sweep of the Dee estuary with the Welsh mountains beyond; Liverpool Bay and Hilbre Island; and the strange coastline near Leasowe, with its ancient sunken forest and lonely lighthouse'.[6] Bradbrook acknowledges that 'the scene is not placed on those links where Lowry played', by which she means the nine-hole course at Caldy and the Royal Liverpool Links at Hoylake, from where the forest and lighthouse are not visible.[7] Although she and Bowker rightly stress Lowry's close observation both fail to account for 'the geography of the imagination', or degree to which he re-arranged and mythologized the landscape:

> On the shore were the remains of an antediluvian forest with ugly black stumps showing, and farther up an old stubby deserted lighthouse. There was an island in the estuary, with a windmill on it like a curious black flower, which you could ride out to at low tide on a donkey. The smoke from freighters outward bound from Liverpool hung low on the horizon.[8]

Lowry has moved his Caldy home to Leasowe (between Hoylake and New Brighton), to get the view (bay, freighters, sunken forest and lighthouse), but has retained the setting of the Royal Liverpool Links at Hoylake (the island to which one might ride is Hilbre, accessible from West Kirby at low tide). Moreover, the details are more than 'precisely observed': the 'antediluvian' forest intimates the novel's Atlantis theme; the lighthouse, the Farolito; the windmill, Don Quixote; and the 'black flower', a song called 'Flores negras' sung in the *Salón Ofélia* (*UTV*, 307). The Consul's future is presaged even in his childhood years.

The golf course with its ominous 'Hell Bunker' also anticipates the Consul's fate. According to Bradbrook,[9] this bunker was 'a well-known hazard' of the eighth hole (a short par 5) of the Royal Liverpool Links at Hoylake. Russell Lowry confirms this, adding that it was filled in

---

6 Bowker, *Pursued by Furies*, p. 8.
7 Bradbrook, *Malcolm Lowry*, p. 30.
8 Malcolm Lowry, *Under the Volcano* (1947) (Harmondsworth: Penguin, 1963), p. 23. Hereafter *UTV*.
9 Bradbrook, *Malcolm Lowry*, p. 153.

before the Second World War,[10] but I am not convinced, for when I visited Hoylake nobody at the club could recall the name. The name was probably transposed from the fourteenth hole of the Old Course at St Andrews, a long par 5 with a huge bunker left of the green. Either way, it foreshadows the dark bunkers of the Farolito in *Under the Volcano,* where the Consul visualizes the reeling universe as a cosmic golf course with himself descending into the *barranca* ('Golf = *gouffre* = gulf') to retrieve lost balls (*UTV*, pp. 206–207).

Lowry did not remember his childhood as a happy one. Russell Lowry recalled that at Malcolm's twenty-first, his 'coming of age', their father, after proposing Malcolm's health in 'Mr Whiteway's admirable but not very stimulating cider', asked for his earliest recollection; to which Malcolm replied: 'As far as I can remember my childhood was one of perpetual gloom. I was either blind, constipated or a cripple. In later years my only pleasure was sneaking off occasionally with Russell to the pictures.' According to Russell, this dropped on the room 'like the second Ice Age'; but nothing happened, 'Father cleared his throat and we moved on to the pudd'.[11] But Lowry in later life returned frequently to the theme, as in the poem 'Autopsy' (1940):

> An autopsy on this childhood then reveals
> That he was flayed at seven, crucified at eleven,
> And he was blind besides and jeered at
> For his blindness. Small wonder that the man
> Is embittered and full of hate …

Lowry would later claim that he was an unwanted baby, a mistake, 'thrown together by a cotton broker in less than 5 minutes. 5 seconds perhaps?'.[12] He told Clarissa Lorenz: 'My nanny used to whip me daily with brambles until I bled. I thought it was the customary thing so I never complained. My parents gave her the sack only after the family gardener told them he saw her hold me upside down over my bath.'[13] The truth seems to be that a beloved nursemaid, Miss Bell, was replaced

---

10 Russell Lowry, 'Clearing up Some Problems', *Malcolm Lowry Review,* 21 and 22 (Fall 1987 and Spring 1988), pp. 100–102.

11 Bradbrook, *Malcolm Lowry,* p. 23.

12 Bowker, *Pursued by Furies,* pp. 6–7.

13 Clarissa Lorenz, 'Call It Misadventure', in Margerie Lowry (ed.), *Malcolm Lowry: Psalms and Songs* (New York: New American Library, 1975), p. 65.

by Miss Long, whom Russell and Malcolm disliked 'for no other reason than that she was not Miss Bell',[14] and that young Malcolm probably had a temper tantrum and was whacked with whatever was handy. From this memory Lowry built a sad tale of suffering, claiming that he had been 'beaten on the genitals with a bramble branch, sexually abused, and held upside down over the cliff's edge'. Bill McConnell was like-wise told of a sadistic nursemaid who wheeled Malcolm's pram along the cliff's edge, above the rolling sea, then tried to smother him.

The 'blindness' had a similar aetiology. In 1920, Lowry suffered inflammation of the eyes and corneal ulceration. A Harley Street specialist scraped his eyeballs in a painful but effective process that brought lasting relief (though he had to wear a patch for a time). Lowry said that the problem lasted four years, and that he was not allowed home because of his disfigurement; his family insisted that it lasted a few weeks only. Earlier, while free-wheeling down the steep King's Drive, Caldy, Lowry had severely gashed his right knee, and minor surgery left a diag-onal scar; this became a wound sustained in Tong warfare. Margerie Lowry claimed in *Psalms and Songs*: 'Malcolm was turned down by the armed forces because of a bad injury to his knee caused by a bullet wound suffered on his earlier trip to China.'[15] Stories of being bullied at school or as a Wolf Cub, whatever their germ of truth, grew in the telling. Lowry later propagated the legend of a first-class degree, despite having done no work for it; in truth, he was lucky to get a Third, and that only because *Ultramarine*, his first novel, published while he was still at Cambridge, was accepted in lieu of other writing. This ongoing fabri-cation was less self-promotion than a compulsive need to reinvent himself. Even in *Under the Volcano* he lacked the surgical detachment to separate himself from his characters; the corollary was that his personal life, the source of all his writing, demanded the metamorphosis of fact into fiction.

That process extended to his parents. Lowry's father, Arthur Osborne Lowry (1870–1945), was the son of a jobbing builder living at 14 Admiral Street, in the respectable lower middle-class suburb of Toxteth Park, Liverpool. Serious and hard working, by nineteen he had advanced to the position of accountant with the cotton-broking firm of A.J. Buston & Co., which had extensive international interests in oil and sugar. After his marriage in 1894 he moved across the Mersey to

14 Bowker, *Pursued by Furies*, p. 10.
15 Lowry, *Psalms and Songs*, p. xii.

various residences in Wallasey and finally to Caldy, rising in the firm and travelling daily to the Liverpool Cotton Exchange from 1912 in a chauffeured Minerva that took him to the Birkenhead ferry. A self-made man, and keen on physical activity, he was by no means the huntin' and shootin' philistine that his wayward son sometimes described him as. A strict Methodist, he disapproved of smoking, drinking or jazz. By his lights he was a good parent, but he lacked a sense of humour and did not relate easily to his sons, each of whom found ways (such as sneaking off to cinemas or listening to jazz) to subvert his authority. Malcolm was a particular disappointment, a 'perpetual source of anxiety to a bewildered father';[16] and was, finally, the only one not to enter the family business. But as Russell Lowry pointed out, 'A much maligned father always paid the bills'.[17]

Malcolm often referred to his father as the 'OM' or 'Old Man', a common enough sobriquet, but the overtones of a sea captain in conjunction with Lowry's irrational fear of authority were enough to demonize him in the private mythology. A 1936 poem entitled 'Prayer' begins: 'Give way, you fiends, and give that man some happiness / Who knelt in Wesleyan prayer to beget a fiend' (*Collected Poems*, no. 64). As Bradbrook notes, his father 'remained for him the figure from his youth; he never imagined the septuagenarian with the bombed offices and suspended business who in 1944 [*sic*] died of cancer of the bowel'.[18] Even in Mexico and Los Angeles Malcolm felt that he was under his father's authority, not only because he was dependent on the monthly allowance that, whatever the provocation, was never suspended, but because his father also paid for lawyers and minders to keep an eye on him. The Consul's pervasive sense of mysterious men in dark glasses spying on him in *Under the Volcano*, then, is not just paranoia (though it is that as well, and equally a manifestation of the daemonic world infiltrating the physical), for it is also a complex invisible chain of command that, no matter where he might be, attached Lowry to Liverpool. Sherrill Grace found, for instance, when compiling Lowry's correspondence, that some of his letters had been forwarded, without his knowledge, from lawyers in Los Angeles to Arthur Lowry in Liverpool, where she discovered them in the Brown, Picton and Hornby Libraries.

16 Lorenz, 'Call It Misadventure', p. 62.
17 Bradbrook, *Malcolm Lowry*, p. 27.
18 Bradbrook, *Malcolm Lowry*, p. 151.

Lowry's relationship with his mother was even more complex. An ineffectual parent, she was not easily loved by any of her children, and Malcolm's dealings with her combine a rejection of her social, religious and personal values with a sense of guilt arising from the lack of her love and his reciprocal coldness. Most of the correspondence between Malcolm and his mother is missing, but he wrote surprisingly regularly, especially after Arthur died. She was one of the first to whom Lowry telegraphed when *Under the Volcano* was accepted in 1947, though this could be construed as a plea for recognition to a previously disappointed parent that his life was not, after all, entirely in vain (his father had died without seeing that success).

Evelyn Boden Lowry (1873–1950) was raised close to her husband, at 113 Handel Street, Liverpool, and shared his wish for betterment and prosperity, but lacked the social skills to achieve them easily. She was the daughter of a master mariner, Lyon Boden, lost at sea in circumstances that were variously described and embellished, by both Evelyn and her son, in the telling. As Lowry told the story to Margerie (who, again, seems to have taken it as gospel), Captain Boden and his command, *The Scottish Isles*, were becalmed in the Indian Ocean, the crew dying of cholera; so the Captain gave orders to a nearby British gunboat to blow up the ship, with him on board. Bradbrook debunks this by saying that Captain Boden had died of cholera, the news relayed to a passing vessel before *The Scottish Isles* vanished and was lost in a storm with all hands.[19] Bowker found that the ship on which John [*sic*] Boden disappeared on 26 April 1884, somewhere in the Indian Ocean, was the *Vice Reine*, of which Boden was not captain but first mate.[20] But Lowry had his myth and told it many times: in *Ultramarine*, 'Through the Panama', *Dark as the Grave*, *October Ferry*, and 'The Forest Path to the Spring'. Its importance was manifold. Firstly, 'Boden' *sounded* Norwegian, which let characters from Dana Hilliot of *Ultramarine* to Sigbjørn Wilderness of the later tales share a Liverpool-Norwegian ancestry, like that of the *Oedipus Tyrannus* on which Dana, and later Hugh Firmin sails (the *Oedipus Tyrannus* reappears in a number of Lowry's later stories). The Liverpool-Norwegian connection was to feature in a novel, *In Ballast to the White Sea*, of which only fragments remain after the 1944 burning of Lowry's Dollarton shack; but scattered

---

19 Bradbrook, *Malcolm Lowry*, p. 25.
20 Bowker, *Pursued by Furies*, p. 4.

comments in his letters reflect these polarities. Secondly, Lowry could choose his romantic maternal heritage over the paternal line of dull respectability; in the 1940s he published poetry under the name of Malcolm Boden Lowry. Thirdly, it let him weave his literary filaments: in 'Through the Panama', a report that his mother is seriously ill leads Martin Trumbaugh to recall the last time he saw her, 'at Rock Ferry Station, Birkenhead (where Nathaniel Hawthorne was Consul)'.[21] Finally, the repressive mother became in *Ultramarine* the impetus for going to sea. Dana recalls his mother saying: 'Why are you so dirty, Dana? My father was always so clean, so spruce. He had his master's certificate before he was twenty-three. When he came ashore he always came in a cab, and wore a top hat ... He was an angel from heaven. He was bringing me a cockatoo.'[22] The dramatic consequence of this is that Dana finally becomes not a seaman, let alone an angel from heaven, but a fireman, a stoker, in the fiery bowels, the infernal Moloch of the ship. Like the Consul in the as yet unwritten *Under the Volcano*, he has chosen hell.

James Stern recalls his first chance meeting Lowry in a Paris bar, each having read and admired the other's book: 'It was I who managed to find words first. "Liverpool?" I uttered. "Ultra-Liverpool?" "Liverpool, yes," he flashed. "Painted across my stern."'[23] In 'Through the Panama', Sigbjørn sees a ship coming from London, calls his countrymen 'rude London bastards', and reflects that he dislikes Londoners anyway, since he comes from Liverpool.[24] Given that Lowry's major protagonists are inevitably transparent projections of himself, it is not surprising that most are from Liverpool or Cheshire (Ethan Llewellyn of *October Ferry* is Welsh and Kennish Drumgold Cosnahan of 'Elephant and Colosseum' is a 'Manxman of distinction',[25] but the point holds). In *Under the Volcano*, Geoffrey Firmin and his half-brother Hugh were orphaned in India, then sent to the Taskersons in Leasowe. The Taskersons represent the family that Lowry would have preferred: 'unprecedented, portentous walkers', and vigorous drinkers (including the mother) who

21 Malcolm Lowry, *Hear Us O Lord from Heaven Thy Dwelling Place* (1961) and *Lunar Caustic* (1963) (Harmondsworth: Penguin, 1979), p. 9.
22 Malcolm Lowry, *Ultramarine* (1933) (Harmondsworth: Penguin, 1974), pp. 110–11. Hereafter *Ultramarine*.
23 Lowry, *Psalms and Songs*, p. 74.
24 Lowry, *Hear Us O Lord*, p. 57.
25 Lowry, *Hear Us O Lord*, p. 48.

yet prided themselves on their 'erect manly carriage' (*UTV*, p. 24). They are modelled on the Furniss family of Hillthorpe (near Caldy): John Furniss, a local lawyer, with his wife Mary raised their eight children (six boys) in 'a free and progressive manner', which meant plenty of walking and drinking.[26] Arthur Lowry strongly disapproved. As Bowker notes, James Furniss had rescued the younger Malcolm from being bullied at 'Braeside', the local day school in West Kirby; and the debt was not forgotten.[27] Abraham Taskerson also incorporates aspects of Conrad Aiken, Lowry's surrogate father, such as poetry and the love of cats (one was named 'Oedipuss Simplex'). Yet Lowry has difficulties in reconciling this liberality with his own Wesleyan upbringing that is also the Consul's cross to bear; the impulse to mythologize all his experience creaks at this point.

Another discrepancy arises with respect to the Q-ships of *Under the Volcano*. During the First World War the Consul was commander of the SS *Samaritan*, the name of which resonates through the book, from the episode of the dying Indian to the Consul's own death. Q-boats, or 'Mystery Ships', were gunboats disguised as merchantmen to tempt submarines to the surface by an apparent surrender. Guns were concealed beneath false hatches, and a 'panic party' would leave the ship, leaving a gun crew on board, waiting for the submarine to present a suitable target. Shortly after the war, a Q-boat came to the Mersey and was opened to the public. Lowry's brother Wilfrid, a part-time officer in the Royal Naval Volunteer Reserve, took Malcolm and Russell to see how the false hatches and guns were lowered and raised. Lowry never forgot this experience. The Consul in his garden, tipsy and nostalgic, recalls the Western Ocean of his soul and the landing at Liverpool, the Liver Building seen once more through the misty rain, and 'those mysterious submarine catchers Q-boats' (*UTV*, p. 135). In Chapter 1, the *Samaritan* is in the Pacific, and somewhere near Volcano Island, Guy Rock and the Euphrosyne Reef a U-boat is destroyed. The location is historically implausible as German U-boats did not operate so far afield and Q-boats were restricted to an arc radiating from Liverpool between Archangel, New York and Gibraltar. Again, Lowry has violated the perfectly wrought surface realism that he valued so highly for the sake of structural and symbolic effects: the anticipation of Hugh's

---

26 Bowker, *Pursued by Furies*, p. 27.
27 Bowker, *Pursued by Furies*, p. 13.

later voyage and the *Samaritan*'s alchemical cargo of 'antimony and quicksilver and wolfram' (*UTV*, p. 38).

By the mid-forties, Lowry was embarked on what he called *The Voyage That Never Ends*, an ambitious fiction that embraced the mundane and occult realms, and their interpenetration. This intention shaped the later writing and may explain why so much was not completed; the voyage, quite literally, could never end. Lowry sporadically offered increasingly sceptical publishers and literary agents blueprints of his grand design, which he constantly revised, so that no simple plan may be offered. Broadly, however, it combined a Dantean three-part structure (Hell, Purgatory and Paradise) with a seven-part pattern of his own devising, with the Mexican writing and especially *Under the Volcano* at its heart. One volume was always to be a voyage out, a revised *Ultramarine*, and it is likely (though the destruction of *In Ballast to the White Sea* makes this speculative) that another would deal with the 'Ordeal' (Lowry was fond of the word) of his Liverpool childhood. Lowry later revised many of his first fictions to make them fit this design, as well as writing new ones that referred to his early years. The rest of this study, then, looks at the Liverpool of Lowry's imagination, first in its own terms and then as it enters, or might have entered, the larger plan.

As Gordon Bowker notes, the 'terrible city' of Liverpool supplied Lowry with two enduring and related visions: '… that of the lunatic city inside which he was to feel trapped and was to suffer, and that of the pathway to the sea and the ocean voyage, the risk-laden escape route from lunacy into uncertainty'.[28] Both were present in the early fictions, and persisted into the later ones. One juvenile effort, 'A Rainy Night', describes a train trip from Yeovil to Liverpool. The narrator, who dislikes his sardine sandwiches, meets Olivsen Christofersen, an 'old' sailor (all of thirty-two), who is on his way to join the *Tasmania* at Liverpool. The train traverses 'the slums of Liverpool', but when it reaches Central Station, the narrator, in the joy of seeing his wife, ignores the seaman, who is found that night dead of starvation in the compartment, even as the narrator's wife finds the uneaten sandwiches.

More promising is 'Enter One in Sumptuous Armour', which opens on the golf course, looking over the Dee, on a freezing day with snow in the bunkers: 'Out there, beyond Hilbre, Lycidas had drowned.'[29]

28 Bowker, *Pursued by Furies*, p. 2.
29 Lowry, *Psalms and Songs*, p. 230.

Returning to school, the narrator describes a drive in the family Minerva across the moors ('Public Footpath to Thingwall') and past small villages (Frankby and the Farmer's Arms, Greasby and the Coach and Horses), through Upton and the Ring o' Bells and on to Birkenhead (the Dolphin, the Blue Peter and the Right Whale). He sees advertisements for the Hippodrome and the Argyle, 'familiar placards that were like friends' before getting off at the Mersey Underground Railway (his father is dropped at James Street) to continue by train to Central and Lime Street: 'Going to school was an insanely complicated business.'[30]

Another piece, 'Goya the Obscure', depicts Liverpool as one of Lowry's cities of dreadful night. Joe Passalique, a trimmer from the *Dimitrios N. Bogliazides*, crosses the Mersey on a sinister ferry (Charon's boat, the infernal tunnel below) to Liverpool, a haunted city of sexual sickness and fear. He has left the sea with a dose of VD and fears to return to his pregnant wife. Walking the streets of Liverpool, he finds himself at the Paradise Street Anatomy Museum, with its dictum, 'Man, Know Thyself', and he envisages the sordid end awaiting him, 'a vicious circle from which there could be no escape'. The vision recurs in *Ultramarine*, in Dana's vision of himself walking down Great Homer Street, stricken with a like disease (*Ultramarine*, p. 165).

Liverpool arouses mixed feelings. 'China' tells of a sailor who spent his life on a vessel plying between Liverpool and Lisbon, and on retiring was only able to say of Lisbon: 'The trams go faster there than in Liverpool.'[31] In 'Through the Panama', an Englishman, 'who had evidently not lived in Liverpool', has the gall to write of Panama, 'It would be difficult to find elsewhere on the earth's surface a place in which so much villainy and disease and moral and physical abomination were concentrated'.[32] In this story, the sand dunes of Willemstadt are like those at Hoylake, 'only infinitely more desolate'; but there is in Curaçao more of a sense of ships and the sea (writes Martin) than in any other part of the world, 'except Liverpool'.[33] 'Elephant and Colosseum' refers to Liverpool as 'that somber and neighboring city' (Margerie's spelling); and the 'Present State of Pompeii' is likened to 'the ruins of Liverpool on a Sunday afternoon'. Yet 'The Forest Path to the Spring' describes a celestial apparition of terrifying beauty as 'a whole blazing Birkenhead

30 Lowry, *Psalms and Songs*, pp. 233, 234.
31 Lowry, *Psalms and Songs*, p. 49.
32 Lowry, *Hear Us O Lord*, p. 59.
33 Lowry, *Hear Us O Lord*, p. 68.

Brocklebank dockside of fiery Herzogin Ceciles'.[34] A rather maudlin late draft of a story called 'Ghostkeeper' is set in Stanley Park, Vancouver, which reminds the protagonist of his birthplace, New Brighton, England, later depicted on screen: 'There's the cathedral! That's Seacombe Pier! That's New Brighton Pier! There used to be a tower only they knocked it down. That's the old prom – called the Ham and Egg Parade. Birkenhead Ales, my God.'[35]

A defining moment for Lowry was his decision in 1927 to go to sea. This forms the substance of *Ultramarine* (1933) and an important thread of *Under the Volcano* (1947), Hugh Firmin's experience replicating that of Dana Hilliot. Arthur Lowry, through his personal contacts with J. Alfred Holt, arranged for Malcolm to be taken on as a deckhand on the SS *Pyrrhus*, a fact that quickly became known to his shipmates, who made pointed comments about doing a good lad out of his job, and bloody toffs who went to sea for experience. Although Lowry had to sign on at the Marine Superintendent's Office, as Dana does on the first page of *Ultramarine* and as Hugh recalls doing, he was driven to the dock on the evening of Friday 13 May in the chauffeured Minerva (*UTV*, p. 161). Next day the *Liverpool Daily Echo* ran the headline 'Rich Boy as Deckhand', quoting Lowry as saying: 'No silk-cushion youth for me. I want to see the world, and rub shoulders with its oddities, and get some experience of life before I go back to Cambridge University.' This did not go down well with the said oddities, who made his trip a misery. The details are recorded in *Ultramarine* with a scrupulous honesty (p. 163), while Hugh in *Under the Volcano* writhes to think of the humiliation that his little publicity stunt has brought him.

The *Pyrrhus* was a freighter of the Blue Funnel Line, Alfred Holt & Co. (Liverpool), built in 1924 by Workman, Clark & Co. of Belfast, with a tonnage of 7,603, a length of 455 feet six inches and a service speed of eleven knots. She was refurbished after the war to carry passengers, but by Lowry's time was cargo only. She would be torpedoed on 17 February 1940 off Cape Finisterre en route from Liverpool to Gibraltar, with the loss of eight lives. The *Oedipus Tyrannus* is fictional, but Blue Funnel ships, distinguished by their tall blue funnels with black tops, were named after Greek heroes. The *Philoctetes* (built 1922) on which Hugh first signs, as well as the *Helenus* (1913), *Menelaus* (1923)

---

34 Lowry, *Hear Us O Lord*, pp. 136, 183, 259.
35 Lowry, *Psalms and Songs*, p. 217.

and *Agamemnon* (1929), called in the poem 'Only God Knows How III' (*Collected Poems*, no. 74) 'Homeric errors', were sister ships of the Blue Funnel Line. Lowry caused his shipmates further grief by calling the *Pyrrhus* a tramp instead of the 'Blue Piper' freighter that she was. Hugh changes in mid-voyage from the *Philoctetes* to the *Oedipus Tyrannus*, because to him she is more of what a ship should be: foul and rusty, with poor food and dysentery, and a forward fo'c'sle; in short, a tramp (*UTV*, p. 169). The *Pyrrhus* was scheduled to sail from Birkenhead for Yokohama via Port Said and Penang on 14 May: this is changed in *Under the Volcano* to Friday 13 May, partly for the ominous overtones of Black Friday, but also for the 'poignant historical coincidence' of Frankie Trumbauer's *For No Reason at All in C* ('for no reason at all at sea'), recorded in New York on that very day.

For the sailors in *Ultramarine*, Liverpool is home: 'ten months and we'll be docked in Liverpool again'; 'how I wish I was back in Liverpool' (*Ultramarine*, pp. 49, 168). Andy and Norman, Norwegians both, give their address as Great Homer Street (a seafarers' home?), while Dana offers 'Sea Road, Port Sunlight'. For Dana, Liverpool means Janet, the 'adored but absent virgin', the good angel in his mind as he is assailed by thoughts of fornication in the brothels of the East.[36] In life she was Tessa Evans, of 26 Thirlmere Street, Wallasey, with whom Lowry played golf, wandered over the Wirral, and visited cinemas in Birkenhead and Liverpool. In the novel she is Janet Travena, of 26 Dornberg Road, New Brighton. Dana thinks of her constantly: waiting at the Crossville bus stop to go to the Hippodrome or the 'twice-nightly' features at the Argyle; walking out on the Saughall Massie Road, with tea at Hubbard and Martin's; the yellow Liscard bus they should have caught but pretended not to see; the ships seen together as they stroll towards Egremont Ferry; and the Mersey ferry boats, as recalled in a letter from Janet that finally arrives, Seacombe emerging from the fog as Liverpool disappears (*Ultramarine*, pp. 27, 98, 31, 63, 130, 145, 169). The romance is adolescent, even mawkish (Hugh Firmin in *Under the Volcano* echoes many of these details, but without the soft sentiment); but it testifies to a Liverpool that Lowry loved, and one that wrought always a strange enchantment.

For there was always the other Liverpool, with its syphilitic streets and derelict human husks staggering down them. That dark side is

---

36 Bowker, *Pursued by Furies*, p. 60.

present in Dana's imagination from the outset, most graphically in the images of ulcerated penises, disfigured foetuses and 'the famous pickled testicles' of the Anatomical Museum in Paradise Street.[37] Douglas Day claims that Lowry's eldest brother, Stuart, aged nineteen, took Malcolm, aged five, and paid the six shillings entry to the 'Syphilis Museum', where pallid plaster casts with their evidence of the ravages of venery made a lasting traumatic impact on Malcolm (the theme, 'first Venus, then Mercury', is iterated in several later works).[38] Russell Lowry, noting that Day invariably gets his skeletons out of the wrong cupboards, corrects the date from 1914 to 1927, when Lowry was eighteen and about to sail on the *Pyrrhus*, 'which made the timing pretty good!'[39] He described the 'Museum' as a cautionary exhibition of pictures, models and specimens, not necessarily syphilitic, aimed at Liverpool's large seafaring fraternity and located in Paradise Street on the fringe of the dock area, in a single dingy room. The entrance fee was sixpence ('six shillings is a twelve-fold exaggeration'). Like most of Paradise Street, the building was destroyed in the air raids of 1940. Muriel Bradbrook says that the museum was part of the 'Flying Angel' headquarters dedicated to the welfare of merchant seaman and warning them of the vile consequences of sexual misadventure.[40] It certainly had that effect on Lowry. In *Ultramarine*, Dana visits in Tsjang-Tsjang a small anatomical museum ('the only one of its kind in Asia') that offers evidence of the iniquities of the fathers as visited upon the sons, and detailed descriptions, which Lowry must have copied or memorized from Paradise Street, of the effects of depravity (*Ultramarine*, pp. 103–104). A little later, an inebriated Dana tells an unidentified seaman from New Brighton of his girl back home and the identical museum there, and begins to sing the shanty, 'As I was walking down Paradise Street' (*Ultramarine*, p. 113). Terror, rather than loyalty to Janet, proves the more effective prophylactic.

The syphilitic strain in *Ultramarine* also owes its origins to Nordahl Grieg's *The Ship Sails On*, which Lowry read in 1927. When young Benjamin Hall joins the *Mignon*, he finds the trip a miserable experience and finally contracts syphilis. At the end of the voyage he climbs over the rail to end it all, but changes his mind and turns to face what life his

---

37 Bowker, *Pursued by Furies*, p. 40.
38 Day, *Malcolm Lowry*, p. 67.
39 Russell Lowry, 'Childhood Agonies', *Malcolm Lowry Newsletter* 7 (Fall 1980), p. 18.
40 Bradbrook, *Malcolm Lowry*, p. 27.

raddled being may find. Lowry 'borrowed' many details from Grieg, whom he later met in Oslo. However, the dominant literary influence on *Ultramarine* was Conrad Aiken's *Blue Voyage* (1927), which Lowry imitated so much that Aiken, both amused and exasperated, suggested that it might better be entitled 'Purple Passage'. Lowry interpreted the dedication to 'C.M.L.' (Clarissa Lorenz) as a mystical message to himself, and the ship's destination of Liverpool as a further confirmation. He wrote to Aiken, and sailed to Boston to meet him and work on *Ultramarine*; he even returned by the *Cedric* (the unnamed ship in *Blue Voyage*), the better to emulate his surrogate father. A third shaping fiction was Herman Melville's *Redburn*, which depicts the trials of the wealthy but naïve young Wellingborough Redburn on his maiden voyage from New York to Liverpool. Like Redburn, Dana Hilliot is one who 'takes the soul to sea' only to find the mildew fallen upon it, a blight that leaves such a scar 'that the air of Paradise might not erase it'.[41] This image returns in 'The Days like Smitten Cymbals of Brass' (*Collected Poems*, no. 196). Dana's task in *Ultramarine*, as Hugh's in *Under the Volcano*, is that of chipping rust off the vessel of the soul. All these works blend as *compañeros* on the unending voyage; Lowry's borrowing is less plagiarism than part of what he termed 'the unimaginable library of the dead' (*Collected Poems*, no. 301) from which all books might be borrowed and in which his own work might be filed, alongside Grieg, Aiken, Melville, and even *Peter Rabbit* (*UTV*, p. 178).

One early poem testifies to Lowry's grand design. 'Peter Gaunt and the Canals' (1936) is written like a dream by Ibsen's Peer Gynt of a world of canals: Suez; Panama; from the White Sea to the Baltic; and from Liverpool to Manchester, by Runcorn and the Ship Canal. Conrad Aiken recalls that the incinerated *In Ballast to the White Sea* included a description of 'a drunken steamboat ride up the Manchester Canal from Liverpool'.[42] In Lowry's greater vision, and the microcosmic manifestations thereof, ships coming from or steaming to Liverpool threw invisible hawsers about the world, bringing humanity together through locks and canals, in a manner reminiscent of Whitman's 'Passage to India'. One specific image of this is a ship with the curious name (a perfect pentameter) of the *Dimitrios N. Bogliazides*, described in *Ultra-*

---

41 Herman Melville, *Redburn* (1849) (Harmondsworth: Penguin, 1976), p. 53.
42 Gordon Bowker (ed.), *Malcolm Lowry Remembered* (London: BBC [Ariel Books], 1985), p. 9.

marine as 'an old Greek bastard of a tramp steamer', bringing a cargo of timber from Archangel to Garston (*Ultramarine*, p. 72). She (almost certainly) would have been part of *In Ballast to the White Sea*; she is mentioned in 'Goya the Obscure'; and she is implicit in 'Hotel Room in Chartres', a ship with 'stacks of timber from Archangel beside her' (*Psalms and Songs*, p. 23). In the poem, 'From Helsinki to Liverpool with Lumber' (*Collected Poems*, no. 77), she steams down the Mersey; in 'Reflection to Windward' (no. 124) she rolls seaward on the high tempestuous seas; and she finally turns up in Lowry's screenplay of Fitzgerald's *Tender is the Night*, where she comes in vain to the rescue of a doomed Dick Diver.[43]

Towards the end of his life, as he was revising 'Enter One in Sumptuous Armour', Lowry still recalled the pull of the sea and its strange enchantment, and how 'filthy, sinister, clap-stricken old Liverpool' was dear to his heart.[44] Liverpool, with the Mersey as its highway to the world, is recalled in a number of poems, such as 'Villaknell' (*Collected Poems*, no. 138), with its reiterated lines: 'But now I see myself a fool … For I was born in Liverpool'. A 'Poem Influenced by John Davenport and Cervantes' (no. 159) laments: 'And youth was born to die in Liverpool'. 'Freighter 1940' (no. 162) depicts the launching of a freighter built in Birkenhead during the blitz, while about her in the Mersey the ferry, 'quite as Charon's boat, knows death' (one was sunk in the bombing), and beneath her in the Birkenhead tunnel, 'men breathe'. Pier Head, on this biting Saturday, is the annex of Dante's hell. Another poem (no. 233) begins: 'Imprisoned in a Liverpool of self / I haunt the gutted arcades of the past'; these arcades are, as Muriel Bradbrook explains,[45] the Goree Piazzas, on the Dock Road, which were also destroyed by bombing in the war, where slaves were reputedly chained before being shipped off to the Americas.

Yet if Liverpool had this infernal aspect, such poems as 'When I am in the purgatory of the unread' (no. 112) affirm that what will survive 'must go back to Pier Head'. The phrase 'the salt gray prop', used in this poem of Liverpool's Pier Head, also appears in a description of Lowry's pier at Dollarton (no. 172), as if to insinuate a mysterious connection between the exiled soul and its port of origin. Dollarton,

---

43 Miguel Mota and Paul Tiessen (eds), *The Cinema of Malcolm Lowry: A Scholarly Edition of Lowry's 'Tender is the Night'* (Vancouver: UBC Press, 1990), p. 239.
44 Bowker, *Pursued by Furies*, p. 41.
45 Bradbrook, *Malcolm Lowry*, p. 4.

Burrard Inlet and Vancouver ('Enochville') reflect the Wirral, the Mersey and Liverpool, with Eden on one side of the estuary and a city of dreadful night on the other; the Shellburn area of Burnaby (opposite Dollarton) is renamed 'Port Boden'; on occasion the 'SHELL' sign might lose its 'S', and a lurid 'HELL' blaze across the waters.[46] In Lowry's later fiction, Dollarton became 'Eridanus', named after a ship of the Astra line that had been driven ashore in a Chinook wind, 'with her cargo of old marble, wine, and cherries-in-brine from Portugal'. With the ghost of the words '*Eridanus* – Liverpool' still visible on her stern, she seems to the narrator of 'Forest Path to the Spring' to comment on himself: '... for I too had been born in that terrible city whose main street is the ocean' (*Hear Us O Lord*, p. 226). Despite a constant threat of eviction, Eridanus is a paradise, in an earth that has become so terrible and foreign that 'a child may be born into its Liverpools' and never learn to appreciate its simple beauty (*Hear Us O Lord*, p. 241). Yet Muriel Bradbrook may be right when she describes the 'Aeolian' unity of 'Forest Path', and calls it 'perhaps the finest thing Lowry wrote' (p. 14); for here, far from (yet inseparably linked to) its Liverpool origins, Lowry's shipwrecked soul finally found refuge.

46 Malcom Lowry, *October Ferry to Gabriola*, ed. Margerie Lowry (New York and Cleveland: World Publishing Co., 1970), p. 15.

4

'Unhomely Moments':
The Fictions of Beryl Bainbridge

Helen Carr

'Being a child lasts for ever; the rest of life soars past on wings.'[1] So Beryl Bainbridge wrote in 1987, and it is a sentiment she has repeated at other times and in other words. Bainbridge began her career as a writer, she says, in order to try to understand her own often painful and unhappy childhood, starting to write books at the age of nine, though her first novel was not published until she was thirty-three. That childhood was spent in the Liverpool area, and even when her books are not set in Liverpool – though many have been – her unvarnished, alarmingly clear-eyed view of the monstrous messiness, self-deception, mingled selfishness and warmth that form the human condition owes much to her experience of growing up there.

Beryl Bainbridge was born in 1934, and brought up in Formby in Lancashire, on the coast just north of the city. Her father's family had lived in the centre of Liverpool, off Scotland Road, but her father wanted his family to come up in the world. Like many other middle-class aspirants of the period and of the post-war years, who moved out of the city to the nearside seaside resorts of the Wirral or the Lancashire coast, he decided to bring up his family away from the working-class streets of central Liverpool where he had spent his youth. Her mother's family, who had lived, as Bainbridge puts it, in a 'suburban villa in West Derby', were regarded as more respectably middle class; her mother had even been sent to a finishing school in Belgium, but their origins too were more dubious – her mother was furious when Beryl's maternal grandmother let slip that she had worked in a lollipop factory in Knotty

1 Beryl Bainbridge, *Forever England: North and South* (London: Duckworth/BBC Books, 1987), p. 164.

Ash when she was eleven.[2] She also tried to suppress the fact that her sisters-in-law had done similarly lowering work, Auntie Margo working in a munitions factory and Auntie Nellie as a cleaner. (The aunts appear under their own names in *The Dressmaker* (1973) – Auntie Margo's usual job was as a dressmaker, though here it's Nellie – a novel set in wartime Liverpool, and the first of Bainbridge's novels to be short-listed for the Booker Prize.) Yet as Bainbridge makes clear in both her fictional and non-fictional accounts, middle-class aspirations did not mean affluence. Her father married her mother in 1926. He was a successful businessman at the time, but went bankrupt shortly afterwards, and anxieties over money fuelled the constant tensions between her parents that seared her early years. Like Harriet in *Harriet Said...* (1972), the first novel she wrote, though not the first she published, she would turn up the wireless, as she always calls it, when she came home from school to mask the sound of their quarrels.

Bainbridge grew up in the years of the Depression, the war, and post-war austerity; the beginnings of a more prosperous world did not appear until she was a young adult. Keeping up appearances was her parents' constant, desperate task. When going out they had to appear respectable, neat and tidy, shoes polished; at home the cups and saucers never matched, they had no pyjamas, only one toothbrush, and in winter, as in so many working- and lower-middle-class households of the period, only one small room was heated. It was just as well they rarely had unexpected visitors; the unheated front room, Bainbridge avers, possibly with some exaggeration, would have put them at risk of frost bite. 'I think,' she has said, 'the biggest change for most people in my life time, more than the Pill or the fact that now nearly everyone has a car and a TV, is reliable hot water, and being warm'.[3] There was some money, but it went towards school fees (she was sent to the well-regarded Merchant Taylors' School in Liverpool), school books, elocution lessons, Latin coaching, dancing classes and music lessons. Bainbridge does not appear to have appreciated these attempts at betterment. She loved going into Liverpool with her father and visiting her more easy-going, less pretentious aunts, though she knew better than to mention these visits to her mother. Her father's nephew Jack was a butcher off the Priory Road, and, much to her mother's ire, her father insisted on visiting Liverpool

2 Bainbridge, *Forever England*, p. 31.
3 'Beryl Bainbridge: Total Immersion in the Past', *Publishers' Weekly*, 11 September 1998.

weekly to buy the Sunday joint from his nephew's shop, going on to drive hard bargains over fish in St John's Market. Beryl would go too, and as they drove in through Seaforth and Bootle and along the dock road, her father, who before the First World War had briefly been to sea and had later been in shipping, would recall the busy docks, numerous shipping lines, and over-flowing warehouses of his youth, stories which would always end with the miseries of life on board, and the virtues of his own saintly mother.

Her father had a violent temper, and though he was never physically violent, he had a harsh tongue, and Bainbridge found her mother's constant unhappiness painful to watch, however irritated she might also be by her snobbishness. Her brother had a nervous breakdown at eighteen, which she puts down to the tense and explosive atmosphere of home. At the time the breakdown was ascribed to the strain of exam-inations, and indeed, if the deprivations endured to enable him to take such examinations caused such ongoing misery, the pressure must have been intense. Bainbridge dealt with it differently. By that age, she had escaped, by what seems to have been a mixture of conscious and uncon-scious design. At fourteen she was expelled from school. Her mother had found what Bainbridge describes as a 'naughty rhyme' in one of her pockets, and went to see the school without even letting her know.[4] It was an extraordinary act. Perhaps she blamed the school, and they would have none of it, but young Beryl was convinced that her mother thought that she was a 'rotten apple' who would infect the whole school, and that she had reported her because she felt it was her moral duty to expose the harm that she might inflict.[5] It can't have improved the atmosphere at home. She was sent off for a year to boarding school, a bewildering experience; the most useful thing she learnt, she says, was that it was not always necessary to shout, as she had had to do at home to be heard over the angry voices. It was a ballet school, and if it didn't do much for her ballet, her tap dancing improved. At sixteen she ran away to London, for a Northerner 'an act of betrayal as well as of folly', as she puts it, the South being regarded as an alien and dangerous place, where people ate dinner instead of tea, and respectable young girls 'could go off to the typing pool after breakfast and be sucked into the white slave trade by tea, never to be heard of again'.[6] She worked for a while in a cinema,

4 Bainbridge, *Forever England*, p. 97.
5 Bainbridge, *Forever England*, p. 97.
6 Bainbridge, *Forever England*, p. 14.

but she was soon back, and joined the Liverpool Playhouse – surprisingly, her father helped her get the job, perhaps keen that at least the elocution classes and the tap dancing should not go to waste – an experience on which she drew in *An Awfully Big Adventure* (1989). Her sense of dramatic structure and the importance of the voice perhaps owe something to her experience as an actress. Among other places, she worked for a while for the Dundee Repertory Theatre, converting during her time there to Catholicism, which she had wanted to do, she says, since she came across Fra Lippo Lippi's paintings at the age of thirteen. Yet that was surely another effort to distance herself from her family and their beliefs; her father was convinced that Catholics were 'worse than bugs'.[7] She was then nineteen; in Scotland, unlike England, one could change religion without parental permission at that age. The height of her acting career was an appearance in the seventh episode of *Coronation Street*, but by twenty-one she had given up the stage (and Catholicism) for marriage and motherhood. Her marriage to the painter Austin Davies broke up after the birth of their second child, but he helped support the children, and in 1963 bought the house for her in Camden Town where she still lives. Her first novel appeared in 1967; her nineteenth will come out next year.

If her early books were written, as she says, 'to get out this business about my mum and dad', that does not mean they are self-pitying; far from it.[8] She is not only interested in understanding what happened to herself – though there are telling explorations of a young woman's dawning and confused sexuality, and conflict with authority figures – but she also wanted to understand how people like her parents had come to be the way they were. In the house where she grew up, there was a photograph of them on honeymoon looking radiantly happy. What went wrong? She wanted to uncover the story, delve into the past, to explore the stages by which people become who they are. Writing was one means by which this could be done; her painting (intriguingly surreal) seems to be another, though she has never done that professionally. Bainbridge's writing career is often seen as two distinct stages – the early work in which she often draws on her own background, mainly set in Liverpool, though sometimes, like *The Bottle Factory Outing* (1974) and *Sweet William* (1975), in London, and then the later books, from the early 1990s onwards, which are much more wide-ranging

7 Bainbridge, *Forever England*, p. 163.
8 Lynn Barber, 'Beryl's Perils', *The Observer*, 18 August 2001.

historical novels. But there are important continuities, and she had in fact much earlier already written two historical novels, so the break is not as neat as is sometimes implied: what goes through them all is that interest in how the past shapes the present, how childhood shapes the adult, the way cultural mores and social habits form personalities and guide their actions, whether in twentieth-century Liverpool or eighteenth-century London, and in tandem with that understanding of causality, a dark sense of the random chanciness of fate, and the terrifying ease with which human beings can bring disaster on themselves.

In her historical novels as in her novels of the Liverpool of her youth, her own experience of life, she says, enters into their making; she writes:

> In my opinion, there is no such thing as the imagination – in the sense we have the power to form images of our own making – for unless we've acquired images, from somewhere, how can we possibly summon them into existence, reformed or not? One can't be born with an imagination. It isn't the same thing at all as a pair of lungs or a toe or a blue eye. It must surely grow with us, built from lost conversations and forgotten events, dependent on impressions and sensations which fall through the mind like shooting stars; gathered from fuzzy remembrances of pictures in story books, of wallpaper patterns, fragments of nursery rhymes and Sunday school parables, whispers in the next room, footsteps in the dark, etc, etc.[9]

She wrote that about the writing of one of her early historical novels, *Watson's Apology* (1984), the story of a clergyman-murderer in the nineteenth century. (He is a creature of the utmost respectability until he kills his wife; such violence lurking beneath surface propriety and piety made it an irresistible theme for Bainbridge.) *Watson's Apology* is preceded by an intriguing 'Author's Note', in which she says,

> This novel is based on a true story ... Almost all the characters are drawn from life, as are the details of the plot ... What has defeated historical enquiry has been the motives of the characters, their conversations and their feelings. These it has been the task of the novelist to supply.[10]

---

9 Bainbridge, *Forever England*, p. 58.
10 Beryl Bainbridge, *Watson's Apology* (London: Duckworth, 1984), p. 6.

This is something, I think, which in some ways applies to all her novels, whether drawn from her life or that of others. She wants to uncover and understand the motivations and emotions of her characters; her extraordinary psychological insight, and her ability to enter into the feelings of those whose lives and beliefs are completely alien to her own, are some of her most striking gifts.

As a literary figure, Beryl Bainbridge has a reputation for eccentricity, something she both cultivates on the one hand and repudiates on the other. Interviewers repeatedly comment on the bizarre interior of her Camden Town house, the statue of St Patrick that greets you, how you have to squeeze past the stuffed water buffalo in the narrow hall, Victorian paintings, figurines and statues everywhere, and a life-size dummy with a Hitler moustache in her bedroom. All these, apart from the latter – they didn't enter the bedroom – were made much of in the South Bank Show in 1998 when she was interviewed at home by Melvyn Bragg; the camera dwelt particularly lovingly on a life-size painting of an elderly, melancholy Queen Victoria, looking indeed a little tipsy, perhaps what attracted Bainbridge. Her love of Victoriana, found through Dickens, is in reaction to her parents' pride in a newly built house in a newly built suburb: 'There is nothing like reading *Bleak House* at an impressionable age in a bungalow,' she says, 'for fixing the mind ever afterwards on garrets and cellars and aspidistra in the parlour.'[11] She employs all her not inconsiderable skills as an actor, Lynn Barber has suggested, to produce an image of unthreatening oddity, something Barber sees as a form of defence against the world, the product of an ongoing need to protect herself from criticism and attack that goes back to her childhood traumas. But if waywardness and a taste for the bizarre are part of her hallmark as one of the North London literati, as a novelist she disputes the label of eccentricity bitterly. As she says indignantly,

> What they don't realise when they say a bit eccentric – and it's the only time I get hot under the collar – is the discipline needed to get something done and something done properly – and in the early days bringing up a family as well. What you need is enormous discipline – eccentricity doesn't count for a flipping thing.[12]

In another interview she insisted, 'I don't see you can be eccentric and

---

11 Bainbridge, *Forever England*, p. 23.
12 Barber, 'Beryl's Perils'.

still pay the bills, and own a house, and baby-sit for six grandchildren every week.'[13] And of course she is right; she is a highly disciplined and productive writer, a perfectionist, throwing away twelve pages for every one she keeps, or rather, perhaps one should say, honing twelve pages down to one. Her books are brief, usually less than 200 pages, her writing sharp and spare, yet psychologically complex, densely plotted, compellingly narrated. Her historical novels are meticulously researched. Yet perhaps her complaint against the label comes partly from a sense of not being taken as seriously as she should be; I would certainly argue that her writing has never gained quite the recognition that it should. That may seem a strange thing to say of a writer who was made a Dame in 2000, the ultimate in establishment recognition, and of someone whose work has been awarded so many prizes, among others the Guardian Fiction Prize for *The Bottle Factory Outing* (1974), the Whitbread Novel Award for *Injury Time* (1977) and for *Every Man for Himself* (1996), and the James Tait Memorial Prize and W.H. Smith Literary Award for *Master Georgie* (1998). She has been short-listed for the Booker five times. But why has she never won the Booker, and why was *According to Queeney* (2001), arguably her most profoundly humane and terrifyingly honest novel, not even short-listed? And why is it, with academics increasingly writing about contemporary literature, that she is so often passed over?

Beryl Bainbridge is engagingly unpretentious, but I don't think it is because she doesn't present herself sufficiently portentously that she has not attracted that kind of scrutiny, nor is it even actually much to do with her personal reputation as a fey eccentric. I would suggest it is more related to the fact that she has never written in ways which fitted in with what was fashionable at a particular moment, or for which there was a ready academic language. One can contrast her with Angela Carter, for example, about whom there are numerous academic articles; funding bodies have been driven to complain about the number of students wanting to write theses on Carter's work. My admiration of Carter is second to none, but I would suggest the academic attention paid to her in recent years has been much facilitated by the fact her work fitted so well into current categories like magic realism, postmodernism, or gender theory; there was a set of literary critical theories to hand. Bainbridge's novels have never fitted in that way. She has always dissociated

13 'Beryl Bainbridge', *Publishers' Weekly*.

herself from feminism, and there has so far been little feminist criticism of her work, though in fact her resistance to seeing women as victims has much in common with Carter herself. Nor could she be accommodated into categories like the postcolonial or the diasporic, though perhaps in the wake of this book that will change – after all, there's increasing discussion of Scottish writing in terms of postcolonialism, so why not Liverpool? And Bainbridge is undoubtedly a writer of the Liverpool diaspora, but so far that's not been a critical category.

So what kind of novels does Bainbridge write? She has said that one of the writers who influenced her most was D.H. Lawrence, particularly his *Sons and Lovers*. Of course, honing down was never Lawrence's style, and there is nothing of what is generally meant by Lawrentian in her writing, but there are ways in which one could see how he was important to her, particularly when she began, as a writer who drew on his own life in a section of society very different from that familiar to the educated classes of his day, who in order to make sense of his own experiences had to go back and unpick the dynamics, desires, tensions and prejudices of the world in which he grew up. There's an inextricable admixture of the autobiographical and ethnographic in such writing, perhaps one of the most significant aspects of the twentieth-century novel, as we've moved to an increasingly culturally diverse and socially mixed society, writers making their worlds legible to readers who may be from very different backgrounds, indeed, making them legible to themselves, finding, in the phrase Toni Morrison quotes from Marie Cardinal, 'the words to say it'.[14] That combination of the autobiographical and ethnographic has surely been a feature of much postcolonial and diasporic writing, from James Joyce and Jean Rhys onwards. There are elements of that fusion in the group of writers that dominated the decade before Bainbridge started writing, the generation known as the angry young men, mainly ex-grammar school boys, writing out of the cultural clash between their backgrounds and the unreceptive establishment world they met, but Bainbridge has little in common with them. On the one hand, though some of them, like John Braine and Alan Sillitoe, certainly helped to put the North on the literary map, the image of northern writers they reinforced was male and working class, characteristics undoubtedly associated in the national mind with the essence of Liverpudlianism. Bainbridge wrote from the

14 Toni Morrison, *Playing in the Dark: Whiteness and the Literary Imagination*
(Cambridge, MA: Harvard University Press, 1992), p. 4.

position of a woman and from the precarious edges of the middle class. But in addition, anger and indignation are not part of her repertoire. The sixties, the decade when satire was reborn and the status quo was mocked rather than railed against, were congenial years for her to launch her writing career. Black comedy is a term reviewers like to use of her writing, useful shorthand, perhaps, though it is debatable whether the phrase quite conveys her mixture of the ironic dissection of banality, compassion and consciousness of human pain. The sixties and seventies were years when Liverpool played a significant part in a powerful critique of the traditional hierarchies that had bolstered British assumptions about class, respectability and authority, a critique that has transformed our culture. Bainbridge's first novel appeared the same year, 1967, as *Sergeant Pepper's Lonely Hearts Club Band*. Her style is different, but equally subversive.

Anna Haycraft, the wife of her publisher for many years, Colin Haycraft of Duckworth, said to Bainbridge when she was first signed on by them in the early seventies, 'Write about what you know, get yourself a good plot and cut out all the adjectives.'[15] Writing about what you know is of course well-established advice – Henry James had famously told Edith Wharton to do just that when she started out as a novelist. Yet Anna Haycraft's comment perhaps suggests that her publishers saw Bainbridge's appeal as a realist, regional writer, a skilful but minor novelist; certainly they paid her very small advances, which may be an indication. Bainbridge remains grateful to Colin Haycraft, but it was after his death that she was able to develop in new ways. 'He was a great mentor, a great teacher,' she has said, 'but in a funny sort of way his death released me to write about more serious things. I couldn't have written the historical books if Colin had been alive, I'd have felt I didn't know enough.'[16] I don't think it is the case that the earlier books are not equally serious in their own way, but the canvas is different; their worlds are sharply and acutely delineated, but they evoke very specific and particular milieus. The later novels range far further – not just in place and social class, but in the width of historical insight. I think one could make a cautious analogy with the changes in Liverpool's own culture over the years, from being, as many places in Britain were in the forties and fifties, inward-looking, concerned with its own immediate world, to a city, as its choice as 2008 European Capital of Culture so

15 'Beryl Bainbridge', *Publishers' Weekly*.
16 Barber, 'Beryl's Perils'.

clearly indicates, with an international perspective, and a sense of its place in a wider history. Liverpool felt very much a separate culture in the years after the war, when I myself was growing up there. As Bainbridge has commented,

> Time was when you could go on an outing to a town barely thirty miles distant from your own and it was like visiting another country. The shops sold different goods and the names painted above the doors were unfamiliar. You could go to Preston for Swedish furniture – though God knows why it had ended up there – to Southport for a frock from the Bon Marché, to Ormskirk for bedding plants, to Pot Williams in Warrington for cups and saucers. Even the people seemed foreign, and the air so heady and strange that you came back giddy.[17]

As this reminds one, Liverpool contrasted itself not just with the South and London, though it certainly did that, but even more so with its neighbours, in my memory at any rate, most frequently and fiercely with Manchester, its twin city in the north-west, with which it felt a deep-seated rivalry and towards which Liverpudlians expressed steady animosity. Liverpool is historically, as John Belchem points out, a very mixed city in its make-up, with numerous Irish, Welsh and Scottish settlers (Bainbridge's father's family were from Scotland), as well as black and Chinese communities, and a comparatively large Jewish population. But that very mixture was perhaps what made it feel a place different from its neighbours, just as its Scouse accent, so unlike that of the rest of Lancashire, has been ascribed to its influx of Irish. This was the world that had formed her parents and that Bainbridge analysed with probing acuity in the earlier work. In the later works, she explores other people's worlds and the larger history of Britain in which all those issues of class and convention that she met in her childhood had their origin.

To return to Anna Haycraft's advice, her second admonition was to find a good plot, something that could pull against the advice to write about the known; life does not often fit itself neatly into plot-lines. As Jean Rhys wryly put it, in irritation at the way her novels were so often read as transparent autobiography, 'a novel has to have shape, and life doesn't have any'.[18] While Bainbridge may draw on aspects of her own experience, it is always crafted and shaped, a skill which is equally or

---

17 Bainbridge, *Forever England*, p. 77.
18 Jean Rhys, *Smile Please* (1979) (London: Penguin, 1981), p. 10.

even more important in the historical novels, where the reader is often aware of the general outcome – the *Titanic* is not going to reach America in *Every Man for Himself,* any more than Scott is going to make it back to England in *The Birthday Boys.* Bainbridge in fact gives her later historical fictions particularly inventive and suggestive structures, as if to draw attention to the fact that though they may be drawn from life, what we are given is art, the novelist's interpretation of how things may have been, and what they meant. For example, in *The Birthday Boys,* she tells the story of Scott's final ill-fated attempt on the South Pole through five first-person accounts, ranging over a period of twenty-one months, one from each of five who were on the last leg of the assault on the Pole. In *Master Georgie,* in which the Liverpool surgeon and keen photographer George Hardy goes with an assortment of followers to the Crimea War, each section is presented as a photographic plate, from the first, '1846: Girl in the Presence of Death' to the sixth, '1854: Smile, Boys, Smile', as one might guess, a darkly ironic title. The Crimea was the first war from which photographs were sent home, staged photographs, not ones of action, and each section is in a way the telling of the story that lay behind a captured moment. In *According to Queeney,* the story of Samuel Johnson and his infatuation with Mrs Thrale, whose eldest daughter Queeney is, the novel is divided into sections with headings from definitions in Johnson's dictionary – for example, the first is 'Crisis *n.f.* The Point in time at which any affair comes to its height', which deals with Johnson's torment as he is attacked by what he calls his 'Black Dog', his fits of terrifying depression, from which Mrs Thrale will for a while rescue him.[19] Each section is dated, the first 1765 and the last 1784, the year of Johnson's death, and the story is interspersed with letters from the grown-up Queeney answering – or more often evading – questions from a Miss Hawkins about Dr Johnson and his relationship with her mother.

From the beginning, many of Bainbridge's novels had dark and unexpected outcomes, so it is perhaps not surprising that when she moved to historical fictions she chose events that had extreme or catastrophic denouements. Something else she may have learnt from Dickens besides her love of garrets and aspidistras was a heightened form of realism, the introduction of unsettling touches of the macabre and the grotesque that disrupt the most mundane and homely of situations. *The Dressmaker,* for example, ends with the ultra-respectable Nellie stabbing an American

19 Beryl Bainbridge, *According to Queeney* (2001) (London: Abacus, 2002), p. 53.

soldier in the neck with her scissors, leaving him with a wound that looks 'as if he had been kissed by a vampire', as he falls to his death.[20] He's been in bed with flighty Margo, though she knows her niece Rita is consumed with a very adolescent love for him, but Nellie only consciously thinks about that later – when she acts she can only register her outrage at his scratching her mother's table with his metal buttons. With great presence of mind, she applies her dressmaking skills to running up a bag in which they put the corpse, and despatches their terrified brother (a butcher who turns faint at the sight of blood) to drive the body to the docks and dispose of it in the water. After which, Nellie has a glass of port.

Bainbridge writes frequently about aspects of life, whether emotional or physical, that most of us tend to filter out, not even allow to come into our consciousness. Does that have something to do with her Liverpool childhood? Perhaps in reaction against her parents' anxious strivings for surface respectability, what she calls their 'mortal terror' of the past coming to light, she is fiercely honest about how things are or have been.[21] She grew up with an acute awareness of the deep poverty in the city itself, something from which a middle-class childhood in the Home Counties would probably have protected her. Recalling the war-time Liverpool of her childhood, she thought of the street urchins who followed the well-paid and smartly dressed American military police who patrolled the streets: '... mimicking their swagger, begging for cigarettes and gum, the children ran behind, legs pocked with the marks of insect bites. A smell clung to them, a mixture of dirt and vermin and cloying odour of damp rags. Even in winter they ran barefoot.'[22] The bare feet are shocking enough, but it is the unflinchingly observed 'pocked' legs and the 'cloying odour' that makes them so disturbingly immediate. In *Master Georgie*, the horrors of the Crimean campaign are searing, as are the extremities endured in the Antarctic in *The Birthday Boys*. But perhaps her ventures into taboo emotions are even more disturbing. Take *Harriet Said...*, for example, which deals with under-age sex, a novel about two friends, twelve and thirteen, in the immediate postwar years in Formby, the action taking place over the summer holidays. The unnamed narrator, the thirteen-year-old, has been sent away to boarding school in disgrace, allegedly because of 'dirty stories' discov-

20 Beryl Bainbridge, *The Dressmaker* (London: Duckworth, 1973), p. 149.
21 Bainbridge, *Forever England,* p. 42.
22 Bainbridge, *Forever England,* p. 173.

ered in her notebook, though she thinks it was really that her parents 'were scared of me and Harriet being so intimate. We were too diffi-cult.'[23] Both sets of parents owe something to Bainbridge's own, deeply concerned with respectability, always quarrelling, generally unhappy. The girls are full of sexual curiosity, persuading lonely adults to tell them about their lives. Harriet is very much the leader, much more knowing and decisive than the narrator. There has been an incident with Italian airmen on the beach, which the parents come to hear about, but they persuade them it was all quite innocent – Harriet is a very convincing liar. The narrator strikes up a friendship with a neighbour in his forties or fifties, named Peter Biggs, and, though Harriet is the most important person in the world for her, gradually begins to feel tenderness and tenta-tive desire for the Tsar, as she calls him. There are exotic touches about him – for Formby in the late forties at any rate – he has been to Greece, and compares her, obliquely, to a Greek statue, and he suggests going to Bordeaux to buy a barrel of wine. He's unhappily married, so he tells her, and she spends much time trying to imagine his earlier life and how his marriage has evolved. One night she and Harriet watch with horror, disgust and fascination as he makes love to his wife on his front room carpet, while they hide in the garden. 'Like an oiled snake, deep delving and twisting, Mrs Biggs poisoned him slowly, rearing and stabbing him convulsively. Her body writhed gently and was still. Ignoring the woman above him the grey Tsar lay as if dead, pinioned limply, eyes wide and staring, speared in a act of contrition.'[24] Harriet conceives a plan, quite what is not clear, even to the narrator. They have an evening at his house while his wife is away, with a friend of his whom Harriet entices, rejects and charms again. To the narrator's immense excitement, the Tsar kisses her a few times, but she has really lost interest in him by the time he has sex with her – she is 'raptureless', though unconcerned: as she says to Harriet – whom she finally succeeds in shocking, for that wasn't part of her plan – 'Just a bit like going to the dentist. Not even as bad.'[25] But events are rapidly spiralling out of control. They visit his house once more, but his wife returns unexpectedly; Harriet tells the narrator to hit her with a stick so they can escape, but when she hits her for a second time she falls dead, and they head home, in a ruse master-minded by Harriet, to put the blame on the hapless Tsar. The sexual

23 Beryl Bainbridge, *Harriet Said...* (London: Duckworth, 1972), p. 10.
24 Bainbridge, *Harriet Said*, p. 62.
25 Bainbridge, *Harriet Said*, p. 148.

elements are presented uncensoriously and matter-of-factly, though the girls' heartless treatment of Peter Biggs – to say nothing of his wife – is rather more shocking, but if Harriet turns out not to control events in the way she and the narrator thought, the girls manipulate the men rather than the other way around. It would probably be thought even more politically incorrect today than it was in the early seventies, when there was much less anxiety about paedophilia, but the presentation of the narrator's attempts to understand the confusing world of adult hypocrisy and desire is brilliantly done. And for all Bainbridge's rejection of theoretical feminism, the girls' refusal to fit in with the requirements of the world of bullying fathers and oppressed mothers could be read in a thoroughly feminist way.

Bainbridge's first historical novel was a typically bold and flamboyant choice; entitled *Young Hitler* (1978), it is about a visit by Adolf Hitler to Liverpool as a young man, to stay with his elder brother, a waiter at the Adelphi Hotel, where Adolf also temporarily though disastrously finds employment. In one sense it is fantasy – Hitler made no such visit – and is one of the most richly comic of her novels, but the paranoia, self-absorption and smouldering resentment of the young Adolf are all too appallingly convincing. It was, however, with *The Birthday Boys* in 1991 that Bainbridge's reputation as a historical novelist really took off. Just as with *Watson's Apology*, it is the motivations that fascinate her. What makes people undergo such hardship and danger, and how do they psychologically cope? Through the comments of their companions, and through the monologues we gradually discover. In the forty-eight pages of his first person account, she makes understandable the Scott whose mixture of idealism and obstinacy, ambition and tender-heartedness, leads to the disastrous end to his expedition. Even more remarkable is her presentation of Captain Oates, whose account ends the book. An old Etonian, an army officer, a keen hunter, a veteran of the Boer Wars (whose excesses he defends), an upholder of the Empire, a man without any intellectual or artistic interests, it would seem impossible for Bainbridge to enter into his mind-set, yet what emerges is a man with vulnerabilities, affections and courage for whom one can feel intense sympathy. Yet for all her compassion and insight, Bainbridge makes one aware that their reckless, possibly foolish bravery is the product of a male culture that still naively moulds itself on the values of adventure stories read by public-school boys. Like the sinking of the *Titanic*, as Bainbridge makes clear in *Every Man for Himself*, Scott's expedition is a self-inflicted tragedy; in different ways the two events signal the collapse of a way of life and a class system that are quite inadequate for a changing world.

In *Master Georgie,* Bainbridge returns to Liverpool. When commenting on the war-time street children of her youth, Bainbridge had pointed out that the 'urchins who roamed the street were not fore-runners of that hippy, happy generation who twined flowers in their hair, but the continuing spectres of Victorian England, waifs and vagrants who in their turn produced another generation of disadvan-taged citizens'.[26] In this novel she goes back to those Victorian spectres, setting the story in the mid-nineteenth century. The first section is told by the twelve-year-old Myrtle, an orphan named after Myrtle Street in which her orphanage was situated, who was taken in as a small child by the well-to-do Hardy family, a small island of affluence among the poverty and destitution of so much of the city. It is 1846; Mr Hardy has died during the afternoon in a brothel, and she and Pompey Jones, a boy from the streets, are called upon to help his son George, then in his twenties, in the struggle to get Mr Hardy's body back into his clothes and home into his own bed before his wife and daughter learn of his death. George says, 'Remember Myrtle, he died in bed from a cessa-tion of the heart', and Myrtle thinks, 'It was, after all, no more than the truth, if one didn't dwell on which particular bed.'[27] George takes a picture of his dead father, with Myrtle beside him. It is the first of many photographs and of many deaths in the book. Other sections are narrated by Pompey Jones, a young man of enterprise if few scruples, a photog-rapher's assistant, first trained by George, and briefly a fire-eater, and Dr Potter, George's brother-in-law, a verbose classical scholar with an interest in geology, incompetent but kindly. As so often with Bain-bridge's novels, the narrators give you their own very partial version of events; the reader must weigh them up and piece them together. They all eventually end up in the Crimea; Myrtle is devoted to George, Pompey attracted to Myrtle, and George loves Pompey. George has dutifully married, but his wife Anne cannot have children, and he has had children by Myrtle, which are passed off as his wife's. A respectable front is as firmly maintained as it would be in Formby a hundred years later. But George, whom the reader only knows through the other char-acters, while he may not be the saint Myrtle thinks him, seems to be no complacent hypocrite. He had been in awe of his father, and is deeply shaken by the nature of his death; his secrets eat into him, and his work

26 Bainbridge, *Forever England*, p. 173.
27 Beryl Bainbridge, *Master Georgie* (1998) (London: Abacus, 1999), p. 33.

as a surgeon, first in the Liverpool slums and then in the Crimea, appears driven by his need, as Dr Potter suggests, to find some prop for his life. There's plenty for him to do: the disregard by the majority of the well-to-do for the lives and well-being of the poor in Liverpool is prelude to the crass disregard for the mass of soldiers by the generals in the Crimea. Mortality through cholera is appalling before the war even begins, and the bungled campaign ends in horrible carnage, though the famous charge of what are described as the 'peacock(s) of the dazzling Light Brigade' has only an intriguingly oblique mention. George is killed by a stray Russian bullet at Inkerman, and the book ends with his still life-like looking corpse being included in a photograph of gallant survivors, to be despatched back to Britain to boost civilian support.

The postcolonial theorist Homi Bhabha has talked of the 'unhomely moments' that he sees in writers like Nadine Gordimer and Toni Morrison, disturbing, disruptive movements in the text which illuminate the relation of 'the traumatic ambivalences of a personal, psychic history to the wider disjunctions of political existence'.[28] I think this could be said to be increasingly true of Bainbridge's work. The dark and the macabre in Bainbridge's work so often shocks one into new realizations of the way the politics of history enter into the most personal aspects of our lives. Her work is compassionate and incisive, humane and funny, but fiercely aware of the forces set in motion by human selfishness and ineptitude. She is a writer of whom Liverpool should be proud.

28 Homi Bhabha, 'Introduction', *The Location of Culture* (London: Routledge, 1994), p. 11.

5

A Man from Elsewhere:
The Liminal Presence of Liverpool in the
Fiction of J.G. Farrell

Ralph Crane

Introduction: locating Liverpool

James Gordon Farrell was born in Liverpool on 25 January 1935 and christened five weeks later on 3 March at the Church of St Mary the Virgin in West Derby. His family, on both sides, had strong Liverpool connections, as Lavinia Greacen details in her excellent biography, *J.G. Farrell: The Making of a Writer*, though neither family had deep Liverpudlian roots. On his father's side the O'Farrells had emigrated from Ireland, dropping the prefix – which identified them as Irish and, misleadingly, as Catholic – when they settled in Liverpool. Farrell's grandfather, Thomas James Farrell, was a successful wine and spirit merchant; his father, William (Bill), born in 1900, was, in Greacen's words, 'shaped by the red-bricked certainties of turn-of-the-century Liverpool'.[1] Bill grew up in Kremlin Drive in Stoneycroft, a respectable suburb, but close enough to the docks for Bill to feel 'the pulse of an invisible empire',[2] a pulse that would later beat through Farrell's three major novels, *Troubles* (1970), *The Siege of Krishnapur* (1973), and *The Singapore Grip* (1978), commonly, though somewhat inaccurately, referred to as his 'empire trilogy', and, in more muted fashion, through his unfinished novel, posthumously published as *The Hill Station* (1981). The Russells on his mother's side journeyed in a contrary direction, moving from London to Liverpool, where her grandfather, a ship's

1 Lavinia Greacen, *J.G. Farrell: The Making of a Writer* (London: Bloomsbury, 1999), pp. 10–11.
2 Greacen, *The Making of a Writer*, p. 11.

captain, was based until his retirement; her father, inspired by the successful example of an uncle, emigrated to Ireland. For Farrell, Ireland seemed destined to be mediated through Liverpool.

J.G. Farrell's parents met aboard the SS *Ranchi*, cruising off the coast of Norway, in 1929. His mother, Prudence Josephine (Jo) Russell, was nineteen; his father Bill, nine years her senior, was on six months' leave from India, where he managed a United Molasses Company factory in Chittagong, Bengal, and staying with his parents in Liverpool. The Liverpool–Dublin ferry allowed Bill to pursue his courtship after he had proposed while still aboard the *Ranchi*. Jo and Bill were married in Rangoon eight months after they first met. Jo returned to England alone for the birth of their first child, Robert, who was born in a nursing home in Reading in April 1932. Bill returned home in 1934 as the Depression hit businesses in all parts of the Empire, and the family moved to Liverpool to be near Bill's terminally ill father, renting a house in West Derby.[3]

Farrell was four years old when he and his family left Liverpool. With the outbreak of the Second World War Liverpool became a target for enemy bombing. Bill, who had been drafted into a factory job, was in Workington in Cumberland; Jo and the boys moved to the relative safety of Southport, where they lived with an elderly widowed relative.[4] J.G. Farrell never lived in Liverpool again. However, though his residential connection with Liverpool was a brief one, and despite the fact that Liverpool is not literally inscribed in his writing in the way, for example, Oxford is in his second novel, *The Lung* (1965), a sense of himself as a man from elsewhere, a liminal position that is in line with being Liverpool-Irish, pervades his writing. Liverpool, like many port cities, is a transitional place, looking out over the Irish Sea and the Atlantic Ocean while turning its back on the rest of the country. Indeed, its geographical proximity to Wales and Ireland emphasizes the sense that, as John Belchem says, it is almost English but not quite, 'in the north of England, but not of it',[5] a city that has been transformed – and set apart from the rest of Lancashire – by its Celtic inflow. Yet despite its prominent Liverpool-Welsh and Liverpool-Irish populations, it is neither quite Welsh nor Irish either. Liverpool, like Farrell's writing, is

3 Greacen, *The Making of a Writer*, pp. 9–20.
4 Greacen, *The Making of a Writer*, p. 22.
5 John Belchem, *Merseypride: Essays in Liverpool Exceptionalism* (Liverpool: Liverpool University Press, 2006), p. 39.

marked by its elsewhere-ness. Similarly, the humour that pulses through the veins of the city – the 'fatalistic humour which sets Liverpool and its inhabitants apart'[6] – and the idiosyncratic ways of seeing things that are characteristic of the Liverpudlian, are evident in all Farrell's writing, though this influence is a tonal one rather than one that can be readily demonstrated through specific examples. Nevertheless, the comic episode in *The Singapore Grip* which describes Miss Olive Kennedy-Walsh being fired from a cannon in the Great World amusement park shortly before the fall of Singapore, or the embarrassment of the Major when he is caught (on two occasions) inspecting the hindquarters of the Blackett family's cat 'for some sign of gender'[7] in the same novel, both capture the sense of humour that was seen as characteristically Liverpudlian and which, by the end of the Second World War, 'was firmly established as Liverpool's response to its psychological, economic and structural problems'.[8]

Interestingly, while Farrell's own literal connections with Liverpool ended at an early age, his connections were maintained incidentally. Liverpool was the gateway to England he passed through in September 1948 on his way to his first term at Rossall School in Fleetwood, on the Lancashire coast north of Blackpool.[9] And, of course, for a boy whose childhood was divided between England and Ireland, the Liverpool–Dublin ferry would remain a presence in his life and also in his fiction: 'Ah, yes, those nightmare journeys back to school in the mail boat over the wintry guinness-black Irish Sea.'[10] In less concrete fashion, his links with the city continued through his relationships with two Liverpool writers, Beryl Bainbridge and Malcolm Lowry, though memories of the city never appear in Farrell's fiction in the same way they appear in both Bainbridge's and Lowry's.

After a period living in France, Farrell returned to England in 1963 and lived for several years in London, writing and earning money (amongst other ways) by reading manuscripts for Hutchinson's. One of the manuscripts he read was *A Weekend with Claude* by the then unknown Beryl Bainbridge, who had been born in Liverpool in 1934, educated at the Merchant Taylors' School there, and worked as an

6 Belchem, *Merseypride*, p. 33.
7 J.G. Farrell, *The Singapore Grip* (1978) (London: Phoenix, 1992), p. 318. Hereafter *Grip*.
8 Belchem, *Merseypride*, p. 51.
9 Greacen, *The Making of a Writer*, p. 39.
10 J.G. Farrell, *The Lung* (London: Hutchinson, 1965), p. 11. Hereafter *Lung*.

actress at the Liverpool Repertory Theatre before moving to North London. "'I read the first page and thought 'this is awful',"" [Farrell] noted, "read the second and thought 'Hmmmm', read the third and couldn't put it down.""[11] *A Weekend with Claude* was published in 1967, and thereafter Farrell laid claim to having discovered Bainbridge's talent. Coincidentally, in 1973, when Farrell's novel *The Siege of Krishnapur* won the Booker Prize, Bainbridge was short-listed for her novel of wartime Liverpool, *The Dressmaker*. And indeed Liverpool has featured in many of Bainbridge's novels, including *An Awfully Big Adventure* (1989), which drew on her experiences as an actress working in Liverpool during the 1950s (later adapted as a film starring Alan Rickman and Hugh Grant), and *Master Georgie* (1998) which won the W.H. Smith Literary Award and the James Tait Black Memorial Prize and chronicles the life of Liverpudlian surgeon and photographer George Hardy in the Crimean War. After Farrell drowned in a freak fishing accident near his home in Bantry Bay on 11 August 1979, Bainbridge was one of his England-based friends who attended a memorial service held at St Bride's in Fleet Street on 19 October 1979.[12]

Malcolm Lowry (1909–57), another writer closely associated with Liverpool, was destined to become the single greatest influence on Farrell's own writing. For Lowry, who was born in Liscard and spent his childhood in Caldy on the Wirrall, Liverpool would be a lasting presence in his writing, notably in his *magnum opus, Under the Volcano* (1947). According to John Spurling, Farrell was always trying to persuade friends to read *Under the Volcano*, one of his favourite novels.[13] And as Chris Ackerley so meticulously details in 'A Fox in the Dongeon: the Presence of Malcolm Lowry in the Early Fiction of J.G. Farrell',[14] Lowry's influence is evident in much of Farrell's writing, particularly in *The Lung* and *A Girl in the Head* (1967).

Liverpool, then, was a presence in Farrell's life and, albeit at times intertextually, in his fiction. I do not want to suggest, however, that his connection with Liverpool is necessarily literally inscribed in his writing;

---

11 Greacen, *The Making of a Writer*, p. 191.
12 Greacen, *The Making of a Writer*, p. 396.
13 John Spurling, 'As Does the Bishop', in J.G. Farrell, *The Hill Station: An Unfinished Novel and an Indian Diary* (with Two Appreciations and a Personal Memoir), ed. John Spurling (1981) (London: Phoenix, 1993), p. 167.
14 In *J.G. Farrell: The Critical Grip*, ed. Ralph J. Crane (Dublin: Four Courts Press, 1998), pp. 19–35.

indeed, the allusions to Liverpool that are found in Lowry's work, or the more direct portraits of the city in Bainbridge's work, are not to be found in Farrell's. So, as I move on to map Farrell's career as a writer, Liverpool will necessarily become a liminal, background presence in this essay – as it was in Farrell's own work.

The early novels: Liverpool as elsewhere

In this section I want to highlight the sense of elsewhere-ness that dominates Farrell's first three novels; indeed, the title of his first published novel, *A Man from Elsewhere* (1963), perfectly captures the sense of being Liverpool-Irish to which I have already alluded. The two men at the centre of this novel, Regan and Sayer, are both specifically described as men from elsewhere, and are the first in a series of displaced male characters that feature in all six of Farrell's completed novels.

A Man from Elsewhere was written in France, where, after graduating from Brasenose College, Oxford in 1960, Farrell had taken up a post as a teacher. It was published in Hutchinson's New Authors Series, and received mixed reviews. The novel hinges on the relationship between the two central male characters, the respected but now terminally ill writer, Regan, and Sayer, a young journalist sent by the Communist Party to investigate and discredit the dying writer who had earlier defected from the Party. The novel is concerned with the aftermath of war, the influence of the past on the present and future, and the opposition between the impersonal communist philosophy of Sayer and the decayed liberal humanism of Regan.[15] Strong influences of Albert Camus, Jean-Paul Sartre, and existentialism are evident in this first novel, as Ronald Binns amongst others has highlighted,[16] not least in the title which clearly and deliberately echoes Camus's *The Outsider* (1942). And though the influence of Samuel Beckett and various English and American writers can be traced in this novel, its intertextual links are primarily to Camus and the French tradition of fiction.

The opposition between Sayer and Regan, which can be read as an Oedipal struggle of the young writer to both absorb and reject the influence of the dying older writer, is also an existential battle for control of the past and the way history is recorded. Anticipating his later, mature

---

15 See Ralph J. Crane and Jennifer Livett, *Troubled Pleasures: The Fiction of J.G. Farrell* (Dublin: Four Courts Press, 1997), p. 38.
16 Ronald Binns, *J.G. Farrell* (London: Methuen, 1986), p. 37.

fiction, these struggles open out into a larger discourse on the nature of heroism. The filmmaker, Luc, for instance, in a scene that would not be out of place in a B-grade movie, attempts to defend a drunken Algerian, but only succeeds in looking ridiculous; Sayer, who saves Gretchen from the unwanted attentions of the youths in the café, later has to be saved by a group of German medical students from the same youths. And neither Luc nor Sayer is prepared to accompany Regan on his potentially suicidal car journey into the village. The heroism associated with knights rescuing damsels (or Algerians) in distress is shown to be out of date; in *A Man from Elsewhere* it is replaced by a Beckettian heroism that gives unheroic people the courage to carry on.

Farrell's second novel, *The Lung*, is very different from *A Man from Elsewhere*, but it does share with the earlier novel the influence of Camus (specifically *The Plague* [1947]) and Beckett, though the greatest intertextual influence on this novel is undoubtedly Malcolm Lowry's *Under the Volcano*, as John Spurling notes in his succinct description of the novel:

> *The Lung* … is a black comedy based on [Farrell's] own experience as a polio victim. The novel is seen entirely through the eyes of its hero, Martin Sands, who is motivated when we first meet him by an irresistible craving for alcohol and a slightly milder one for women. The aggressive, threatening circumstances of the world and its powerful interests have become, inevitably through such eyes, a blurred background of silly or insufficiently loving people (especially Sands' ex-wife), out of which, like a thunderbolt from Jove, the crippling disease suddenly emerges to strike our man almost dead. Farrell must by this stage have read Malcolm Lowry's *Under the Volcano* (which always remained one of his favourite books), since in the early chapters, before he catches polio, the drunken, divorced, cynical Sands bears such a resemblance to Lowry's Consul. However, unlike the Consul (that latter-day Faust), Sands is essentially a comic figure and Farrell's triumph is to keep him so through all the vicissitudes of his gradual cure in a private hospital.[17]

The influence of *Under the Volcano* can also be seen in the temporally circular form of *The Lung*, which begins and ends at Easter, and 'in Martin's dark glasses, in his drunkenness, in the effects on him of his wife's infidelity, in the repeated animal imagery, and in the symbolic sign in the

---

17 Spurling, 'As Does the Bishop', p. 157.

hospital gardens which points down to the earth (the grave or hell)'.[18]

The novel begins with Sands attending a wedding with his ex-wife, and ends with him leaving hospital in the company of the daughter of his ex-wife, and the possibility of another wedding: 'I married my ex-stepdaughter and we had ten children and lived happily ever after. It was just terrible' (*Lung*, p. 207). In the intervening year Sands has suffered a frightening attack of polio, a period of medical treatment inside an iron lung, and all sorts of indignities and embarrassments related to his physical condition. Yet in this novel, too, the central character displays a strong Beckettian desire to continue to exist, even if there is no certainty that anything outside will be any better than his experiences inside the hospital.

Time and illness are both significant tropes in these early novels, and would become major preoccupations in Farrell's later work, where disease operates as a metaphor for the dying empire in his empire triptych. In *The Lung*, too, Farrell's use of comedy and the grotesque, which continues through to his last completed novel, *The Singapore Grip*, is developed, in such extraordinary scenes as that which describes Sands's seduction of Marigold with the help of a pair of scissors to compensate for the weakness of his arms and hands. But despite the comedy of this second novel, the bleakness of *A Man from Elsewhere* is not entirely left behind. As Sands prepares to leave the hospital at the end of the novel, he discovers that Monica, the young girl he had befriended, has leukaemia, and as he thinks about her later he wonders if 'she isn't better off dead' (*Lung*, p. 206).

Critics agree that these first two novels are not Farrell's best, but both are, nevertheless, significant for the way they introduce many of the themes that would be developed in his later fiction.

Both the title of Farrell's next novel, *A Girl in the Head*, and its focus on another alienated central male character, are suggestive of the sense of elsewhere that characterized his first two novels. *A Girl in the Head* focuses on the adventures of Count Boris Slattery in the English seaside town of Maidenhair Bay during a single summer. Boris (who may not be an impoverished Anglo-Polish aristocrat at all, but Mick Slattery from Limerick), alighted from a train at Maidenhair Bay, 'the cemetery of all initiative and endeavour'[19] years ago, and, following an accidental act of

18 Crane and Livett, *Troubled Pleasures*, p. 45.
19 J.G. Farrell, *A Girl in the Head* (1967) (London: Fontana, 1981), p. 15. Hereafter *Girl in the Head*.

heroism, married Flower, eldest daughter of the middle-class Dongeon family with whom he now lives in a decaying Victorian mansion named 'Boscobel'. The house is named after the home of the elderly relative in Southport with whom Farrell had lived for some time after escaping Liverpool soon after the outbreak of the Second World War.

The sense of alienation, or elsewhere, that characterized the first two novels is again strong in this book, as is the sense of imprisonment that was developed in *The Lung*. As the summer passes, stifled by the dull routine of existence that he believes is the human condition, Boris waits for time to pass, and for the coming of Inez, the girl in his head that gives the book its title. And while Boris waits, he also watches – the beach, through windows, through a hole in the floor of his room, at the circus. These acts of voyeurism again set him apart, reflecting his position as an outsider, a man from elsewhere.

There is, of course, a strong intertextual link between this novel and Nabokov's *Lolita* (1955), which, as Ronald Binns points out, is 'the classic account of "a girl in the head"'.[20] But while Boris (in his pursuit of Inez) is in many respects a benign version of Nabokov's Humbert Humbert, he is even more like Lowry's Consul. Like the Consul, 'Boris wears dark glasses, carries a silver flask of brandy around with him, is followed by a stray dog and is unnerved by a sunflower staring at him.'[21] And like Lowry's Consul, Boris represents a sense of potential wasted, and also a sense that heroic achievement is an illusion. Boris's reward for accidentally saving Granny Marie-Thé's life is to be imprisoned (as he sees it) in the middle-class purgatory of the Dongeon household.

According to George Brock, who wrote a profile of Farrell following the publication of *The Singapore Grip*, Farrell 'prefer[ed] to disown his first three novels and dismiss them as "casting around"'.[22] And perhaps as a consequence, all three novels are now out of print, though second-hand copies of *A Girl in the Head* are relatively accessible. This authorial reflection on the early works – as apprentice pieces that were eclipsed by the later empire novels of the 1970s – is an invitation for readers and critics to underestimate both the quality (certainly in the case of *A Girl in the Head*) and importance of these novels. And while there is undoubtedly a shift in genres after the first three novels, many of the themes introduced and developed in these early fictions are further explored in

20 Binns, *J. G. Farrell*, p. 42.
21 Binns, *J. G. Farrell*, p. 41–42.
22 Gordon Brock, 'Epitaph for Empire', *Observer Magazine*, 24 September 1978, p. 73.

Farrell's major novels, the historical fictions which make up his empire triptych.

The empire triptych: Liverpool as a gateway to empire

In the fiction that followed *A Girl in the Head*, Farrell moved away from the contemporary settings of his first three novels to the past, and to a form of historical fiction that would confirm him among the most important of Britain's post-imperial, twentieth-century novelists. *Troubles*, which won the Faber Memorial Prize in 1970, *The Siege of Krishnapur*, which won the Booker Prize in 1973, and *The Singapore Grip* brought him both critical and commercial success. In this final section of my essay, as I move on to look at this triptych of empire novels, I want, particularly, to suggest that Farrell's Liverpool-Irish background allowed him to take on empire and colonialism from an ambivalent position, somewhere between colonizer and colonized, or what, borrowing from Bhabha's influential work *The Location of Culture* (1994), might be called a 'third space', a space from which one can question essentialist positions of identity, empire, and so on. As Bhabha explains, 'It is that Third Space, though unrepresentable in itself, which constitutes the discursive conditions of enunciation that ensure that the meaning and symbols of culture have no primordial unity or fixity; that even the same signs can be appropriated, translated, rehistoricized and read anew'.[23] While Farrell's Irishness obviously situates him in a position of ambivalence ideal for exploring the tension between colonizer and colonized, it is worth considering that what John Belchem terms 'Liverpool's apartness'[24] might also have contributed, albeit unknowingly, to Farrell's representation of empire.

Collectively, these three novels map the decline of the British Empire, while each focuses on a significant historical moment in the dismantling of the empire on which (at least for a time) the sun never set: the Irish civil war of 1919–21; the Indian mutiny of 1857–58; and the fall of Singapore to the Japanese in 1942. (And the decay of empire is mirrored in the corresponding decline of Liverpool, whose fortunes as a port were linked to the fortunes of Britain's empire.) The first panel in Farrell's

23 Homi Bhabha, *The Location of Culture* (London and New York: Routledge, 1994), p. 37.
24 Belchem, *Merseypride*, p. 31.

triptych, *Troubles*, tells the tragicomic tale of the shell-shocked Major Brendan Archer's extended visit to the decaying Majestic Hotel, where, having travelled to Ireland in order to claim his bride, Angela, he finds himself caught up in the Irish struggle for independence. Ronald Binns suggests that *Troubles* is 'arguably Farrell's masterpiece',[25] while the Irish novelist John Banville is unequivocal in his judgement, declaring that '*Troubles* is surely his masterpiece, and the book of his that is certain to endure'.[26] Traces of Lowry can still be found in this novel, but the influences on this work perhaps inevitably include a number of Irish writers; echoes of W.B. Yeats, Sean O'Casey, Elizabeth Bowen and Iris Murdoch can all be found in the novel.[27] The novel also fits into the Big House tradition of Irish writing, as Ronald Tamplin amply demonstrates in his essay on '*Troubles* and the Irish Tradition'.[28]

The novel begins after the First World War, when the Major travels to Ireland to visit his fiancée and meet her family, the Spencers, who own the enormous, crumbling Majestic Hotel, sited on a promontory near the fictional town of Kilnalough in County Wexford. As the novel progresses, the decaying edifice literally begins to fall apart as it increasingly becomes a symbol of British rule in Ireland, and in a more general sense of the Victorian–Edwardian ideology of empire to which, like many Anglo-Irish 'Big House' families, the symbolically named Edward Spencer (whose name recalls the sixteenth-century poet and Irish planter, Edmund Spenser, who in his *A View of the Present State of Ireland* [1596] advocates a brutal military solution to the Irish problem) still clung.

The Major catches up with Angela, at a bizarre tea party soon after his arrival, but is never able to track her down again, although he spends a great deal of time searching for her in the endless corridors and rooms of the hotel. His daily explorations in pursuit of his bride are conducted against the backdrop of Irish politics, the rumours of Sinn Fein reprisals against Irish people who work for the British, and so on. But after he learns of Angela's illness and death (of leukaemia), the 'troubles' move increasingly into the foreground as the Major becomes involved with

25 Binns, *J.G. Farrell*, p. 45.
26 John Banville, 'Introduction', in J.G. Farrell, *Troubles* (New York: New York Review of Books, 2002), p. vii.
27 See Crane and Livett, *Troubled Pleasures*, p. 69.
28 Ronald Tamplin, '*Troubles* and the Irish Tradition', in *J.G. Farrell: The Critical Grip*, ed. Ralph J. Crane (Dublin: Four Courts Press, 1998), pp. 48–64.

Angela's friend Sarah Devlin, an Irish-Catholic girl. Significantly, while the Anglo-Irish Angela dies of a blood disease early in the novel, Sarah, who appears to be semi-paralysed when we first meet her, gains in health and strength as the novel progresses.

At the outset, the Major appears to sympathize with the views of his host, Edward Spencer, and is particularly frustrated by what he sees as 'a war without battles or trenches'.[29] But as the novel progresses he begins to question the easy distinctions Edward (like the British govern-ment) makes between Irish 'rebels' and English 'soldiers', until, by the end of the novel he understands the difference between the English glorification of war as a noble sport, and the far more practical methods employed by the Irish to remove the British army occupying their country. This can be seen in a passage late in the novel when Edward shoots dead a young Sinn Feiner caught trying to blow up the statue of Queen Victoria in front of the Majestic. The Major is horrified when he realizes that Edward has been using the statue to attract his quarry, that he didn't see the Irish as people at all, but as 'a species of game' (*Troubles*, p. 417) to be hunted and shot.

The difficulty of understanding this conflict is emphasized throughout the novel as Farrell repeatedly demonstrates the problems of telling one side from the other. Are Edward and his family the mad Irish, as the Major early in the novel, and the visiting undergraduates see them, or are they British and the enemy, as Sarah and Sinn Fein see them? Were those involved in the 1916 Easter rebellion traitors attacking the English who were defending them from the Germans, or heroes fighting an army of occupation? The confusion is such that late in the novel the Major admits that he is unsure which side he is on, and although he still supports Edward, he does so out of loyalty rather than conviction; his confidence in the civilizing power of the British in Ireland has been utterly eroded. And though there is no material evidence, it is tempting to speculate here that the Major's divided loyalties may reflect Farrell's own Liverpool-Irish background and sense of dislocation, to which Caroline Moorehead draws attention in a profile published a week before the publication of *The Singapore Grip* when she explains that '[a]t school he was addressed as an Irish boy; in Ireland he felt English'.[30]

---

29 J.G. Farrell, *Troubles* (1970) (London: Phoenix, 1993), p. 169. Hereafter *Troubles*.
30 Caroline Moorehead, 'Writing in the Dark, and Not a Detail Missed', *The Times*, 9 September 1978, p. 12.

The Major's vanishing confidence in the ideology of empire is echoed in *The Siege of Krishnapur* when, towards the end of the siege, the central character of that novel, the Collector, realizes that 'even if a relief now came, in many different ways it would be too late' because 'India itself was now a different place; the fiction of happy natives being led forward along the road to civilization could no longer be sustained'.[31] In *The Siege of Krishnapur* Farrell turned to another significant moment in the decline of the British Empire, one which chronologically precedes *Troubles*, and where the obvious physical threat to the British residents of northern India is symbolic of a philosophical threat to the empire that would gain momentum over the next hundred years.

The action of this novel, set during the Indian Mutiny of 1857–58, takes place in the fictitious town of Krishnapur where a group of British administrators, members of the local military garrison, and their families, are besieged in the Residency. Under the command of the Collector, Mr Hopkins, they hold out for three months against repeated sepoy attacks before a relief force arrives to rescue them. The events of Farrell's novel are loosely based on the siege of Lucknow (June–November 1857), and Farrell draws on both historical and fictional accounts of that siege in his rewriting of the Mutiny. In his treatment of the siege he parodies the romantic adventure fiction of the nineteenth century, in particular the conventions of the Mutiny novel, to question and undermine the imperial ideology of the day.

This is nowhere more evident than in an important scene which concludes the action of the siege itself. The general in charge of the relief force, after seeing the 'extraordinary collection of scarecrows' (*Krishnapur*, p. 307) who come out to greet his men, wonders how this significant moment in history will be recorded:

> Even when allowances were made, the 'heroes of Krishnapur', as he did not doubt they would soon be called, were a pretty rum lot. And he would have to pose for hours, holding a sword and perched on a trestle or wooden horse while some artist-wallah depicted 'The Relief of Krishnapur'! He must remember to insist on being in the foreground, however; then it would not be so bad. With luck this wretched selection of 'heroes' would be given the soft pedal ... an

---

31 J.G. Farrell, *The Siege of Krishnapur* (1973) (London: Phoenix, 1993), pp. 225–26. Hereafter *Krishnapur*.

indistinct crowd of corpses and a few grateful faces, cannons and prancing horses would be best. (*Krishnapur*, pp. 310–11)

This description, which deliberately recalls Thomas Jones Barker's famous painting, 'The Relief of Lucknow', shows how the moment was presented to the world, and at the same time demonstrates the absurdity of the way history is recorded. The painting is a distortion of the reality of the event, as Farrell emphasizes by having the general 'pos[e] for hours' on a wooden trestle defending the values of empire.

Indeed Farrell subverts the rhetoric of empire throughout this novel by relentlessly undermining both the heroic and romantic conventions of the Mutiny novel. Heroic conventions are challenged, for example, in his presentation of the hearty Harry Dunstaple and the romantic Fleury, through the loutish behaviour of Mr Rayne, Lieutenant Cutter, and others, and through the cynicism of the Magistrate, who, in response to a stirring speech from the Collector towards the end of the siege, is heard to say (referring to Shakespeare's *Henry V*), 'I suppose he's going to tell us that gentleman now abed in England will be sorry that they're not here' (*Krishnapur*, p. 281). And the romantic conventions of the genre are constantly undermined by the heat, the flies, and the smells that accompany any moment of intimacy, though the smell that they have become accustomed to does prevent Lieutenant Stapleton, a former admirer of Louise, from coming between her and Fleury when he arrives with the relief force.

Unlike the authors of conventional Mutiny novels, Farrell does not celebrate the end of the siege as a victory; there are no fanfares when the relieving troops arrive, only a few ragged, starving survivors. Farrell shows that while the British may have survived this particular skirmish, they have already begun to lose the ideological war that would continue for almost a century, and would be brought to a sharp conclusion by Farrell in the third panel of his empire triptych, *The Singapore Grip*.

At one point in that novel a photograph the Frenchman Dupigny looks at while sitting in the Penang Swimming Club

showed a group of ladies and gentlemen, assembled this time for a picnic, perhaps. The padre was there looking young and vigorous, a watch-chain visible against his black waistcoat and with a white sun-helmet on his head. The ladies were still sitting in the rickshaws that had brought them; but only one coolie had remained to appear in the picture and there he was, still gripping the shafts as if he had only just trundled his fair cargo up. The European standing beside the rick-shaw had reached out a hand as the photograph was being taken and forced the coolie's head down so that only his straw hat and not his face should be visible in the picture. (*Grip*, p. 305)

The 'confident assumption of superiority embodied in that hand forcing the coolie to hide his face' (*Grip*, p. 305) that was still felt at the time the photograph was taken, around 1910, is no longer tenable in 1941, in the face of the looming Japanese victory in Malaya and Singapore. As Dupigny concludes, 'Whatever happened with the Japanese the old colonial life in the East, the European's hand on the coolie's straw hat, was finished' (*Grip*, p. 305). The fall of Singapore in 1942 would mark the end of the century-long decline of empire that Farrell had mapped through three novels.

Through the concerns of Matthew Webb, who arrives in Singapore having inherited his father's business interests, and the Major (from *Troubles*, who returns as a minor character in this novel), considerable emphasis is placed on the way Blackett and Webb Ltd treat their native workforce, and, more generally, the way the colonial enterprise exploits its colonies. While the representatives of empire in *The Siege of Krishnapur* and *Troubles* can at least be seen as misguided in their zeal for empire, businessmen like Walter Blackett can only be seen as ruthless in their economic exploitation of the colony of Singapore. Matthew's unease in his unfamiliar, exploitative role is manifested in the severe bout of fever he suffers soon after his arrival, an illness that he speculates might be 'the Singapore Grip!' (*Grip*, p. 204), and which during the course of the novel infects the more sensitive members of the colonial community, who, like the Major in *Troubles* and the Collector in *The Siege of Krishnapur*, are not immune to the suffering of the colonized. The illness, of course, is colonialism itself, and the economic grip of colonialism on this part of the world is the condition the novel inves-tigates. Various explanations of the phrase 'the Singapore Grip' are offered during the course of the novel, but the one that seems most convincing comes late in the piece when Matthew triumphantly announces to his American friend, Jim Ehrendorf:

'I *know* what it is! It's the grip of our Western culture and economy on the Far East ... It's the stranglehold of capital on the traditional cultures of Malaya, China, Burma, Java, Indo-China and even India herself! It's the doing of things *our* way ... I mean, it's the pursuit of self-interest rather than of the *common* interest!' ...

Ehrendorf sighed, thinking that in any case the Singapore Grip was about to be pried loose, if that was what it was. (*Grip*, p. 523)

Matthew's evident unease about the activities of Blackett and Webb Ltd in particular, and of western countries more generally, reflects the concerns the Collector in *The Siege of Krishnapur* had about progress. In the imperial context, progress, economic or otherwise, is what benefits the colonizer, not the colonized. The railways are the prime example, and the one Matthew turns to in one of his many philosophical discussions with Ehrendorf:

'I suppose you're talking about railways ... In our African colonies something like three-quarters of all loans raised by the colonial governments are for railways. True, they're useful for administration ... but what they're mainly useful for is opening up great tracts of land to be developed as plantations by Europeans. In other words, it's done not for the natives' benefit but for ours!' (*Grip*, p. 459)

Self-interest, not the common interest, is the motive which drives a colonial power; everything is done for the benefit of the colonizing power, for the moguls of the rubber industry rather than for the colonized native workforce.

The fall of Singapore is portrayed as a significant event which – like the Troubles in Ireland that led to the division of the country and the Mutiny in India, after which control of the country passed into the hands of the Crown – marked a major turning point in the fortunes of the British Empire. The fall of Singapore delivered a fatal blow to what was in the 1940s already a misguided confidence in empire, as Farrell makes clear: 'This Sunday, then, was the last day of the defence of Singapore, the last day of freedom for the British who remained on the Island ... almost, you might say with hindsight, the last day of the British Empire in these parts' (*Grip*, p. 585). As he draws the novel to a close, Farrell uses the privileged position of hindsight to survey the post-empire period and comment on the lack of change that has occurred since Singapore's independence:

That man behind the newspaper, if it were Ehrendorf, let us say, and if he happened to remember his arguments of years ago with Matthew about colonialism and tropical agriculture, might he not, as his eye was caught by that headline 'Plantation work pays less than one dollar a day', have said to himself that nothing very much had changed, after all, despite that tremendous upheaval in the Far East? That if even after independence in these Third World countries, it is *still* like that, then something has gone wrong, that some other, perhaps native, élite has merely replaced the British? If it *were* Ehrendorf might he not have recalled that remark of Adamson's (passed on to him by Matthew) about King William and the boatman who asked who had won the battle ('What's it to you? You'll still be a boatman')? (*Grip*, p. 598)

There is a strong sense here – as in each of the earlier empire novels – that although the empire itself would crumble, the untenable moral and political values on which it was built would survive.[32] The authorial presence lurking behind that passage perhaps reflects Farrell's own experience of visiting Saigon in 1975 as part of his research for *The Singapore Grip*, just as the presence of Ehrendorf, an American, may signal the way the United States would, in the later decades of the twentieth century, move to fill the colonial void left by the British and French.

Coda

The links between Liverpool and Britain's empire that I suggested earlier are implicit in Farrell's three historical fictions are finally made explicit in Farrell's last-completed novel, *The Singapore Grip*. Specifically, in this novel the demise of the British Empire echoes the economic decline of Liverpool, which once vaunted itself as the second metropolis of the empire, and 'aspired to combine commerce, culture, and civilisation',[33] but which would become, by the 1980s, Britain's most deprived city.

Early in the novel, the reader is introduced, as his visitors have been for a number of years, to a series of paintings that hang on Walter Blackett's drawing room wall. The paintings, which depict the rise of Blackett and Webb Ltd, show cargo being loaded in the East – in Rangoon, Calcutta, Penang, Malacca, and Singapore itself. In one painting, 'by a more sophisticated hand, the ship had arrived in Liverpool and was being unloaded again' (*Grip*, p. 11).

32 See Laurence Bristow-Smith, '"Tomorrow Is Another Day": The Essential James G. Farrell', *Critical Quarterly*, 25.2 (1983), p. 51.
33 Belchem, *Merseyside*, p. 38.

The paintings are, of course, there to provide a history of the rise of Blackett and Webb, of Singapore, and of Britain's empire in the east; but they also segue neatly into the history of Liverpool. Here, albeit fleetingly, through a series of paintings hanging on a drawing-room wall in Singapore, Farrell carefully links the economic progress of Liverpool to that of empire. Through these paintings Farrell concisely reveals the exploitative economic history of the empire which drove the growth of both ports, and highlights the importance of Liverpool as a point of departure and return in the business of empire. And while Liverpool's commercial and mercantile significance is, as Belchem notes, often over-looked in economic histories and 'industrial' novels that privilege the manufacturing north – Charles Dickens's *Hard Times* (1854), set in the fictional northern industrial city of Cokestown and based on the author's impressions of Preston, is a good example – Farrell reminds us of the city's former importance as a seaport and commercial centre of the empire, equal to (if not surpassing) even London.

6

The Figure in the Carpet:
An Interview with Terence Davies

Michael Murphy

Terence Davies was born in Liverpool in 1945 and he grew up in a working-class Catholic family, the youngest of seven surviving children. After leaving school aged sixteen he worked for ten years as a clerk in a shipping office and as a bookkeeper before leaving the city and attending Coventry Drama School. While there he wrote the screenplay for Children *(1976), the first part of the* Terence Davies Trilogy. *Davies next went to the National Film School, and over the following seven years wrote and directed* Madonna and Child *(1980) and* Death and Transfiguration *(1983). With* Distant Voices, Still Lives *(1988) and* The Long Day Closes *(1992) Davies continued to draw on his childhood experiences in Liverpool. The two films marked him out as arguably the most important and distinctive British film-maker since Michael Powell. Davies subsequently adapted and directed two novels by American authors: John Kennedy Toole's* The Neon Bible *(1995), and Edith Wharton's* The House of Mirth *(2000), which won a best-actress award for Gillian Anderson and a string of nominations for Best Director.*

Davies's output has been sporadic but is characterized by an extraordinary ability to realize the emotional content of a scene through colour, music, framing, lighting, and an inherent sense of rhythm and movement. Central to his oeuvre is a cinematic depiction of memory that examines the ways in which we inhabit a world of familial and social ritual, while experiencing an inner life that is often painfully at odds with the collective. His films occupy a territory which explores on the one hand family history and personal terrors, and on the other the liberating and visionary experience of cinema. As such he is part of a tradition that includes Jean Genet, Max Ophuls, Sergo Paradjanov and Pier Paolo Pasolini.

Davies has written one novel, Hallelujah Now *(1984), and his first five screenplays were published as* A Modest Pageant *(Faber & Faber, 1992). At the time of this interview, plans for a film adaptation of Lewis Grassic Gibbon's*

Sunset Song *had fallen through, with the BBC, Channel 4 and the UK Film Council all having turned down at the last stage his funding applications. He lives in London, where I interviewed him on 8 May 2006 at Kettners Restaurant, Soho.*

MM: The films that you are perhaps best known for are set in Liverpool in the forties and fifties. Can you say something about your early experiences and how they later propelled you to becoming a film maker?

TD: They are of extremes that, funnily enough, reflect my personality. I either love something or I hate it. There's very little grey area. It was one of incredible violence. My father was absolutely psychotic and ill – he was dying with stomach cancer and died at home. The body was in the house for ten days after he died. So, repression and terror. I was constantly terrified. On one occasion he threatened to kill me and I didn't move for four hours. And then after he died, I was taken to the movies – to see *Singin' in the Rain*. It was my first film. What a revelation! How can you not fall in love with cinema when that's your first film! And I can remember bursting into tears when it came to him [Gene Kelly] singing 'Singin' in the Rain'. My sister Eileen who had taken me asked why I was crying, and I said, 'He just looks so happy.' That was a huge revelation. And then our house became like a magnet. Everybody came. It really just drew people. And then my mum began to live, we all began to live. We had nothing, but in those days you lived like a community and did things together. There was lots of street life, I remember, but I also remember running out into the street in the morning – or any time, really – and thinking, 'I must remember how the street looks today.' I'd look at things and I'd remember with *such* intensity ... Oddly, someone described my response to cinema as a religious experience and I now think it actually was. Because I was also a practising Catholic – I was until I was twenty-two – so the intensity of those experiences which were all terribly extreme when I think about them now, have coloured the way I am, the way I think, certainly the way I think emotionally. And whilst I don't have a photographic memory, I have a very good memory for emotional recall. I can remember how things felt, and I do think that's really important because –

MM: You mean in terms of how things emotionally felt, or physically?

TD: Both. Absolutely both. I know exactly how I felt. I mean, films, for instance, I can remember where I saw them, the route I took, where I sat, and whether I went on my own or with someone. It's that vivid.

Not for all films but for a lot of them. It was an intense atmosphere in which I grew up, allied to the fact that my brothers and sisters, and my mother, talked about my father as, I think, a kind of therapy. And I listened. When you are the youngest of ten, you listen because no one's interested in your opinion.

MM: How long did this idyllic period after your father's death last?

TD: It lasted from the age of seven to eleven. It was ecstatic. I was in a permanent state of ecstasy. I was sick with happiness.

MM: Listening to you, I'm reminded of what Proust said about the only paradises being those we have lost. I wonder how much making films became a way of reclaiming or documenting those years?

TD: It wasn't conscious. There was an enormous need to revisit them. In terms of *Distant Voices, Still Lives*, just to try and chart the suffering that went on. There were a lot of things I left out. Nobody would have believed them because he [Davies's father] was so extreme. But *The Long Day Closes*, I mean, I just wanted to try and do precisely what you have just said: recapture the lost paradises. The last time I was happy. I've never been happy since. I've had moments of happiness but most of the time there's a *huge* sense of loss.

MM: What comes across in the films is that the family survives because of the mother. I just wonder how big a presence you felt women to be in that society? Of course it wasn't that long after the war and women had had the experience of all kinds of independence.

TD: But you didn't think of it, you know, in terms of women in society or anything like that. My family was the centre of the world. I thought they were the most unique people in the world and no one was as interesting, *no one*. They had wonderful friends – and I loved seeing them – but my family was extra-special. But because I was gay – and I didn't know that of course at the time – like a lot of gay men I get on with women. I love the company of women. I think they are funny, especially northern women. I love to hear their banter. Friday nights were just sensational because they would come in and I'd be sent to buy make-up, they'd get made up, they'd press their frocks with a flat iron … The smell of pan-stick and *Evening in Paris* … I can still smell it now! It's as vivid now as it was then! My brothers less so because, like a lot of gay men, I'm not easy with men. I'm afraid of them. I was afraid of my father. And so I'm afraid of them, I always feel inferior. I've always wanted to be big and muscular.

MM: That moment near the beginning of *The Long Day Closes* where Bud is looking out of his bedroom window at the half-naked builders across the road, there's clearly something homoerotic there, but the person whose eye he catches is his brother. What for you is that moment? Is it a desire *for* the men or to be like them, to be *part* of that community?

TD: It's mixed. The initial feeling was terror. The first time it happened was the summer after I left primary school when I was eleven. It was a hot summer and I hadn't gone to the pictures. And I was up in the back bedroom and they were building this wall in a garage called 'Smittens' [*laughs*]. Awful. And I saw his flesh for the first time and it was instinctive. I should not be looking at a man like this.

MM: And then there's the moment when Bud hears someone laughing. He clearly associates the laughter with a kind of ridicule, a comment on what he's feeling emotionally, and he turns away from the window and sits down in his room. That's the moment when he thinks, 'I shouldn't be looking.' I read it as a kind of portrait of the artist as a young man: it's the moment when he realizes that looking is going to be very much a part of his life.

TD: And at that moment, you know, it completely destroyed any happiness that I ever had. It destroyed it in that moment. I just knew it was wrong. I knew you shouldn't look like this, and my brother asking me to wash his back, I mean, I cannot tell you how difficult that was. I played it in the film as though he [Bud] doesn't respond at all but it was awful because I thought, 'Everyone will know. Everyone *must* know.' So it was a pivotal moment, certainly, in my development; and probably stunted it because it was at that point I thought that whatever 'it' is has got to be absolutely controlled. It cannot be given in to. And I didn't know what 'it' was.

MM: Do you think this sense of things having to be controlled has fed into the aesthetic of your films, which, for all the passion, are very, very controlled. Would you connect the two things?

TD: Yes, I think … I think … I think I'd call it probably not controlled in the same way as I mean it for my personal life but it's rigorously organized. It needs to be, for me. Do I know why? I suspect I don't. It's not that I want to control other people, but when something is right I feel it. I don't know it, I *feel* it. And if the frame is a centimetre off, *I know*. I don't know how I know, but I know and it has to look like *that*.

MM: If it's 'off' it takes you back to being eleven and knowing that the way you are looking out of the window causes things to go off kilter, that you shouldn't have looked like that?

TD: Yeah.

MM: That's interesting. Because I was recently watching *Peeping Tom* again, and what put me in mind of your films is the fact that the central character who records the suffering of women, the terror in their eyes, does so because he has had the same thing done to him by his father, who then gives him a film camera. It just seemed a perfect metaphor for your films. The fear that your father instilled in you was almost like him saying, *Here is your subject matter. Here is the frame of reference within which you are going to work.*

TD: I'd never thought of it like that. The sort of films I was brought up on were the American musical and British comedy. And what were called 'women's pictures'. Like *Love Is a Many Splendoured Thing* or *Letter from an Unknown Woman*. Y'know. So I never even thought I would make films because people from working-class families just *didn't*. It was a completely different attitude, y'know. It was people who were posh and went to university who made films and not people like me. What your history does is inform the way you see the world. Now that may mean that when you have children of your own you may be a tyrant or it may mean that you are more loving. It can go either way. Just because you've had a nasty father doesn't mean you are going to be nasty.

MM: But there is a keen interest in fear in the lives of your characters. I'm thinking of Tucker – not so much the bullying scene at the beginning of the *Trilogy* as the scene when he's waiting in line for the school medical examination and he thinks that his being gay is going to be discovered by the doctor. There's real terror there.

TD: Most of the time I *was* frightened. Of the world. And also just simple things like taking your clothes off. I had never taken my clothes off in public. Y'know. I hated it. I can't do it now. I hated the way I looked, and I hated what I felt to be a canker in the soul. I still have that. I still feel it has ruined my life. I wish I was just ordinary. I just want an ordinary life. I wanted it then, I still want it now. And probably I will die wanting it. It's the nature of the world as it's manifested in small things, like having to go for a medical examination.

MM: I'm interested in what you say about the horror of the world being made manifest in small things. It's a small detail, and it only appears in the script of *Distant Voices, Still Lives*, but when the father turns up at the front door, having discharged himself from hospital – even though he's dying – the description you give is of him being like a Belsen victim. I'm wondering at what point your generation became aware of what had been happening during the war? Or was it that the familiar – familial

– things around you were so fearful that they blocked out what was happening out there in the world?

TD: For me it was. I don't know what it was like for the others. But when you're that young the world is the house, and your family, and school and the street. There's nothing else. And then it becomes extended by the cinema and the church. But that's all your life, I mean, and if somebody is dominating it, you know, or subverting it, or doing whatever, then not only is that your entire world but you *think* that is the world. You know, I couldn't, I couldn't understand when my friend Albert Drake, his father wasn't doing that. Mr Drake took us on the ferry. I thought, well, why didn't my dad do that? Mr Drake was very gentle. A very tall gentle man. They were from a large family, too. So it was a shock, finding out that other people didn't do this. Other people don't live like this.

MM: What makes the father in *Distant Voices* so terrifying is his vulnerability. I mean, there's the scene in the film that reminds me of *Whistle Down the Wind* – the musical version of which is playing just down the road from here –

TD: By Andrew Rice Pudding [*laughs*].

MM: – where the children are looking down on the German soldier who they think is Christ. And there's the scene in *Distant Voices* where the children are terrified in case they are caught looking at the father as he currycombs a horse while singing 'While Irish Eyes Are Smiling'. The film is saying at this point: 'This is the father he *might* have been.' And that, too, is terrifying. Why doesn't *my* father take me on the ferry? I don't want to keep bringing things back to the autobiographical, but how difficult was it to allow yourself at that point in the film to create a sympathetic father figure, to allow that kind of humanity to what otherwise is a Gothic monster?

TD: The scene you just quote, my sisters and brothers didn't do that, it was me. He still had a horse, then, up near Bowler Street, and I climbed up and looked down on him. It was the only time I saw him happy. And that was the only song he ever sang. Because my mother was Irish, although he used to berate her for that. She was of Irish extraction. She was born in Liverpool. So … You … Again, it comes down to that kind of refraction of saying: I saw him, on one occasion looking happy; it would be interesting if my two oldest sisters and an older brother saw it rather than me because it's appropriate for the story. It takes us back to an aesthetic truth rather than a realistic one. The single beating that he gives her [the mother] has to stand for all the beatings he gave her from 1929 to 1952. Because you can't keep on doing it all the time. And then how do you make it powerful? By running a love song underneath it.

MM: Just picking up on what you say there about how the aesthetic *refracts* experience, there's also the way in which that refraction sends those energies into all the other films. If what we're talking about is the imminent threat of violence, the danger of a character stepping *slightly* out of line and the full weight of society falling down on them, then it's present with Tucker throughout the *Trilogy*; and it's there with Lily [*The House of Mirth*]. Very early on in the film ... In the commentary on the DVD, we're only minutes into the film and you say, '*That's* the mistake she made.' After that we are just waiting for her to fall. Is it as simple as saying –

TD: No, really, you've just crystallized what I simply didn't know. Because I am afraid of the world. I am afraid of its arbitrariness. It really does terrify me. When you have something like a novel as structured and as great as *The House of Mirth*, where ... This is what terrifies me about the book, this is why I think it really is one of the great, *great* novels, there are all these rules, no one tells you what they are, but transgress them and retribution is swift. It's different if you know what the rules are, then you can say, 'Well, that's fine, I don't agree with that, I'm going to do it anyway,' but if you don't know –

MM: Isn't part of the terror with Lily that she *does* know –

TD: No, she doesn't.

MM: You think not?

TD: No. What she does, she misinterprets. She thinks, 'If I charm that will be enough.' But it's *not*. What she doesn't realize is: here is this surface meaning. The subtextual meaning is: you can have all sorts of peccadilloes, fuck as much as you like, as long as no one finds out, as long as you play the game. What you can't do is play part of the game and then be – shock, horror – 'Oh, you know, I didn't realize that was going on.' *It doesn't work like that.* And she's horrified because she thought it did. It's equally true when you are told what the structures are. In the Catholic Church you have this thing called a soul, so you shouldn't do this or this, otherwise it'll be in danger. That's terrifying.

MM: And that's where the real interest in community and society comes from in your films and which is there all the time, whether it be the microcosm of the playground in the *Trilogy*, war-time Liverpool in *Distant Voices*, small-town America in *Neon Bible* or, moving to the other extreme, New York in *The House of Mirth*. In every film there is a loner figure, somebody on the outside – I mean, this is one of the things that makes the father in *Distant Voices* such a very interesting figure in terms of the other films. He in many ways is the person on the outside, the one for whom we have sympathy, who we want to see survive. Do you think you need the social aspect there because you have an essentially tragic view and you can't just have tragedy of individuals?

TD: My view of life *is* essentially tragic. And what you've just said is very accurate. I can't really add to it, except to say I don't feel part of the world, as such. I don't. As much as I love my family, I'm an outsider. You know, I speak in this peculiar way – I lost my accent by the time I was eleven – you know, I'm reasonably intelligent, so I have taught myself –

MM: When you say you've *lost* your accent, it suggests it's there to be re-found. You must have trained the accent out of yourself –

TD: O no, absolutely, *absolutely* by accident. I have a very acute ear. It started off by being imitative. One of my brothers went into the army. Then *Round the Horne* was on [the radio]. No, no – it was *Beyond Our Ken* and then *Round the Horne*. I'd only have to listen to it twice, I could remember most of the programme and I'd write it down. When I listened, what I think happened was I heard … I must have heard someone speaking in a particular way that I thought was beautiful and just started imitating it.

MM: So this was the Beeb –

TD: Almost certainly.

MM: You've said you felt like an outsider, so this would be a way, if you like, of being *received* –

TD: At the time you just thought they spoke beautifully. When I was doing the research for *Distant Voices* and the *Long Day Closes*, there was *Family Favourites* introduced by Jean Metcalf … At the time I was still a child. I just thought she spoke beautifully. People don't *hear* words, they *feel* them. Or you hear it so deeply, it's felt. Which is why I pick up a foreign language so quickly. The problem is I never know what I'm saying. Which is a bit of a drawback [*laughs*]. People always say, 'It's a really good accent.'

MM: An interesting way to explore a menu.

TD [*laughs*]

MM: As well as that sense of individuals under threat of violence, it seems as well that … that the communities you are drawn towards also feel themselves threatened. The kids in the playground must be threatened by Tucker in some way; in *Neon Bible*, I mean, there's that terrifying scene of the lynching; even in *The House of Mirth*, there's something in Lily that threatens …

TD: I'm not a political person. I'm more interested in the way things affect ordinary or, in *The House of Mirth*, rich people. When you are in something, whether it's school or the family, the street or the Church, there's a dynamic there that can't be broken. Or it can be broken at your peril. But if … Two things can happen: either you can't see it and transgress; or you can see it, and inevitably you're alienated from it because you don't agree with it and it destroys you in a different sort of way. When I grew up, a working-class person had a specific role. And was a specific *thing*. I was none of those *things*. I was gay. I was having a terrible spiritual time. I'd lost my accent. And I had intelligence. Not trained. I trained myself. That alienates you from the very people that you love. I'd do anything for them, and they'd do anything for me. But it's like Nora in *A Doll's House* saying, 'I waited for the miracle and it did not come.' And Torvald has no idea what she means. And that's the tragedy. And she's shocked to her core – just like Lily finds integrity. She's found integrity. And once you've found it, you can't lose it. It's like once you've lost your virginity, you can't get it back.

MM: Or your accent.

TD: Or your accent. [*laughs*]. *Werk!*

MM: Good try [*both laugh*].

MM: Is there not a third way –

TD: [*laughing*] O, probably –

MM: Because that, or so it seems to me, is what you're saying in *The Long Day Closes*, that Bud has found that other way through the *gaze*. Through art. What we see through his eyes is the film he is going to grow up to make. Again it takes us back to Proust: all Marcel's experiences become the novel he plans to write. I don't get that same tragic sense with Bud. He's not going to become Tucker. Or Lily. He is going to survive.

TD: But he's not going to be *happy*. And he *isn't*. Something's *gone*. It might even be the first sense of love. I mean not in the sexual sense, but in a truly pure sense that you love someone because you love them. Perhaps we are all essentially alone.

MM: So the sunset that Bud watches, those darkening clouds, are more like a coffin lid being nailed down over those four years, those four idyllic years –

TD: Yeah –

MM: The light is dying, is it?

TD: Yeah. It is. It's gone. And at the end it goes. Because they did. And so I withdrew into cinema and reading, to a certain extent, praying until my knees bled. Then going to the cinema became religious. I couldn't bear anyone to talk. I started going on my own, that way I thought no one could talk and break the spell.

MM: Which is interesting again, then, in terms of that motif in your early work to do with the communal rites and rituals of the Catholic Church, the Christian calendar and festivals. Because though you say you lost your faith in your twenties, the films go back and invest a great deal in the Church. Was that done with a sense of nostalgia?

TD: No, it was completely instinctive. I think we've gone too far now with any kind of authority being despised. That's a recipe for disaster. But in those days anyone in authority you just automatically believed in. You did as you were told.

MM: What it also does is subsume the lives of individual character within much bigger narratives – whether religious or to do with class. There are times in the films when the narrative is 'suspended' while these other rituals and traditions take over.

TD: But they don't so much take over as become part of the pattern, you know. And they are part of the pattern, you know. You don't eat meat on a Friday; you fast Saturday night in order to take Communion the next day. You go to Palm Sunday mass and midnight mass. And then there are the rituals of the family. The insurance man coming every Friday. Mr Spall came for twenty-seven years and when he stopped coming it was like someone *dying*. My brothers going to the match on a Saturday. I used to love listening to the sports reports just for the sound and rhythm of, you know, Queen of the South, Sheffield Wednesday, Accrington Stanley. And also Peter O'Sullivan's *wonder-ful* voice. Michael O'Hare doing the Grand National. This little Bakelite radio. The pattern was so interwoven that one didn't think, 'I'm going to Church,' 'I'm going to school,' it was all part of that ritual. It's only when you stand outside the pattern like the discovery of [T.S. Eliot's] the *Four Quartets* on television over four nights in the sixties, with Alec Guinness reading them from memory, I mean, they were revelatory, you know. I didn't understand them but I went out and bought them. I read them at least once a month now. Because they're about the nature of time and memory, the very questioning of the pattern, the fabric. Once you look at the pattern you can no longer accept it – because then you know it's a pattern.

MM: How important, then, was leaving Liverpool to your increasing awareness and rejection of the pattern, and the knowledge that you didn't fit in?

TD: When you're part of the pattern, it's a great comfort. It fulfils. It wasn't until later, as I grew as a person, as my inner life grew … Then you do change, you become estranged from the pattern. You do long for it, but it can become stultifying as well. When I go back there now, yes, I see that pattern as stultifying. It's where I grew up, and the Liverpool I know has vanished. It comes back to that line in the *Four Quartets* where Eliot says, 'For the roses have the look of flowers that are looked at.' The difference being that what at one time was simply looked at becomes changed by having looked.

MM: I'm reminded of the title sequence to *The Long Day Closes* where you show a vase full of flowers. Did you have the Eliot in mind?

TD: I'm sure it was. I'm sure you're right. Again, it was just something that I felt instinctively.

MM: So you think it would have been impossible to have stayed in Liverpool and become an artist?

TD: Yes. Had I been heterosexual, you know, I may have gone the same route as everybody else. I wasn't, and so I was already outside the pattern. And as soon as I realized I was gay – and of course in those days it was a criminal offence – then you are outside it forever. I've always felt outside. Even as a child, immersed in my family, I don't know, something happens, even then I knew … I wasn't conscious of it. I watched all the time. Even then I was an outsider.

MM: And it was easier to be an outsider in a metropolis like London?

TD: No, it's not. Because it's not just like being an outsider; it's being an outsider on life. That makes for a spiritual loneliness that nothing can fulfil. Just recently I've been reading a lot of Emily Dickinson. There's a three-stanza poem which sums up exactly what I've come to:

> I reason, earth is short –
> And anguish – absolute –
> And many hurt,
> But, what of that?

> I reason, we could die –
> The best Vitality
> Cannot excell Decay,
> But, what of that?

> I reason, that in heaven –

Somehow, it will be even –
Some new Equation, given –
But, what of that?

MM: *Distant Voices, Still Lives* is at long last being restored and released on DVD. How do you feel about those films now? What do they mean to you? Will you be coming back to them as an 'outsider'?

TD: A lot of the time, I don't feel I had anything to do with them. I feel like the also-ran. I haven't got the Oscar. I can't get a film off the ground. But then I think, and it's a dreadful cliché [*laughs*], that if *The House of Mirth* does end up being the last film I make, it's really not such a bad film on which to end.

7

'Every Time a Thing Is Possessed, It Vanishes':The Poetry of Brian Patten

Stan Smith

The floss of temporal things

Returning briefly to Liverpool in 2005, Brian Patten explained, in an interview with *Nerve*, a local magazine describing itself as 'Promoting grassroots arts and culture on Merseyside':

> I started writing because I was quite isolated. My family didn't talk to each other, it was one of those nightmare families. My father had left.
>
> I grew up in a quite violent and strange house and I just felt very isolated, so I started writing to try and articulate my own feelings really you know. I wasn't thinking about whether it was poetry or not, I was just trying to articulate what was going on inside me. I had one teacher at school, a guy called Mr Sutcliffe, who was really ace and he was inspirational to me. That was at a school called Sefton Park Secondary Modern; I think there is a little Norwegian supermarket there now.[1]

The unprepossessing detail is characteristic of Patten's writing: the disarming confessional, and the ability to stand simultaneously both outside and within the lived experience; the lack of resentment at personal deprivation, recognizing both its gratuitousness, for the individual, and its cultural determination, never quite establishing, in the words of 'A Love Poem', 'why all that's commonplace / Comes to seem unique';[2] the insistence on local particularity, moving from the warmth

---

1 Darren Guy, 'Liverpool's Poetic Hero', interview with Brian Patten, *Nerve* 5, Spring 2005 (Liverpool: Catalyst Media). No pagination.
2 Brian Patten, *Vanishing Trick* (London: Allen & Unwin, 1976), p. 9. Hereafter *VT*.

of that acknowledgment to the slightly comic intimation of mortality in the school's conversion into the improbable precision of a 'Norwegian' supermarket.

Characteristic, too, is the careful indignation, fusing cynicism and idealism, which amounts to an intervention later in the interview, when asked what he thought of Liverpool being designated European City of Culture:

> Well there's going to be an awful lot of money floating around. I hope they can keep hold of it ... They did this poetry competition with Radio Merseyside about 'Poems on the Sea' or something. They only got fifty/sixty entries, and you know who they got to organize it? Not a local magazine, but a PR company in Manchester. I was really pissed off. It could have been organized by your magazine, or someone else's magazine, at least someone based in Liverpool.

Patten's words align themselves with the dissenting tones of the magazine's editorial, which, claiming to be 'the only local voice for those who have been silenced by the mainstream media', observes that 'Liverpool artists have less funding and a smaller voice since the Capital of Culture award, which favours corporate blandness', while citing 'a report released in March 2005 [which] states that between 65% and 70% of children are living in poverty in some areas of Liverpool'.

Brian Patten was himself born in 1946 into an impoverished working-class, soon-to-be single-parent family in the Sefton Park area of Liverpool.[3] The Penguin UK Authors website quotes him to the effect that, growing up on a street called Wavertree Vale, 'The street's name was my first lesson in irony. ... It was a treeless street that crouched in the shadows cast by huge gasometers.'[4] The discrepancy between how things are named and what they are, between a language which dissembles reality and the nature of that 'real', touches a division at the core of Patten's poetry, where disenchanted social observation jostles with a gift for conjuring visionary fantasy from the ordinary street. In the play between the two modes the poetry finds its modestly impassioned distinction. Central to Patten's work is the peculiar dialectic between individual isolation, in an environment felt to be 'quite violent and

---

3 For biographical information, see Linda Cookson, *Brian Patten* (Plymouth: Northcote House, 1977), and the various Patten websites.

4 Penguin UK Authors website: Brian Patten.

strange', and a populist sense of communal identity, with its local loyal-ties, which has always just been lost but hovers perpetually on the verge of possible recovery. Elegiac sorrow for this collective loss underlies and underwrites the poetry's sense of personal dispossession.

Patten left Sefton Park Secondary Modern School in 1961 to work as a cub reporter on a local newspaper, the *Bootle Times*. A year later, after meeting Roger McGough and Adrian Henri, who became his fellow performers at poetry venues around Liverpool, he set up his own poetry magazine, *Underdog*, which ran to eight issues (the first issue appears to be lost). The title of the magazine is significant. Under the eleven-plus educational system which prevailed at the time, school selection at secondary level, though ostensibly competitive, by and large reproduced the class stratification of the 'affluent society' forged in the 1950s on the back of postwar economic recovery. The system, only partially replaced by the programme of comprehensive education initi-ated in the 1960s, all too often cast the excluded majority who had failed to 'make it' to the elite grammar or technical schools as 'underdogs', for whom the secondary modern fulfilled the function of pedagogic sink estate. Asked by the interviewer about the academic critics who slated *The Mersey Sound*,[5] the 1967 Penguin Modern Poets anthology which first brought the three poets to a national and international readership, Patten summed up the populism underlying his ideas about both poetry and education with an aphorism of Adrian Mitchell's: 'Most people ignore most poetry, because most poetry ignores most people.'

As a major port, Liverpool in the late 1950s and the 1960s shared in the growth of world trade generated by the long postwar boom. In retro-spect, the boom years can be seen as an intermission between periods of extended economic decline, underlined in the 1970s by extensive contractions and closures in Liverpool's docks and shipping industry. The collapse of the city's economic infrastructure exacerbated the prob-lems of long-term unemployment which issued in 1981 in the Toxteth Riots, in the simmering resentments of the Thatcher years, and, for a time, the capture of the city's Labour Party and Council by the hard-left Militant Tendency. Interpolated into the *longue durée* of decline, the 1960s' boom years were always vulnerable to the shifts of the global market. If the poems of *The Mersey Sound* speak with the irreverent

---

5 Adrian Henri, Roger McGough and Brian Patten, *The Mersey Sound* (Harmonds-worth: Penguin Modern Poets, 1967; revised and enlarged edition, 1974). Hereafter *MS*.

proletarian-chic of the clamorous youth culture from which they emerged, they whisper also of its fragility and transience. The insouciant, combative gaiety of this moment is everywhere shadowed by the tone of elegy. The verse collectively evinces a suspicion that, in breaking free from the taboos and prohibitions of traditional working-class culture, something precious has also been forfeited, and a sense, too, of a present shot through with premonitions of further loss, when the youthful revels are all ended.

Adrian Henri's 'Tonight at Noon', for example, which opens *The Mersey Sound*, offers a vision of the world turned upside down, where 'Poets get their poems in the Top 20' and 'there's jobs for everyone and nobody wants them' (*MS*, pp. 11–12). But its euphoric moment cannot be sustained, as the oxymoronic temporal telescoping of the title suggests. In similar vein, McGough's poem, 'At Lunchtime A Story of Love' (*MS*, pp. 69–70), imagines a morning busload of passengers, persuaded by the poet that 'the world was going to end at lunchtime', engaging in a last-minute orgy of public love-making. Returning home on the evening bus, a little embarrassed because the world has not in fact ended, the same passengers jump at the poet's suggestion that 'we could always pretend', to initiate another outbreak of 'naughty things'. In the following weeks the epidemic spreads to every bus in the world, collective connivance in the fantasy of apocalypse licensing a carnival of promiscuity. As to the world ending, the poem concludes, 'It still hasn't. / Although in a way it has.' The paradoxes of a time turned inside-out inscribe both these visions of Liverpudlian Cockagne in the same make-believe realm as the hobo's dream of the Big Rock Candy Mountain, located, as the title of one of Patten's contributions to the book puts it, 'Somewhere Between Heaven and Woolworths' (*MS*, p. 103). In contrast, the comic apocalyptic inversions of Patten's 'Prosepoem Towards a Definition of Itself' (*MS*, pp. 107–108) have a different vision of final things, arguing, 'Poetry should seek out pale and lyrical couples and wander with them into stables, neglected bedrooms and engineless cars for a final Good Time.' The innocuous 'final' inserts its chill into all supposedly 'good' times. (In *Little Johnny's Confession*, where the poem first appeared, the point is underlined by additional reference to Dantescan 'unsafe forests' and the extension of capitalization to 'A Final Good Time'.)[6] Patten's contributions to *The Mersey Sound* are suffused

6 Brian Patten, *Little Johnny's Confession* (London: Allen & Unwin, 1967), p. 18. Hereafter *LJC*.

with a darker, Keatsian melancholia that has heard the insinuating whisper in the garden of earthly delights: *Et in Arcadia ego*.

The division of Patten's verse into two selections a decade apart, *Love Poems* (1981) and what the publishers call its 'companion volume', *Grinning Jack* (1990), implies a conscious dualism between the epiphanic moment and sad accommodation to a volatile quotidian, made palatable by an acerbic gallows humour.[7] It is not, however, a division that holds up, for the two moods interpenetrate and sustain each throughout the poetry. The title *Grinning Jack* is clarified in 'Staring at the Crowd', originally published in *Grave Gossip*,[8] a volume dedicated to a recently dead friend and much possessed with death, as its title indicates. The phrase refers to the grinning rictus of the death's-head, the skeleton at the feast of the senses 'that every man / ignores as calmly as he can':

> Who'll kiss us on the cheek and blow
> The floss of temporal things away.
> It's Grinning Jack I see today,
> And once seen he'll never go away. (*GJ*, p.125)

Beneath Liverpool's upsurge of cultural exuberance in the 1960s lurked an abiding melancholy, witnessed by the way in which the breathless vignettes of the Beatles' 'Penny Lane', for example, were called to account by the lonely crowds of 'Eleanor Rigby'. The heady enthusiasm, the exhilaration at a new start, coexisted with a deeper intuition of mortality and decline. Patten's verse reacted angrily at times to the way whole communities could be sidelined, reinvented as a version of pastoral, and then relegated once again to marginality and obscurity. Some of this anger seemed to arise from remorse at his own complicity in the processes of supersession, as he was to admit thirty years later in 'The Betrayal':

> By the time I got where I had no intention of going
> Half a lifetime had passed.
> I'd sleepwalked so long. While I dozed
> Houses outside which gas-lamps had spluttered

---

7 Brian Patten, *Love Poems* (London: Allen & Unwin, 1981); *Grinning Jack* (London: Unwin Hyman, 1990; this edition, London, Flamingo, 1995). Hereafter *GJ*.
8 Brian Patten, *Grave Gossip* (London: Allen & Unwin, 1979). Hereafter *GG*.

Were pulled down and replaced,
And my background was wiped from the face of the earth.[9]

This sense of betrayal at not recording the vanished lives of family and neighbours, whom the poem describes, in a significant metaphor, as 'The loose change history spent without caring', is seen, too, in the same volume's reproachfully entitled 'Neighbourhood Watch'. His one-time contemporaries on his native street, 'refugees from / the way things are supposed to be', whom he failed to watch over, have departed, as property development turned their homes into marketable commodities, so that 'One by one the souls of these houses and their tenants / have been undone by the fingers of bankers' (*A*, pp. 20–21). In *Storm Damage* the title of one poem asks of his sixties generation, thirty years on, 'Where are all those long-haired optimists now?' What the poem mourns, brooding over the 'yellow, infantile magazines / That celebrated ghost-revolutions', finding 'So much hoped for, so little altered', is the tragicomedy of incorporation, old protest songs regurgitated as muzak in crematoria (his generation is already dying), while what were once community workshops now appear on the stock market as listed companies. Yet there is a kind of paradox here, for if protest and revolt are ephemeral, one thing remains permanent: power. 'The same truncheons' still rise and fall, becoming, in a swift elision, the orchestral batons 'conducting / Man's history, ignoring / His passing fashions, his illusions.'[10] 'A Bird-Brained View of Power' (*GG*, p. 24), rehearses the poet's paranoiac sense of responsibility for all this. 'Job Hunting' confirms his sense of the transience of those carnivalesque moments celebrated in *The Mersey Sound*, as his children play a game 'called job hunting' among the ruins of broken machinery and cranes, coming back clutching 'Nuts, bolts, the broken vizor / Of a welder's mask' they have prised from the ground, to ask, 'Daddy, / Is this a job, can we keep it?' (*SD*, p. 49), no doubt a deliberate evocation of Yosser Hughes's desperate plea, 'I can do that. Gizza job.'

'It would be easy to blame an age, / Blame fashions that infiltrate and cause / What was thought constant to change', admits the speaker of 'Tristan, Waking in His Wood, Panics'.[11] But the poem goes on to

9 Brian Patten, *Armada* (London, Flamingo, 1996), p. 16. Hereafter *A*.

10 Brian Patten, *Storm Damage* (London: Unwin Hyman, 1988; this edition, London, Flamingo, 1995), p. 28. Hereafter *SD*.

11 Brian Patten, *The Irrelevant Song* (London: Allen & Unwin, 1971), p. 46. Hereafter *TIS*.

suggest that it was his proprietary dream of a future that brought about this change – hence the panic of the title. The poetry of 'the Mersey Sound', the snappily punning formula reminding, implicitly, that an estuary silts up unless its shallows are dredged, raised questions about the apparent success story in which it shared, questions about the ultimate ownership of a local identity appropriated and marketed as a commodity, a people's culture cashed in as 'pop culture'. 'Nobody born in this city,' Patten confided to the *Liverpool Daily Post* in 1975, 'can ever really leave. The city is within them … Its images and memories are so powerful they will remain within me forever; Liverpool I carry within me, from the first breath to the last'.[12] Across Patten's anxious intuitions of class and cultural dispossession falls the shadow of a darker history. Liverpool's prosperity had been founded on the Atlantic slave trade – on the violent uprooting of individuals from their own time and place, the transubstantiation of human beings into merchandise, as an everyday business. Once the hub of a global commerce in human lives, the city discovered, in the marginalization that accompanied its 'Final Good Time', a fate that seemed at times like an ironic return of the repressed. On this troubled stage, Patten's poetry could find a contemporary personal setting in which to perform once again the ancient topoi of pastoral, *tempus edax rerum* and *carpe diem* ('Time devours all things' and 'seize the day'), in an isolation at once strange and familiar, metaphysical and intimate.

So ordinary a thing as loss

Patten's favourite time is not that of final things but of false starts, those ordinary dawns full of equivocation and ambiguity, where the world lies all before us, but will probably disappoint. Of his twenty-six poems in the original *Mersey Sound,* nine contain the word 'dawn' and three of them have the word in the title, while another three, speaking of early waking, call up the same transitional moment. In 'The Fruitful Lady of Dawn' (*MS*, p. 123) the eponymous female figure 'cannot fathom out / whose dawn she belongs in'. She appears to be a transient partner, who, though she 'approaches breakfast as she would a lover', joyful at being alive, is unable to understand 'why a sentence made of kisses' is succeeded by 'the image of somebody wandering alone through semi-colons', just passing through. In 'In a New Kind of Dawn' (*MS*, p. 124) someone, not necessarily the poet, readjusting his conscience,

---

12 Quoted in Cookson, *Brian Patten*, p. 12.

dreams of lives he would have swum through had he been strong enough. 'On the Dawn Boat' (*MS*, p. 124), recalling Robert Creeley's minimalist lyrics, finds the poet waking to think about the many warnings and signs he has witnessed, none able to lead him away from where he is, or where he might or should be. All these dawn moments juxtapose indicative and subjunctive moods, seeing the actual emerge out of the suppression of all those alternative possibilities which remain unrealized and unfulfilled, and laced with a kind of diffuse guilt about their very indeterminacy. Linked with the motif of dawn is that of dusk: two poems in *The Mersey Sound* speak directly of evening and another of the sun going down. In several, a rainy autumn or winter is the prevailing season. The dawn motif is repeated endlessly throughout Patten's oeuvre. But these poems are not traditional aubades, full of the promise of renewal and rejuvenation. Rather, the characteristic experience of dawn is of separation and loss, as in 'Song for Last Year's Wife', in his first collection, *Little Johnny's Confession*:

> I imagine you,
> waking in another city, touched
> by this same hour. So ordinary
> a thing as loss comes now and touches me. (*LJC*, p. 34)

The anaphora 'touched / touches' renders the emptiness of loss oddly tangible, in imagination restoring wishful contact between the former lovers, though the poem knows it is an illusion, knows that, though his spies tell him her 'body's as firm … as alive, warm and inviting' as before, it is only her ghost that winter, in 'its isolation from other seasons', sends him 'to witness / when I wake'. 'A Creature to Tell the Time By' in the same volume speaks of a woman he created for himself; 'woken with her / at dawn', the revelation he encounters is that, inside both of them, 'the green love that grew there yesterday / was dead' (*LJC*, p. 22). 'The Transformation' looks at a similar scene from the point of view of the woman, apparently another casual partner, watching, 'still half asleep, / How dawn ignites a room', and observing, of her sleeping lover, how 'His body distant from your own / Has by the dawn been changed', recognizing, finally, for all her hopes that something more may have grown from this brief encounter, 'How dawn mishapes [*sic*] a room, / And all your confidence by the light is drained' (*TIS*, p. 39). Departure is the unspoken premise of all these elusive and illusory moments.

Patten's early poetry often situates itself at the fag end of some allegedly wild all-night party, as, for example, 'Party Piece', which opens his section of *The Mersey Sound* (*MS*, p. 95). In it, a young man, distanced into the third person, proposes to a girl he's met at a party that, 'Now this place has emptied', they should 'make gentle pornography with each other', 'While the partygoers go out / & the dawn creeps in, / Like a stranger.' The biblical resonance (the day of the Lord coming like a thief in the night) is probably too heavy an association for such a light poem to carry, but the moral reservations are not hard to discern beneath the slight lyric grace. This is not the innocently sensuous dawn of the traditional aubade, but a rather more jaded scenario. Though love-making is presented as a moment of mutual tenderness, 'gentle' does not totally mute the impact of 'pornography', which, even if playfully used, calls up the sexual consumerism of what Richard Hoggart had recently characterized, in *The Uses of Literacy* (1957), as 'The Newer Mass Art: Sex in Shiny Packets'.[13] Though the speaker advises against thinking about 'how cold this place has become', the adjective links physical and emotional temperatures, preparing the way for the final vision of desolation, in which the two casual partners diverge for ever: 'later, he caught a bus and she a train, / And all there was between them then / was rain'. The preposition 'between' hovers itself between linking and sundering, sharing and separating. The excited vision, earlier, of them unclipping their minds and letting tumble free 'The mad, mangled crocodiles of love' is an unsettling image, full of latent violence, a consumerist voracity, the woodbines amid which they make love are not Keatsian flora but stubbed-out cigarette butts, and the 'guinness stains' of a drunken debauch gesture towards other, deeper and harder-to-remove stains, moral and emotional, again with a religious undertone deriving from the theology of Patten's Catholic childhood.

The darker narrative of such parties is spelt out in the plangent 'Portrait of a Young Girl Raped at a Suburban Party', 'already ten minutes' pregnant', in the satiric 'Party Notes',[14] or, more lyrically ambivalent, in 'Somewhere Between Heaven and Woolworths, A Song' (*MS*, p. 103; *TIS*, p. 45). In the latter, the woman who keeps kingfishers in their cages and goldfish in their bowls, though still 'lovely', is afraid of growing old. For her, the sexual act has been exploitation. If 'There

13 Richard Hoggart, *The Uses of Literacy* (Harmondsworth: Penguin, 1957), ch. 8, pp. 246-72.
14 Brian Patten, *Notes to the Hurrying Man* (London: Allen & Unwin, 1969), pp. 25, 31. Hereafter *NTTHM*.

were numerous men that loved her', such 'love' is debased to the mere sexual act. These men were in reality 'more cruel than kind', their alleged love 'an act in isolation, / A form of pantomime', not only a theatrical act but one that topples into a grotesque ludic parody of the real thing. The woman's apparently blasé attitude towards all this is at the same time a self-protection against recognizing how she has been used, forgetting the feelings shared at all-night parties but retaining a vision of heaven, a lost moment of fulfilment which was always a deception, a gimcrack delight of the kind sold in any five-and-dime store:

> For among the songs and the dancing
> She was once open wide,
> A girl dressed in denim
> With the boys dressed in lies.

There is a kind of transcendence here, crying out from the text, something indicated by the earlier 'shared'. Open wide, sexually available, she was also open to the universe, her vulnerability a kind of generous, needy innocence that triumphs over the serpent in the garden. The true location of the human, the poem implies, is in that middle ground, 'somewhere between', of mortal persistence. The ambivalently defiant openness here is not unrelated to that in 'Her Advice' (*VT*, p. 36). Here it is the woman whose words comprise two-thirds of the poem who makes all the running, casting her male addressee as a 'Dreamer, unlike myself', calling him away from the window where he is star-gazing, urging him not to 'drift too far from me' as 'In other rooms the party's growing old'. 'Heaven left alone will not grow bored', she advises, to which, in deliberative retrospect, he can only respond, twice, that 'she was right', though – a major qualification – 'our longings do not end with what she says'.

Patten's own longings are to recover that utopian, time-transcending moment of untrammelled being which may hide even amidst the debris of a party growing old, that 'place not far away' which 'It takes a lot of trust to reach' spoken of in the beautiful brief lyric 'Something Never Lost' (*GG*, p. 50). *The Irrelevant Song* is preoccupied with such ontological searchings. In 'At Four O'Clock in the Morning' two casual lovers 'in present time ... rest' as in a 'completed', time-stopped world. In fact, 'all is temporary and ... changeable, / So in this bed my love you lie, / Temporary beyond imaginings'. The windows are already 'freaked with dawn', and shrill bird-song 'reminds / each of a separate knowledge'. Unlike children, they are aware of the 'human weight' of words that become 'false and monstrous' as soon as uttered (picking up that equivocal verb 'lie'). If, enjoining silence, he can say 'enough words are used' here, it is because the words are 'used' in a further sense, second-hand, worn down and blunted, recalling an imaginary lost authenticity which is always 'Yesterday's echo' (*TIS*, p. 19). 'The Morning's Got a Sleepy Head' acknowledges that for both lovers, 'The gap one makes in leaving is not filled', yet each persists in casting the other, impossibly, as the presence that will bring existence to completion, filling its consuming lack with self-presence (*TIS*, p. 27). But, as 'Through All Your Abstract Reasoning' asks, 'struck so by another's identity / how can you hold on to any revelation?' (*TIS*, p. 24). 'Because There Were No Revelations At Hand', however, finds 'the lack of anything revealed to be / A revelation of a kind' (*TIS*, p. 23).

In the earliest poetry, a lost arcadian innocence, in which the self was at one with its 'completed' world, is symbolized by the comic book superheroes of childhood. 'Where Are You Now Superman?' speaks of these heroes having been killed off 'simply because we grew up', leaving the possibility that, somewhere else, they still abide, impervious to cynicism, for new generations of children who have not yet stumbled out of Eden (*LJC*, p. 20). (Ironically, Superman is faithlessly replaced by Batman as top nostalgic icon in the revised version of the poem published in *The Mersey Sound*.) The paradox of identity for Patten, first explored in the 'Little Johnny' poems, is that the subject is constructed in a process of acculturation in which it is dispossessed in the very process of entering into 'separate knowledge' – knowledge of the self as separate, and as separated. At the core of the self is an absence, a void yearning to be filled, and it is this sense of the self as *lack* which underlies both the longed-for enchantments and the rueful disenchantments of his love poems. 'Johnny Learns the Language', a poem added to the sequence in later editions of *Little Johnny's Confession* and in *Grinning Jack*, confesses that, in entering into discourse, he also 'began to understand / how words were the nets in which / what I was floundered'. To his parents, Johnny announces:

> I am learning your language.
> 'Loss', 'Defeat', 'Regret' –
> Without understanding
> You would have these be
> the blueprints for my future. (*GJ*, p. 10)

'When Into Sudden Beds' (*TIS*, p. 42) sees the pursuit of sexual encounter as a futile attempt to escape this lack in which the self is founded, seeking to 'share / 'For habit's sake some human warmth', a strategy which only serves to 'ignite some loss', recalling in dream that other who can be defined only negatively, as one 'who is now gone'. Forced to turn 'with a larger sympathy than once you owned', he finds himself unable to reciprocate, 'When for love you're asked to pay in kind, / And find you are not large enough to turn.' The elusive logic itself turns on that repeated 'turn', for what happens in this turning is the conversion of a discourse of commercial transactions into a different kind of exchange, a mutual giving, 'in kind' – the word suggesting both kindliness and kinship, reinforced by that tactility which is a repeated trope of the love poetry ('Whatever's touched, shoulder, thigh or breast'). The venal barter of mutually exploitative intercourse turns potentially into something quite different, for only love can pay 'in kind' for love. That he is not 'large enough to turn' brings out the full subversive force of 'owned' in this 'larger sympathy than once you owned'. For, if its immediate meaning is 'acknowledged', 'owned up to', it also raises questions of ownership, of self-possession, and of what it means to be one's 'own' self – questions integral to the evolution of Patten's poetry.

What did we ever own?

Most of the poems in *The Irrelevant Song* are attributed to a persona, William, who appears to be the grown-up, disenchanted successor to Little Johnny. The eponymous opening poem of the volume, casting the lyric I of the subsequent poems in the third person, describes the context in which 'William's Songs' are generated. William, another dawn-riser, writes his love songs 'On seaside proms before the people had risen', 'Yet however early he had risen / The spaces beside him / Would be left vacant', and the frosty light would gather inside him most mornings, until 'His loss grew branches' and 'Across his tongue / The world's tastes skated' (*TIS*, p. 11). Like those 'girls waking in early rooms / Possessed by dreams that would not suit you', William is himself possessed by an impossible dream of fulfilment until, his songs 'Fled into an irretrievable country', he is compelled to disown 'the Daughter of Sadness' in whom he had founded his fantasy of fulfilment, in a world which now seems to have 'Relinquished any meaning' (*TIS*, pp. 15–16). This is a complex fable, its internal contradictions acknowledged in that auto-referential admission, halfway through, 'And so a story changes' (*TIS*, p. 13). In an interview, Patten advised would-be story-tellers: 'Always know at least one important thing about your character that you do not reveal in your story. Give them a secret that stays a secret between you and them.'[15] All Patten's poetry presents a universe where an essential secret is withheld for its subject, leaving him aware only that, in the words of 'Perhaps', 'so much will have been missed / That has never been missed', leaving him 'hungry and baffled' (*SD*, p. 29). So it is with William here. The secret of *The Irrelevant Song* is hinted at in the multiple resonances of that word 'possessed', linked to the concept of 'disowning' and to an almost subliminal imagery of consumption, of tasting and eating. To be 'possessed' is not to be oneself, but to be in thrall whether to a dream, a passion, demons, or another person. In this last sense, one is also owned. To disown another, then, as here, is to free them from one's own fantasy of them. Central to the whole sequence is the idea of a subjective emptiness, founded in inexplicable loss, which seeks to fill its void by hungrily consuming the world, only to find that 'the sad endings you pursue / Are but things completed' (*TIS*, p. 13), that the urge to possess only expands the devouring emptiness.

'What did we ever own that hadn't / the quality of seasons, / their numerous dyings?' asks 'Winter Song' (*TIS*, p. 31). 'The Outgoing Song' correlates 'all things that / you owned and were broken by', in an extension of Proudhon's axiom that property is theft, to suggest that possession alienates the subject who owns as much as the object appro-priated, dispossessing both the possessor and the possessed (*TIS*, p. 30). The edgy confessional of 'Tristan, Waking in His Wood, Panics' acknowledges that 'Every time a thing is owned, / Every time a thing is possessed, / It vanishes' (*TIS*, p. 46), for to own a thing or a person is to rob them of their existence in and for themselves, in Sartre's terms, not only as *ensoi* but as *poursoi*. Possession turns the 'thing' into *a* posses-sion, no longer itself. But if, in the last word of this poem, loss is 'irretrievable', it is seen here as the consequence not of defeat but of the triumphs with which the poem opened, where Tristan, begging not to be allowed to win yet again, reiterates the word 'want' three times, while protesting that he does not 'want to possess'. Tristan, like his author, is 'familiar with opposites', and the traction between possessing and wanting here gives away the secret these poems imagine to lie at the heart of being, the unfulfillable voracious craving of wanting not to want

15 Penguin UK Authors website: Brian Patten: interview.

(*TIS*, p. 46). 'The Outgoing Song' reveals this same paradoxical relation between self and world, for if, in being reduced to quietness and
impassivity, he finds himself emptied of desire, small worries spilling out
from him, the poem ends with anxious questions about 'this want, this
reaching out' which reverses the movement outward, seeking to engulf
even the outgoing song itself (*TIS*, p. 30).

'Poem Written in the Street on a Rainy Evening' (*TIS*, p. 43) likewise deals in the paradoxes of possession, in a dream of restoration where
'Everything I lost was found again', his heart moving 'Through the
darkest objects laughing'. Here, a language of consumption surrepti-
tiously unites the order of things and of subjective being. His joy is
'gobbled up' by dull surroundings, but the world is a feast spread before
him, 'suddenly made edible', with forever in which to taste it. The
imagery imputes a sacramental communion with the real, in which he
tastes the world as wine in his mouth. 'Someone Coming Back' makes
similar correlations, opening 'Now that the summer has emptied / and
laughter's warned against possessions', but ending with the morning
demanding, of the subject who contemplates it, 'O taste me! Taste me
please!' (*TIS*, p. 22). In 'The Song' Patten had written of cities where
dreams are 'eaten with breakfast' challenged by a bird song that represents unfettered being. Though he speaks initially of turning the song
into a possession, his hands scooping it up to send to a lover, her eyes
trapping it, the poem closes with a different image, in which hands and
eyes become the song's hosts, nurturing without possessing, finding it

> Presumptuous to offer as unique those things
> we own in common; yet how common the heart
> that without touching or wishing to own it,
> lets the song nest there. (*NTTHM*, p. 37)

Such tentative owning in common suggests an alternative way of
accessing the world to that of possessive consumerism. Which is only
to the good, since Patten's universe leaks. As in traditional pastoral, the
day cannot really be seized, cannot, in some Faustian compact, be
commanded to be still. Leakage is one of his favourite metaphors, often
linked to another, that of 'drifting', and each interchangeably applied to
both internal and external worlds. Into his songs 'there leaked / More
awkward celebrations', we read in 'The Irrelevant Song' (*TIS*, p. 16). In
'Towards Evening and Tired of the Place', he speaks of himself as 'Adrift
in places where nothing has yet happened' (*VT*, p. 35), the subject's

passivity intimately related to his dependence on events, on things happening, rather than on deeds, him doing things. In 'Sometimes It Happens' in the same volume, 'A fountain empties itself into the grass' in implicit analogy for how the self relates to days and loves that drain away. Here, dreams flare up, then suddenly vanish, as do the years, 'Quicker than a minute'; things cease to matter even as he is wondering whether they matter, until caring itself is past, leaving the self with nothing (*VT*, p. 31). This is reality's 'Vanishing Trick', as in the title poem of the volume, where he watches his lover gathering up 'longings mistakenly scattered' with her clothes, moving away as she 'talk[s] of going as if going were the smallest matter'. 'In the morning', he reflects, 'bodies evaporate and nothing / can quite hold them together':

> Suddenly everything changes.
> Less than a second passes and nothing's the same.
> Something that clung a moment ago lets go as if
> all its clinging meant nothing. (*VT*, p. 12)

In the opening poem of the volume, 'A Love Poem', 'Adrift on the taste of you', he finds himself baffled as he wonders why in this particular woman, with her body 'Harbouring loneliness', the commonplace comes to seem unique, 'And though down my spine one answer leaks / It does not bother to explain itself' (*VT*, p. 9). In 'You Have Gone to Sleep', 'Something not anchored in love drifts out of reach', while 'Into the voice leaks bitterness', because 'A moment ago I found / Your mouth on mine was counterfeit.' Now it is a planet that drifts out of reach, and 'Tomorrow something else might wake / What's gone to sleep' (*VT*, p. 10).

In observing this 'sleep ... full of exhaustions' (*VT*, p. 10), the poem initiates a leitmotiv that was to dominate Patten's next volume, *Grave Gossip*, in 1979, which, in its depiction of being exhausted even 'by what had not yet happened' ('Hopeful', *GG*, p. 47), recalls the argument of John Barth's essay 'The Literature of Exhaustion', reprinted to renewed critical interest a couple of years previously.[16] Barth proposed that contemporary society, having suffered the 'used-upness' of all literary and cultural modes, the exhaustion of traditional historical narra-

---

16 John Barth, 'The Literature of Exhaustion', *Atlantic Monthly*, August 1967, reprinted in Malcolm Bradbury (ed.), *The Novel Today: Contemporary Writers on Modern Fiction* (London: Fontana, 1977), pp. 70–83.

tives, could now find originality only in the ironic recycling of past forms and figurations, the renewal of cliché as self-conscious discourse. The poem 'The Common Denominator, Or, The Ground-Floor Tenant's Only Poem' acknowledges as much in its own self-justification: 'At a clouded intellect I've hurled / All the clichéd answers in the world' (*GG*, p. 22) . The volume runs through a whole series of reconfigured literary clichés to body forth the general exhaustion, from the nightingale / poetry analogy ('Absurd and clichéd as it sounds', *GG*, p. 24), through a series which reworks a slyly jaundiced Brer Rabbit, to Dante's classic epiphanies in the dark wood of mid-life crisis. That Patten has Barth directly in mind is confirmed by the verbal echoes in 'The Right Mask', where, challenged by a poem wanting to be written to don a series of Yeatsian masks in order to write it, he replies of each suggested persona in turn that 'I've used it already ... I've exhausted it ... It's all used up' (*GG*, p. 34).[17]

Grave Gossip queries the use of 'dragging the body and all / its loose desires and its ghost connections' through the world ('The Purpose is Ecstasy', *GG*, p. 52). But in fact it deploys remarkable originality in reworking the very played-outness of this culture of recycled clichés and ghost-written speech, where illustrious ghosts gossip among the bookcases and, in two related poems, the poet finds himself 'Trapped' in library archives and in the offices of a metaphysical as well as real 'Poetry Society' (*GG*, pp. 27, 28). An astonishing number of dead men (and occasionally women) of letters are summoned up by name in the book's literary séances: Baudelaire, Rimbaud, Shakespeare, Donne, Gray, Blake, John Clare, Coleridge and Wordsworth, Keats, Dickinson and Stevie Smith, Woolf and Dylan Thomas, Auden, Betjeman, even McGonagall and a still-living Larkin, while Whitman is invoked in the theme-setting title 'I Studied Telephones Constantly' (*GG*, pp. 10–13), and many more are evoked by implication, including that Dante who presides over all this whole infernal underworld of letters. 'It is a dubious honour getting to know the dead', Patten observes in 'The Last Gift' (*GG*, p. 47). Defining himself in the book's final poem, 'Assembling a Prayer', as 'One of Death's little camp followers', he reports that he has finally 'learnt how to throw away the tragic books'(*GG*, pp. 54–55). But these poems are all in a sense dead letters, sent but uncollected, to

17 For a further consideration of these themes in *The Irrelevant Song* and *Grave Gossip*, see Stan Smith, *Inviolable Voice: History and Twentieth-Century Poetry* (Dublin: Gill & Macmillan; Atlantic Highlands, NJ: Humanities Press, 1982), pp. 193–99.

the literary dead, analogous to all those misplaced calls from 'ghost phones' of which 'I Studied Telephones Constantly' speaks, lingering in telephone exchanges 'where the operators sleep-walk among the babble' (GG, p. 13). In the punning suggestiveness of the book's title, all this is 'grave gossip', serious gossip about the living and the dead, but also gossip that the grave itself broadcasts, as messages leak between worlds, and the two title words themselves switch between adjective, noun and verb:

> I was listening to the grave gossip.
> Terror leaked from the mouth's pit. (GG, p. 13)

In gossip, language itself leaks. But if 'Death owns everyone's telephone number' (professing lurking within possessing), the line calls up that recurrent topos of Patten's verse reiterated in the question and answer which close the poem:

> How many telephone numbers does the night possess?
> The night has as many telephone numbers as stars. (GG, p. 13)

The cover photo of *Grave Gossip*, in what is surely a deliberate recollection of one of the most vivid sequences accompanying the 'Eleanor Rigby' track in the Beatles' animation *Yellow Submarine* (1968), depicts Patten himself in a public phone box, his hand raised against the glass as if on the verge of panicking that he might be trapped inside. Or it may be that it is the conversation, in which we can never share, that induces the anxious body language. The image is telling in its very ambiguity.

Cargoes

Armada (1996), Patten's most recent non-children's book, makes periodic returns to Liverpool, following his mother's hospitalization with a haemorrhage, and her subsequent death, occasioning a reconsideration of the place where he grew up and its determining influences. As Linda Cookson has noted, the collection is full of nautical allusions, 'concerned in many ways with journeys into the unknown', not only as 'a metaphor for human experience', but also suggesting 'a further world, as yet undiscovered, beyond that horizon'. Cookson quotes Patten's explanation that the book's title is not a specific reference to the Spanish Armada. Without the prefix 'A' or 'The', he says, the word can be given a new resonance. It can be defamiliarised and opened up. At the moment of death, in the micro-second between being and non-being, perhaps consciousness enters a state that can be called *armada*, in which all an individual's million fragments of memory, all thoughts, all sensations simultaneously weigh anchor and set sail across unknowable space and time.[18]

As always with Patten, it is in this liminal moment that we can glimpse an evanescent meaning. The self here is both fleeting and multiple, as in those poems of Whitman ('I am large, I contain multitudes') whom he links in his *Nerve* interview with Arthur Rimbaud, the poet who first articulated the modern sense of a human subjectivity not identical with itself – '*Je est un autre*'.

The title poem recalls how in infancy, accompanied by his mother, he would launch a 'child's armada' of twig and paper-tissue ships on the local pond (there is an implicit analogy with the launch of this collection of poems), till 'all came to ruin and were on flame / in that dusk-red pond', afire with the setting sun. The spatial dynamics of the scene are worth considering. Like all ships leaving Liverpool, this fleet has to sail west, into the sunset, and it is toward the western horizon that the child is looking, as in the well-known painting of *The Boyhood of Drake*. As in other poems, however, the mother stands behind the boy, assumed but unseen, preoccupied with her own separate concerns, impatient to be going. Now, cutting to the present, she repeats on her hospital bed that impatience to be gone. Her skin, touched, reminds him of the pond's cool surface, as she waits to be blown out of reach like one of those paper boats, while his 'heart burns as that armada burnt, / long, long ago'. Heat and cool merge here as, in the psychic economy of the poem, he becomes both the observer watching his mother's small boat depart, and the whole armada that goes down in a collective shipwreck.

Balancing this, 'Ghost Ship', the penultimate poem of the Armada sequence, combines echoes of the Ancient Mariner and the Flying Dutchman to evoke the long-dead 'one who fathered me' (not quite the same as a father), figured as perpetually leaving port for the open seas (*A*, p. 33). A merchant seaman whom Stella Patten left after she discovered he had sired children by two other women, his father is now joined by the newly dead mother as the determining absence within which the self constructs a provisional identity, to leave the poet, as the

18 Quoted in Cookson, *Brian Patten*, pp. 73–74.

title of the preceding poem indicates, for ever 'In The Dark' (*A*, p. 32). His youth, this poem says, recalling the motifs of earlier volumes, has 'drifted out the skeleton', but has 'left its baggage'. The latter idea intersects in several poems with the nautical motif, in ambiguous figuration of the nature of identity. Most obviously, this occurs in 'Inattention', which opens with a child sitting on a doorstep in the sun, reading a book while behind him, in the room, a woman sits writing a letter. The poem reproduces the emotional topography of 'The Armada'. The shadow of the gasometer across the waste ground in front of him slowly lengthens throughout the poem, so he is facing west into a declining sun; the mother behind him is preoccupied with her own concerns. But the child hasn't noticed any of this, engrossed in the 'unfamiliar' and 'wondrous' words of his book, as 'Over and over, as if it were a spell, he repeats the word *cargo*', sending his imaginary ships out on an ocean where phosphate clings to rusting propellers and whales rise like islands. In imagination abandoning the book, he becomes 'the captain of a great ship and its cargo of treasure'. In fantasy he is the custodian of this cargo, but a syntactic ambiguity subliminally allows him to be cargo as well as captain. And indeed, in the house behind him, 'a woman is packing belongings. / Another book, an encyclopedia of regrets, is banished to its own space'. In that book, it is the mother who is in charge of a cargo which includes the child, himself a possession ('belongings') to be packed and transported to another place (*A*, p. 22).

The child's dependent, secondary role in the parents' lives is indicated by the ambiguous spatiality of 'The Eavesdropper', where he sits in his 'vantage point on the top stair / of a house that no longer exists', eavesdropping on his parents' rows 'like a cabin boy who listens in secret / To the crew of a great, creaking ship', both look-out and spy, outside and above it yet inescapably implicated (*A*, p. 18). In several poems, Patten casts his mother as the victim of a philandering first and a violent, abusive second husband (recollected, 'a terrible dummy' in his coffin, in 'Stepfather', *A*, p. 25). But she is also the victim of a wider, systemic oppression, of those inequalities of class and culture which condemned her to a life of drudgery, a mother at eighteen, living with her parents in a cramped terraced house, suffering what Patten calls the 'crushed hopes' and 'stifled longings' of an impoverished working-class family.[19] 'Cinders', the opening poem of *Armada*, with its appalling pun on cremation in the title, identifies her with the downtrodden Cinderella

19 Quoted in Cookson, *Brian Patten*, pp. 1–2.

of pantomime, 'sweeping kitchens'; but in her case 'life was never a fairytale' and no fairy godmother ever appeared to rescue her (*A*, p. 13). (Noticeably, there is no Prince Charming in this narrative, nor even a Buttons.) In a similar vein, 'Echoes' speaks of his grandmother, her legs crushed by a wartime bomb and her 'soul crushed by iron callipers' which are 'like a ball and chain', the clunking of which 'echoes through my history / And imprisons me' (*A*, p. 19). The imagery of a historic bondage recurs in 'What I Need for the Present' (*A*, p. 43), which, rejecting a series of unwanted presents, portrays them as 'your box of fetters', and the present itself as a place of incarceration. 'Sick Equation' speaks of drifting with the crowd, 'One among the many whose dreams of flight / Weighed down the soul' under the shadow of the albatross (*A*, pp. 44–45); 'Why Things Remained the Same' (*A*, pp. 64–65) laments 'the weight of the baggage I carried', 'hauled from place to place'; while 'In Perspective' (*A*, p. 78) decides that the bones in his pockets have weighed him down long enough. In these poems, the self has become its own baggage, the heavy cargo it is forced to haul around. The poetry veers between a sense of the self as full of accumulated junk it needs to cast off, as in 'No' (*SD*, p. 34), and, alternatively, as the 'corroded', empty being of 'Salvage Operation', abandoned by 'Those parts of myself I let escape', who feels driven to dive down and recover them from 'the currents of the mutable self / Where all that was lost might still drift, / Battered, but salvageable' (*SD*, p. 68). Identity is simultaneously possessed and dispossessed, as for those human cargoes once transported across the Atlantic by the same armadas of coffin ships that brought prosperity to Liverpool.

That subliminal associations with a systemic subjection lurk within Patten's poetry is suggested by the two concluding poems of *The Irrelevant Song*. 'The Pessimistic Song' considers 'the flesh that loves have illuminated', 'the dreams, the possessions, the long bodies already surrendered / the longings that build their houses in tomorrow' to be 'chains now', from which deliverance lies only in renunciation: 'they're all in a sack and tied up together. / Fling them away then' (*TIS*, p. 61). More equivocally, the book's final poem, 'Meat', wants to give the reader 'something / that bleeds as it leaves my hand / and enters yours', something that in its bleeding 'demands to be called real', translated in the process from exchangeable commodity to the subject and site of revelation. The poem speaks of a whole creation which is nothing but meat, 'the active ingredient, / the thing that bothers history'. Meat, the material being in which subjectivity is founded, is 'the sole inventor of paradise', but is nevertheless 'the thing denied entrance into heaven, / awkward and perishable', both 'the splendid meat' and 'the blemished meat', that 'weeps over its temporariness'. The appalling secret at the heart of all transcendent visions is that to be human is to share in that universal carnality to which carnival perpetually bids adieu, to be possessed by the body of the world. Grace then lies in acknowledgment of 'the meat you are' (*TIS*, p. 62).[20]

20 A more jocund variation on this theme can be found in 'School Note' in the same volume (*TIS*, p. 57).

8

Finding a Rhyme for Alphabet Soup:
An Interview with Roger McGough

Deryn Rees-Jones

Roger McGough was born in Litherland in 1937. Educated at St Mary's College, Crosby, he graduated from the University of Hull in 1957and then returned to Liverpool to teach. With Mike McCartney (later McGear), John Gorman, and Adrian Henri he performed as The Liverpool One Fat Lady, All Electric Show, *before forming, with McCartney and Gorman,* The Scaffold. *'Lily the Pink' was a number one in the UK Singles Chart in 1968 for five weeks. McGough published his first volume of poetry,* Summer with Monika, *in 1967 and two collections with Adrian Henri and Brian Patten,* The Liverpool Scene *and* The Mersey Sound. *Peter Forbes has described McGough as having 'articulated a Liverpudlian Beat ethos as confidently as the Beatles recreated American R&B in their own image' suggesting that 'his defining trait is skepticism ... Clichés are regularly invoked, mocked and treated to sardonic modulations ... and although the comic effects give the impression of light verse there is a philosophical angst in his work.' McGough has continued to write poems for adults and children, while also developing a successful career in TV and radio. He has received two BAFTA awards, for his films* Kurt, Mungo, BP and Me *(1984) and* The Elements *(1993), two Signal Poetry Awards (1984 and 1998) and a Cholmondley Award (1999). He is a Fellow of the Royal Society of Literature. His* Collected Poems *was published in 2003 (London: Viking).* Said and Done: The Autobiography *was published in 2005.*

DR-J: Can you start by talking about what being a writer who comes from Liverpool means to you?

RM: I suppose in a sense I feel Liverpudlian very strongly, almost as if it's easier to be Liverpudlian than to be English. That was enforced by coming from an Irish immigrant family and going to a Catholic school in Liverpool – a very tight community in Liverpool, very close knit.

Close knit can be good but there is also a sense of people watching each other. And of course you come over to England and you lie low, you don't call attention to yourself. In school I was taught by the Irish Christian Brothers. We were taught Gaelic, we were taught to write our names and spellings in Gaelic, and a couple of boys I was in school with joined the IRA. When we were doing English history there was always a feeling as a Catholic that we were slightly on the wrong side of things. So learning about the Armada, and the fact that 'we' defeated it, we wondered what would have happened if it had been the other way around. We would have been better off because we'd have been living in a Catholic country ... It was easier to be Liverpudlian than English. It's changed now, it's less parochial. I also think about what John Updike said, that everyone in New York assumes everyone in New York wants to be a New Yorker as well. And the Liverpool thing, you assume everyone wants to be a Scouser. So there's a sense that you're always on the lookout for heroes and any connection with Liverpool – the actors Rex Harrison and John Gregson, for example (although they didn't sound Liverpudlian) – and trying to find literary heroes later on. But that was more difficult. There's a strong sense of that partly because you were very hemmed in. We knew we were Catholics and there were Protestants down the road. There were the Orange Day parades, but there wasn't any fighting. My friends were Catholic and Protestant. It was never violent, unlike Belfast.

I was the first of my family to go to university. What jobs were here? Teaching was on offer ... People going away to sea was part of life at school and a lot of friends who didn't do well at fifteen, went into something connected with the sea, such as a purser or an engineer or stayed on dry land to work in a shipping office. We knew people whose marriages stayed steady for so long because when you had a row you went away in the hope that when you came back all would be forgiven and forgotten.

DR-J: You talk about that longing for that exotic other life in your poem 'Alphabet Soup'.

RM: My father had been to sea and particularly loved wide-open spaces. He actually signed the forms to emigrate to New Zealand but my mother wasn't keen so I never got to be an antipodean poet. Funnily enough I had an email from Manjimup library, the place mentioned in the poem, asking had we been there. I had to explain that, though I'd been to Perth and Southern Australia, I hadn't been there, and that I'd chosen the town because it rhymed with soup! In fact when I did leave

Liverpool I went to Hull. We all went to Hull University mob handed. Six of us from the same class. We met up with people who weren't from Liverpool so we stuck together to ward them off. We wouldn't wear blazers. We were rebels, suspicious of southerners and suede shoes. I suppose we were seen as this edgy rather noisy group but we probably wished we could integrate, which we did after a year or so. Over the years when I've travelled, at book signings, people come over and say they're from Liverpool, and there are all sorts of links. I enjoy that, but other writers find that quite funny …

DR-J: How do you feel about being thought of as a Liverpool poet?

RM: The tag Liverpool poet – what does that mean? Because there are other Liverpool poets, as you know – Paul Farley, Matt Simpson, Jamie McKendrick. But when it was applied to the three of us it was used, not geographically, but rather as a reference to class. Often by critics in a demeaning way. From the beginning there was always a label – 'pop poets'. Initially that was put on because Adrian, in particular, used references to TV commercials and Adrian was a pop painter using images and slogans from the world of advertising. But then it had a pop music element to it because of Liverpool and the burgeoning music scene. And we still get that Beat poet title. It was always a sort of way of distancing you from *poetry*. That sense of us being cheeky, funny, not too serious. 'Performance poets'. One critic likened us to 'a three headed pantomime horse' and another referred to us as 'small town Manto-vanis'. We were easy targets. They thought we weren't going to be around very long anyway. We were pigeon-holed as an interesting sociological rather than literary movement. And so it was a name that was as much an albatross as anything. Brian and I didn't like the title of the book, *The Mersey Sound*, but we knew it would help sell the book.

DR-J: How much did you feel you were reacting against that definition?

RM: No, not reacting against. I started writing late, I was eighteen, at university, doing Geography and French, when I started reading Rimbaud, Baudelaire, listening to Dylan Thomas, being excited by poetry, and I found I could do it. Until then I had wanted to be an artist but realized I wasn't good enough.

DR-J: Reading through the *Collected Poems*, there are actually lots of poems about poets and being a poet. Do you think of poets as occu-pying a quite special place?

RM: What drew me to poetry was the need to internalize, a sense of the spiritual and the search towards meaning. Trying to make sense of the world around me, I suppose, using words as stepping stones. I do see the poet as outsider – not in an arrogant, 'gazing in on the masses' sort of way, but as someone who can appreciate the values of silence and solitude (although, in my case, only for short periods). When I started writing I was going to send poems to *Torch*, the university magazine, and I looked through it and I thought, they're not going to publish these, they are not difficult enough. Even now I look at *Poetry Review* and I think I'm not writing poetry. Maybe I'm not writing poetry. Of course it's a wider church, but sometimes you've got to be very single-minded and get on with what you do, the way you do it. Quite early on I brought humour into the verse, partly perhaps because of a working-class fear of being regarded as intellectual and sensitive. It took me a while to welcome humour into my poetic armoury and see it as a gift. To many critics in this country, though, it is one they could do without.

DR-J: Is there a distinction between writing that is for the page and writing that is for performance for you?

RM: Again there's that 'performance poets' tag, the implication being that the writing can be sloppy and sentimental, just as long as you please the audience. In fact I never consciously write for performance. A poem has to be perfect on the page, and I write and rewrite *ad gloriam*. When writing, too, I speak the words softly so that the sounds are pleasing. Generally, when you are writing lyrics, the music's there anyway. You know there's a tune. It's a different skill, but poets have to work in a darker, quieter room. I've been doing the two together almost since the beginning, and then writing *became* a performance, it was part of the same thing. I write to make sense of the world as you see it, and language is that way you do it. Writing is such a pure thing. I describe it sometimes in terms of masculinity and femininity. The writing is internal, still and feminine, whereas it's the masculine part that gets up and performs it, the showing off part of it, and I've always been embarrassed by that side of the process. In fact, I've always been wary of becoming too good at performing poetry in case the poet gets sidelined. It's the poem first, then the poet, then the performer.

DR-J: Do poems and song lyrics come from the same *emotional* place?

RM: Can do, I suppose, but with a song you know you're reaching a wider audience. You're writing it, knowing that someone will be singing it, drawing attention to what you're doing, but a poet doesn't do that when they write. It's not as attention seeking.

DR-J: You don't have a sense of an audience when you're writing a poem, then?

RM: No, not really, I don't think I do. Occasionally, writing for TV and radio, you know you're writing something that will have a one-off life. I spend time but you know that the audience isn't going to be critical in a way in which other poems for the page are. It makes you think in a different way.

DR-J: A lot of the poems are very personal.

RM: Yes, they are, yes. It became a way, at first, of dealing with teenage angst, religious, philosophical stuff, facing up to the idea of death and loss. You get very sentimental. I've always been bordering on the sentimental, it's an emotion I'm not dismissive of. Comedy came later on.

DR-J: Do your family read your poems?

RM: Years ago I did a newspaper interview and mentioned the fact that when growing up we had an outside toilet, and two of my aunties rang my sister saying that I shouldn't bring the family into disrepute, that it was a very clean house and that my mother was a wonderful person. More seriously, I have heard over the years how certain poems about relatives upset surviving members of the family, and this worries me, because I have always tried to be honest in my portraits, if not necessarily truthful, and they were all written with affection.

DR-J: Are there things you wouldn't read aloud?

RM: Yeah …

DR-J: Why is that?

RM: Oh, the twelve-poem sequence 'Holiday on Death Row', for instance, which I still find too shocking in a way. They came out of a painful experience and were somehow cleansing at the time, but it's a time and place I don't care to revisit. For different reasons I very rarely read 'Summer with Monika', though I do occasionally when Andy Roberts provides the music. The poems belong to a younger man than me. Also 'The Lesson', once a poem popular with teachers and kids, which, after the classroom tragedy in Dunblane, was put into the drawer.

DR-J: One of the things about the *Collected Poems* I love is that you have resisted organizing it chronologically. The book begins with poems about family and ends with them, and there is a real sense that in shaping forty years of poems you are presenting the reader with a new narrative of your preoccupations. One of those preoccupations is a negotiation of masculinity which is constantly being addressed across the decades. Poems about being a father, about what it is like to have sons, or 'In at the Kill', about having a daughter. I wonder if you could talk about how much that was or is an issue for you as a poet? Whether poetry was seen as middle class, effeminate?

RM: We were told it was. It wasn't part of my life, no books of poetry, people didn't read it, or speak it, it wasn't my world. Had I scraped through and done English Literature in sixth form it might have been different. All poets seemed to be dead, Protestant, middle class, so when I became interested in art and drama, and the poetry happened, I didn't know where it had come from. I wasn't part of a group, no friend wrote poetry, there was no-one to show it to, and so for years poetry became my best-kept secret.

DR-J: Are there poems that people ask you to read?

RM: Yes, and someone (Phil Bowen actually, who wrote a book about the Mersey Poets) recently compiled a list of his 'Top Twenty' poems, with which I'm pretty well in agreement. Here it is, in no particular order:

'The Way Things Are'
'Hearts and Flowers'
'Defying Gravity'
'The Identification'
'Survivor'
'40-Love'
'In Case of Fire'
'Squaring Up'
'Ex Patria'
'Cinders'
'The Railings'
'Let Me Die a Youngman's Death'
'Summer with Monika'
'Waving at Trains'
'At Lunchtime'
'5 Car Family'
'The Terrible Outside'
'Vinegar'
'Everyday Eclipses'
'Payback Time'

DR-J: There are lots of political poems in the book, ones about class, about the environment. Were they written close together?

RM: Some were, one poem sparks off another, but I don't think I've been political enough, compared, say, to Tony Harrison or Adrian Mitchell. My output of environmental poems though, particularly in my children's collections, has been pretty consistent.

DR-J: You live in London now. Do you have a sense of Liverpool being a very changed place? There's a strong sense in the work of lots of Liverpool writers that it's important to leave. Do you think of yourself as a poet of place, or is there a sense that you are a poet interested in people, their idiosyncrasies, and that it's that humour and surreal take on things that ultimately makes you a Liverpool writer?

RM: What a wonderfully complex question to end with! The answer is that I don't honestly know. I grew up at a time when, despite the Beatles boom, most young people with get-up-and-go got up and went. You were proud to have been born in the city but the grass seemed greener elsewhere, and there was a natural urge to travel and to experience life outside. Had it not been for 'The Scaffold' I think I might have moved south earlier; as things turned out I didn't leave until my forties. I believe that not only is Liverpool a changed place but that the country is too, and there is a lesser sense of the capital being the magnet that it once was. I wonder if I was a young poet writing in Liverpool now whether I'd feel the same urge to move away.

9

Rewriting the Narrative:
Liverpool Women Writers

Terry Phillips

In the preface to *Merseypride: Essays in Liverpool Exceptionalism*, John Belchem draws attention to the way in which 'Liverpool's past has been characterised as different'.[1] While he argues that 'Liverpool's apartness ... is crucial to its identity', he concedes that it has both been seen as 'an external imposition, an unmerited stigma' and 'upheld (and inflated) in self-referential myth'. The thrust of Belchem's argument is that Liverpool's exceptionalism is neither a matter for pride nor stigma but is explicable, largely in terms of its identity as a maritime city. Belchem goes on to offer a brief historical survey which includes a consideration of the fluctuating economic fortunes of Liverpool. In this chapter I focus both on the representation of Liverpool and on the representation of Liverpool women at various stages of the city's twentieth-century history, from its Edwardian heyday, through the depression of the interwar years, the German bombing campaign of the Second World War, the economic downturn of the 1980s and 90s to the contemporary resurgence of the city, within novels written by women over the last thirty years. The texts which I will be considering focus particularly on the effects of these economic fortunes on the female inhabitants of the city, whether as wives and daughters of seafarers, dock workers or wealthy merchants, and in some cases as members of the Liverpool-Irish community, which as Belchem points out have tended in recent years to be written out of the history of the Irish diaspora by Irish revisionist historians.[2]

1 John Belchem, *Merseypride: Essays in Liverpool Exceptionalism* (Liverpool: Liverpool University Press, 2000), p. xi.
2 Belchem, *Merseypride*, p. xiv.

My starting point is the publishing phenomenon of Helen Forrester. The first volume of her four-volume autobiography about her childhood in Liverpool, *Twopence to Cross the Mersey*, published in 1974, was an early success in a nostalgia market, based on location, but by no means confined to Liverpool.[3] Forrester followed with three more volumes, published in 1979, 1981 and 1985, and two fictional texts written alongside them, *Liverpool Daisy* (1979) and *Three Women of Liverpool* (1984). Her later substantial output of fiction includes four further novels about Liverpool, whose popularity undoubtedly owes something to the success of the autobiographies. The publication dates of the retrospective fiction of Forrester, and particularly the autobiographies, are also important in that they largely coincide with a downturn in the economic fortunes of Liverpool, following on from the brief cultural renaissance of the 1960s, which brought the city renewed, if temporary, confidence. However, for Liverpudlian readers it may well carry the trap of invitation into a shared victimhood, something of the sense of 'external imposition' to which Belchem refers, and the lack of economic analysis, which is my main criticism of all these texts, compounds this.[4]

While the success of Forrester's autobiographical and fictional texts set in Liverpool is at least in part due to their appeal to a sense of local identity, her attitude to the city is ambivalent, and in the autobiographical texts largely that of an outsider. The outsider's view is encapsulated by the first words of *Twopence to Cross the Mersey* (the title of which refers to the price of escape out of Liverpool), 'Liverpool is a city through which visitors pass on their way to other places' (p. 7). The young Helen is an exile, constantly haunted by the memory of two other places, the comfortable south which she has left behind and the Wirral, tantalizingly near and far where her estranged grandmother lives and where she was a childhood visitor. After a number of years in Liverpool, she revealingly comments to her friend, referring to her southern

---

3 Helen Forrester, *Twopence to Cross the Mersey* (1974) (London: HarperCollins, 1993), p. 7. Hereafter *Twopence*.

4 See, for example, the comments of Eleanor Bron who played the role of Helen in a musical adaptation of *Twopence to Cross the Mersey*: 'I didn't realise until now that Helen Forrester had this huge following ... It's more than nostalgia. There is a harder edge. Many in the audience will see it as a reflection of something they have experienced' ('Arts: Twopence for Your Thoughts; Joe Riley Talks to Eleanor Bron about Her Latest Role', *Liverpool Echo*, 16 September 2005, p. 11).

childhood, 'I used to do that at home.'[5] The final volume, *Lime Street at Two*, published in 1985, sees Helen making her home in Wirral at last, and ultimately welcoming her escape.[6] In Forrester's writing and that of some of her imitators, Liverpool, like other cities, functions as part of the violent hierarchy of urban over rural which characterizes aspects of English cultural inheritance.

The extent to which, in the autobiographies, Forrester analyses the diverse landscape of this initially alien city is debatable. She undoubtedly attempts some kind of interpretation of the poverty she sees around her, but a close examination of the texts reveals gaps and contradictions. She comments on mass unemployment (*Miss*, p. 9) and points out the 'rock-bottom wages' for labouring in Liverpool which are insufficient to pay the rent.[7] Nevertheless, while she observes accurately the fact that most of Liverpool's workforce is employed on a casual basis and recognizes this as the cause of the apparent fecklessness which ensues (*Twopence*, p. 95), in an older critical voice she speaks of 'the labour unrest rampant in the docks of Liverpool forty years later' and attributes it, not to the casual nature of labour which still persisted after that forty-year gap, but to the influence of communism, which she always distrusts. Indeed, theoretical analyses do not appeal to her: 'Sometimes the theories and interpretations of statistics made me laugh, and I thought of the shrewd exploiters of social assistance amongst whom I lived.' Again the later voice intrudes to comment, with no specified source of evidence: 'Now, three generations later, this swindling has become an art, and some people live very comfortably from it' (*Waters*, p. 127).

Nevertheless, the progress of the four volumes is almost, though not quite, the story of a conversion, a movement from the perspective of a horrified outsider to that of a resident, with a degree of pride in the city. Although the tone of alienation suggested in the opening and best-known volume is never quite shaken off, in the final volume, she tells us with an air of pride on behalf of her first fiancé, Harry O'Dwyer, that 'men had sailed from Bootle since ... A.D. 613' (*Lime Street*, p. 9). When St Nicholas's Church is bombed she feels the loss —'It was part of our

---

5   Helen Forrester, *Liverpool Miss* (1979) (London: Fontana, 1982), p. 286. Hereafter *Miss*.

6   Helen Forrester, *Lime Street at Two* (1985) (London: Fontana, 1986), p. 181. Hereafter *Lime Street*.

7   Helen Forrester, *By the Waters of Liverpool* (1981) (London: HarperCollins, 1993). Hereafter *Waters*.

waterfront, part of our heritage' – in a way she could never have felt it in the earlier volumes (*Lime Street*, p. 69). Her conversion, if such we may call it, appears to be a product of two influences, the acquisition of friends, and the appreciation of the resilience of many of her neighbours. When her father joins the dole queue shortly after his arrival in Liverpool, he is greeted with friendliness and advice. He came home 'marvelling at their sheer resilience and good nature in such adversity' (*Twopence*, p. 95). Later, during the war, Helen comes to admire the messenger boys who take enormous risks; the cleaners who still turn up to put damaged offices in order; the tram drivers who drive their vehicles through the burning city; the Red Cross workers who write to soldiers; and the 'marvellously inventive, skilled workmen … [who] found ways to hook up telephones, lay water pipes and electric cables and mend the huge sewers' (*Lime Street*, pp. 27, 38, 59, 67, 113). Furthermore, the texts, even from the start, do find space, albeit limited, to speak of sources of pride in Liverpool's heritage. Early on, the narrative evokes the magnificence of Liverpool Cathedral as well as the opulence of Bold Street (*Twopence*, pp. 107, 108), and some of Helen's happiest experiences are at the Liverpool Playhouse, courtesy of a local philanthropist; she lists the internationally renowned actors and actresses she saw there (*Miss*, p. 289).

Forrester's two earliest fictional texts about Liverpool link closely, though differently, with the autobiographies. The fictional *Three Women of Liverpool* shares much of its subject matter with the autobiographical *Lime Street at Two*, and in fact was published in the preceding year. These two texts are the only ones to deal with the war-time bombing of Liverpool and express something of the sense deeply and with some justification felt by Liverpudlians, that their contribution to Britain's survival in the Second World War was largely ignored.[8] While the plucky East Ender has entered English cultural memory, the equally plucky inhabitants of Bootle and other devastated parts of Merseyside are forgotten outside the region in favour of very different stereotypes.[9] That Forrester is concerned with issues of representation is indicated in

---

8   Helen Forrester, *Three Women of Liverpool* (1984) (London: HarperCollins, 1990). Hereafter *Three Women*.

9   In Liverpool and the neighbouring boroughs the death toll was 3,875, with 7,144 seriously injured. Out of a total of 282,000 homes, 10,840 were destroyed and a further 184,840 damaged. See Peter Aughton, *Liverpool, a People's History* (Preston: Carnegie, 1993), pp. 187–89.

Lime Street at Two, when, on meeting an airman from another part of the country, she tells him, 'People forget that London isn't the only target' (*Lime Street*, p. 187). *Three Women of Liverpool* emphasizes the extent of the devastation of what is variously described as the 'doomed port' and 'the stricken city' which the enemy aims to wipe out (*Three Women*, pp. 64, 121). The destruction of some of Liverpool's great landmarks and commercial enterprises is described (*Three Women*, pp. 71, 192) and the sheer extent of loss in concentrated areas represented by the sailor from Seaforth who had to identify fourteen bodies (*Three Women*, p. 202), as well as the effects on day-to-day lives of such events as the destruction of the Dairy (*Three Women*, pp. 56, 58).

The other early fictional text, *Liverpool Daisy*, was published in the same year as the second volume of the autobiographies, *Liverpool Miss*, and features a central character whose circumstances are totally different from those of the young Helen, but whose fate, and whose struggle against it, at a deeper level reflect Helen's own struggle. If Forrester's representation of Liverpool is affectionately ambivalent, her representation of women is uncompromisingly radical. Her untutored feminism is born directly of her own experience. She represents herself as increasingly rebelling against her parents, initially in her struggle to obtain work, against the wishes of her mother, who does everything she can to stop her (*Miss*, pp. 43, 55). She constantly comments on the inequality with her brothers, 'boys needed rest; girls could manage without' (*Miss*, p. 167), and rejects the notion of sacrifice, that age-old method of repression for women within the family (*Miss*, p. 254). Her interest in obtaining a career for herself is initially born not of any theoretical belief in the right of women to have one, but rather of her image of her own body as inadequate, which she deems will preclude marriage, the only form of escape. Such a view is of course absorbed from the prevailing ideology of the woman as object of gaze and pleaser of the male gazer who becomes her provider. Nevertheless it may be deemed a fortunate error as it leads Helen to win for herself a well-paid post as a personal secretary, before she does eventually achieve her childhood ambition of escape from Liverpool via marriage, still the escape route for the majority of women.

In *Liverpool Daisy,* written one must suppose in parallel to *Liverpool Miss*, Forrester chose to invent a character totally different from herself, lower class, Liverpool-born and of Irish extraction, a woman who has two children in prison and who says of her son's crime, the manslaughter of an Orangeman on 12 July, 'Serve them right if they got stabbed.'[10] The Irish stereotype is writ large: their quarrelsomeness and violence; the stinking squalor in which they exist. Nevertheless, out of this unpromising background steps a strong, if unorthodox heroine. Daisy discovers by chance the earning power that can be derived from a limited form of prostitution (*Daisy*, pp. 53–63).[11] Daisy, like Helen initially lacks self-esteem. Her body is characterized as fat: 'She was normally a cheerful woman, though often aggressive, and her hearty laugh would make her great breasts shake in unison' (*Daisy*, p. 32). Her new career improves not only her finances but her self-esteem: '"He thought I was worth three bob," she marvelled' (*Daisy*, p. 95). Arguably the dangers are underplayed and Daisy's rather select group of clients a little romanticized. In spite of rediscovering a pride in her sexual attractiveness (her husband spends most of his time at sea and most of his shore life drinking), when she meets up with Ivy, a more conventional prostitute, who advises her to wear more alluring clothes and paint her face, she reflects, 'She wasn't a whore like this woman and she didn't want to look like one' (*Daisy*, p. 170). When Ivy introduces her to the alarming lifestyle of a full-time prostitute, Daisy reacts not as the hardened aggressive matriarch she is, but as the young Helen might have done (*Daisy*, pp. 173–77). As in other novels the significant characters are all female, their menfolk spending much of the time absent, at sea, seeking work or in the pub, the typical scenario of the port matriarchy. The women's lives are harsh, and being instinctive survivors rather than theoretical feminists, they expect to be beaten from time to time (*Daisy*, pp. 132, 183).

It is unsurprising that strong women recur in all Forrester's fiction. Daisy can be seen as the Helen who might have been if she had been born into the circumstances of the very different women she observes around her. Such women are traditional matriarchs, women who are regarded as being subservient to their husbands and having few acknowledged rights and no public role, and yet who wield a great deal of actual power, though at great cost to themselves. While such matriarchy is

---

10 Helen Forrester, *Liverpool Daisy* (1979) (London: Fontana/Collins, 1990), p. 33. Hereafter *Daisy*.

11 On the prevalence of prostitution in Liverpool, see Paula Bartley, who, speaking of a slightly earlier period, comments that 'it was commonly accepted that London, ports (such as Liverpool) and army towns (such as Colchester) held the highest number of prostitutes … For example, in 1881 police sent for trial 5,942 women in London, 4,615 in Liverpool, 2,091 in Manchester and 477 in Birmingham' (*Prostitution: Prevention and Reform in England, 1860–1914* [London: Routledge, 2000]), p. 3).

often associated with the Irish rural communities from which many of them come or are descended, it in fact has much more to do with their lives in the port city. As Manuel remarks in *The Liverpool Basque*, 'Ports from which men go to sea are matriarchal societies; it is women who are in charge' (*Basque*, p. 22).[12]

The plight of middle-class women may well have different roots, although it is evident that Forrester saw parallels between the repression of working-class and middle-class women. Two of Forrester's later, strongly feminist novels, feature women from her own class. *Yes, Mama* (1988), the only one of Forrester's novels to be set exclusively in the Edwardian heyday of Liverpool, demonstrates that even amid apparent affluence women often suffer. The plot centres on the illegitimate Alicia, whose upper-middle-class mother avoids her and whose legal father tolerates her in the house only in order to retain respectability.[13] As her parents fall ill, Alicia comes to the same bitter realization as the Helen of the biographies, that she is there to serve only her parents and other relatives' needs, and the same determined resolution that she will not grow old as a single woman in one of their houses (*Mama*, p. 212).

However, the fictional heroine who most closely resembles Helen is Celia in *Mourning Doves* (1996), who, like her creator, is suddenly reduced to poverty.[14] Like Helen (and Daisy), she has been presented with a negative body image. Having believed her parents' false explanation that she is delicate, she accepts being withdrawn from Miss Ecclestone's Day School for Young Ladies (*Doves*, pp. 136–37) Any previous desire on Celia's part to rebel has remained largely unexpressed, as 'Church and custom had reinforced her parents' declaration that it was her duty as a good churchwoman and devoted daughter to care for them when they grew old' (*Doves*, p. 58). Forrester is unequivocal in her condemnation of the ideologies which kept women in their place, a marked contrast to her more ambivalent attitude to socio-economic issues. Celia's awakening begins when the family are forced, by her

---

12 For a discussion of the role of women within a port community, and their previous exclusion from political affairs, though in this case focusing on casualized dock labour, see 'The Women of the Waterfront', in Michael Lavalette and Jane Kennedy, *Solidarity on the Waterfront: The Liverpool Lock Out of 1995/6* (Birkenhead: Liver Press, 1996), pp. 45–65.

13 Helen Forrester, *Yes, Mama* (1988) (London: HarperCollins, 1994). Hereafter *Mama*.

14 Helen Forrester, *Mourning Doves* (1996) (London: HarperCollins, 1997). Hereafter *Doves*.

father's death and the revelation of his substantial debts, to move into a dilapidated uncared for property in Meols. In terms of gender analysis, the text is more advanced than the autobiographies, subjecting the 'career' of marriage to a much more searching examination. Celia's widowed sister, Edna, has made a marriage suited to her status to 'a domineering man, a selfish man at best, a bully determined that she should bear more children', who on her refusal to comply takes a Brazilian mistress (*Doves*, p. 145). Celia's friend Phyllis not only does not have the knowledge to prevent annual conceptions, but knowing nothing of the facts of life, finds sex with a clumsy husband both painful, and shocking, so that 'neither she nor Celia, therefore, had any idea that intercourse could be pleasurable' (*Doves*, p. 77). This is Forrester's most completely feminist text, analysing the educational and sexual repression of women, the complicity of the previous generation of women and the liberating effects of the First World War.

Of Forrester's four later Liverpool novels, published after the completion of the autobiographies and the two earlier novels, two remain to be considered in order to complete a consideration of Forrester's portrayal of Liverpool. *The Liverpool Basque*, published in 1994, is exceptional in having a male central character but nevertheless is the novel which most closely resembles her stance of retrospection in the autobiographies.[15] Manuel Echaniz is a Canadian citizen, aged eighty-four, who reflects on his childhood and upbringing in Liverpool. He comes from a seafaring family and consequently there is more attention to Liverpool's maritime character. His attitude to Liverpool reveals some of the ambivalence of Forrester's other texts. His identity is always two-fold: 'the essence of himself – was Liverpool Basque' (*Basque*, p. 6). Later, on holiday with his father's family in the Pyrenees, he forms the belief which stays with him forever that 'his father came from the most beautiful place on earth'. The South, the Wirral, the Pyrenees figure as Liverpool's recurring others in Forrester's writing. However, as the novel progresses, the older Manuel immerses himself deeper and deeper into the Liverpool experience, and seems to lose his grip on the present. Ultimately and inevitably he returns to Liverpool, and the only logical conclusion of such backward turning, death. After a good lunch with too much brandy Manuel and his old Basque friend, Arnador, die under the wheels of a lorry on the Dock Road (*Basque*, p. 373). The link

---

15 Helen Forrester, *The Liverpool Basque* (London: HarperCollins, 1994). Hereafter *Basque*.

between the two Canadians, Forrester and the fictional Manuel, is that they both seek to recover the past by writing. Did Forrester use Manuel to indulge a nostalgia for Liverpool and for the past she always resisted, seeing too clearly its inevitable result?

If Forrester ultimately resists too close an identification with Liverpool, by representing Manuel as returning only to die, her latest Liverpool novel, *A Cuppa Tea and An Aspirin* (2003), shows evidence of a more sympathetically radical analysis of the city. This novel draws much closer to the 'shiftless' class Forrester observes from the outside in the autobiographies.[16] The family of Martha Connolly, eleven people who live, cook and sleep in one single room in one of Liverpool's infamous courts, is the most deprived group described in any of Forrester's texts. Early in the novel she offers an analysis of the casual dock labour scheme, pointing out that the surplus of unskilled labour on Merseyside meant that powerful business interests were happy to maintain the system (*Cuppa Tea*, pp. 26–27). Later there is a critical implication to the description of a nurse who recognizes malnutrition, 'that polite, political word which covered the fact of starvation', but 'consoled herself with the usual argument against more welfare: the dire situation of many of her patients was not helped by their own hopeless improvidence' (*Cuppa Tea*, p. 168). This is as close as Forrester comes to radical economic analysis, but there is too little evidence to suggest a radicalization of her views. Taking her writing as a whole, while she cannot be accused of romanticizing the past, as many writers of this kind of fiction do, and she manifests an admirable desire for justice and sympathy for the poor, she never quite reaches down to root causes. A consequence is that her portrayal of Liverpool makes some contribution to the contemporary, or at least recent portrayal of its population as feckless.

The popularity of Forrester's texts apparently inspired a series of imitators, who, in their representation of Liverpool, reflect something of Forrester's ambivalence.[17] Lyn Andrews's *The Leaving of Liverpool* is

---

16 Helen Forrester, *A Cuppa Tea and An Aspirin* (2003) (London: HarperCollins, 2004). Hereafter *Cuppa Tea*.

17 Charlene Rooke, in an interview with Forrester, observes that 'a whole cottage industry of women writers trying to emulate her success has sprung up in Liverpool' ('Helen Forrester's Life Reads Like a Dickens Tale – or Like One of Her Own Novels', *New Trail Alumni Magazine*, Autumn 1997, http://www.ualberta.ca/ ALUMNI/newtrail/97-2/forrester.html. Accessed 17 June 2006).

built to some extent around the notion of escape.[18] Yet the central character's farewell to the city is to some extent ambiguous: 'this great sprawling metropolis with its elegant, gracious buildings and wide thoroughfares, its slums and its squalor, the mighty river its highway and lifeblood' (*Leaving*, p. 381). There is little analysis of the economic situation which drives Emily to her regretful departure. She leaves for America, where her brothers have succeeded economically, and there is an unstated implication that real enterprise is no longer possible in the old world of Liverpool (*Leaving*, p. 371). The unfavourable contrast of Liverpool with elsewhere is not confined to the enterprise of the new world but to the community values of North Wales villages, many of whose inhabitants were, like Emily's stepfather Albert, drawn into Liverpool (*Leaving*, p. 359).

In Katie Flynn's *Two Penn'orth of Sky*, the preference for the rural over the urban is strongly suggested, particularly by the sojourn of the prematurely widowed central character, Emmy, at a sanatorium in Llandudno.[19] When Emmy returns to Nightingale Court from the Welsh sanatorium, its full horror is presented in Gothic terms: 'The archway loomed like an enormous black mouth, wanting to drag her down and gobble her up.' But then she sees the people within: 'And now she saw the other side of Nightingale Court as people came streaming out of their houses' (*Sky*, p. 312). However, the text makes a clear distinction between the deserving and the undeserving poor, represented by Emmy's friend Beryl, whose family are clean and hard working, and 'Mrs' Telford, of dubious morality and licentious drinking habits. The text refers to the inhabitants of the Court as 'victims of poverty' (*Sky*, p. 41) but offers no analysis of the causes of poverty, thus like Forrester contributing something to negative stereotypes of the city. While these texts feature strong women characters, they leave largely unexplored the issues of the role of women which Forrester addresses so directly.

While nostalgia novels after the manner of Forrester have proliferated, there are novels which reflect recent and contemporary Liverpool, such as the crime novels of Margaret Murphy, whose first novel was published in 1996. In what follows, I intend to focus on those of her best-known novels which use Liverpool as a setting. Murphy's treatment of Liverpool is primarily as setting rather than subject matter. In *Past Reason*, the representation is overshadowed by the legacy of one of

18 Lyn Andrews, *The Leaving of Liverpool* (Reading: Corgi, 1994). Hereafter *Leaving*.
19 Katie Flynn, *Two Penn'orth of Sky* (London: Arrow, 2004). Hereafter *Sky*.

Liverpool's most depressing decades, the 1980s and its aftermath.[20] One character reflects on this legacy: 'He had dealt with Saturday-night drunks, the riots of the 1980s, and more recently, the drug addicts and their gun-carrying pushers' (*Reason*, p. 66). It may of course be seen as a summary of a policeman's life in any post-industrial city. Unsurprisingly, the novel, unlike the social commentaries on deprivation of Forrester and her imitators, gives some limited space to the leafy suburbs. The severely traumatized half-French child, Alain, whose discovery in the street gives rise to the action, comes from an elegant and affluent household in Mossley Hill.

The landscape, both actual and metaphorical, of *Dying Embers*, published a year later in 2000,[21] the plot of which centres on the murder of a sixth former from an inner city school in Liverpool, is bleaker. This time the depressing urban landscape is placed in a historical and economic context, which focuses on the peaks and troughs of Liverpool's twentieth-century history and reflects a fall away from the optimism of the post-war decades. Derelict flats are described as 'built in the fifties as shining new symbols of hope, replacements for the back-to-backs flattened during the Blitz, now empty and falling down' (*Embers*, p. 32). A feature of Murphy's treatment of Liverpool which distinguishes it from that of the writers considered above is that it is less inward looking, in that it places Liverpool in a wider context, in this case that of post-industrial Britain. Vince, a policeman who has transferred from London, is haunted by the memory of a young crazed drug addict leaping to his death (*Embers*, pp. 297, 335) and there is reference to the fact that 'over half of all teenagers in Britain' dabbled in drugs at some time (*Embers*, p. 145).

In *The Dispossessed*, published in 2004, after two novels set in Chester, Murphy returns to a Liverpool setting, which has crucial differences.[22] The title refers to the asylum seekers to be found in Liverpool and every large city, the murder of one of whom, a young Afghan, initiates the action. The plot broadens beyond Liverpool and reveals a scam based on the sale of identities directed from Dover. In Liverpool it is set against an at least partially regenerated background. One of the local gang leaders observes that 'the new millennium had brought an optimism to

20 Margaret Murphy, *Past Reason* (London: Pan Books, 2000). Hereafter *Reason*.
21 Margaret Murphy, *Dying Embers* (London: Macmillan, 2000). Hereafter *Embers*.
22 Margaret Murphy, *The Dispossessed* (2004) (London: Hodder & Stoughton, 2005). Hereafter *Dispossessed*.

the city: ambitious redevelopment projects, new money, inner city regeneration' (*Dispossessed*, p. 355). There are descriptions of landmarks and tourist sites, such as the cathedrals and the regenerated Albert Dock, as well as affluent Cressington Park (*Dispossessed*, pp. 193, 339). Of course, the city still has its darker side, represented not only by the underworld, which preys on the vulnerable, but by Jez and his young friends, who engage in petty thieving and vandalism until one night they are tragically caught up in the criminals' net (*Dispossessed*, p. 103). Like several of Murphy's plots *The Dispossessed* offers a surface interpretation, in this case one which falsely connects the murder of the Afghan woman, four unidentified immigrants and a Lithuanian to local anti-immigrant unrest. It is an interpretation which is fastened upon by the media. 'Tensions between the local and refugee communities have mounted …' comments one TV reporter, in a report which has the potential to become a self-fulfilling prophecy (*Dispossessed*, p. 155).

The importance of representation suggested by the incident of the TV report is more explicitly raised in *Now You See Me*, the plot of which centres on cyber fraud and more explicitly raises the question of representation, both of the locality and the individual.[23] Developing the trend begun in *The Dispossessed*, the Liverpool of *Now You See Me* combines a positive view of a pleasant and thriving city with reminders of its petty and more serious crime. There are descriptions of the investigating officer Rickman's comfortable house in a pleasant area of Mossley Hill and of the regenerated waterfront (*Now*, pp. 56, 67) alongside reminders of 'local scalls' (*Now*, p. 293). As in the preceding novels there is the by now almost obligatory reference to the Toxteth Riots (*Now*, p. 307), but for the first time that other notorious feature of Liverpool in the 1980s makes its appearance: 'the Hatton era', when the Militant Tendency dominated Liverpool City Council. Oddly, the villain of the novel, Patrick Doran, is described as being 'an enforcer with the rag-tag army of lefties who ruled Liverpool City Council in the 1980s' (*Now*, p. 253); oddly because this particular chapter in his career is never followed up and has no relevance to the novel. It is noteworthy that the references to the Militant era are somewhat superficial and do not explore the important political, social and economic questions that lay behind it: the balance of power between local and central government, local democracy, monetarism, and the question of those left behind by

---

23 Margaret Murphy, *Now You See Me* (London: Hodder & Stoughton, 2005). Hereafter *Now*.

the Thatcher revolution.[24] The novel as a crime novel set two decades later offers not analysis but representation. However, the narrative itself shows an interesting metafictional awareness of the way such representation functions. Kieran Jago, an extremely successful local solicitor who represents a very minor villain, makes an interesting justification to the investigating officer for his apparently altruistic act. Foster expects 'the usual partisan doctrine of common experience, cultural heritage – Irish immigration, English repression, the dual religions of football and church' (*Now*, p. 328). However, Jago refers to a more general stereotype: 'I'm not talking about The Beatles, Ferry 'Cross the Mersey and all that me-eye …That cheery scouser crap is rooted in a mythical culture of a different millennium' (*Now*, p. 328). Jago's preferred representational stereotype is different again: 'Liverpool as it is now, in the twenty-first century: expansion, new money, Urban Splash, the Tate Gallery, European Capital of Culture.' However, Jago argues, there are local people in whose experience 'Liverpool … means dirt, poverty, drugs, street crime, burglary' (*Now*, p. 329).

These four versions of Liverpool each have a certain validity and their proximity in the text serves to foreground the issue. The first representation focuses exclusively on the Liverpool Irish community, from which Murphy's characters predominantly come, but it is only one community. The Liverpool-born cyber villain's real name emerges as Ceri Owen. Its Welshness passes without comment, as does that of 'Megan', her assumed name, and here is perhaps an unmarked indication of the limits of representation, which has excluded Liverpool's Welsh element. Individual and group representation are subject to the same limits. In discussing Megan/Ceri, Foster, consciously quoting media-speak, opines that perhaps she returned to Liverpool for 'The vibrant night life? The footie? The fabulous waterfront?' (*Now*, p. 374). Foster's ironic tone suggests an awareness that the reputation of a city is just that, a matter of representation rather than of fact.

Murphy writes of a social context in which women's aspirations are clearly much greater than they were in the eras of which Forrester writes. Her texts reflect this greater self-consciousness, together with an awareness that the struggle is not yet over. The police forces who figure in her novels demonstrate aspects of sexism and related prejudice. In *Dying Embers*, Vince, the gay policeman, is the victim of the coarse humour

---

24 For a discussion of the issues surrounding the events of 1984–85, see Michael Parkinson, *Liverpool on the Brink* (Berkshire: Policy Journals, 1985).

of his unattractive colleagues after two of them 'out' him. Perhaps as an act of poetic justice, it is Vince who solves the crime. In *Past Reason*, there is Weston, who is rather too interested in his female colleague's legs (*Reason*, p. 13); the policeman who responds to the central character's business-like approach by speculating on her sexuality (*Reason*, p. 99); and his colleague who is prejudiced against 'tarts who called themselves "Miz"' (*Reason*, p. 100). The women in the novel prove more than capable of holding their own. Weston's colleague comments sharply, 'Got an eyeful, have you?' (*Reason*, p. 157). *The Dispossessed* and *Now You See Me* chart the sparring of the sexist police officer Foster and DCC Naomi Hart, whom he clearly finds attractive: 'Every time she began to think she might get to like him, Foster said something that alienated and infuriated her' (*Dispossessed*, p. 138), while in *Now You See Me*, when, having seen the equipment in her flat, he asks if she has a boyfriend, she caustically asks, 'Did you think a love of gadgets was exclusive to the Y-chromosome?' (*Now*, p. 222).

Murphy offers not only a critique of sexism, but a more subtle analysis of gender issues. *Past Reason*, like all Murphy's crime thrillers, depends on rational and patient police methods to uncover solutions. There is no Miss Marple figure to celebrate the virtues of intuition. The values that are celebrated, which might stereotypically be regarded as female, are possessed by both Jenny and Mike, the Social Services Liaison Officer, who 'moved easily between the different groups, comfortable at each level, approachable and warm'.

The foregoing demonstrates a shift in both the representation of Liverpool and the representation of women. In Forrester's texts, though less so in her imitators, women display enormous strength, but within traditional roles. While they rarely step out of these roles, many of them articulate resistance to what society expects of them, and the narratives are shaped to express both the resistance of down-trodden middle-class women and the strength of working-class matriarchal figures. Forrester and her imitators represent Liverpool as a site of exile, an area to be escaped, often opposed to a rural idyll and by implication different from the rest of the world, a view which may indeed be regarded, as Belchem suggests, as an outside imposition. Forrester herself is of course partially implicated in such an imposition as an outsider, and together with her imitators accepts a view of the city based on conventional binaries of rural/urban and privilege/deprivation.

In contrast Murphy's texts betray a much greater awareness of the process of representation itself. Her female characters, women of a later age, demonstrate a more self-conscious awareness of themselves as women and of issues of gender and sexuality which have entered the public domain. A similar self-consciousness marks her portrayal of Liverpool as an area to be celebrated and understood, in a more sophisticated analysis of representation, as perhaps not so remarkably different from the rest of contemporary Britain. A character in *Now You See Me* reflects on the cyber villain: 'Perhaps it was all about control: she wrote her own narrative, and in doing so, rewrote her past' (*Now*, p. 374). This rewriting of narrative and rewriting of the past is of course an unending process. Belchem's starting point in the preface to *Merseypride* is Ramsay Muir's 1907 *A History of Liverpool*, which sought to make Liverpool's absence of a glorious past a source of inverse pride. Belchem comments on how subsequent histories have glossed over the role of the slave trade and the contribution of settlers from overseas.[25] Liverpool in the twenty-first century, with the aid of the Capital of Culture designation, has once more begun the rewriting of its own narrative, which will hopefully redress these omissions, but yet will remain a narrative no more nor less accurate than the narratives of its past.

25 Belchem, *Merseypride*, p. xiii.

10

Jumping Off:
An Interview with Linda Grant

George Szirtes

Linda Grant was born in Liverpool in 1951, the daughter of Russian and Polish Jewish immigrants. She read English at the University of York and completed an MA at McMaster University, Ontario, Canada, where she lived from 1977 to 1984. In 1985 she returned to Britain and became a journalist. Between 1995 and 2000 she was a feature writer for the Guardian, *and was for five years a columnist on the* Jewish Chronicle. *Her first novel,* The Cast Iron Shore *(1996), won the David Higham Prize for Fiction and was shortlisted for the Guardian Fiction Prize. Her second,* When I Lived in Modern Times *(2000), set in Palestine immediately after the Second World War, won the Orange Prize for Fiction and was short-listed for the Jewish Quarterly Literary Prize for Fiction. Her novel* Still Here *(2002), set in Liverpool, tells the story of a middle-aged English woman and her relationship with an American architect. Her non-fiction includes* Sexing the Millennium: A Political History of the Sexual Revolution *(1993) and* Remind Me Who I Am Again *(1998), an account of her mother's dementia, which won the MIND Book of the Year/Allen Lane Award. Her most recent book is* The People on the Street: A Writer's View of Israel *(2006), winner of the 2006 Lettre Ulysses Award. Grant's writing has been described as illustrating 'the manner in which ideas, ideals and idealism can inform our own sense of who we are ... Grant excels at the creation of recognizable characters who refuse to be passive; who won't accept the drift of time and their own ultimate inconsequence. She is a realist, and a passionate believer in the very idea of belief' (Garan Holcombe).*

GS: What are your first memories of Liverpool? In which part of Liverpool did you live? Say something about your house, your street, your neighbours.

LG: My grandparents on both sides came to England at the turn of the twentieth century from Poland and Ukraine and like the rest of the Jewish community settled in an area called Brownlow Hill, in the city centre, near the Adelphi Hotel. Most people moved out to the suburbs after the war – to two areas, Childwall, where I lived until I was eight, and then Allerton. They were both very leafy neighbourhoods, physically very attractive, with a lot of the red sandstone that's characteristic of the city. My first home was near Childwall woods, a rather lovely semi-detached corner house at the beginning of a short cul-de-sac with a garden next to it, a swing, and a coal hole, because we still had coal fires. I particularly remember the strange white glittery stone in the rockery and a gardener telling me that if you split it there was gold inside. In 1959, we moved to a detached house in Allerton, near the park, which was decorated in that style I am rather fond of – nouveau riche, eighteenth-century ornate. The house backed onto allotments with a marvellous view across it to a very exclusive road, a kind of millionaire's row. And a short walk away was a brand new synagogue, which opened the year we moved there and my parents were founder members.

GS: Where did your father work in Liverpool and did you ever see him at work? Did you go shopping with your mother?

LG: My father was a hairdresser's supplier. He made shampoo and perm lotion and setting lotion which he supplied to hairdressers in Liverpool and the North West. I often saw him in his 'premises' as he called them, at the foot of Brownlow Hill, where he had a 'factory' (essentially a yard at the back, where he mixed up the chemicals.) Shopping was my mother's whole life, and the strongest recollections I have from childhood are of trailing around after her through the major department stores, and particularly Cripps on Bold Street, which was an exclusive shop selling London fashions.

GS: How aware were you, and how early, of your family's Jewishness? And of a Jewish community or milieu in your area?

LG: Ours was a totally Jewish household, from the mezuzah on the front door to the two sets of china and cutlery in the kitchen and the ubiquitous collection box for the Jewish National Fund on the mantelpiece and its ever changing map outline. My parents lived entirely inside the Jewish community; they didn't know anyone who was not Jewish and would have been afraid to. They considered the world outside the Jewish community to be threatening, and in essence anti-Semitic, which had some substance because in 1947 there were anti-Semitic riots in Liverpool.

GS: Were your family treated any differently as Jews as far as you were/are aware? How were Jews regarded then, as far as you knew?

LG: I never experienced any anti-Semitism growing up in Liverpool. I suspect it was there, but I simply never came across it. Maybe I was lucky.

GS: Can you say something of the range of Jewish life in the city (e.g. religious: from Orthodox through liberal and purely cultural; social: from working class and poor through the various classes).

LG: Liverpool Jewish life was pretty traditional. Most people were members of the United Synagogue, Orthodox enough in that women sat upstairs, and most people I knew kept kosher. There was a Reform synagogue, but no-one I knew was a member. No Charedi. As for the Hampstead Jewish intellectual type, if they existed, I never met them.

GS: What schools did you go to? What kinds of school were they? How wide a range of Liverpool society were you aware of there? What was the physical fabric of school like, and the journey there?

LG: I went to a school called Belvedere, its primary school, then its secondary school, which was part of the Girls' Public Day School Trust – direct grant. This was pretty unusual because the school was on the edge of Toxteth, in Liverpool 8. It had been set up in the nineteenth century to provide an academic education for the daughters of the merchants, insurers, and ship owners etc. who lived in the Princes Park areas. This was the first time I came in contact with the Liverpool middle class, and a very small number of girls on scholarship; overall, it was a middle-class experience. The school was in a series of early Victorian houses, connected by passageways, again looking out over Princes Park. It was quite a journey to get there, a bus to Garston, which was one of the toughest areas of the city, changing and then another bus to Toxteth. That was when I really saw what the city was.

GS: How much licence did you have in your early to middle secondary school years to make friends, wander around, and be parts of various kinds of social life?

LG: I was not given licence, I took it. I could see the suburban Jewish ghetto closing in, and I ran for my life.

GS: In your novel *Still Here*, the central female character is part of a wealthy, influential, philanthropic family. Was your family anything like this? How well known was your father's business?

LG: My family were absolutely nothing like the Rebicks. The mother was based on the mother of a girl I was at school with, Marianne Ellenbogen, née Strauss, about whom a book was written, *The Past in Hiding*, by Mark Roseman. But the brother in the novel, Sam, was very much like some of the people I knew who loyally stayed behind in Liverpool and made a real contribution to the city, specifically one who was the solicitor defending the Toxteth rioters. My father's business began to fail in the 1960s, because women stopped having their hair shampooed and set two or three times a week, and a perm every three months. My father was born in 1904, so by this time he was in his sixties and trapped in work he now hated. Far from being philanthropists, we were struggling to keep our head above water.

GS: As a growing girl how aware were you of Liverpool music, literature (I think of McGough, Henri, Patten chiefly but others too) and sport (Everton/Liverpool)?

LG: At the end of my first term at secondary school, Christmas 1962, the leaving sixth form performed a panto, a kind of skit show of their own devising. One of the girls was going out with one of the Beatles (I think George, but I'm not sure) and she managed to get him to lend her their leather jackets, the ones they'd worn in Hamburg, while they mimed to 'Love Me Do' which had been released a couple of months earlier. Even in the first year we knew about the Beatles, though I've no idea how – it just filtered down the school and we were all in the hall at lunchtime, doing the Cavern Stomp. I think it was the following year that I started to skive off school at lunchtime saying I was feeling sick, or had a dentist's appointment, and going to the Cavern's lunchtime sessions. The Beatles were still occasionally playing there in the evenings but the lunchtime sessions had the cream of the Mersey Sound. It was more or less obligatory to wear a denim skirt, a brown or black polo neck jumper and round-toed patent shoes, so I would carry these to school in my satchel and change into them in the toilets of a café in town. By the time I was doing O levels, a friend and I used to go every afternoon, from school to the Picton Library in the city centre, revise, and then get changed and go to the Philharmonic Hotel or O'Connor's, which were the two pubs where Roger, Brian and Adrian hung out, and I got to know them fairly well, because I was a young girl who wanted to be a poet, was writing poetry, and had won a citywide poetry contest. A lot of writers were coming up to Liverpool because of the arts scene, just to see what was going on, and I was absolutely in the middle of all that. As for sport, I was totally oblivious, though I did go to a World Cup match at Anfield in 1966 – no idea who was playing.

GS: In what ways did the Catholic/Protestant divide affect you? How far did you notice it?

LG: My mother's birthday was 12 July, Orange Lodge Day, when the Protestants marched through the city centre, and so we always knew that 'you don't go into town on Mum's birthday' because there were fights between Catholics and Protestants. My parents strongly supported the Catholic cause, were supporters of a united Ireland and the Catholics in the north. I think this was because, being Jewish, they instinctively supported the underdog even though they were politically right wing, Tory voters.

GS: Were you aware of the distinctness of Liverpool as a city? Its cosmopolitan/immigrant population?

LG: My parents were en route to America. It was never their idea that they should settle in Liverpool. Like a lot of Jewish immigrants to Britain, they had bought what they thought was a ticket to New York but found themselves dumped in Liverpool. There was a sense in which we still felt that we were en route somewhere else. Aged seventeen, my father went to sea on the SS *Laconia* as a baker and jumped ship at New York in 1923, staying there until 1929 when he returned for a holiday that never ended. He married (not my mother, a first marriage) and had a daughter, and somehow he never went back to America until a short trip in the early sixties. America was the lost paradise for my father, and for the rest of his life he compared Britain unfavourably with the United States. I always felt that we were somehow stranded on the wrong side of the Atlantic. My father was a natural American, large, loud and boastful. America was his place and New York his city. Liverpool was the jumping off point. I always feel that our family has spent a hundred years trying to get to America without ever quite succeeding. The middle-class population of Liverpool is quite small, so being middle class there was not like growing up in the Home Counties, and anyway, as a family we were only one generation away from tenements. The docks, the sea, the memory of the blitz, all were part of the fabric of growing up. Liverpool always felt to me as if it was not in England, nor the North either, oddly. It was a port and its back was turned away against the land, looking outwards across the Atlantic. I always felt we were a bit of America that had somehow broken off, and in some ways I think that's why I am incapable of being anti-American.

GS: How much did you know of Liverpool's history?

LG: Something, but not as much as I should. We certainly didn't study it in school, though we knew about the slave trade, sugar. I knew about Gladstone, and every time I am going past Huskisson Street I remember that it was named after William Huskisson MP – the first person ever to be killed by a train.

GS: What did you know of the political life in the city?

LG: Liverpool was, improbably, a Liberal city for most of the fifties and sixties, but by the seventies it became solidly Labour. The dockers and the car workers at Ford's Halewood plant were a major impact on city life – but to be honest, I was too busy writing poetry to pay too much attention to any of that.

GS: Do you think there is something about Liverpool that fosters poetry, or conversely is antithetical to the novel? What made you change from poetry to prose, and did leaving the city influence the decision?

LG: I wrote poetry because there was a kind of poetry boom in the sixties, not just in Liverpool, and because I was a teenager, and teenagers don't tend to write novels. I left when I was nineteen, around the time I stopped writing poetry, but I didn't publish my first novel until I was in my forties. I think I'm a natural prose writer, not a poet, but I don't think the city had anything to do with that at all.

GS: *Still Here* anticipates the re-development of Liverpool in advance of 2008. What for you defines Liverpool culturally?

LG: Liverpool for me is the vitality and spirit of its people, the great beauty of its architecture – not just the city centre civic architecture, but the sandstone suburbs. The parks, the galleries, the Philharmonic orchestra. But mainly it's the indomitable spirit of the people, the general bolshiness, the lack of timidity or social deference. All of which are needed somewhere in the soul to make art.

11

Ramsey Campbell's Haunted Liverpool

Andy Sawyer

At the age of fourteen Ramsey Campbell found a paperback collection of stories by H.P. Lovecraft in a Liverpool sweet shop. The discovery of the collection, Campbell has gone on record as saying, 'made me a writer',[1] providing a template which he would at first imitate and then explore creatively to develop a series of award-winning short stories and novels, such as *The Parasite* (1980), *Incarnate* (1983), *The Hungry Moon* (1986), *Ancient Images* (1989), *The Long Lost* (1993) and most recently *Secret Stories* (2005).

Lovecraft, as Campbell would only later discover, was, like himself, someone whose weird fiction was partly an attempt to deal with profound personal difficulties. In the introduction to *The Face That Must Die* (1983), Campbell described his own upbringing in what some would call a severely dysfunctional family and others something like an extract from his own fiction. There are, however, other resonances between the two as writers whose fictions map the tensions between geography, topography and consciousness. In other words, each writer uses setting to express both a series of personal and social anxieties and a more existential response to Pascal's terrifying 'infinite immensity of spaces whereof I know nothing'.[2] Or, to put it even more into words which could also have been written by a horror writer, 'If you gaze for long into an abyss, the abyss gazes also into you.'[3]

---

1 Ramsey Campbell, *Ramsey Campbell, Probably* (Harrogate: PS Publishing, 2002), p. 286. Hereafter *RCP*.
2 Blaise Pascal, *Pensées*, ed. J.M. Cohen (Harmondsworth: Penguin, 1961), p. 57.
3 Friedrich Nietzsche, *Beyond Good and Evil*, ed. Marion Faber (Oxford, Oxford University Press, 1998), p. 68.

At the age of four Campbell had himself encountered the abyss staring back at him from a children's annual featuring the popular cartoon character Rupert Bear and a story involving a macabre Christmas tree. A chance glimpse a few years later in a Southport shop of a copy of *Weird Tales* (the magazine with which, as he was to learn, Lovecraft was most closely associated) left him with an image of horror which grew more exaggerated over the years. His obsession with it may also have been fed by the fact that his mother had forbidden him to buy the magazine. (When he was seventeen Campbell found the *Weird Tales* issue which had terrified and attracted him ten years earlier, only to discover the cover was much less horrific than he'd remembered.) These images, fused with others from cinema and prose fiction, seemed to express and exploit his inner fears. Before he was ten, Campbell had discovered many of the great names of supernatural fiction: Lovecraft, Sheridan Le Fanu, M.R. James, Ray Bradbury, Robert Aickmann, and many others in anthologies borrowed from his local library. He had also begun writing his own horror and science fiction.

Campbell began to seek out the pulp fiction magazines which at that time could be obtained from market stalls, specialist dealers, corner shops and disreputable vendors in more lurid material. The popular American magazines of the thirties, forties and fifties were distributed irregularly and haphazardly, shipped across the Atlantic as ballast and distributed in market stalls, Woolworth's and a small network of specialist dealers. These dealers would also obtain magazines on subscription or (during the post-war period of currency restrictions) organize barter systems by which fans would swap material across the Atlantic. Some magazines had British reprint editions. *Weird Tales* was one, a British equivalent running from 1949 to 1954 with more or less identical contents but with British advertisements. For people in search of original material the wait could be frustrating. Similarly the chances of obtaining a specific issue. British bookseller Ken Slater recalls being told, 'I will hold any I get for you, but I can't select my orders; they come in bundles' (personal communication, 26 September 2006). Even reprint editions were beyond the pocket money economy of most readers.

Merseyside was almost certainly one of the conduits through which American magazines originally entered the country. Not only was Liverpool one of the country's major ports, but individuals in the mercantile trades may have brought magazines back from the United States in the same way as individuals were reported (although Bill Harry, founder of *Mersey Beat* newspaper, plays this down) to have brought American music across in the 1950s and early 1960s. Certainly the period saw a considerable overlap between science fiction and popular music enthusiasts. Harry was also a member of the Liverpool science fiction group for a while and had issued his own fanzine, *Biped*, in 1955. The roots of science fiction and fantastic literature in Liverpool struck deeper, however, with the city being one of the first in Britain to develop a science fiction fan group, some of whom actively became involved in the import and distribution of magazines. Perhaps as a result Liverpool became home to a number of important writers in the field – not all of whom, however, were aware of the existence of others.

Merseyside's place in the history of science fiction and fantastic literature dates back at least as far as the Wirral-born philosopher and writer Olaf Stapledon (1886–1950), second only to H.G. Wells as a speculative writer. At the time of writing his epic future history *Last and First Men* (1930) Stapledon had almost certainly never come across the first generation of American science fiction magazines then being produced, seeing himself as belonging exclusively to the British tradition of Wells. Ironically, from the mid-1920s Wells was being used to justify the new literature of 'scientifiction' in America, with many of his early scientific romances being reprinted in Hugo Gernsback's *Amazing Stories*, the first magazine dedicated to what was later to be called science fiction.

A philosopher and social reformer (he taught Extension classes for the University of Liverpool and the Workers' Educational Association), Stapledon's influence upon British science fiction extends through the cosmic visions of Arthur C. Clarke and Brian W. Aldiss to another Liverpudlian, Stephen Baxter, who in many ways developed the tradition of Stapledon's speculations about time, space and human evolution. (Rather neatly, Baxter, although ten years younger, attended the same school, St Edward's Grammar School, as Ramsey Campbell.) Unknown to Stapledon, shortly after the publication of *Last and First Men* a group of Liverpool fans formed the ambitiously titled 'Universal Science Circle', whose president, Colin H. Askham, and secretary, Les Johnson, became associated with the British Interplanetary Society, formed in 1933 by Philip E. Cleator to educate a largely sceptical public in the coming reality of space travel. Also involved in the early years of the society – still in existence today – were Liverpool authors Eric Frank Russell and David McIlwain (better known under his pseudonym Charles Eric Maine). In 1937, Russell accompanied Les Johnson to the first British science fiction convention in Leeds, and by then Johnson was part of the Milcross Book Service, based in Brownlow Hill, which traded books and magazines to the British science fiction community until the 1950s. Later writers associated with Merseyside include Douglas R. Mason, a Wallasey head teacher and a prolific writer of science fiction novels during the 1960s and 1970s; Rob Grant and Doug Naylor, responsible for the 1980s science fiction comedy *Red Dwarf*; actor/writer/director Ken Campbell, who, although not a Liverpudlian, founded the 'Science Fiction Theatre of Liverpool' in the 1970s, which adapted various science fiction classics for dramatization at the Everyman Theatre; and another multi-talented horror writer/director/artist, Clive Barker, who (like Grant and Naylor) attended Liverpool University and was encouraged in his desire to write horror after a school visit by Ramsey Campbell.[4]

Few of these writers used Liverpool or Merseyside as the setting for their fiction. There were exceptions. The 'Seagate' of G.G. Pendarves's 1937 short story 'Thing of Darkness' (published, like much of her work, in *Weird Tales* magazine) is a thinly disguised Parkgate, while Douglas R. Mason set several novels in 'Wirral City' – sometimes an orbiting satellite, sometimes a metropolis. It is Campbell, however, who has most consistently returned to explore the literal and metaphorical undercurrents and underworlds of the region. The remainder of this chapter, then, will explore how the tradition of a realist depiction of place and the transrealism of plot, so often found in supernatural fiction, operates in the way Campbell takes the Lovecraftian tradition of mapping the sublime upon the mundane and made Liverpool and the Merseyside region a threshold between the exterior and interior worlds.

Early in 1962, Campbell (then better known by his first name John) attended a meeting of the Liverpool Science Fiction Group (a separate venture from the earlier group which, however, had helped with its inception in 1951) at its premises in Bold Street. '[W]ith a name like *that* we just had to have him as a member,' wrote club member John Roles in the Spring 1962 edition of the Liverpool group fanzine *Bastion*.[5] (The rather more famous John W. Campbell was then editor of *Analog* – formerly *Astounding* – which since the 1930s had been an influential science fiction magazine.) The Liverpool group was at the time one of the most active branches of science fiction fandom, and proved a

---

4 Douglas E. Winter, *Clive Barker: The Dark Fantastic* (London: HarperCollins, 2001), pp. 61–62.

5 Eric Bentcliffe (ed.), *Bastion*, 3 (Spring 1962) (Liverpool: Liverpool Science Fiction Group), p. 39.

congenial and supportive group. Campbell's stories were published in fanzines and, encouraged by friends, he sent examples of his work to August Derleth, H.P. Lovecraft's friend and executor. Derleth offered trenchant but encouraging advice. This resulted in the inclusion of Campbell's 'The Church in High Street' in an anthology, *Dark Mind, Dark Heart* (1962). Two years later Campbell's first book, *The Inhabitant of the Lake*, was published by Derleth's Arkham House imprint.

Although Campbell has been amusingly frank about his 'second-hand Lovecraft', quoting some of the more overblown passages in his introduction to the reprinting of some of his earliest stories in *Cold Print* (1985), they remain (unlike many Lovecraft imitations) the writing of someone working through his influences to find his own distinctive voice. This voice began more fully to emerge in his second collection, *Demons by Daylight* (1973), the publication of which saw Campbell giving up his job working in Liverpool libraries (he had previously worked in a tax office) to become a full-time writer. It was also a time when Campbell was extending the range of his influences, working his way through such non-genre writers as Vladimir Nabokov and Graham Greene, as well as watching the films of Alfred Hitchcock and Ingmar Bergman.

Before continuing to examine Campbell, it will be useful to return briefly to particular aspects of his debt to H.P. Lovecraft.

Howard Philips Lovecraft was born in Providence, Rhode Island in 1890. As mentioned earlier, his family life was severely dysfunctional. His father died in a mental asylum from 'general paresis', almost certainly as a result of syphilis. Lovecraft was brought up by his possessive, neurotic mother until her death in 1921, following which he lived with two aunts. Family wealth meant that the young Lovecraft did not have to work. The declining value of the inheritance, however, and his own failure to earn a living as a writer, meant that by his death in 1937 he was living in humiliating poverty. He devoted his life to scholarship and literature – which in practice meant becoming an autodidact of immensely wide if not always deep knowledge, writing weird and supernatural fiction, revising and ghost-writing the fiction of considerably less talented others, and carrying on an immense and fascinating correspondence with friends established through the amateur journalism movement and the early fandom associated with the magazine *Weird Tales* in which much of his fiction was published. Sometimes dismissed as an overly neurotic, barely literate writer of pulp-Gothic shockers, on closer examination Lovecraft becomes a writer of annoyingly contradictory but fascinating and genuine gifts. Recent re-packagings of his work by Penguin Modern Classics (edited by S.T. Joshi), the Library of America (edited by Peter Straub), and the enthusiasm of cult French novelist Michel Houellebecq, have helped foster a reappraisal of Lovecraft that reaches beyond the confines of the horror-reading fraternity.

The geography and topography of Lovecraft's fiction is easily traced onto the New England he knew. Essex County, Massachusetts and his birthplace Providence are the locations of the Miskatonic Valley and the coastal towns of Kingsport, Dunwich, Innsmouth and Arkham, where Miskatonic University with its curious collection of occult texts is situated. In addition, 'real' places, often connected to incidences of eighteenth-century puritan hysteria at outbreaks of 'witchcraft', are frequently mentioned. Miskatonic Valley is a region of isolated farmhouses and haunted forests. We read, then, in 'The Colour out of Space' that 'West of Arkham, the hills rise wild, and there are valleys with deep woods that no axe has ever cut ... The old folk have gone away and foreigners do not like to live there.'[6] In contrast, the coastal towns are a mixture of antiquity (which in Lovecraft means culture) and decay (for which we read immigration and in-breeding). The roots of all this in Lovecraft are explored more fully in S.T. Joshi's *A Dreamer and a Visionary* (Liverpool: Liverpool University Press, 2001), but it seems clear that part of the creation of his 'Miskatonic Valley' landscape and the archaic, brooding language with which he describes it has to do with an outer displacement of paranoia. The landscape reflects an interior turmoil – a whole range of personal and social anxieties involving cultural, racial, or class phobias, his personal isolation from the economic mainstream and his dislike of much of the culture of the twentieth century, and the Gothic/Puritan literary tradition that influenced him and to which he undoubtedly belongs.

Such a fusion of locality and personality is by no means confined to Lovecraft. More recently, Stephen King's Maine, with the fictional towns of Castle Rock and Derry serving as sites for various conflicts between good and evil, recalls Lovecraft's own New England setting. More important to Campbell is how M.R. James and his circle created a world of antiquarian scholars and vicars in Cambridge colleges and the landscapes of the East Anglian Fenlands and Norfolk coastline. With his sly humour and restrained language, James established the model of the

---

6   H.P. Lovecraft, 'The Call of Cthulhu' (1928), in S.T. Joshi (ed.), *The Call of Cthulhu and Other Weird Tales* (London: Penguin, 1999), p. 170.

'English ghost story'. It is to Lovecraft and James, then, that we should turn in looking for those writers who initially influenced Campbell in his experimentations with the genre.

Campbell describes his debt to Lovecraft as one which progressed from surface imitation to explorations of the underlying sense of wonder and orchestrated structure in his stories: 'It's easy to imitate Lovecraft's style, or at least to convince oneself that one has done so; it's far more difficult to imitate his sense of structure' (*RCP*, p. 289). His early stories copied slavishly, right down to using Lovecraft's own locale. American locations provided a sense of displacement (both as foreign and as in fact *fictional*) at the same time as retaining a necessary familiarity. Lovecraft's own anglophilia provides a further frame of reference. The disadvantage of such an approach, of course, was that Campbell knew little about New England. As a result his version of the Miskatonic Valley was simple pastiche. August Derleth suggested he remedy this ('Chasing the Unknown', *RCP*, p. 289), with the result that the stories Campbell eventually published in *The Inhabitant of the Lake* are set in the Severn Valley in Gloucestershire and the surrounding Cotswolds. We can still discern here the influence of the seaport/rural mixture of Lovecraft's imaginary towns of Temphill, Brichester and Goatswood. As Campbell worked through his debt to Lovecraft, Brichester was to prove the most important. Thus the stories collected in his next book, *Demons by Daylight* (1973), follow the classic Lovecraftian pattern of fictionalizing a real location. It soon becomes clear, then, that Campbell's 'Severn Valley' is actually Merseyside, with Brichester in these early stories being Lovecraft's Arkham projected onto Liverpool.

Other influences were becoming equally important. 'In the mid-60s,' Campbell says, 'I went to the movies nearly every night for years. I was actually going into areas which had been bombed out, blitzed streets, and you had maybe a cinema and several blocks of abandoned houses around them.'[7] Such a landscape was fertile ground for a mind primed on Lovecraft's antiquarian images of cosmic fear and the intrusion of the supernatural into the modern urban settings of Fritz Leiber's Chicago and San Francisco. Once we have noted the correspondence between Brichester and Liverpool, it becomes apparent just how present the city and its locations are even here in Campbell's first book. 'The Inhabitant of the Lake' refers to a 'Bold Street'. The story also contains a 'Mercy

---

7   S.T. Joshi, *The Count of Thirty: A Tribute to Ramsey Campbell* (West Warwick, RI: Necronomicon Press, 1993), p. 13.

Hill' (the echo of 'Mersey' is clear), a place name that crops up again in 'The Horror from the Bridge'. What becomes apparent, then, is how Campbell moved from using plots and settings reminiscent of Lovecraft, to developing his own narrative voice and topos. The significance of this was clearly apparent to Campbell, who has commented on how 'writing about [Lovecraft's] creations had been a way to avoid dealing with my own fears' (*RCP*, p. 291). The fictionalizing of Liverpool therefore enabled him to write about his own anxieties in a lightly disguised version of the everyday world. 'The Franklyn Paragraphs', in *Demons by Daylight*, is part of this continuing transition from 'Brichester' to 'Liverpool': a Brichester writer of horror fiction, Erroll Undercliffe, tells the story while Campbell himself appears as narrator, describing the communications between himself and Undercliffe. Also included in this hall-of-mirrors-like structure are references to Campbell's previous books and to real people well known in the circles of the British horror fraternity. The following story, 'The Interloper', written as if by the same fictional Undercliffe, shows Campbell's Liverpool struggling to emerge from the shadow of Brichester. It is a strongly autobiographical story, one Campbell has called 'a strange kind of revenge on the sort of schooling I'd had to suffer at the hands of Christian Brothers' (*RCP*, p. 427). Through this and subsequent stories in the book we are beginning to see a realist depiction of Liverpool in the post-war era: the grey depression of poverty, slums, wrecked communities, economic decline, insular snobbishness, prejudice and authoritarianism, and an isolated pseudo-intelligentsia. It is a region which, in its paranoid isolation and desperate anxiety, reflects, emotionally, Lovecraft's own invented geography, *without*, significantly, Lovecraft's terrifying racial prejudices.

Campbell's increasing awareness that Lovecraft's use of supernaturalism and setting provided the tools by which he could explore his own personal relationship with his environment becomes ever clearer as the face of a recognizable Merseyside emerges. The eldritch terrors that rise up in Campbell's stories become less imitations of a foreign model than carefully constructed pictures of the mingled fear and awe which arises as the impersonal shadows lurking behind modern life are imagined as having solid form. And in this, they are closer to the heart of Lovecraft's own careful unification of 'the realistic and the fantastic, the personal and the cosmic' (*RCP*, p. 231) than any pastiche.

Consequently, later stories show horror – or, more accurately, a profound anxiety about the nightmarish aspects of contemporary reality – seeping into the lives of individuals in recognizable Merseyside locations. 'Call First' (1975), one of a series of short stories that attempts to evoke the macabre humour of 1950s' horror comics, features a scenario found in several other stories/novels of the time: a sinister library user who turns out to be a black magician, his haunted castle being replaced by the more mundane trappings of a public library and a seedy house. 'The Man in the Underpass' (1975) evokes old gods under the streets of Tuebrook, while 'The Companion' (1976), in which a ride on a ghost train by a man who finds something – or someone – taking his hand, was inspired by Campbell's memories of the fairground at New Brighton. 'Mackintosh Willy' (1979) weaves a story of a murder/haunting out of some graffiti Campbell observed in a bus shelter near Newsham Park. 'The Ferries' (1982), meanwhile, is derived from the view across the Dee marshes at Parkgate. A Wirral setting also dominates 'The Depths', this time Neston and Birkenhead. Neither is Merseyside limited to making an appearance in Campbell's shorter fiction. *The Influence* (1988) features Queenie, a Liverpool matriarch; *The Face That Must Die* (1979, rev. 1983), though a non-supernatural tale, remains relentless in its exploration of the mind of a paranoid killer from Cantrill Farm, a location that struck Campbell as nightmarish enough in itself to need nothing but description to evoke the alienation of the central character, Horridge. The grotesque and horrific here arises from a macabre humour that, fittingly for a city with Liverpool's reputation, arises from a specifically *linguistic* humour. Thus Horridge's dislocation and alienation make themselves manifest in sadistic puns. 'A Street Was Chosen' (1991) achieves its unsettling effect by recounting a series of increasing cruelties in the passive-voice style of a scientific report. Public readings of this story frequently result in laughter from the audience, not least because of the incongruity between the restrained, objective language and the awful things that are being done to the characters.

Humour, especially slapstick, produces its effects through incongruity, often violent incongruity, and exaggeration. If a pompous man slipping on a banana skin is funny, do we laugh at a pompous man being murdered by a maniac with a blow torch? In *The Count of Eleven* (1991), in which the latter takes place, we are forced to confront uneasily our own responses as we sympathize with the tribulations of Jack Orchard while simultaneously recoiling from his actions. The accidents Jack suffers recall the carefully staged slapstick routines of Laurel and Hardy films (the duo are referenced here and elsewhere in Campbell's fiction) and we are reminded that both horror and humour are ways in which our image of what is right and appropriate in the world is undermined. Indeed, in writing about slapstick comedy, Andrew Stott, while he does not discuss horror, nevertheless uses language that describes a slapstick routine in exactly the same way as we might recount the events of a horror story:

> The slapstick protagonist is continually prone to attack ... At the heart of slapstick is the conceit that the laws of physics are locally mutable, that the world can rebel against you, or that a person can be suddenly stripped of their ability to control their environment or anticipate how it will behave.[8]

Interestingly, Campbell has himself said that he would have liked to be a stand-up comedian:

> Assuming I'm not already and just don't know it ... I do like to put jokes in my stories ... Part of the business of writing horror fiction, I suppose, is to have the courage to risk the absurd. Humour and horror tend to meet in the grotesque – a thin dividing line where the writer hopes to control the reader's emotions.[9]

He has also remarked on how jokes 'force you to look again at things you've taken for granted'.[10] While words like 'bleak' and 'joyless' have been applied to Campbell's vision, it is important to note that the apparent relentlessness is a form of satire – and some of Campbell's most relentless satire is directed at those readers of horror who see its only function as providing an ever-increasing intensity of sadistic image. This hesitation or oscillation between humour and horror is often a reflection of the oscillation between the fantastic and realism in Campbell's plots. At the heart of horror is our uncertainty about our place in the world.

The paranoid puns of Campbell's 1983 preferred version of *The Face That Must Die* (an over-enthusiastic editor had cut most of them on first publication in 1979) enact the connections between Jack Orchard's

---

8   Andrew Stott, *Comedy* (London: Routledge, 2004), p. 93.

9   Douglas E. Winter (ed.), *Faces of Fear: Encounters with the Creators of Modern Horror* (London: Pan, 1990), p. 100.

10 Andy Sawyer, 'Ramsey Campbell Interviewed', *Vector*, 151 (August/September 1989), pp. 8–10.

chaotic interior world and his apparently random affliction. The repeated refrain of the music hall tag 'you have to laugh' is part of this consciously uneasy use of humour as a defence mechanism. Possibly there *is* some malevolent force which is piling ill-luck upon Orchard for its own amusement (the Biblical story of Job is explicitly referenced); or perhaps his obsessive punning is a sign of mounting insanity. Conversely, in the surreal grotesquerie of *Needing Ghosts* (1990) there are scenes, such as Mottershead's talk in a library (he is, apparently, a writer who has woken one morning with no idea who he is, what he is doing, and why), which collapse all the boundaries between nightmarish illogic and absurd humour. At such moments the reader is left to attempt to decide whether what is being told is a grimly hysterical satire of a writer's life or an altogether darker study of madness. Again, central to Campbell's depiction of this is his fictionalized Liverpool.

The first overtly 'Liverpool' story, 'The Cellars' (1965), used the common horror motif of an intrusion from underground in its invention of a system of 'catacombs' beneath Liverpool. Based on the extensive system of cellars under Rumford Place shown to Campbell by a friend, the catacombs of the story unconciously echo the 'Williamson Tunnels' in Edge Hill, created by the businessman Joseph Williamson in the early nineteenth century, possibly as a job creation scheme for soldiers returning from the Napoleonic Wars, possibly because of a belief that Armageddon was on its way. Campbell has said that at the time of writing 'The Cellars' he was unaware of Williamson's tunnels, and that the ones in the story were based on 'an extensive system of cellars… under Rumford Place' (personal communication, 31 May 2006). Nevertheless there is a history of people associating them with the supernatural. Charles Hand, writing in 1916, describes what he saw of these tunnels as a 'nightmare maze … grotesque beyond description'. James Stonehouse, writing in 1846 only a few years after Williamson's death, includes in his manuscript a sketch which (because of a trick of perspective) gives the viewer a sense of something monstrous at the end of the tunnel.[11] The 'cellars' of Campbell's story are more mundane, but because of this ordinariness, more frightening.

A bored office worker, Julie, is asked by a colleague, Vic, to visit with him some catacombs he has heard about near the river. They have been out together previously, but his apparent shyness blocked any further development towards a relationship. Nevertheless, they cross Liverpool

---

11 See http://www.williamsontunnels.com/articles.htm

together – a wintry, grey city, grimy and rain-soaked. Their journey is noted by named locations: Church Street, the Victoria Monument, and Exchange Flags. At this point they lose their way, signalled by their wandering through a maze of now unnamed streets. By this point the couple are both in and out of the known city. Eventually they discover a trapdoor, under which are steps leading down into darkness. They go into the vaults, left decaying by lack of use. By candle-light they explore what appears to be an office with a table and telephone now left amorphous and spongy by moss, fungus and cobwebs. Vic has earlier described his interest in the catacombs as 'curiosity, morbid of course, since it's me', and his morbidity is emphasized by the way he plays upon Julie's fears. When they reach a pair of vast iron doors sealed by an iron beam which has come loose from its holdings in the wall, Vic fantasizes about what may be behind them: 'It's as though something came from that place beyond, whatever's through those doors, and shut them in with the mould … made pets of them, perhaps, or collected them … Imagine what they looked like if they ever escaped … You could scream all you like down here, nobody would hear you.'[12] On the way out, Vic thrusts his hand, coated in 'leprous' candle wax, towards Julie's face.

The next day, Julie needs to borrow some money and thinks of Vic. He is busy on the telephone and she decides to approach him later, meets a former boyfriend, goes out with him, and forgets about borrowing money from Vic. She never thinks of seeing him again. Some time later, however, she is shopping with a friend, Alice, who tells her that Vic has not been at work for weeks. When colleagues call round to Vic's house, his nervous mother slams the door in their faces. There is a hint of something grotesque and half-seen, but at this point Julie is clearly no longer interested in Vic, so Alice changes the subject. A fortnight later, it is Valentine's Day. The dateless Julie is resigned to a dreary evening at home. Boarding the ferry at the Pier Head to cross to Birkenhead she hears a deck hand teasing a mate about some 'muddy hunchback' he is supposed to have seen. Arriving home, she sees that the day's downpour has left a bush on the green opposite her home looking bedraggled, as if a figure were peering from behind it. Her mother has gone out, so she makes some coffee and listens to records. The rain lashing against the window makes her think she sees a plump figure crossing the green, but she dismisses this and settles down to read her Valentine cards. One

---

12 Ramsey Campbell, *The Height of the Scream* (1976) (London: Millington, 1978), p. 105. Hereafter *Scream*.

– the largest – is 'written in a hand so magnified and unsteady that she assumed it was the work of an illiterate or cripple' (*Scream*, p. 111), and on the envelope is a blob of white mould.

What we are led to expect by these clues, and the physical desolation of the exterior world – the Mersey's 'thick wrinkled water from which the rain extracted bubbles like the last breath of the drowned' (*Scream*, p. 109) and the 'stern rectangular frames imprisoning windows and doors' (*Scream*, p. 110) of Julie's street – *happens*. In the silence after her records have finished, she hears someone padding around outside her house. A face peers through a window. Frightened, she dashes up to her room where she sees 'a humped figure progressing painfully away from her, toward the river' (*Scream*, p. 113). By the time it has fallen into the water, she is downstairs, waiting impatiently for another of her boyfriends to answer his phone.

By this time, we have long understood that although Julie is the focalizer, the story is about Vic and that we have been led along a conventional path only to be disappointed if what the reader wanted was a stalk-and-slash tale. Such stories are often revenge fantasies in which women are punished for being sexually active, and Julie is certainly something of a tease, but any punishment she receives is temporary. Instead, the embodiment of location has overwhelmed Vic's fantasies. The horror leaks or intrudes into the real world in a fashion typical of a Lovecraft or M.R. James story, only here it is more obviously connected with character. The story tells us – by implication – that Vic has returned to the catacombs and been trapped by monstrosities lurking underground or in some way infected by the mould, which has turned him into the physical embodiment of his inner self: morbid, shambling and alone.

Such 'lower depths' also feature in 'The Interloper', written three years later but once again set in the Brichester of its supposed author, Erroll Undercliffe. The central character is a schoolboy, John (Campbell's first name) who is persecuted by a sadistic teacher. With a friend, Dave, he decides to spend lunch at the Catacombs, strongly reminiscent of the Cavern club, the centre of Merseybeat in the late 1950s, early 1960s: 'In the side street they could hear beneath their feet a pounding drum, a blurred electric guitar. Somewhere down there were The Catacombs.'[13] The boys go into a nearby building, descending past

---

13 Ramsey Campbell, *Demons by Daylight* (1973) (London: Star, 1990), pp. 64–65. Hereafter *Demons*.

cobwebbed alcoves to a 'circular vaulted chamber' with a pool in its centre. Beyond the pool is a rack of clothes, including a pinstripe suit with an orange handkerchief in the jacket pocket. Investigating, Dave is caught by some creature which jets 'from what must have been a mouth a pouring stream of white' (*Demons*, p. 68). John flees, past the alcoves where previously unidentified forms now seem to be trapped people, and gets back to the surface. But when he returns to school he notices that the Inspector – whose impending visit has been driving the awful teacher, Scott, to greater acts of petty cruelty – has arrived, wearing a pinstripe suit with an orange handkerchief, just like that he had noticed in the catacombs, and that his garments are covered with cobwebs. John is sick with fear, and under pretence of taking him to the school nurse to be treated, the Inspector escorts him back to the catacombs.

Two further early stories established the sense of place which Campbell was to make his own. 'Concussion', from *Demons by Daylight*, is technically science fiction – a time-slip story that confuses past and future – beginning in a bland future of weather control and rectangular housing blocks, and fashions that are suggestive of the early 1960s. This, and the oblique narrative (returning by bus to Liverpool to die, Kirk notices that the young woman sitting near him is the same Anne with whom he had an idyllic affair over fifty years earlier), makes it a complex narrative to unravel. Does Kirk dream Anne? Does the blow to her head caused by Kirk's attempt to speak to her somehow send part of her back to the past? Furthermore, having broken his glasses Kirk spends much of the story unable to see much of his surroundings, with the result that this dislocating haze becomes divorced from time and place. Where, exactly, does the story take place? When Kirk tries to track Anne down he discovers that her street in Southend has not even been built.

For all its dislocations, there remains a strong sense of place in 'Concussion', especially in its evocation of semi-rural Wirral suburbia. Conversely 'Litter', from *The Height of the Scream* (1976), is a 'Brichester' story clearly overlain upon Liverpool. The narrator works for the local radio station and frequently crosses the market on his way home. The market is a location he dislikes because of its lack of personality: 'This place is about the least haunted I've ever encountered … if you dig into most cultures you'll find the notion of the genius loci. What sort of spirit could this place have?' (*Scream*, pp. 133–34). Yet it is the litter scattered around the market that *becomes* the 'haunt'. 'Litter' overturns what many imitators of Lovecraft mistakenly believe to be the heart of the fiction – the pseudo-history that brings the intrusion into the real world. What is underneath this market, returning us to 'The Cellars' and 'The Interloper', is desolation and isolation: neither a comforting, cosy heritage nor an excuse for the meaninglessness of people's lives.

This sense of the abyss that lies at the heart of such localities comes to the fore in several of Campbell's more recent novels. *The Darkest Part of the Wood* (2003) returns to the earlier Brichester, though here it is less a 'version' of Liverpool than, like Lovecraft's Arkham, a kind of consensus space which exists only in order that the story may be told. We expect a certain kind of story, and we are given it, but with deeper resonances. The earlier 'Brichester' stories of haunted places, ominous histories and threatening intrusions are recalled. Before the events recounted in the narrative take place, we are told about an American professor, Lennox Price, who came to Goodmanswood to investigate the stories associated with it and discovered a hallucinogenic moss that spawned a cult. Price and some of the cult members are now insane, while his wife, an artist, and one daughter and her son live nearby. The story begins, then, with the return to Britain of his second daughter Sylvia, who is pregnant. The name she wishes to give the child is similar to that of a sixteenth-century sorcerer. Local children tell tales of the 'sticky man'.[14] Lennox is killed after apparently trying to abduct Sylvia. The link between Lennox and the mage Nathanial Selcouth becomes stronger when Selcouth's journal is found. Lennox's grandson Sam, injured when he fell out of a tree during a protest over the building of a by-pass, is offered a publishing job, but finds himself unable to leave the vicinity. At the centre of everything is the wood, small in area but with a sinister history as far back as records can be traced.

While there appears little here that is specifically Liverpudlian in origin, nevertheless *The Darkest Part of the Wood* revisits some of Campbell's earliest influences. The ambulant Christmas tree from his childhood reading of 'Rupert Bear' annuals reappears in Chapter 15. Again, the sense of the numinous, the 'delightful horror' to be found in special, *old* places marks the internal displacement of dysfunctional family relationships. Although laced with Lovecraftian awe, Arkham-like settings and characters, such as the sorcerer who raises the being that is the source of the 'Goodman' legend, the convenient cosiness the Mythos has come to offer is eschewed. It is as if Campbell is going back

---

14 Ramsey Campbell, *The Darkest Part of the Woods* (New York: Tor, 2003), p. 65. Hereafter *Darkest*.

to first principles to present Brichester as a symbolic location in its own right, neither a displaced Liverpool nor simply a metaphor for disordered personalities but a wider landscape of the mind. Goodmanswood, like the medieval legend of the Green Man, suggests the violent and alien aspects of nature with the accompanying terror of being lost in the wood figuring as the lurking demons of the subconscious. The Price family, as artists, scientists, librarians or writers, are concerned first with exploring reality, and then playing with it. Their horror is that they succeed.

With its banal location and even more banal characters, *The Overnight* (2003) is the deliberate opposite of such fertile symbolism. Instead, it returns to the nothingness at the heart of modern living implied by 'Litter'. In a newly established retail park in an area known as 'Fenny Meadows', the staff of the Texts bookshop are opening the newest branch. The American manager, Woody, is using a fake mixture of management-textbook cheerfulness and autocracy to motivate his staff (single-parent Jill; Mad and Ross, who have just split up as a couple; gay Jake and homophobic Greg; book-loving Wilf; Connie, who is beginning an affair with Jill's ex-husband; and club-going Gavin) to prepare for a visit by senior management. Business itself – partly because of the fog which blankets the area, partly because of the location itself – is poor, the staff discontented, and Woody's attempts to raise morale and productivity are inhibited because of his crassness. A number of minor incidents – a false alarm, mysteriously untidy shelves, a number of videos returned as faulty – develop into a crescendo of unsettling events. Nigel finds opening up the store on his own increases his fear of the dark. Publicity for events, including an in-store reading by a writer, the meaninglessness of whose book is matched only by his arrogance, is marred by glitches, resulting in misspellings and errant apostrophes. Lorraine, meanwhile, is knocked down by a car thief and killed; while an encounter with a bullying former schoolmate who reminds him of his dyslexia results in Wilf being fired for losing his temper. Against the odds, Woody orders his staff to work overnight to make sure that the store is in perfect condition for the management inspection. At this point, all that has previously remained glimpses of forms half-seen steps terrifyingly into view.

Much of what happens can be read as the kind of macabre comedy discussed earlier. But behind this lies the essential blankness of modern off-motorway retail park environments: the identical chain stores, the staff who do not really want to be there and the customers who want to be there even less. There is really nothing to describe in the area. Even the horrors are amorphous, difficult to pinpoint. Campbell may not directly have had in mind the development of retail outlets on Speke Boulevard (the novel's dedication mentions that he worked at the Borders bookshop in Cheshire Oaks, near Ellesmere Port, before writing the book), but his satire of the kind of development to be found all over Britain may also include also phenomena like the optimism of the city's re-named 'John Lennon Airport', with its slogan 'Above us only sky' taken from Lennon's 'Imagine'. The story asks us to imagine not perhaps what lies above but beneath Liverpool's re-branding of itself.

A local historian may hint at Fenny Meadows' macabre past, but essentially there is no past to speak of. All we can piece together is the isolation of a place which, like the 'Brichester' market of 'Litter', has no personality and is haunted by presences which lack definition. Even the bookshop can only offer a range of *products*: when ordering his staff to recommend a book as they greet customers, Woody advises them to suggest 'anything'. Individual enthusiasm counts for nothing. In any case, only the dyslexic Wilf actually *likes* reading. The globalized root-lessness of Texts and Fenny Meadows also separates the *fictional* location from the real location it is built on. Because of the fog and the delib-erate avoidance of concrete description we can't (even if we know the real life location) *recognize* the place. Only readers familiar with the setting would bother to check the precise geographical reference which puts Fenny Meadows off the M62, locating it between Liverpool and Manchester rather than the Ellesmere Port location of Cheshire Oaks. Who, we might think, would notice that one such location is different from another?

Yet in each novel there is a kind of resolution. One character in *The Darkest Part of the Woods* escapes the locality. The ending of *The Overnight* suggests that horrors are not to be mindlessly fled from or revelled in but confronted. There is bleakness and alienation in Campbell, but while he never avoids the logical conclusions of his settings, there can also be opportunities for redemption. It is this, perhaps, which is his greatest difference from his mentor, Lovecraft. While concepts like 'catharsis' are too frequently over-simplified justifications for our desire to be confronted in fiction by the horrific and disturbing, Campbell has nearly always presented horror as a tension, an expression of anxiety rather than sadism. Indeed his condemnation of the brutal and sadistic in fiction has run parallel to his critique of those who would censor material which confronts and presents our transgressive impulses. Increasingly, in Campbell's fiction, the gaze into the abyss has become a dialogue with it.

Campbell's most recent novel, *Secret Stories* (2005),[15] is his most 'Liverpudlian' for some years. The story of a young writer (in character not unlike the dysfunctional young men of his early Brichester/Liverpool tales) who wins a short story competition in a Merseyside magazine, it soon becomes clear that Dudley has actually committed the murders he writes about. Not the least of Campbell's achievements here is that while Dudley's fellow-characters are nearly all stereotypes, suggesting a Liverpool clinging stubbornly to its own sentimental-reactionary image of itself (the separatist-feminist comedian; the father, a poet, who spouts working-class platitudes), we come to realize that they are *right*. Dudley is no sympathetic anti-hero but a monster. The character we feel the greatest sympathy for is the one who in earlier fictions *would* be the monster: Dudley's clinging, possessive, guilt-ridden mother, who in some way has created her appalling son but has done so out of love. Here, Campbell's use of locality and domesticity in a story of 'realistic' horror confronts what he has given us of his biography in a remarkably uncanny way, almost as if we are being asked to consider how far the author's success lies in the fact that he is *writing* the story while his protagonist is *living* it. We are also confronted with an extreme version of how we, as individuals, live secret, hidden, interior lives. Conventionally, we would empathize with Dudley, to the extent that, as with Horridge in *The Face That Must Die*, Campbell is forcing us to listen to the voice and viewpoint of the monstrous rather than dismiss it as 'alien'. But the tables are quickly turned, and the characters who seem to represent the priggish and pretentious aspects of social life have a viewpoint too. The killing joke of the novel is that one of the things we are forced to confront is this easy classification of how individuals, classes or cities see themselves into sentimental stereotype. By the end of the book what we may have seen as heavy-handed satire is something much more subtle, and it is tempting to see Campbell's Liverpool peering knowingly back at him as he writes himself upon it.

15 Ramsey Campbell, *Secret Stories* (Harrogate: PS Publishing, 2005). Titled *Secret Story* for the American edition.

12

'We Are a City That Just Likes to Talk': An Interview with Alan Bleasdale

Julia Hallam

Voted the city's most popular writer by a readers' poll conducted by Liverpool City Libraries in 2003, Bleasdale's dramas, alongside those of his contemporaries Willy Russell and Jimmy McGovern, epitomize for many people the essence of 'Liverpool style'. Throughout a career spanning over thirty years, Bleasdale has written fifteen stage plays, fourteen works for television, a film and two novels, but it is for the memorable characters in television dramas, such as Boys from the Blackstuff *and* GBH, *that he is most well known. Considered by many critics his finest work, these 'state of the nation' dramas situated Bleasdale amongst the foremost political dramatists of his generation. Bleasdale's work is characterized by the depth and complexity of his male characters: anxious, tormented individuals often coping with the entrapment, despair and madness created by unemployment in the 1980s and the shift in gender roles that accompanied changing patterns of employment in the 1990s. As the 1990s progressed, Bleasdale expanded his repertoire, moving away from political dramas and exploring such genres as the crime thriller and classic novel adaptation. With the release on DVD in July 2006 of his work for Channel Four,* GBH, *Jake's* Progress *and* Melissa, *he was in a contemplative mood and agreed to discuss the relationship of his background to his work and the question of whether there is something that could be called a unique Liverpool style.*

★ ★ ★

Bleasdale began by talking about his early life, not in Liverpool as he quickly points out, but in Huyton, 'where I could see the borders of Liverpool from my bedroom window'. His parents were from large Liverpool families and had grown up in the dockland housing areas either side of the Pier Head, Mill Street and Scotland Road.

'My father was the last of thirteen children born in 1917, my mother the last of ten children born in 1918. My father was born six months after my grandfather died in 1917, so my grandmother with her thirteen children lived just off Scotland Road and brought up thirteen children. Three of them died in the 1920s due to diphtheria, polio and flu epidemics. She brought them up in extreme poverty with no man at her side, my father never knew his father.'

Describing himself as a late developer, Bleasdale wrote his first stories in his early twenties but it wasn't until he created the character of Scully that he found his own voice.

'One of the reasons I started writing was because my mother was a great reader of American detective stories. She was often not very well so I would go to Huyton library with a list of books she wanted me to get for her, so when other kids were reading *My Friend Flicka* I was reading *Farewell My Lovely* and *The Big Sleep*. She was a big fan of Raymond Chandler and Dashiel Hammett and Perry Mason and Ellery Queen ... from there I went on to read all the Conan Doyle, Sherlock Holmes. I passed the eleven-plus in 1957. [At that time] there was a huge number of children and no places in Catholic grammar schools ... Like many people my father came back from the Second World War and nine months later a child was born. My father didn't want me to go to a Jesuit school, he'd been beaten by Jesuits. I had tremendous support from my parents; I didn't have their knowledge 'cause it wasn't given to them because of the times in which they were born and brought up. My mother passed the eleven-plus but because her mother was required to get a uniform, shoes ... for no fault of their own, they weren't educated; but they were both very intelligent.

'I didn't have a [grammar school] place unless I went to Widnes Wade Deacon, about forty or fifty of us were bussed in every day from Huyton. Nothing changes, we all thought the lads from Widnes and Warrington were thick and they all thought we were robbers and scallywags because we were from Liverpool as far as they were concerned. I didn't by any stretch of the imagination have anything resembling an academic career, I was always bottom of the class until I was fourteen when a teacher called Trevor Williams, who was born and brought up in Bootle and then went to university and got an honours degree in English Literature, arrived at our school, and he spoke like we all spoke. He had this passion and love of literature and it was a tremendous boost. Finally after all those barren years, somebody was talking to me about something that I knew that I loved. He was talking not necessarily in the same language but in the same dialect. It sounds inward looking, but we had teachers who'd condemn you by where you'd come from. He was a man who'd come through all that, he was a huge influence on me, I owe an awful lot to him. He introduced me to Steinbeck, to Orwell and to Hemmingway and Graham Greene and all those great writers. I owe a tremendous debt to Trevor, you can't do it on your own. I had the love and support of my parents, when I went to Padgate teacher training college in Warrington. There was a guy there, Lewis Britton, and he was the complete opposite of Trevor Williams, a total academic, very middle class and educated and eccentric and slightly daft. Him and his wife and six children were wardens of the hostel we were in. I tried to introduce them to Bob Dylan and he tried to introduce me to T.S. Eliot and there was a meeting of slightly mad minds ...

'In the forties and fifties we were still a big sailing city and facing west, to America. One of the things about Liverpool at the time was everyone knew someone, family or friend in the merchant navy who went over to New York ... I knew this guy called John Sloan, and his dad came back – this was 1956, '57, '58, with Chuck Berry, Bo Diddley, Little Richard and Elvis Presley and no-one had ever heard stuff like this. I love rock'n'roll and rhythm'n'blues and I don't think if you were born in Hemel Hempstead you got rhythm'n'blues like we did. I'm probably the only person in Liverpool a similar age to the Beatles who claims never to have met any of the Beatles. It was one shilling and threepence to get into the Cavern at lunchtime and get a bowl of soup, and sometimes you'd sag off because a really good band would be on, so I did see the Beatles when Cilla Black was the cloakroom attendant. I remember the first time I saw Brian and Roger and Adrian in '68 or '69, we went to see them at the Liverpool Everyman and I thought Patten and McGough brilliantly funny and I was immensely jealous. By the time I saw them they were well established, I was always the late developer.'

Bleasdale found his first voice in 1968: 'My own voice, the Scully character, was the voices of all the characters I'd grown up with, the scallywags and all the decent people who came from Huyton.' It was another two years until he had enough confidence to try to find an audience for his work. By then he was preparing to leave the UK to take up a teaching post in the Gilbert and Ellice Islands in the Western Pacific the following spring:

'My wife and I got married on Boxing Day 1970 and came back from honeymoon, it was New Year's Eve about seven o'clock, I went down to Radio Merseyside, I gave the receptionist this envelope with my name and address on it and seven short stories inside and said if there's anyone here who might want to read these ... I didn't have any copies.'

It was some weeks before he heard anything.

'The head of Radio Merseyside had a big box full of stuff like I'd written and he said to this kid straight out of university, "Go through that lot," and he was looking through them in despair (I still do this because every so often you find a gem) and about half way down he found my work. I was working in Farnborough in Hampshire at the time, three weeks away from going away. Just before we flew out, a bloke in Radio Merseyside rang my mother. Of course straight away she could see the Nobel Prize ...'

Bleasdale was invited to read his stories on air, a remarkable opportunity, but with no car and absolutely no money for travel, he had to refuse. Then the head of Radio Merseyside rang him and said, 'OK you can hire a car for one day and get the petrol.' He hired a car for thirteen pounds fifteen shillings, got up at six o'clock and drove all the way to Liverpool and read out his short stories.
Three of the stories were Scully stories.

'That day a woman called Barbara McDonald who worked for Radio Manchester and also for Radio Four and Jim Walker, a producer from *World in Action* were in Liverpool. They put the radio on, heard one of my Scully stories and rang Radio Merseyside and said, "We don't know who this bloke was but he's really, really good and must keep going."'

Bleasdale met McDonald and Walker in Manchester before he went away. Their encouragement convinced him to keep writing while he was away teaching in the Gilbert and Ellice Islands.

'I loved teaching there, the Polynesian kids were just fantastic, but school finished at quarter to one 'cause it was so hot. Everyone else went sailing or fishing or just got drunk but I wasn't interested in any of them then, so I started to write my first Scully novel; I wrote about the back streets of Huyton on a tropical Pacific island. I was lucky, by

1975 I'd got my first novel published and then I got my first television play accepted by a guy called Barry Hanshaw, who phoned me up and said, "We don't think this is very good but there's something there somewhere so we'll do it." Those days are over now, you know. Barry reckoned there was something there and he gave me a director called Les Blair who worked with improvisation and Les Blair educated me too, in his way. It was only a half-hour play for BBC Birmingham but it had Alison Steadman. A proper education is so important, not just to get your O level but for the world, the life, the job that you do.

'Then I was offered a film by BBC Birmingham and I realized that anyone who walked the streets of Liverpool in the mid to late seventies or read the *Guardian* knew that unemployment was going to be the biggest political question of the time and that it was going to affect the people on the streets, the craftsmen, the workers, the tradesmen. I wrote the original *Black Stuff*, and it was at that time when I found more voices than the one I already had. This was mainly because I was working in the theatre as well with a wonderful woman called Caroline Smith who ran the Playhouse Upstairs. She took me to Manchester in 1975 and because it was a community theatre, the university theatre in Manchester (the Contact Theatre), I had to find more voices, other voices than the Liverpool voice I already had. I wrote five stage plays for her, all of them were not remotely Liverpool voices, they were Lancashire or Manchester. Caroline was a great help to me; she taught me everything: she taught me theatre manners, she taught me how to approach actors and directors, how to approach work, how to approach an audience and she played an equally important part to Trevor and Lewis. They were there when I didn't know what I was doing, when I was beginning to know what I was doing. She made me realize exactly what I had to do and how important that was. I use the word manners deliberately, there's no point in shouting and screaming and howling at people, it doesn't achieve anything. Caroline was wonderful about the mechanics of theatre; I always lacked the mechanics. So basically I served an apprenticeship under Caroline. I wrote five plays for her, I had a great company of actors; lots of the actors I worked with at the Contact Theatre I worked with for many years afterwards.

'I had considerable success in the north-west and elsewhere with the plays, but I loved writing for television immediately. I knew novels 'cause I read them all my life since I was seven, and I knew cinema because me Nana used to take me to the pictures, and I went the pictures with me Mum and Dad all the time, so I loved film and I loved books.

I never set foot in a theatre until I was nineteen. I went to the Theatre in the Round in Stoke and thought, "Is this what it's like?" 'cause I'd seen Brian Rix farces on the telly at Christmas with what I now know is proscenium arch, and actually I saw a very good production of Pinter's *Homecoming*. I did get excited by theatre but in my heart of hearts I knew instinctively I could write film because that's what I knew. Film and television is what I watched with my Mum and Dad (Dad worked seven days a week and did murderous shifts), I watched the television, watched the films and read books, I never went the theatre, so when I got to write television it was something that I fully instictively understood.'

In the mid-1980s, Bleasdale and Willy Russell took up residency as artistic directors at the Liverpool Playhouse; for some critics, the two writers epitomized the 'voice' of Liverpool at that time.

'I'd just done *Boys from the Blackstuff*, *Having a Ball* was a big success; Willy Russell had just done *John, Paul, George, Ringo and Bert* and *Educating Rita* and *Blood Brothers* came out. We were all identified with the Playhouse success but actually we didn't deserve to be because Chris Bond and Bill Morison did the day-to-day stuff and that was agreed. Basically they put the shifts in and we put the shifts in at home writing plays, that's what happened. Willy and I are contrasting human beings and very different writers. He writes about escape and I write about staying where you are and going mad, and I think by and large Willy gets it right, better to escape than go mad. I've got a lousy eye, I'd never be a director, I don't see things but I hear things and I hear them instinctively and lock them away. I really don't see things. My wife Julie sometimes changes things around in the house but I don't notice, I say to her when did you do that? But I hear things, and I kind of like collect them, it's not something I ever developed, it's just something that's there. I find rhythm. I'm no good on the dance floor but I always find rhythm when I go to the typewriter, it's a natural thing, it's a bit like Kenny Dalglish being able to turn and swivel in the six-yard box … If you told him he had to do that on film, he wouldn't be able to do it. I've seen Kenny Dalglish trying to be natural taking a penalty shot on film and he stubbed his foot four times because he had to think about it; for him in his situation you don't have to think and you just rely on what is there, what your natural ability is. So no eye but an ear; I never worry about character and speech, what I worry about are the things I'm no good at like me eyes, the visual side of writing and the plot, these are things I work at the most 'cause I know they're my weaknesses. I worry terribly about getting a visual image that's worth seeing on film because otherwise, do it on the radio. I worry about plot, I'm not good at crosswords or puzzles or jigsaws, I don't have that, so I have to really, really work hard at that, worry about that. I go through endless drafts trying to make a plot.

'After *Boys from the Blackstuff*, *Scully* and *The Monocled Mutineer*, I wanted to hide away for a while. I thought, for want of a better expression, I'd got a fourth gear with that work and I knew that maybe there was a fifth gear knocking about so I wanted to get it but I didn't want to do it in public 'cause I thought I might fall flat on my face. So from 1985 to 1990 I hid away completely. I did it for two reasons, one a creative reason, I started writing what became *GBH*, the great British holiday, the great British novel. I wrote it as a novel and I got over two thousand pages and thought that I was only half way through and I did think the great British public wouldn't want to read a four-thousand-page novel by me; Jeffrey Archer maybe, but not me. The other reason was because our oldest boy became very ill, physically ill, he developed epilepsy. He's completely recovered now and is in excellent shape but it was an extremely traumatic time in our lives and so I disappeared and ran away upstairs. I was always at home but sometimes I was lost in myself, pretty selfish really, you come downstairs and have your tea but you're still upstairs writing. So I spent those years trying to make sure he was OK and also trying to find something that was outside of what I understood. I understood the *Boys from the Blackstuff* and I understood *Scully*; my grandfather died in the First World War so I understood *The Monocled Mutineer*. We have a letter in my family from grandfather George that says, "I know I'm going into battle and I know I'm not going to survive and the child that you're carrying, if it's a boy child, I'd like you to call him George." I got accused and attacked for being a Marxist millionaire who was working for Russia in the *Daily Mail*, they thought I had some kind of political manifesto but actually in the book that is published of *The Monocled Mutineer* the dedication is to my father, "To my father who never had a father", so that was why I wrote it, that's where I was coming from.

'I knew when I was writing *GBH* that fundamentalism was going to be the big issue. Militant has died and all that politics is gone now but what I knew, like what I knew about how unemployment would be a severe and dreadful problem for the working classes of this city, any city in the eighties some years before, you could see it in the manner in which Militant, whose political philosophy I don't have a great deal of argument with, but the manner in which they conducted themselves. It was grievous and vile and unpleasant and that was just the tip of this enormous iceberg ... it drives me. I didn't vote till I was thirty-eight and I never marched in my life until February 2003 with the Iraqi war, all our family marched. I'm not a marcher but I knew that was one of the most grievous mistakes of any century. The whole argument in *GBH* is centred on the Michael Palin/Jim Nelson speech at the end of *GBH* when he says to that crowd and mob, "Why don't you read more than one book, read two books three books, go to the library, join the library don't just read the one book and say that's the book for me." Unfortunately it seems to me that these people in positions of the power in the world now have only read the one book, in fact I don't think Bush has read any books!

'I wrote the beginning of *Boys* and *GBH* in a blind fury about what was happening. *Boys* I started and completed writing during the Callaghan government but I certainly wrote *GBH* through the Thatcher government and through the Militant years in Liverpool. I wept with anger, then lost interest in anger and found drama and I think that Dickens did the same. Dickens wrote the start of *Oliver Twist* in a blind fury. When I was asked by ITV to do *Oliver Twist* I was more than half way through writing *Running Scared* for the BBC. Saying yes could well have been one of the biggest mistakes of my life. I decided to stop *Running Scared* thinking that nothing would change, the people in position of power at the BBC wouldn't change, that our society wouldn't change that much because it was pretty dreadful. I thought I would never be asked to write a Dickens ever again. It was my teacher at school who told me about Dickens; *Oliver Twist* was one of those books that was on the way through to finding Steinbeck and Orwell. I said, "Yes, I'll do it," and basically what happened is that I got really really scared and thought what am doing? I spent three months not having the courage to get into the same playground as Charles Dickens, let alone pretend that I was *in* the same playground as Charles Dickens, as every great playwright that's ever lived. The only way I could actually approach it was to try and write ... Because I always wanted to know how Oliver Twist's mother really got pregnant and there's one line that said Oliver Twist's father went to Rome and died. His first wife was in the city at the same time and he leaves that up to you and I thought, "S—, she murdered him!" Whether he ever realized, I don't think he did, but I thought, "Hello, there's a clue," so I wrote the back-story to give me the confidence to start with Dickens. So as you know the first two hours don't exist except in my imagination and one line of Chapter 34. The people from ITV read it and really liked it so it gave me the confidence to try and get into the big boys' playground for a little while. But the other reason I wanted to write it that much is much more important … our eldest boy's illness. I wanted to write about epilepsy but I didn't want to write about it in that kind of socio-political play for today, "My son's suffering from epilepsy, he's fallen down in the street and the police think he's drugged" and all that, I didn't want to do that. When I read *Oliver Twist* I realized that Monks, although it's never spelled out, has falling down fits, and I thought, "Oliver's half-brother is an epileptic," and that's why I created Monks from a very vague and not particularly well-drawn character. I created Monks, Marc Warren's character and his mother, Lindsay Duncan's character, they don't really exist like but it gave me that opportunity. I guess I was exorcising my ghosts and terrors yet again.

'I did come back to Liverpool … while I was doing *Jake's Progress*, *Melissa* and *Oliver Twist*, I was working on *Running Scared*. What I wanted to do was *Boys from the Blackstuff* came out in 1981, *GBH* in 1991; I wrote a series the length of *GBH* (longer than *Boys*) between 1996 and 2001 that would basically be going back ten years and taking the pulse of the nation. At the time the BBC were unbelievably running scared, they kept trying to cut it and cut it and in the end they took me down from the length I wanted it to be … How I try to explain it is, at the moment I'm just over fourteen stone, my ideal weight is thirteen stone; if I exercise and go on a diet and lose weight, I get to my fighting weight, which is thirteen stone. What the BBC wanted to do was get me down to eleven and a half stone, so the only way to do that is to take one of my legs off. And a one-legged boxer has never won a fight. I'll take the fat, I'll strip everything out of it but don't take the bones away from me. It was murder, it was probably the most heartbreaking time in my what's laughingly been described as a career. It was a huge loss to me. I'd like to think it's due to the way British television has developed but there again there are people who've had success who are extremely talented so I don't know, I doubt it. I always had the most tremendous support from Barry Hanson and David Rose and Michael Wearing in the seventies, in the eighties I had great support from Richard Broke and Les Chatfield and various people; then in the nineties I went to heaven when Michael Grade, John Willis and Peter Ansorge were at Channel 4. By the time I completed *Running Scared* the people who bought me back to the BBC, Peter Salmon and Tessa Ross, they'd both left their jobs and it was a case of new people wanting to prove themselves and not pick up other people's work.'

In answer to the question, 'Is there something identifiable amongst Liverpool dramatists as a Liverpool style?', Bleasdale paused.

'Yes, I think … there's clearly obvious lyricism and love of words of the Irish and the misery of the Welsh and the fact we were a city, a famous and rich and successful city that was built on casual labour and people became very casual about their labour. Even in my time I remember my uncle who worked on the docks in the Dingle, he would go down with six thousand men to the pen on the south docks and there'd only be six hundred jobs so five thousand four hundred men would walk back up the hill and they'd go and have the *craic* and they'd talk. I think Liverpool became not a literate city but a very articulate city, it became dependent upon words … If you listen, it's very interesting. John Lennon's a classic example of the Liverpool voice in that you always go in sharp and fast because you want to make your point, you break into a conversation then it tails away, it withers, he's made his point and it's quite witty, then he quietens down. I always think of Lennon when I think of Liverpool for many reasons, it's that kind of "get in there" fast and I think that's very much how people talk … It's no surprise that dialogue is my great strength because I've listened to these people all me life. I don't think that people like Willy and myself and Jimmy McGovern or people like Stephen Butchard, who I think is a remarkable writer, we haven't got the same voice but I know we're listening to the same voices, we're listening to what our backgrounds and what our heritage is. We are a city that just likes to talk.'

13

'Culture Is Ordinary': The Legacy of the Scottie Road and Liverpool 8 Writers

Sandra Courtman

At a time when Liverpool's culture is being acknowledged and celebrated, we should ask whose culture and what sort of peoples have created the modern city of Liverpool. Arguably, it is the working-class ethos of the city that has contributed most significantly to the city's image and its growth. This is particularly noticeable in the wide attention given to a number of working-class voices that have emerged from the city in recent decades and gained national prominence. What has received less attention, however, are the writers' groups that have fostered some of these authors. It is the aim of this chapter to address this. Drawing on material from the archives of the Federation of Working-Class Writers and Community Publishers (FWWCP), and on correspondence and interviews with founding members, I will explore the precise reasons for the inception of one of these groups, Scotland Road Writers (Scottie Road), and its ability over two decades to bridge Liverpool's race/class divide.

In 1958 Raymond Williams published 'Culture Is Ordinary' in which he argues that the need to create, record and share experience is a common impulse.[1] Williams restores the notion of cultural growth as being intrinsic to all groups, not just the middle class or those with a university education. He is helping us to recognize an important thesis that underpins this chapter: working-class people express their own

---

1 'Culture is ordinary: that is the first fact. Every human society has its own shape, its own purposes, its own meanings. Every human society expresses these, in institutions, and in arts and learning. The making of a society is the finding of common meanings and directions, and its growth is an active debate and amendment under the pressures of experience, contact, and discovery, writing themselves into the land' (Raymond Williams, *Resources of Hope* [London: MacGibbon & Kee, 1958], p. 75).

forms of cultural and political growth in various creative and dynamic ways and their expression can to be driven by an all-too-often bitter life experience.

In June 2000 I visited the Phoenix Adult Education Centre in Liverpool 8 to meet with founding members of Scotland Road Writers. I had heard that the writers' group had forged an alliance between activists and black migrants who joined Scottie Road in the early 1970s. I wanted to explore how, in a city with a reputation for social division, recent black arrivals to Liverpool joined with descendants of Irish immigrants to create a forum for creative expression. This alliance between black and white working class in Liverpool might be considered unusual given the city's troubled history of racial tension. In 2000, the same year as my visit, Caryl Phillips published *The Atlantic Sound*, in which he described his journeys within the Atlantic slave trade 'triangle' of the Caribbean, Britain and North America. Writing of a Liverpool with entrenched attitudes to its black constituents, Phillips records how Stephen, a young black Liverpudlian, told him: 'It's a segregated city. The whites have their bit and we have our bit, and that's it. Which is weird for a place which has one of the most multicultural histories of any town in Britain.'[2] When Phillips spends the morning strolling through Liverpool visiting cafés and landmark buildings, he realizes: 'I have not encountered a single black person. Where on earth is Liverpool's black population?'[3] A black resident reinforces this point in his observation, 'Every time I go into the city centre it never ceases to amaze me. I don't see black faces working in the department stores. I don't see anybody looking like me.'[4]

I need to draw attention to these observations because this paradox was also evident on my visit to Liverpool 8. Arriving at a community centre in one of the poorest parts of the city, I expected to see a type of ethnic mix that I was familiar with in Birmingham, Sheffield and Manchester. However, there were no black or Asian faces, and our discussion about this historical moment of class and race solidarity took place in an all-white group. When I asked about this, there were feelings that the racial divide in Liverpool was intractable. This chapter, then, explores this paradox in relation to a group of dynamic working-

2   Caryl Phillips, *The Atlantic Sound* (London: Faber, 2000), p. 79.
3   Phillips, *The Atlantic Sound*, p. 85.
4   'Racism? It's Endemic Here', *The Observer*, 4 December 2005, *Guardian* online archive, http://www.guardian.co.uk/race/story/0,,1555305,00html. Accessed 17 July 2006.

class writers from the Caribbean, South Asia and Africa and their meeting with a community of much earlier Irish immigrants. The areas around Scotland Road had provided a home for the many starving Irish immigrants who arrived in Liverpool in the early nineteenth century. As John Belchem explains: 'By 1870 there were 18 Catholic parishes in Liverpool served by 64 priests; by 1914 the number of parishes had risen to 24 of which 16 were clustered in the Scotland, Vauxhall and Everton areas.'[5] This is a meeting of two specific histories of settlement and migrant labour. Even given these differences, black and Irish people shared the experience of poverty in the 1970s and recognized a need for expression.

In its broader context, Scottie Road was not unique in its manifesto for political and cultural change. The group was instrumental in the formation of the FWWCP (in existence since 1976 and now an international organization of community writers). As a national network they were able to bid for funding to create opportunities for writers to develop their literacy and creative talent. The literacy projects of the FWWCP were inspired by Paolo Freire (1921–97), a Brazilian educationalist who published *Pedagogy of the Oppressed* in 1972. Freire's doctrine teaches that the process of liberation begins with the oppressed first *speaking* then *writing* his or her own words.[6] The FWWCP embraced his idea that it was important to make a 'safe' space for working-class writers, such as those in the Scotland Road area. Therefore the group encouraged the racially and ethnically excluded to meet and write about a liminal existence where, as Phillips recognizes, 'the line between creativity and self-destruction is etched vaguely on the sand'.[7]

What community writing groups publish is often immediately undervalued in conventional literary terms. A good example of this is the Manchester-based *Voices*, in which contributions from the Scottie Road Group were published in the 1970s. When it came to applying for Arts Council Funding, the magazine was subjected to a literary scrutiny it had never anticipated. As Blake Morrison wrote in his unpublished report to the Arts Council in 1980:

5 Frank Boyce, 'From Victorian "Little Ireland" to Heritage Trail: Catholicism, Community and Change in Liverpool's Docklands', cited in John Belchem, *Merseypride: Essays in Liverpool Exceptionalism* (Liverpool: Liverpool University Press, rev. edn 2006), p. 110.
6 Paolo Friere, *Pegagogy of the Oppressed*, trans. Myra Bergman Ramos (London: Penguin, 1996).
7 Phillips, *The Atlantic Sound*, p. 80.

The weakness of the magazine had been to print bad poems and articles simply because they express 'good', i.e. politically acceptable, opinions: shallow and overt propagandising has been more common than work of literary merit .... I noticed a definite improvement both in the contributions to, and the production of *Voices* between the first issue of 1975 and the recent *Voices* 20 [1980].[8]

In his influential work connecting social class and aesthetic taste, *Distinction: A Social Critique of the Judgement of Taste* (1979), Pierre Bourdieu explains how such judgements recognize the emergence of 'literary merit'. Part of the process identifies aesthetic achievement as having a distance from the realities of everyday existence: 'The pure aesthetic is rooted in an ethic, or rather, an ethos of elective distance from the necessities of the natural and social world.'[9] The Scottie Road Group and other founding member groups of the FWWCP were never concerned with an objective standard of 'literary merit' divorced from politics. On the contrary, they formed because they *needed* to write about the material realities of their everyday struggles. When they made the decision to seek funding from the Arts Council, it inevitably brought them into conflict with establishment rubrics of literary value. Community-published reminiscences are not often of interest to literary critics (although they are to historians), on the grounds that the rough form of the work often gives them little currency outside the world of their author and an immediate readership. When the FWWCP initially sought funding from the Arts Council in 1976, there was a fierce debate about the organization's relationship to notions of 'literature'. At the time of the funding bid, Jim McGuigan was engaged in research for his thesis 'The State and Serious Writing: Arts Council Intervention in the English Literary Field'. McGuigan's presence at the Arts Council meeting led him to conclude: 'The circularity of the discourse of "serious" writing is quite dizzying. It is virtually impossible to interrupt this interplay of shared and unexamined assumptions without calling the whole notion into question.'[10]

---

8   Blake Morrison, cited in the editorial of *Voices* 22, Autumn 1980.

9   Pierre Bourdieu, 'Distinction: A Social Critique of the Judgement of Taste' (1979), in Vincent Leitch *et al.* (eds), *The Norton Anthology of Theory and Criticism* (London: W.W. Norton, 2001), p. 1813.

10 Jim McGuigan, 'The State and Serious Writing: Arts Council Intervention in the English Literary Field' (unpublished doctoral thesis, University of Leicester, 1984), p. 232.

The FWWCP opposed the Arts Council's assertion that the writing was parochial and should be funded as such through regional community arts projects. Melvyn Bragg, who chaired the Arts Council committee during the FWWCP's bid for funding, supported the application but only on the grounds that it might promote good reading habits: 'Apart from the chairman, the committee was entirely opposed to supporting the FWWCP in any way. Bragg said that he was not impressed with the writing but he did feel that the FWWCP was doing a potentially good job in encouraging working-class people to read literature.'[11] The Arts Council's circular argument on funding the FWWCP illustrates that there are irresolvable difficulties in attempting to deal with community publications as if they were mainstream writing.

We might look to the origins of working-class writers' groups formed in the 1970s as a response to material deprivations and to their members' growing sense of disaffection. This disaffection has its historical roots in Liverpool's relationship with both its black population and its Irish settlers and produces a need for a safe space to express frustration, anger and loneliness. The Scottie Road writers' group acts as a powerful conduit for this disaffection. The writing they produced can give us an insight into a long history of conflict arising from the different interests held by political and racial groups. Their debates were unequivocally political and arise out of the shared meanings of extreme poverty and feelings of isolation. For the Scottie Road group, it was a sense of powerlessness brought about by poor housing and rent increases that brought people together initially.

Whilst poor people might find themselves unavoidably thrown together by their circumstances, an alliance between black and white working-class people is not usually emphasized in histories of the 1970s. Ron Ramdin's study, *The Making of the Black Working Class in Britain*, writes of the division between the state and black youth during the period;[12] and in 1981 television viewers became familiar with media images of angry black youth in such areas as Toxteth facing riot police. Liverpool was constructed in the national imagination as a war zone.

11 McGuigan, 'The State and Serious Writing', p. 220. McGuigan was an observer at Arts Council meetings to determine funding and reveals these in a chapter which goes into some detail on the Federation's bid for funds and the committee's (chaired by Melvyn Bragg) response (pp. 223–44).
12 Ron Ramdin, *The Making of the Black Working Class in Britain* (Aldershot: Wildwood, 1987).

Under Thatcherite policies, it became a place where 'the former grand industrial city of the north, was succumbing to the prevailing blight of violence, unemployment, poverty and depression at a rate that was far in excess of other British cities'.[13]

When Caryl Phillips writes of his feeling that Liverpool has always been an inhospitable place for black visitors, he is drawing on research into its treatment of the human cargo of the slave trade. He is also drawing on some bitter personal experience. As a supporter of Leeds United football club he often visited the city as a teenager. When he tried to strike up a conversation with Everton fans, he was told to 'Fuck off! We're Scousers and we don't talk to niggers.'[14] In the 1970s, the football terraces were a register of unmediated prejudice and a place where racist feelings went unchecked. Chanting directed towards Liverpool's black football players, as for example in 'He's black, he's scouse, he will rob your fucking house,' homogenizes Liverpool's diverse ethnic and religious communities in an image of working class poverty where black immigrants, white Irish Catholic (Scousers) blend to become irredeemably criminal.[15] Ironically, this 'outsider's' chant is ignorant of Diane Frost's assertion that 'the notion of "Scouseness" was, and still is, something Black Liverpudlians are excluded from since to be "Scouse" is to be white and working class'.[16]

The Scottie Road group provided a counter-culture to this historical trend of racial division. The alliance of black writers and a settled white population relied on a shared experience of cultural isolation and exclusion. Liverpool's Irish migrant population had from the nineteenth century been ghettoized and their presence within the city constructed within a discourse of criminality and immorality that strikes a chord with contemporary reports from the West Indies. James Froude, for example, who visited Barbados in 1888, reported that African Caribbean people 'sin only as animals', and described the Irish as 'more like tribes of squalid apes than human beings'.[17] In 1881, Edward Augustus Freeman trav-

13 Phillips, *The Atlantic Sound*, p. 77.

14 Phillips, *The Atlantic Sound*, p. 77.

15 I heard of this football chant from prisoner-students from Liverpool when I was teaching in the education department of HMP Sudbury, Derbyshire.

16 Diane Frost cited in Belchem, *Merseypride*, p. 64.

17 James Froude, 'The English in the West Indies: or The Bow of Ulysses', in Elleke Boehmer, *Empire Writing: An Anthology of Colonial Literature* (Oxford: Oxford University Press), p. 114; and in Robert Winder, *Bloody Foreigners: The Story of Immigration to Britain* (London: Little, Brown, 2004), p. 152.

elled to America and wrote: 'This would be a grand land if only every Irishman would kill a Negro, and be hanged for it.'[18] Here Irish and Negro are lumped together as 'the problem' and expected to involve each other in the solution. Of course, the homogenization of black and Irish immigrants as uneducated, immoral and lawless belies the richness and diversity of their contribution to culture. In *Bloody Foreigners*, Robert Winder reminds us:

It has long been all too easy to refer to 'the Irish' when we mean only 'the Irish poor'. It is as if the successful Irish, the witty Irish, the ambitious Irish, the entrepreneurial Irish, the thrifty Irish do not count, truly as Irish. One of the side-effects of such talk is to decorate the whole idea of immigration with associations of degradation and cruelty.[19]

The converse is more usual in that it is an immigrant population that enriches cultural growth. It was the sheer number of West Indian arrivals in the post-1948 era that has helped to create post-colonial/multicultural Britain. This generation has come to be known as the Windrush generation after the first of many ships, the SS *Empire Windrush*, docked at Tilbury in 1948 with 492 West Indian hopefuls on board. The arrival of West Indians impacted profoundly on post-war British music, theatre, comedy, literature and style. Post-colonial Britain is vibrant because of the resilience and creativity of its various immigrants. When it comes to Liverpool, however, its cultural relationship to its black and Irish population seems to be complicated by patterns of much earlier relations with migrant labour. Liverpool had considerable importance as a slave port, however, and according to John Belchem it is 'now one of the least ethnically diverse of British cities with small numbers of the post-1945 "new commonwealth" migrants'.[20]

The Scottie Road Writers first met in 1973. Initially the group was convened by David Evans, an action/research lecturer in Liverpool University's Institute of Extension Studies with a brief to work in inner cities. David Evans was born in Queenstown, South Africa, and as a white activist in the 1960s was imprisoned for five years by the apartheid

18 Cited in Winder, *Bloody Foreigners*, p. 158.
19 Winder, *Bloody Foreigners*, p. 163.
20 Belchem, *Merseypride*, p. xxvii.

government. After being placed under house arrest, he left South Africa for England. He had been running a free literature class in Scottie Road when Frank Keelan, an unemployed electrician and chair of the Heriot Street Tenants' Association, approached him to form a writers' group. David Evans came to Scottie Road as a published fiction writer with a background in journalism. This experience would prove valuable as he began to encourage writers and help them bring about change in the community. Subsequently, he went on to co-found a separate group in Toxteth called Liverpool 8.

One of the founder members of Scottie Road, Barbara Shane, remembers how David Evans helped them to focus their writing: '[It was] about writing leaflets, about expressing the discontent of his community. So within a matter of months, people were actually comparing their writing around the injustices of the Fair Rents Act, about the shoddy housing we had.'[21]

The group were careful not to promote a party political line but rather 'hoped that the whole life around Scottie Road would come out in the writing'. Initially, there was little choice but to finance their own publications, collecting small contributions that were reimbursed when copies were printed and sold. The 1975 issue of *Voices* began its editorial with the explanation that 'with an utterly empty purse and an appeal for £150' they were eventually able to print the names of people and the sums that had made it possible. Given that many of the contributors were struggling financially, even a relatively small investment indicated the value that the community placed on seeing their work published and distributed more widely.

Undoubtedly, the courage and strength of the group would go on to facilitate alliances between black and white writers. The fact that the workshop was held in a staunchly white Catholic area of Liverpool is significant because the group gave readings, taking writers into pubs where they might not have been accepted as individuals. This area has a long history of intolerance that Jimmy McGovern, a one-time member of the group, and Stephen Frears explore in their film set in Liverpool in the 1930s. *Liam* (2000) traces the consequences of unemployment to reveal how powerlessness and despair fuel racism and sectarianism. Community relations in the 1970s were no less complex and David

21 Barbara Shane and Barbara Blanche, discussion with founding members of 'Scottie Road' writers' group, Phoenix Adult Education Centre, Liverpool 8, 28 June 2000. All further citations refer to this meeting.

Evans questions whether Scottie Road 'was a hotbed of aggressive racism. That was not my experience of it, though obviously there was both racism and ignorance about race.'[22]

Barbara Blanche remembers how public readings entailed a personal risk:

> We actually went into the local pubs with the writers' workshop and Jimmy McGovern would stand up and read his latest short story to a whole audience of people and some people would stop playing pool and wonder what they were listening to. And others would send pool cues [whizzing] over our heads.

She goes on to relate how black writers were inspired by these readings:

> And the other amazing thing was that we had some black writers came to Scotland Road because they didn't have anywhere else to go. We worked with them to eventually establish their own Liverpool 8 writers' workshop ... In those days, and it still is, Scotland Road was a very white Catholic community. And there was no tolerance for anybody other than, you know, local white Catholics.

These performances might act as more than inspiration; they could also establish a sense of solidarity for marginalized people:

> We had to utilize our position in that community to defend them [black writers] to come in and do those [readings]. Because if they had come in without a linkage ... if that's the right word, well, they just wouldn't have come into that community. Never the twain will meet.

David Evans does not recall any black writers formally joining the Scottie Road group but writes of how it provided the catalyst for the Liverpool 8 group in Toxteth:

> What happened was that Scottie's activities and first publication were noted by Dorothy Kuya, a black working class woman and community activist attached to the Community Relations Council. In 1975 she got hold of me and said that she was getting demands for a writers' workshop in Liverpool 8 (Toxteth). Together we started a group

---

22 David Evans, e-mail to the author, 3 February 2007.

which was multi-ethnic, including members of the Windrush generation and some Liverpool-born black people with Caribbean and African ancestors, some mixed heritage people, an Asian woman and one or two whites.

It's true that in time L8 and Scottie workshops did meet in Scotland Road, a wonderful occasion in which much in common was found and an event which preluded joint readings and participation in the Federation. The two groups remained distinct however, though whites came into the L8 group.[23]

Dorothy Kuya and her sister Norma Igbesoko founded Liverpool 8 with contributions from Cheryl Dudt, of Asian descent, and Liverpool-born black, Levi Tafari, now one of Britain's leading dub poets. Liverpool 8 also included Jamaicans, such as Henry Dixon, Lloyd Thomas and Hugh White, who drew Tommy Doyle of Scottie Road into anti-racist campaigning.[24] This was a dynamic moment in the history of Liverpool's race relations, showing that creative expression could unite and challenge people. The activities of Liverpool 8 are also part a cultural shift in the 1970s towards an autonomous black British identity of which Stuart Hall can write:

Young black people in London today are marginalized, fragmented, unenfranchised, disadvantaged, and dispersed. And yet, they look as if they *own* the territory ... what is it about that long discovery–rediscovery of identity among blacks in this migrant situation which allows them to lay a kind of *claim* to certain parts of the earth which aren't theirs with quiet certainty?[25]

Liverpool 8's Levi Tafari is a prime example of how this territorial confidence has also evolved outside of the metropolis, and Tafari has praised the part that Liverpool 8 played in giving him the strength to write. Liverpool writers and performers have been instrumental in claiming a new cultural space for black Britons so that performers like Tafari and Birmingham's Benjamin Zephaniah are now valued as the new urban griots. Tafari connects this experience with poets on the other side of the Black Atlantic:

23 David Evans, e-mail to the author, 3 February 2007.
24 David Evans, e-mail to the author, 3 February 2007.
25 Stuart Hall cited in Beth Sarah Wright, 'Dub Poet Lekka Mi', in Kwesi Owusu (ed.), *Black British Culture and Society* (London: Routledge, 2000), p. 275.

Cos we might be living inna a different country
But dhe struggle is dhe same where ever we may be …
Word Sound and Power come to set we free! Set we free![26]

This confidence was born out of the cultural dynamism of the early 1970s. Scottie Road and Liverpool 8 also led to an interest in drama which prompted Merseyside Arts and Liverpool University to fund playwriting workshops for working-class writers. Alan Bleasdale, Willie Russell and Bill Morrison were involved in encouraging new working-class talent through the playwriting workshops. Jimmy McGovern is the best known but not the only successful writer to emerge from that initiative. Work in and for the community included the Vauxy Theatre, originated by Chris Darwin in Scotland Road.[27] Barbara Shane explains:

> It was a time of turbulence but for us it was a time of hope. Things were moving. It was just after the sixties and there was all those student movements in Paris and all those activities. And people thought there could be change but [we] learned our hard lesson since.

Historically, a working-class culture has not been able to assume a standard of its members' literacy and therefore has promoted alternative means of expressing ideas and stories by means of an oral culture. Raymond Williams writes about how his Welsh working-class family were very accomplished in this respect:

> At home we met and made music, listened to it, recited and listened to poems, valued fine language. I have heard better music and better poems since; there is a world to draw on. But I know, from most ordinary experience, that the interest is there, the capacity is there.[28]

What emerges from Scottie Road, and other groups who later joined the FWWCP, is something that every community arts worker and prison educator encounters. Ordinary working people with a scant or non-existent literary education and few artistic pretensions write poetry, prose and life-writing having apparently had no literary role models and often with little or no encouragement from parents or teachers. These

---

26 Levi Tafari, 'Duboetry', cited in Wright, 'Dub Poet Lekka Mi', p. 286.
27 David Evans, e-mail to the author, 3 February 2007.
28 Williams, *Resources of Hope*, p. 77.

writers are part of a tradition of cultural expression firmly outside mainstream culture. Ken Worpole explains how in the early years of the FWWCP, the oral and the literary impacted on each other in creative, if non-standard, ways:

> ... a lot of work was very good because it was coming from that storytelling tradition, a very ordered rhythmical tradition. You had the kind of ballad tradition. All those kinds of things and it worked very well in a large setting but on paper it didn't look so good ... The way you negotiated with the Arts Council was through something called the book and a standard of literature and there were bound to be cultural misunderstandings.[29]

It was a tradition that was very strong in the Irish community. Barbara Shane remembers how her mother passed on her love of poetry:

> She was unlettered, she was unlearned but she liked poetry and she'd quote poetry to us all the time ... My eldest sisters they learned poetry by rote. So we got into the habit of thinking in poems, you know. And I thought, all of us have worked in factories, we have all worked in services – the image we are getting of ourselves is people who are stupid and thick and this is all we're fit for. But there is more to us than that. So we decided to take action in the field of education and one of the things that came out was Scotland Road writers' workshop because we knew people wrote, you know, even if they wouldn't admit it.

For people from this oral story-telling/political ballad tradition, moving from the oral to the written would sometimes involve secrecy. Barbara Shane remembers how, combined with 'a lot of political turbulence around Scotland Road', the need to write contributed to the beginnings of the group:

> That's why we started ... because it's not the part of the general ethos to write but as you go round you get to know people who drag a crumpled piece of paper out of their pockets with a poem on it. So we knew that there were people who were desperate to express themselves.

29 Author's interview with Ken Worpole, London, 28 June 1995.

For writers in this situation, what might be considered as 'odd' behaviour in terms of the class/cultural norm may even be considered an act of betrayal. This has both psychological and practical effects. Here is Barbara Shane again:

> There was an awful lot of overcrowding and the family group didn't want you to go away from the group on your own. In a sense they felt rejected and also there was no really, as you say, safe space – there was nowhere in the home that was sufficiently private.

In times of distress, Ken Worpole says, 'people do reach for the pen as much as they reach for the glass and that is quite interesting'.[30] But when they begin to bring private material into the public arena of the workshop and submit it for publication, there is a potential cost to their relationship within their family and community. He concludes:

> [There is always a] question of to what extent people can expose private fears and differences. I know when we started publishing at Centreprise, some of the early books created a lot of local controversy amongst families of people who had written. Other family members would come along and say, 'You shouldn't have written that. You shouldn't pull out skeletons in the cupboard.' You know … when people describe very graphic poverty, other family members coming along saying, 'You don't parade your poverty – hide it.'

Interestingly, in a recent interview about *The Street* (2006), Jimmy McGovern recognized the sensitivities of his local 'Scouse' community and set the series in Manchester where it would be less likely to reinforce a stereotype:

> It's actually set up here in Manchester but I had thoughts initially of a street off Kensington – that's Kensington, Merseyside, *not* Kensington, London! But there are always problems on Merseyside because if you portray a character on screen who's a thief, say, then you're compounding a stereotype. Our city is very sensitive about how Scousers are portrayed.[31]

30 Worpole, interview, 28 June 1995.
31 'The Street', interview with Jimmy McGovern for BBC Liverpool. http://www. bbc.co.uk/liverpool/content/articles/2006/02/20/200206_inside-out-street. Accessed 24 July 2006.

However, in terms of experiences that are normally kept within a closely knit community, McGovern is well known for his courage in drama-tizing material that many writers would regard as too sensitive – as seen in two films for television, *Hillsborough* (1996) and *Sunday* (2002).

As a member of the Scottie Road group in the 1970s, McGovern published some of his earliest pieces in *Voices*. The FWWCP archives suggest both how hard he has worked to become recognized as a writer and how much he still draws on work that allowed him to explore some of the social, religious and political motifs that would later come to distinguish his writing.

In 'Confession: 1958', published in *Voices* in 1979, he writes about experiences that would emerge again in his psychologically complex play *Priest* (1994), and in the film *Liam* (2000). The following extract was published when he was part of the Scottie Road writers' group. The story is written from a child's point of view where, in a stream of consciousness, he relates a terrified reaction to seeing his mother naked:

> He opened the door and heard the splashing of water in a bowl and the splashing of water on an oilcloth floor and the slapping of foot on a wet floor and he smelt the smell of Lifebuoy and cool air, all at the same time, and he saw his mam there naked with her head and neck flashing round to look at him through her hair. She was stooped over, drying herself, with the towel between her legs and her hair all wet and tatty and long and falling down nearly straight to her waist and he saw in a hot flash the other hair, all black and curly and he knew his mam was deformed and how terrible it was for him to see her and her deformity ...[32]

The child is tortured by the encounter but it is unavoidable because his mother lacks, as if to reinforce Barbara Shane's point, anywhere to wash in private. This experience is also depicted in *Liam* and indicates how important Scottie Road was to the writer's development.

By the 1980s this type of cultural activity would be considered an historical anomaly but would nevertheless have some residual effects. Thatcherite policies and post-modernity fragment communities rather than unite them through the search for the 'common meanings' of culture, religion and politics that Williams writes about in 'Culture Is

---

32 Jimmy McGovern, 'Confession: 1958', *Voices* 20, Autumn 1979, p. 33.

Ordinary'. McGovern has acknowledged his debt to another writer, Alan Bleasdale, who shows very powerfully how a Liverpool community fights to retain traditional working-class values when faced with the devastation of mass unemployment. In Bleasdale's cult television series *Boys from the Blackstuff* (1981) we see traditional values disappearing under the pressure of ideological change. The Rt Reverend David Sheppard, Anglican Bishop of Liverpool from 1975 to 1997, said about the series, 'It's about people with great gifts and abilities being robbed of the chance to use them.'[33] Bleasdale's blend of melodrama and humour illuminates the destruction of the humanity of characters who are not usually represented in mainstream culture. This enabled him to say something profound about the break-up of traditional communities on Merseyside. However, what people usually remember about the series, and what made it universally popular, is its sharp, warm and subversive sense of humour and a type of creative resilience that seems to be a distinctive and yet 'ordinary' part of Liverpool culture. Working-class writers, whether mainstream like Bleasdale and McGovern, or those that remain community published, teach us that there is a real cultural value in the representation of different types of experience. When I asked Ken Worpole what impact the FWWCP writers' groups might have had on mainstream culture, he was emphatic about its effects:

Oh I think it has had a tremendous impact. I really do. First I think it made people feel looser about forms. You can't imagine the rise of stand up comedy, the rise of oral poetry or story telling. It wouldn't have happened the way it did without these kinds of movements.[34]

Performance poetry and stand-up comedy are not the only legacies of this movement. We should not underestimate the importance of what David Evans calls the 'ripple effect':

Scotland Road and Liverpool 8 inspired a group of women on Cantril Farm housing estate to start their own workshop. Central to this was Maria O'Reilly whose mother was Liverpudlian and her father African. This kind of ripple effect resulted in other groups on Merseyside and was to lead to the Second Chance to Learn course installing

---

33 Bleasdale, 'Introduction', *Boys From the Black Stuff*, p. 15.
34 Worpole, interview, 28 June 1995.

a writers' workshop in a programme that was essentially social studies and history based.[35]

The influence of these examples on the community was pervasive, and undoubtedly influenced the introduction of creative writing courses into colleges and universities on Merseyside and elsewhere. It may also have inspired people like Scottie Road's Eddie Barrett to become a tutor. Currently creative writing is a major growth area, with increasing numbers of courses being offered at all levels up to PhD. We should value the part that Scottie Road and Liverpool 8 played in this movement, because, far from being partisan and parochial, their activities form part of a cultural shift in the 1970s that was able to put writing on the agenda for everyone and to move groups of writers (working class, immigrants, women) from the margins to the centre.

Acknowledgements

I am indebted to the people who gave generously of their time and who allowed me access to rare textual materials that made this research possible. With thanks in particular to Jimmy McGovern for permission to cite his work; and David Evans, convenor of Scottie Road, whose responses to an earlier draft enriched this research. I thank Barbara Blanche and Barbara Shane, founder members of Scottie Road Writers Group, who were willing to share their oral history of this group. Tim Diggles, Steve Oakley, Nick Pollard, Dorothy Blake, Roger Mills, Ken Worpole, Rebecca O'Rourke. I thank members of the Phoenix Adult Education Centre: Ritchie Hunter (tutor) and Changing Direction Group members – Lynn Richardson, Carol Connolly, Anne Slater, Edie Chalkey, Joyce Nimmo, Anne Greenall, Jean Knowles, Arthur F. Bowling, and Norma Lee – who were kind enough to take part in the discussion about working-class writing.

35 David Evans, e-mail to the author, 3 February 2007.

14

'I've Got a Theory about Scousers': Jimmy McGovern and Lynda La Plante

Philip Smith

In Jimmy McGovern's *The Lakes* (BBC, 1997–99), the central character, Danny Kavanagh, leaves home looking for work. His search takes him to the Lake District where he is interviewed for a job helping in the kitchens of the Ullswater Hotel. When questioned about his health he replies, 'I've got an infectious laugh.' The chef, realizing Danny is from Liverpool, counters: 'Think you're a comedian? ... I've got a theory about Scousers. You're all descended from the bastard children of slave owners, so you can't help it, sitting by while all the others do the work.' His words deliberately echo an earlier declaration by the hotel's owner: 'Do you want to hear my theory about Scousers? Bone idle. It's not your fault you understand, it's in your genes. You're all descended from the feckless Irish. Half starved, you get on a boat, you get as far as Liverpool and say, "Sod that, I'm not going any further, this'll do."' With this comic repetition, McGovern simultaneously foregrounds and defuses the locals' prejudice and, what is more, that of many of the series' viewers. By making Danny the most eloquent character in the series, he counters such familiar negative stereotypes with an equally familiar positive one: that of the garrulous Scouse rogue with the trademark patter who, when asked if Liverpool is rough, responds, 'Everywhere you go they stop you and ask you if you've got a weapon and if you say no they give you one to take in.'

The Lakes draws on McGovern's own experiences of employment in the Lake District as a young man, and these exchanges hint at a persistent, formal dynamic in his work. McGovern conducts a dialogue with the familiar and the customary and twists it into something new. It is a strategy which also helps define his relationship with genre, making it feel urgent rather than comfortable. As such it is productive to view

McGovern's writing alongside that of another television dramatist from Liverpool, Lynda La Plante. Both are prolific, both came to prominence in the early eighties, and both helped renew mainstream television drama by engaging with genre. But where McGovern's writing obviously bears the city's imprint, La Plante's, at least superficially, is defined by its absence.

Lynda La Plante grew up in Crosby, the daughter of a sales manager, and left Merseyside at the age of sixteen to train as an actor at RADA. Despite her assertion that 'Liverpool is still very important to me', the city rarely features in her writing.[1] Instead there is an emphasis on London, America and metropolitan female achievement which may, in part, be read as a flight from the world of the 'feckless' male Scouser referenced by McGovern in *The Lakes*. Frequently there is little exposition of the back story of La Plante's strong female protagonists. In an echo of the aspirational Thatcherism of the 1980s, it is where her characters are going, not where they come from, which is freighted with significance. This is first evident in *Widows* (ITV, 1983), La Plante's earliest work for television, which, despite its non-star cast and unknown author, was an extraordinary success, commanding over eleven million viewers.

Widows was conceived while La Plante was playing a prostitute in *The Gentle Touch* (ITV, 1980–84), and was born out of her frustration at being typecast in a range of similarly forgettable parts. The series was therefore a conscious attempt to expand the range of female roles in genre drama. As such its impact can still be felt today. High production values, the use of long lenses, and a 'neo-noir' lighting scheme which emphasizes shadow and contrast, manifest its aspirations to the cinematic. It opens with the attempted heist of a security van. As the van crosses Waterloo Bridge in London and enters an underpass, the robbery begins, only to unravel catastrophically. Brakes screech, cars crash and flames burst forth in an action sequence with a nod to Hollywood (undermined only by a continuity error in the positioning of one of the vehicles, which momentarily destroys the illusion of invisible editing). With this scene as a 'hook', *Widows* delivers on the genre promises of the action/crime series. But this pact with the audience is soon subverted. It appears the botched heist has left no survivors, so Dolly Rawlins (played by Ann Mitchell), the gang leader's widow, assembles

---

1   Quoted in Tony Barrett, 'I Had Given up Hope of Ever Having a Family of My Own', *Liverpool Echo*, 27 September 2004.

a team of women to take their place. She intends to use her husband's
ledgers (which contain details of his criminal activity) to plan another
job. These texts become key to the series' deconstruction of the social
formation of gender identity, positing it as a learnt code ripe for appro-
priation: 'We're going to pull a raid and I don't want us getting hurt.
We're not big strong fellas, we're women, but we gotta learn to think
like men.' Armed with this insider's knowledge the widows succeed
and, following the example of Ronnie Biggs, the most notorious of the
Great Train Robbers, escape with their proceeds to Brazil.

On the one hand there is an element of the stunt about this. It allows
the series to feel distinctive whilst still delivering the conventional narrative beats of the crime genre (clandestine scheming, the raid, the flight
from the law). Nevertheless, the focus on gender and identity was
genuinely innovative and helped strip away hard-boiled clichés. In
previous crime dramas women were frequently little more than adorn-
ments: the wives and lovers of police and thieves. A police raid, in a
series like *The Professionals* (ITV, 1977–83) would often reveal a criminal fleeing out the window while a young woman rushed to adjust her
underwear. In *Widows* it is the men who provide the window dressing:
bungling their attempts to catch Dolly and her crew or supplying the
required sinister mood as they lurk in the shadows. The viewer is invited
to share the women's relish at their liberation. One widow, Linda
Perelli, declares: 'I feel like I'm ticking all over, my heart's thumping
like crazy ... but I feel alive though.' Another, Shirley Miller, faced with
the transition from beauty queen contestant to gangster, initially worries
about her abilities: 'I can't handle shooters.' Following their successful
raid, however, she parodies the trite platitudes expected of the beauty
pageant: 'I love reading, writing and robbing banks.' In place of car
chases and fist fights, there is a continued emphasis on interiority and
female space: Dolly evades police surveillance by visiting a women-only
health spa or her hairdresser (the male officers stake out the front of the
building but she escapes from the back).

The inversion of gender roles, though more than a trite gimmick, is
not always smoothly handled. Both La Plante and the director Ian
Toynton occasionally seem a little flat-footed, unsure how to handle the
fresh narrative possibilities which have been unleashed. Interestingly,
this uncertainty is clearest in the most visually rewarding scenes in the
series. A sequence of the widows preparing for the robbery is juxtaposed
with black and white flashbacks of Harry and his men training. What
passes for realism on television (low key performances, motivated

camera movement, a subdued colour palette) is displaced by outbursts of expressionism (emphasized by a discordant score and overtly photographic composition) reminiscent of European independent cinema. This rupture is more self-conscious than earlier formal slippages (such as the heightened noir lighting scheme at the lock-up where the widows meet), as if stalking the script is an awareness of its own radical departure from both genre and gender convention. In some respects it is possible to see the gender politics of *Widows* as a reaction to the rise and domination of Thatcherism. A simplistic parallel can, of course, be drawn between a strong female leader and La Plante's strong female leads, but here the textual response is much more nuanced and layered. There is a simultaneous relish at the creation of dynamic female roles and an uncertainty as to how to direct this new-found agency. Something of the same can be said of La Plante herself, who doggedly refuses to endorse any kind of feminist reading of her work, while delighting in the pioneering female roles she has created.

Whatever its ambivalent gender politics, *Widows* demonstrated the possibility of formal innovation within the broadcasting duopoly of the BBC and ITV. The arrival of Channel Four a year earlier in 1982 marked a more dramatic evolution of the television ecology. The new channel did not simply represent extra 'bandwidth': the Broadcasting Act of 1980 stipulated it should 'encourage innovation and experiment in the form and content of programmes'. Doubters suggested that a genre like soap opera sat strangely with such a remit. But *Brookside* (C4, 1982–2003), for which Jimmy McGovern wrote over eighty episodes, brought a renewed complexity and vigour to the genre, refashioning it for a brash decade. It felt contemporary and spoke with a distinctive Scouse swagger.

Raymond Williams has argued that because of their apparent mundanity, soaps have often been ascribed less cultural significance than the single play: 'Since their origins in commercial radio in the 1930's, many serials have been dismissed as "soap opera". Yet their persistence and popularity is significant, in a period in which, in so much traditionally serious drama and fiction, there has been a widespread withdrawal from general social experience.'[2] However, by the early eighties there was a growing sense that soaps like *Coronation Street* (ITV, 1960–) and *Crossroads* (ITV, 1964–88, 2001–03) were themselves

2 Raymond Williams, *Television: Technology and Cultural Form* (London: Routledge, 1974), p. 58.

neither subtle nor supple enough to represent 'general social experience'; itself an increasingly contentious concept. As the Thatcherite
onslaught began, with the social ferment of mass unemployment, the
miners' strike, rioting in Brixton and Toxteth, financial deregulation
and the Falklands conflict, the fictional inhabitants of soap land appeared
marooned in the ether, waving a long goodbye to external reality.

Brookside, set in an anonymous, newly built estate on the edge of
Liverpool, fed on this sense of dislocation and rupture. It made other
soaps feel arthritic; creaking and wheezing as they found adjusting to
the contradictory energies of social liberalism and economic monetarism
almost as difficult as the working-class communities they sought to
represent. Often crude, sometimes unsuccessful, *Brookside* attempted to
renew the genre by addressing the perceived reality of this fractured
world. Memorable storylines dealt with abortion, rape, AIDS, unemployment and domestic abuse. McGovern wrote of the rise of the
Militant Tendency and a world 'moving so far to the right it was impossible to stand still for a moment'.[3] Of all the new voices *Brookside* brought
to the screen (Frank Clark, Kay Mellor, Frank Cottrell Boyce), his
writing shouted loudest and hit the hardest. According to John Yorke,
a senior drama commissioner at the BBC, 'You could tell within five
minutes if it was a Jimmy McGovern episode because someone was
punching someone.'[4]

McGovern, the fifth of nine children, grew up in Greenside, Liverpool: 'It used to be a slum area but today it's a beautiful little street with
wonderful little houses – built by the Militant Tendency!'[5] As a child
he had a stammer and was educated by the Jesuits at St Francis Xavier
College, which he describes as a 'truly awful' experience: 'It's where I
learnt how to cry to avoid punishment.'[6] McGovern would later move
from job to job before teaching for three years at Quarry Bank School
(now Calderstones Comprehensive). He became involved with the
Scotland Road writers' workshop, completing several plays which
helped secure him a job on *Brookside*.

Schooled in socialism, his writing for Brookside often had a potent
political edge, even if agitprop posturing could occasionally render its

3   Interviewed on 'Left of Frame: The Rise and Fall of Radical TV Drama', BBC4
    Time Shift, 2 February 2006.
4   Quoted in Ian Burrell, 'Television Drama', *Independent*, 27 March 2006.
5   Quoted in Paddy Shennan, 'Jimmy Tells It Like It Is', *Liverpool Echo*, 9 April 2003.
6   Paddy Shennan, 'Jimmy Tells It'.

earliest incarnations reductively issue-based. McGovern would later acknowledge this characteristic of some of his first scripts. Reflecting on an episode broadcast after the highly contentious sinking of the Argentinean cruiser *The General Belgrano* during the Falklands conflict, he comments: 'I had me *Belgrano* speech, about a lot of young men dying in the south Atlantic to cheer us up and re-elect Thatcher, and I kept putting it in and they kept taking it out, and eventually Bobby Grant did make that speech, but ... you learn your characters have to have free will.'[7]

Unlike the residents of *Coronation Street* or *Crossroads*, the inhabitants of *Brookside* swore, watched television, used the toilet and talked politics. It was shot on the same portable video cameras used by news crews: not pretty but cheap, and signifying an aesthetic of authenticity. According to Phil Redmond, founder and chief executive of Mersey Television which produced the show, 'People used to say to me: "It's different from other soaps – it's more real, it's like the news or a football match." ... That was exactly the sort of reaction I wanted to hear.'[8] There were no wobbly walls or overlit sets; instead Redmond, a former quantity surveyor, bought thirteen houses on a new estate for £25,000 each. Seven became offices and six were cabled for filming, allowing speedy lighting set-ups. The *Brookside* production line was a model of efficiency which would have put a smile on the face of any management consultant. On a typical day sixty episodes would be being prepped, shot or edited, and after four months the site and equipment had paid for themselves.

At its peak, *Brookside* was watched by over eight million people and it was an essential training ground for McGovern: 'It taught me everything I know; it was a brilliant time.'[9] He mastered the skill of combining multiple plot strands with economy and style, and soon learnt to express class and emotional conflict not as bloodless ideology, but as the beating heart of drama. However, the flow charts and team writing brought their own frustrations: 'If I came up with a great story say I might be allowed to start that story off but it's played over fourteen, sixteen weeks and other writers get a hold of it and they haven't got my interests. A lot of them are totally apolitical.'[10]

7 Quoted in Robert Crampton, 'Scouse Grit: Jimmy McGovern', *Times Magazine,* 11 March 1995.

8 Geoff Tibbals, *Phil Redmond's* Brookside*: The First Ten Years* (London: Boxtree, 1992), p. 6.

9 Shennan, 'Jimmy Tells It'.

10 BBC4 *Time Shift.*

Another factor behind McGovern's decision to leave the soap in 1988 was the gravitational pull generated by broadcaster and producers which dragged the show towards ever more sensational storylines. This is a constant force in the soap universe, producing a short-term dividend in terms of higher audiences but ultimately risking viewer loyalty when the melodrama becomes tiresome. Redmond's stated aims that he 'wanted to show life as it is' sat increasingly uneasily with plots which included an armed siege, the outbreak of an Ebola-like virus, a bizarre cult making the close its headquarters, and the transformation of Lindsay Corkhill from struggling single mother into a lesbian gangster. Ratings slumped to one and a half million viewers, and *Brookside* disappeared into a black hole of self-parody before being axed by Channel 4 in 2003. In his column in the *Liverpool Echo*, McGovern wrote: 'In *Brookside*'s fate lies a lesson for all the soaps: keep it real.'[11]

This slide into melodrama with its stereotypical characters, exaggerated emotions and simplistic conflicts dogs much genre television including La Plante's sequel to *Widows*. *Widows II* (ITV, 1985) gained an audience of over thirteen million viewers, but all too often it appeared to have abandoned its predecessor's carefully wrought sense of reality en route to Rio, like a piece of lost luggage in a Heathrow departure lounge. The opening episode seemed preoccupied with the luxury life style of villas, swimming pools and white Rolls Royces enjoyed by the widows in Brazil – a response, perhaps, to glossy American imported drama of the period such as *Dallas* (BBC, 1978–91) and *Dynasty* (BBC, 1982–89). This airport novel idyll is disrupted by Harry Rawlins. Dolly's husband, as we discovered late in the first series, survived the disastrous heist only to betray her: 'He's alive, living with Jimmy Nunn's bitch. Tell me how he could do that to me because all I ever did was love him … And even worse I still do.' Harry wants to get his hands on the money the widows stole and his threatening presence drives the plot. The women become passive figures, ciphers almost, defined by their attempts to avoid detection, their sense of agency lost as they run headlong into a narrative cul de sac.

Widows II is early evidence of a strand in La Plante's fiction which, as Julia Hallam argues,

abandons sociological realism altogether in favour of intertextuality and the highly wrought emotional landscape of glossy prime-time

11 Jimmy McGovern, 'Real Reason for Close Closing', *Liverpool Echo*, 17 June 2003.

melodrama. Here high production values, musical underscore and contrived plots create a form of drama more readily associated with popular American formats where the focus is on individual tragedy and personal circumstances rather than socially extended commentary.[12]

The uneasy negotiation between this soft focus escapism and an almost journalistic rigour is the defining tension of La Plante's oeuvre. Her most accomplished drama, *Prime Suspect* (ITV, 1991), tells the story of DCI Jane Tennison's fight to lead a murder enquiry in the face of institutional opposition and benefits from meticulous research. In effect what *Brookside* did for soap, *Prime Suspect* does for the police procedural. La Plante took a flagging genre, dusted it down, injected a dose of authenticity and revitalized the form for a new decade. The cold, bruised flesh of prostitute Della Mornay is one key signifier of La Plante's claim on the real, her naked corpse the first of many to be dragged from the urban wastelands of the author's imagination and ferried to the clinical certainty of the forensic lab. Here we learn Mornay had a rare blood group (the first clue in the hunt for the killer) and that the time of death can be accurately determined using her watch, smashed during the attack. The importance placed on evidence and the matter of fact tone of the gowned pathologist (which barely wavers when he announces Mornay has 'semen in virtually every orifice') contribute to an atmosphere of controlled unpleasantness that artfully conveys an unflinching naturalism. We have come a long way from the reassuringly anaemic *Dixon of Dock Green* (BBC, 1955–76). Indeed *Prime Suspect* can be read as the logical conclusion of a desire to reclaim 'reality', in all its ugly detail, for the police procedural. In this respect its roots can be traced back to a series such as *Z Cars* (BBC 1962–78), perhaps the first British police drama which attempted to import a greater sense of documentary realism to the genre, with its challenging (for the time) portrayal of policing in the fictional Merseyside community of Newtown.

Prime Suspect's construction of this reality comes with a definite aesthetic. It builds on the noir touches of *Widows*, expressing them in a more cinematic language: roving steadicam, rain-drenched scrublands and the use of shallow depth of field with blown-out highlights are all designed to immerse us in a world of crime and punishment. This visual

12 Julia Hallam, *Lynda La Plante* (Manchester: Manchester University Press, 2005), p. 114.

style is carefully contained, its artifice disguised, reinforcing rather than overwhelming the documentary aura of facts and proof which grounds male violence and the adrenalized search for the killer in the realm of necessary detail, clues and cold, hard fact. The rhythm and flow of police life are delivered with fine nuance, and the carefully choreographed scenes succeed in appearing as unstructured as verité film-making. This observational tone, reinforced by the slow, considered pace of the series as a whole, is epitomized by one scene in which we follow DS Bill Otley into the operations room to announce the death of his superior, DCI Shefford. The camera lingers on the assembled officers' faces before slowly panning through 360 degrees as a respectful silence falls on the room, broken only when the phones begin to ring and the officers hesitantly return to their required duties while Otley, pain and loss written on his face, walks away.

Shefford's death creates an opportunity for Jane Tennison (played, in a career-defining role, by Helen Mirren). Tennison insists she should replace him and head the murder enquiry but she is rejected by her superior: 'Now, Inspector, is not the time to shove your women's rights down my throat.' Despite La Plante's attempt to drain any overt politics from her work, there is little doubt that a significant proportion of *Prime Suspect*'s impact comes from its robust dissection of policing and gender. The film enjoys Tennison's eventual empowerment, inviting the viewer to do the same. Later, when she is promoted, the narrative acquires a rewarding intricacy in which institutional sexism is revealed to mask a deeper corruption. As the corpse of another unfortunate prostitute hits the mortuary slab, Tennison discovers Shefford had been a client of both victims. Senior male officers close ranks and conspire to undermine her for 'running around the country trying to rake up dirt' on Shefford. This story of struggle in the workplace plays as if the police procedural is beginning to cross-fertilize with the soap and soon we are introduced to Tennison's emotional hinterland. She smokes, drinks and, according to one senior officer, has 'got balls', but we also witness her struggling in the kitchen and neglecting her father on his birthday, snapping at him as she replays her television appearance on *Crime Night*.

La Plante's script is aware that, after each domestic hiatus, the viewer, like Tennison herself, will return to the chase with renewed vigour. Soon Shefford's implication in the murders is revealed as a red herring, one of the narrative pleasures of detective fiction. But the friction arising from Tennison's search jeopardizes her position: 'I've not quite had the theatrical "you've got 24 hours", but unless we find something soon

I'm on traffic.' When the threat is implemented, her officers, won over by her determination and professionalism, refuse to accept Tennison's replacement. Informed of this by her superior, she waits for him to leave before wiping a tear from her eye and proceeding to nail the real killer: a post-feminist image replete with tough vulnerability. By the climax of the series Tennison's mastery appears complete and the genre successfully reworked, having set a new benchmark in terms of careful plotting, visual fluency and strong performances from an impressive cast including Ralph Fiennes, Zoë Wanamaker and Tom Wilkinson.

Prime Suspect has gone on to become a returning franchise, with a seventh and final instalment broadcast in autumn 2006. The programme earned La Plante a BAFTA in 1991 when she beat fellow Liverpudlian Alan Bleasdale. Bleasdale had been nominated for the highly regarded *GBH* (C4, 1991), a response to events in Liverpool in the 1980s, when members of the Militant Tendency gained control of the city council. His defeat was taken by some as a sign that television was abandoning signature, authored pieces and descending into a morass of genre. It can just as easily be read as indicator that genre fiction itself was becoming increasingly sophisticated. The latter argument was reinforced by Jimmy McGovern's breakthrough drama *Cracker* in 1993 (the same year which saw La Plante's impressive *Prime Suspect III*). *Cracker* (ITV, 1993–96, 2006) freed McGovern from the team writing constraints of *Brookside*. It allowed him to develop his distinctive voice by installing a radical interiority at the centre of the police procedural in the shape of Fitz (played by Robbie Coltrane), a psychological profiler brought in to help 'crack' difficult cases. But where La Plante fetishizes accuracy, McGovern uses the form to deliver an electrifying intensity, with Fitz dominating murder investigations and aggressively confronting suspects in a way which would get him slung out of a genuine police station. Moreover, Fitz propels each case forwards not by hunting for material clues but by relocating the crime scene, frequently, as in *Men Should Weep*, transposing it to the workings of the male psyche:

> Show me a man and I will show you a potential killer, a potential rapist. I am one for goodness sake. I don't do anything about it myself of course because I'm frightened of other men, frightened of being caught, because I'm the product of several thousand years of so called civilisation, but I think he's still inside me: the killer, the rapist, buried deep, growling occasionally just like the tomcat in the alley.

When the morgue begins to fill, the id and the ego are the 'prime suspects' hauled in by Fitz for interrogation, while, by examining his own submerged desires, he seeks to cast light on the criminal mind. 'Motive. That's the important thing. Motive. What drives people to do the things they do? What are they getting out of it?' *Cracker*, informed by Fitz and McGovern's Catholicism, complicates motive, enlarging the procedural's accepted repertoire of cause and effect: if we are *all* guilty, any black and white division between good and evil disappears. This may make for simplistic theology but it provides the raw material for strong drama: *Cracker* thrives on the moral negotiations we conduct with our primitive selves, and the hunt for hidden motives displaces the standard hunt for the criminal. As Fitz says: 'It's the truth that counts not the result.'

If McGovern creates a moralistic universe, he then gleefully muddies the water, splashing around in the nether recesses of the id and conceding a deeper complexity. *To Be a Somebody*, for example, is a subtle meditation on the erosion of working-class identity. Robert Carlyle plays Albie Kinsella, who becomes a skinhead and embarks on a killing spree after the death of his father. Albie's father had been traumatized by the Hillsborough football disaster in which ninety-six fans were crushed to death during the 1989 FA Cup semi-final between Liverpool and Nottingham Forest. McGovern would later return to this tragic event in a drama-documentary, entitled simply *Hillsborough* (1996). Its use here illustrates how his fiction, unlike La Plante's, overtly engages with Liverpool and uses lived experience to combine the personal and political. Hillsborough becomes the catalyst which allows us to see that Albie, unlike his father, is both mainstream and marginalized, a relic of a dying Labour community ignored in an era of identity politics. Albie's first victim is an Asian shopkeeper who refused to help him when he was short of cash: 'Do you remember me you robbing Paki bastard? Treat people like scum they start acting like scum, I'm a socialist me, trade unionist, voted labour all me bloody life, I've marched for the likes of you, but you just see me in my clobber and you see me as scum.' Albie articulates his fury at being stereotyped by affirming his own racist prejudices, a contradiction which accentuates the horror of the violence. Here, as elsewhere in McGovern's work, the political engagement is deliberately uncomfortable and creates an unusually sophisticated portrait of an individual forged from conflicting tensions, rather than a character manoeuvred onto a page to deliver a necessary plot point.

Fitz, like Albie, is defined by the impulses which pull him apart. La Plante's *Prime Suspect* may have infused the police procedural with some of the customary, mechanical concerns of the soap, but where it had touches of *Coronation Street*, the alcohol- and gambling-fuelled disaster which is Fitz's private life has its roots in the early, caustic, fists-flailing episodes of *Brookside*. Fitz is described by his brother as 'a Glasgow man, hard drinking, hard living and the graveyards are full of them'. He says of himself, 'I drink too much, I smoke too much, I gamble too much, I *am* too much.' McGovern has written of his own heavy drinking and gambling, but there is a deeper parallel between author and character, both of whom attempt to shape a story from apparently random events and inarticulate desires. In effect, Fitz provides a metanarrative which riffs on the ensuing complexity of McGovern's desire to allow his characters 'free will'. He is at his finest in the interrogation room eyeballing a suspect, where the close-up, a conventional indicator of emotional honesty, becomes instead a barrier (representing the lies and self-delusions of the suspect) which Fitz must overcome in order to establish a more profound truth and attribution of guilt. In interrogating the police procedural and bringing to the genre a new understanding of its own latent potential, McGovern's script performs a parallel process.

La Plante and McGovern became established brand name writers at a time when the four terrestrial broadcasters were increasingly relying on genre fiction. They had shown the possibilities of formal reinvention, but almost inevitably, as the flashing blue lights swept across the schedule, quality declined. Peter Ansorge, former head of drama serials and series at Channel 4, may be a touch sweeping but highlights a genuine concern when he writes:

> The police series that now dominate our screens are plot-led and curiously characterless. The dialogue is entirely functional, there to provide information that is free from any worrying sub-text. The stories are often copied from previously successful shows, particularly *Prime Suspect* and *Cracker*, which may explain a proliferation of serial rapists in the programmes that is totally out of proportion to their actual presence in the United Kingdom.[13]

13 Peter Ansorge, *From Liverpool to Los Angeles: On Writing for Theatre, Film and Television* (London: Faber & Faber, 1997), p. 93.

Like *Prime Suspect, Cracker* became a returning franchise with new writers contributing episodes to the second and third series: confirmation that high profile dramas were increasingly seen as intellectual properties ripe for exploitation in the UK and abroad.[14] Indeed, *Cracker* and *Widows* were both remade for the American market, although neither enjoyed the success of the original. They were, in a phrase sometimes used to describe failed transatlantic remakes, 'lost over Denver'. A dispute between La Plante and producers Granada concerning an American version of *Prime Suspect* also contributed to her decision to establish a production company in the summer of 1994. Writers, she realized, had little control over their creations, 'I didn't own it. I was just for hire.'[15] The *Prime Suspect* franchise would continue but without its original author.

There is, however, no necessary corollary between creative control and quality. Indeed it is possible to make a case that writer/producers often lack perspective on their own work, and despite La Plante's undoubted skills in characterization, structure and dialogue, a significant number of her subsequent productions failed to live up to the promise of *Prime Suspect*. *She's Out* (ITV, 1995) extended the *Widows* franchise by returning to the character of Dolly Rawlins, who, after being released from Holloway Prison, assembles a new gang of female criminals and is determined (in that gambit beloved of crime writers) to pull one last job before she goes straight. On a technical level Mitchell's performance is difficult to fault but all too often she finds herself lost in a scenario of baroque complexity (women on horseback restage the Great Train Robbery to fund the building of an orphanage). Other characters feel second hand and the mockney dialogue is at times past its sell-by date ('What's his game then?', 'You never said nuffin' about that prune-faced bitch being in on this.') None of which seemed to deter La Plante's loyal audience, but did prompt much critical smirking. 'More like a Weed than a Plante' read the headline of one review.[16]

---

14 Three series of *Cracker* and a feature-length special were broadcast between 1993 and 1996. Paul Abbott and Ted Whitehead contributed scripts from series two. A one-off special scripted by McGovern was broadcast in Autumn 2006. *Prime Suspect VII*, written by Frank Deasy and directed by Philip Martin, was also broadcast in late 2006. Helen Mirren has stated this will be the final time she plays the role of Tennison.

15 Quoted in Mark Lawson, 'Queen of the Inside Track', *Guardian*, 17 October 1998.

16 Adam Sweeting, 'More Like a Weed Than a Plante', *Guardian*, 25 June 1998.

Further indications of a leaning toward the melodramatic came with *Bella Mafia* (CBS, 1997), adapted by La Plante from her novel of the same name. This American mini-series benefits from a large budget and a fine cast (including Vanessa Redgrave, Nastassja Kinski and Peter Bogdanovich), and with its Italian-American entanglement it confirmed La Plante's ambition to work on a larger canvas. Unfortunately, this tale of the bloody revenge wreaked by the women of the Sicilian Luciano clan after the murder of their husbands all too often lurches towards the clichéd. Vintage black Mercedes gleam in the sun, reflecting fake tan images of ersatz Mafiosi who mouth lines like, 'Your skin is so soft, come on momma don't cry, give me that perfect smile.' *Killer Net* (C4, 1998), a tartrazine-fuelled 'youth' romp peppered with random nudity and swearing, which ostensibly warns of the dangers of internet criminality but suffers from attention deficit disorder, also disappointed. As did *Mind Games* (ITV, 2001), starring Fiona Shaw as DI O'Neil, a psychological profiler with a difference. O'Neil, a former nun, draws on her 'deep Christian faith' to pioneer new profiling methods and 'uses her innate spirituality as a way of confronting the twisted mind of a killer'.[17] These drastic departures from La Plante's initial realist manifesto lack both agility and authority, a tendency which has prompted one television critic to award her the soubriquet 'Losta La Plot'.[18] But these dramas represent only one aspect of La Plante's work: others, such as the initially impressive *Trial and Retribution* (ITV, 1997–), indicate it would be reductive to read them as an indication of serial decline.

While a significant proportion of La Plante's later dramas shout loudly but shun daily reality, McGovern's fiction has with time become more intense and personal. If religion in *Mind Games* feels like a gimmick, in *The Lakes*, perhaps McGovern's most accomplished work, it provides an unexpected, brooding intensity which warps the pastoral form. At a time when *Hamish Macbeth* (BBC, 1995–7) and *Heartbeat* (ITV, 1992–) were pulling crime drama towards rural nostalgia, McGovern dragged the pastoral in the opposite direction, removing any sense of heritage or nostalgia from his depiction of the Lake District. The lead character, Danny Kavanagh, unlike many of his fictional predecessors, quits Liverpool with its high unemployment to seek his fortune in the country. But the lakes provide no escape from urban pressures, merely concealing

17 Description of 'Mind Games' from La Plante Productions' website http://www. laplanteproductions.com
18 Jim Shelley, 'Call the Cops', *Guardian Guide*, 1 April 2006.

them behind thick stone cottage walls. The countryside, according to the hotel's chef has become the city's dependent playground:

> This is Wordsworth country, Danny, millions of people come here all looking for a bit of Nature. They clog up our roads. They stomp all over our fells. They pack our bars. They buy up our houses. Oh the hotels and restaurants spring up, but the mines, the quarries close down. The farms get turned into timeshare complexes. So for people like me Danny, *local* people like me, there's nothing left to do but look after this urban filth. We get to depend on this urban filth.

Danny falls in love with Emma, a local girl, and a familiar narrative arc of sex, unplanned pregnancy and hasty marriage unfolds. The crackling tensions within the village (and the repeated intrusion of the 'urban filth' in the form of hotel guests and staff) combine to give *The Lakes* a distinctive energy even before its superficially conventional plot is pulled apart by death. While Danny is in charge of a boathouse three girls drown. The villagers turn on him alleging he pocketed money from children who should never have been let out on the water. The truth surfaces only gradually: Danny, like Fitz, is a gambler. He was phoning through a bet when the girls stole the boat. He refuses to disclose his alibi, fearing it might save his reputation only to wreck his marriage (he has promised Emma his wages will not be wasted on the horses but used to support their child).

As the series culminates in a coroner's inquest into the death of the drowned girls, McGovern masterfully raises the stakes. Guilt spreads through the village: the drowned girls would have been in school if their teacher had not neglected them to confront his adulterous wife. Gradually the village's superficial propriety falls away and the plot circumstantially implicates a series of villagers in the girls' deaths. There are echoes of a lost Eden but this is no religious tract, here even the priest, like McGovern, is a sceptic: 'They're all up there on a cloud are they, all the billions who've died and been slaughtered, gassed, blown to bits? They're all up there on a cloud playing their harps. It's a fairy tale. Reality is a little girl, nose, mouth, caked in mud. Dead.'

The Lakes, while bedded in realism, achieves a wider, more nuanced tonal range than other genre fiction, frequently deploying moments of rich expressionism, such as its opening, spiralling top shot, which reveals Danny Kavanagh lying on his bed, intercut with sudden flashes forward to bodies flailing in the water. Elsewhere Danny communes with

Nature, the birds circling overhead in scenes reminiscent of *Kes* (Loach, 1969), and we hear him voice fragments of poetry from Gerard Manley Hopkins and W.H. Auden. These fragments provide a complementary meaning system to the events unfolding in the valley below (the 'urban filth' monologue, for example, can be read as a prose response to the 'artificial wilderness' of a stanza from Auden's *The Shield of Achilles* quoted in voice-over). The director David Blair handles these moments with a light touch, capturing a heightened reality which feels earned by the script rather than over stylized. Extensive use of long lenses (with repeated action often filmed on 85 mm, 135 mm and 300 mm[19] lenses then cut together) lends a knowing vitality to the scenes with the young hotel workers and locals. Military jets roar overhead, presenting Nature as conquered and hinting at more disturbing, human energies. Key conversations are shot in silhouette as the moral conflicts develop and the camera continually circles as if trying to penetrate the characters' souls.

McGovern's sequel, *The Lakes 2* (BBC, 1999), lost much of its predecessor's poetry, appearing crude in comparison. Its storyline (centring on murder, rape and madness) bore the fingerprints of melodrama. While this did not result in the perverse pyrotechnic display of La Plante's *Killer Net* or *Bella Mafia*, there is little light and shade, more primary colour. The multi-stranded narrative, however, is arguably the form most suited to McGovern's incendiary talents. His writing skills, honed on *Brookside*, seem to revel in the dynamic possibilities and reach of the densely plotted episodes of *Cracker*, the first series of *The Lakes* or the overlapping stories of *The Street* (BBC, 2006). *The Street's* opening tale of Angela Quinn's affair with a neighbour (traumatically cut short by a traffic accident in which her lover collides with her child), illustrates McGovern's continued ability to wring comedy, passion and tragedy from the everyday. Subsequent episodes (overseen, if not all scripted by McGovern) develop into a rich portrait of life on a single street.

There is a customary hierarchy in film and television, at the apex of which sits the feature film and at the bottom the soap. McGovern seems

19 The 'normal' field of vision of the human eye is said to equate approximately to a 50 mm lens (when shooting on 35 mm film). Focal lengths greater than this narrow the field of vision and are described as long lenses. Longer focal lengths tend to isolate subjects rather than featuring them in their context because of their shallower depth of field. Rapid pans on a long lens have a distinctive energy because of this which cannot be achieved in the same way using a wide-angle lens.

to merge the most rewarding elements of both forms in his multi-stranded serials, which allow him the screen time to pursue complex stories featuring a large cast but avoid the schematic gravitas of soap opera. Indeed his own feature films, while admirable works in themselves, feel either a touch slight and conventional (*Priest*, 1994; *Liam*, 2000) or overcooked (*Heart*, 1999) in comparison. Similarly his trio of drama-documentaries (*Hillsborough* (ITV, 1996), *Dockers* (C4, 1999) and *Sunday* (C4, 2002)) are exceptional films but they are marked by a minor, if necessary, stifling of his own voice; the result perhaps of intense research. McGovern has written that 'the process of writing a drama-doc is as important as the drama-doc itself. It must empower the powerless,'[20] and while his respect for the victims of Hillsborough and Bloody Sunday or the striking Liverpool dockers may be admirable, these factual pieces by their very nature demand a curtailing of his imaginative powers.

If McGovern is particularly adept at working within the serial form, the institutional structure and discipline afforded by the police procedural continue to provide the framework for La Plante's most involving work *Trial and Retribution* (first broadcast in 1997, with filming beginning on a fourteenth instalment in 2006) marked a definite return to form. It has the slowness and sense of detail of her strongest dramas, and was innovative in its fusing of the procedural with the courtroom drama. Each episode builds to a final act which follows the arrested suspect's progress through the criminal justice system and often provides a trenchant indictment of institutional failure. Police and viewer look on as complacent lawyers, judges and the Crown Prosecution Service struggle either to convict or inflict proper punishment. Inevitably, the franchise in its many iterations includes weaker moments in which the attempt to meld two genres can appear broken-backed or the plot hackneyed. A case in point is *Trial and Retribution IX*, in which the perpetrator is eventually tracked down once the police realize he is mimicking the methods of American serial killer Ted Bundy. The charitable might deem this intertextuality, the less forgiving lazy writing. Equally, its chief formal innovation, the repeated use of split screen, can cut both ways. At its best it fractures the viewer's perspective (sometimes into a dozen separate images), denying omniscience and provoking telling questions about point of view in a kind of prime time reworking of Peter Greenaway's *Prospero's Books* (1991). Such techniques, however, can also

20 Jimmy McGovern, 'The Power of Truth', *Guardian*, 10 June 2004.

disguise limp storytelling, serving as a smokescreen for a story that lacks sufficient conviction, meandering instead through conflicting testimony until it stumbles on a conclusion.

Trial and Retribution's continued attempt to refashion genre and render it more than easily digestible fodder is commendable; but its mixed success in stretching the form suggest that the police procedural, as redefined by La Plante is, if not yet exhausted, certainly tiring. Leo Braudy has argued: 'Genre films essentially ask the audience, "Do you still want to believe this?" Popularity is the audience answering, "Yes."' Change in genres occurs when the audience says, "That's too infantile a form of what we believe. Show us something more complicated."'[21] In this respect it is significant that the recent series which most profoundly echoes *Prime Suspect*, La Plante's breakthrough work, is the high concept time travel drama *Life on Mars* (BBC, 2006) featuring the detective Sam Tyler, who, after a car crash, appears to have travelled back in time to the 1970s where (like DCI Tennison before him) he has both to educate and earn the respect of a team of hostile, old-fashioned coppers. This superficially unpromising scenario is surprisingly effective at toying with notions of progress, political correctness and childhood identity, as if suggesting that a more tangential genre intervention is now required to realize ambitions higher than those found in the current plethora of derivative crime dramas. In this respect *Life on Mars* walks an interesting tightrope. It explicitly critiques social attitudes prevalent in the 1970s whilst playing with the period's genre expectations. And while it enjoys the shorthand provided by these conventions (savouring its illicit trespass into the realm of the politically incorrect), the series' attempt to remake the genre for the twenty-first century reveals an implicit desire for a synthesis of the old and new (a fusion of pre- and post-Thatcherite attitudes which avoids confronting the intervening decades). But while the dynamics of the drama frequently subvert the intentions of the writer and director, in its own way *Life on Mars* is a *Cracker* or *Prime Suspect* for a new decade, proof of the continuing potential of the police procedural and genre drama as a whole which both McGovern and La Plante helped unlock. Their own careers, however, may also be read as testament to the ambivalence of genre, which, once mastered, always hovers on the margins waiting to make its presence felt.

---

21 Leo Braudy, *The World in a Frame: What We See in Films* (New York: Anchor Press/ Doubleday, 1977), p. 179.

15

Manners, Mores and Musicality:
An Interview with Willy Russell

John Bennett

This interview with Willy Russell was recorded at the Cornerstone Building of Liverpool Hope University in May 2006. Willy Russell is an alumnus of the university, having previously tried careers in hairdressing and labouring. He is the author of some of the most successful and much-performed stage plays of recent decades, including Stags and Hens *(1978),* Educating Rita *(1980),* Shirley Valentine *(1986) and the West End musical* Blood Brothers *(1983). He has adapted his stage plays for the cinema, and has a string of highly successful original TV commissions to his credit:* Our Day Out *(1977),* Daughters of Albion *(1979),* One Summer *(1984) and* Terraces *(1993). 'His plays tell stories of dreams, aspirations, escape and the pursuit of happiness. His characters strive to flee from a deadly, stifling environment and achieve something finer – or at least they dream of doing so.'[1]*

JB: Commentators invariably describe you as a 'Liverpool playwright' but later work, such as your novel *The Wrong Boy* (2000) and the album *Hoovering the Moon* (2004), make me see you as a much more of a polymath.

WR: The 'Liverpool' tag is something that one is never going to be able to shake. The fact that I work primarily as a dramatist, that I write for performance is probably completely bound up with 'Liverpool-ness', what being a Liverpudlian is. All the most well-known Liverpool forms are in the spoken rather than the written word. That's not to omit or overlook such writers as Beryl Bainbridge, Ramsey Campbell and other

---

1 Ros Merkin, 'Willy Russell', in John Bull (ed.), *The Dictionary of Literary Biography: British and Irish Dramatists Since World War II* (San Francisco and London: Bruccoli Clark Layman, 2001), p. 246.

very good writers of prose, but when thinking of Liverpool and writing I think that the first artists who come to mind are those from a spoken/sung rather than literary background – firstly the post-war comedians: the Tommy Handleys, the Arthur Askeys, the Ted Rays. They didn't use the Liverpool accent because it wasn't acceptable at that point, and so they would adopt either a lower-middle-class accent or either a vaguely northern idiom. But although this first wave of Liverpool comedians were not remotely 'Scouse' in their language or their comedy, nevertheless the work came out of a certain kind of Liverpool observation of the world, an irreverence, a capacity for put-down and for pricking pomposity. Then, of course, after that you had the massive explosion of Merseybeat. But again it wasn't something which was essentially a written form – it was song. Interestingly, when the poets emerged from Liverpool, Adrian Henri, Roger McGough, Brian Patten, they wrote primarily for performance, for the spoken word, the fact of it going down in a book being (then) just a means of recording the poem. Then, of course, the playwrights and screenwriters, the Alun Owens, the Neville Smiths, John McGraths and then people like myself, Alan [Bleasdale], Jim Morris, Jimmy McGovern – all of us writing for performance and the spoken-ness which is absolutely of Liverpool. Had we all, from Ted Ray to Jimmy McGovern, been born and brought up in Ashby-de-la-Zouch, there would have been a very different outcome. There is something to do with the nature of the spoken language in Liverpool that is as the sky and the light must have been to the impressionists. So why does it continue to irk me when journalists/commentators use the 'Liverpool' tag? Probably because I'm being too sensitive. But I suspect that in the description 'Liverpool writer' I discern journalistic sloppiness or, worse, an intention to diminish or reduce.

JB: Given the lengthy catalogue of writers and performers that you have just mentioned, is there any one person that you admire in particular?

WR: I toured with the poets in the nineties and I would be on stage every night listening to Brian Patten and he would break me into pieces – his poetry would cripple me and then at the same time I'd be sitting there when Roger [McGough] was at the microphone and be dazzled by his playfulness and his wit and deeply moved by Adrian [Henri] and his iconoclasm. Alan [Bleasdale] moved me to tears and had me howling with laughter and admiration at his audacity. Jimmy [McGovern] is often sublime. But to say that I have got an absolute favourite, no. They all terrify me, intimidate me, inspire me – and depress me with the depth and breadth of their talent.

JB: The Everyman Theatre in Hope Street played an important role in establishing you as a playwright, staging such early work as *When the Reds* (1973), *John, Paul, George, Ringo and Bert* (1974), *Breezeblock Park* (1975), *Stags and Hens* (1978) and *Shirley Valentine* (1986). It is an important venue for the city and its history and your relationship with it has some, albeit limited, documentation; what is less well known, and fascinates me, is the artistic significance of the lively bar and restaurant beneath the theatre, the equally famous Everyman Bistro.

WR: It is very interesting, the Bistro – prior to the Martin Jenkins/Terry Hands days towards the end of their regime is when I first went to the Everyman and went in the Bistro, and it was very much the kind of place where you booked a table and you went for a meal, and I was immediately and totally intimidated because it was the sort of place where young (ish), middle-class, university-educated, arts-speaking, arts-practising, or wanna-be arts-practising people, met. My impression was that it wasn't for the likes of me. You didn't hear people with accents in there and I didn't really go back; I was deeply intimidated in there. Once [John] McGrath and [Alan] Dossor had started to carve out this new Everyman, a theatre which was presenting work designed to be acutely relevant to the city in which it existed, there was a change downstairs, and this must have coincided with the arrival of Paddy Byrne and Dave Scott – what happened was after the show you could go down to this bistro and drink. To drink in there you had to buy an Everyman hamburger, and if you had this cloakroom ticket for a hamburger – it was just a way of getting around the licensing laws – (and the hamburgers were horrendous really) but it allowed you to drink after hours and this was fantastic in Liverpool. We were nineteen, twenty – so to have a place where you didn't have to have a full meal but you could go and drink and smoke was a small kind of paradise. What it did do, probably more immediately and effectively than was happening upstairs in the theatre, was break down the class situation, because what you got was a kind of diluting of the middle class, university, arty, educated crowd who were now mingling with the kind of aspirant secondary modern kids, like me, who still talked with something of an accent but were nevertheless more concerned with things artistic/musical/cultural than with the stereotypical football, fights and shagging. For me the Bistro was a place where I could legitimately 'talk seriously'. I'm sure lots of futures were hatched out down there. Nobody talks about the Everyman Bistro but it is of vital importance. For me the Everyman, both theatre and Bistro – was as important, as potent and as sexy a place to be as the Cavern. My first ever professional job at the Everyman was to take a play which was set in Hull and was built around the fortunes of a central character called Ray whose life was mirrored by the success or otherwise of Hull City football club; *The Tigers Are Coming OK* was the original script by Alan Plater and it had been quite a success in Hull but, as was the Everyman's practice at the time, if somebody had a regional success in Hull, or Stoke or Newcastle, or wherever, the Everyman would get the script and have a look at it and see if that particular piece could be taken, re-located to Liverpool and be made into a play that was relevant to the Everyman and to Liverpool. I was offered Alan's play and turned it into a play for Liverpool [*When the Reds*], but, as I said, my perception of the original Plater play was that it was really quite successful over in Hull and there was a sense that Hull, theatrically at that time, was really buzzing.

JB: That's fascinating because I think Hull and the Hull Truck Theatre Company and their pioneering combination of live music and improvisation had a major impact on British theatre in the early seventies but is now perceived by some commentators as less interesting, perhaps less fashionable and certainly having less popular cultural impact. John Godber [current artistic director of Hull Truck Theatre Company] often observes that the North East has never had a major television soap based in the area whereas the North West has had *Brookside* and *Coronation Street*. Also musically, Hull may have given the world the Housemartins in the mid-eighties but Liverpool has produced a more enduring 'famous four'; and the direct inspiration for your first major success at the Everyman.

WR: When *John, Paul, George, Ringo and Bert* happened it was a very, very different time to today. Liverpool had completely and utterly turned its back on the Beatles – they were a group that had split up, end of story. There was no idea at the time that they would ever become this massive cultural feature of Liverpool life; this is 1974, the Beatles had been this huge phenomenon. The Beatle thing happened and they were then dead and gone, all one knew was that there were a few people kind of propping up bars and still being boring about 'When I was this for the Beatles,' or 'When I was that for the Beatles' – no one wanted to hear those stories because they weren't really about the Beatles, they were about drawing attention to whoever was speaking, so it was in that atmosphere that I was approached to write my piece. The theatre, in fact, had no interest whatsoever in the Beatles and I'm sure that the reason my play happened was because Manchester Contact theatre did a documentary about the Beatles. We schlepped up to Manchester to watch this show because the idea again was that Alan Dossor was going to ask me to adapt it. Now he knew nothing of my history as a Cavern-goer and my knowing everything there was to know about the Beatles at that time, so I sat down in this audience and watched a stunning performance from Bernard Hill as John Lennon, but the rest of the show, it made the fatal mistake of using dialogue that was culled from biographies and which of course resulted in very literary, stilted language. And I said – 'Hey I'm only a young writer' – I'd only done one adaptation [*When the Reds*] and a pub show [*Sam O' Shanker*] – but I know this story and rather than adapting what I've just seen I want to write my own Beatles play. I know it must have come across as pure arrogance, but I must have sounded convincing because Dossor took a chance and commissioned this barely proven writer to create this large scale, main stage show. When it became known that I was working on this play about the Beatles a lot of people started to say to me, 'Oh, you must talk to so and so,' various people in Liverpool who were known to have had associations with the Beatles. But I didn't talk to any of them, I didn't want to be made a slave to the facts as mediated by someone else. I wanted to present my own take on the phenomenon that was the Beatles – although I did very consciously write it in the style that the Everyman had established for itself – the 'house style' in which music and comedy, the stylized and the naturalistic, the traditional and the wildly experimental and irreverent were all harnessed and made into the totality of performance that was so recognizably Everyman. Years later, when writing *Blood Brothers*, it was perfectly natural for me to assume again that particular Everyman house style – a style which, I must emphasize, was never ever presented as something which could stand in place of content. The Everyman house style was there to serve the content of the plays.

JB: Your next play for the Everyman was *Breezeblock Park* (1975), which later transferred to London. Is it right to categorize *Breezeblock Park* as a very different kind of play?

WR: It was a very determined decision on my part – once I'd come up with the play – to revel in the fact of making a well-made play, a play that observed the unities of time, place and action in a way that a great majority of the 'Made in Liverpool' Everyman plays didn't – I'd been down to the West End as the play about the Beatles had transferred and I had seen my first Ayckbourn, I'd seen *Norman Conquests* (1974, London production) and I'd witnessed broadly middle-class audiences having their manners beautifully presented before them and then dissected, with scalpel-like precision. And of course I saw that people who are having their dubious manners and mores paraded before them don't, as one might expect, recoil in shock and horror, but revel absolutely in this process, almost wetting themselves at seeing their own manners and behaviour so expertly portrayed. And of course, the fact is that it's never themselves they're watching – it's always the neighbour or the aunt or the uncle or the work colleague. And even though the experience is one in which there is an implicit criticism of a way of living, it is still, nevertheless, also a celebration – a coming together in a theatre of a group of people who broadly share a certain way of life and the assumptions and behaviours that go with it. Watching that first Ayckbourn I do recall clearly thinking wouldn't it be brilliant (and really radical!) to do the same thing at the Everyman but for an audience that shared a different way of living, a working-class rather than middle-class culture. At the time there was a tendency in some aspects of the Everyman's work to go, 'The workers are plotting the revolution as we speak – the factories of Kirkby will be worker-led tomorrow.' My first-hand experience of working-class living told me that this was largely university-inspired bollocks, and that rather than plotting the revolution most working people of my experience were just getting on with their lives as best they could. And I knew that this was an audience that would recognize and relate to seeing its own mores and manners depicted in a theatre – hence *Breezeblock Park*, which was a very conscious attempt to write something which did not conform to the kind of Everyman house style of the time and which owed far more to the tradition of the naturalistic, well-made play. I just knew that this audience would love to see its own bad manners paraded before it so *Breezeblock* was a very definite attempt to do something different.

JB: I think that you are generous with your expertise, working with students at Liverpool Hope [Willy Russell is Visiting Professor in Contemporary Theatre at the university and is a regular contributor to the city centre campus's Cornerstone Festival of Performance], teaching for the Arvon Foundation and mentoring new writers for television. Does that mean that you believe you can be taught to be a writer?

WR: No. You can't be taught to have that indefinable thing that makes a writer. But if you do have that within you, and once you have acknowledged and located it, then I think you can learn a lot; you can learn a lot about the particular play you're writing at that time, or the book, there is always more to be learned but there is no guarantee that what you learned in the writing of one play will do anything for you in the writing of the next play. We know what not to do and yet we still all make the same bloody mistakes! You can't equate it to brick-laying – once a man has learned to lay a good line of bricks the chances are he will never lay a terribly bad line of bricks again – now that is not true of playwrights; playwrights of the highest quality can write the most magical play and then the next play can be a total piece of garbage because, when you start again, you are going out to create something that does not yet exist, it is new. There are certain principles, there are certain unwritten laws and rules which will apply to everything that is written but that doesn't help you.

JB: After *Breezeblock Park* you wrote *One for the Road* (1976) and *Stags and Hens* (1978) and then *Educating Rita* (1980). In this new era of mass higher education, do you think that *Rita* can now only be staged as a period piece, that it was very much of its time?

WR: We did a revival at the Liverpool Playhouse in 2002 and we made the decision to allow the audience to decide the period in which it was taking place – by that I mean we did not specifically set it in the year it was written and the year, at that time, that it was taking place. But what I didn't want to do was set it as though it was definitely in 2002. I didn't want to introduce the mobile phone, I didn't want to introduce the word processor, etcetera, probably most of all I didn't want to have to deal with the fact that higher education, adult educa-tion, is now so very, very different in terms of political correctness, health and safety factors that you probably couldn't have the central situ-ation of the play in which this woman gains an education. Although, thinking about it, the fact is that even in its original conception the situ-ation was something of a cheat! Even in the Open University you never had a degree course that takes place over a single year (which is what the time span in *Rita* appears to be) and, certainly, it would be unusual for a student to attend one, two tutorials a week. That was the case in 1980 when the play was first staged and then subsequently seen just about everywhere. But I never heard anyone, anywhere, ever say 'hold on, the facts of this play are wrong'. If one achieves a truth then the mere facts will look after themselves. And so although the world of education is (factually) rather different today, the truth of a woman's struggle to find herself through education remains the same truth that it always was and always will be because that kind of inner need/yearning is a universal thing and therefore beyond time and the fashions and dictates of a particular period.

JB: Have you found the inherent musicality of the Liverpool accent, the distinctive cadences and rhythms, helpful in your writing?

WR: I'm working with Alan Parker [on the screenplay for *Blood Brothers*] at the moment; he was saying what's so rich about the Liverpool idiom is that it can be light and flutey and musical and charming but it can be so violent, it can be so heavy. Parker walked into a pub and there was swearing in Scouse and he was immediately nervous and I can understand that but maybe a sense of the musicality of the tongue is something that I can't comment upon because it's just always been there, I take it for granted.

JB: In the introduction to one of your television plays, *Daughters of Albion* (1979), there is a quotation from you, cited by the editor of the collection, that states, 'Literature is an invention by the middle-classes for their own benefit. The working-classes haven't accepted literacy yet, which is why it is so difficult to teach working-class kids whose traditions are in the spoken word.'[2] In the twenty-first-century climate of increased access to all aspects of culture, do you still hold that view?

WR: There's a difficulty in answering that question because that was spoken at a time when you still had a broadly based recognizable working class in this country. Within that working class you may have had all kinds of divisions as there always have been. And something which commentators have never really understood was that there were sub-classes within this – the assumption was that because you're all working class, because you lived in council housing, because you worked in factories, you were the same. Not true – our end of the street wouldn't mix with the common end of the street, people who worked in offices were different from those on the factory floor, the skilled workers superior to the unskilled – all kinds of divisions and sub-divisions. But when it come to certain attitudes and values, they would be shared by all these groups who no matter what their differences in perceived status all subscribed to being part of a wider thing called 'the working class'. When Thatcher introduced 'buy your own council house' she shattered that so totally because once people become home-owners they become, if you like, individual and that is why it is very difficult today to have the kind of community, the kind of society which

2 Cited by Ray Speakman, *Opportunity Knocks? Two Plays: Willy Russell and Polly Teale* (London: Heinemann Floodlights, 1986), p. 1.

was in place when I made those particular comments. You don't have the same broad-based working class that goes to similar jobs, lives fairly similar lifestyles, – that's gone, and what I think there is now is probably a broad market-place class which is also to do with the absolute triumph of capitalism; there's nothing in the way now. No matter what we might think of the Marxist–Leninist movement, there was an alternative philosophy but it has now gone, for years nobody has been able to even mention that kind of opposition to capitalism without being completely sneered at and derided, and we know because of the opening up of appalling versions of Marxist–Leninism that it too was no real alternative, but without an alternative to capitalism you have a consumerism which has just become completely rampant. The seeds of it were there in '78 but it's now so all-pervasive. It's in a speech in *Educating Rita* where Rita says of her husband, 'He thinks we've got choice already: choice between Everton an' Liverpool, choosin' which washing powder, choosin' between one lousy school an' the next, between lousy jobs or the dole, choosin' between Stork and butter.'[3] If anybody tells you that they are giving you more choice – check your wallet! Because they are taking your money and they are lowering your standards; it is the most beautiful con. But what it means is that we don't have the same recognizable, identifiable mass class that existed still in '78. You have a situation now where people wouldn't proudly say, 'Yes, I'm working-class,' that's gone. But what there now is, is a consumer class – and its inevitable offspring, the entrenched underclass. So, my fear is not that the working class, or what is now the working class, has still not embraced literacy. Frankly I'm more concerned at how the middle classes appear to have abandoned literacy! Anyone working in education knows that the standard of literacy is appalling compared with what it was thirty years ago. I happen to think that that fact is bound up with the rapacious capitalism/consumerism I've already alluded to. I'm not saying it's the whole story. But I know when I talk to groups of people, if I come to an institute of education, of higher education or even further education, I know that when I address students I make assumptions about the level of literacy and understanding amongst these people and I'm so wide of the mark. So often the references I make are met with blank, uncomprehending stares. When talking to those who are studying drama I assume that they will have at least the beginning

3 Willy Russell, *Plays One: Breezeblock park, Our Day Out, Stags and Hens, Educating Rita* (London: Methuen, 1996), p. 316.

of a body of knowledge and that I can therefore use a level of language and reference that will be largely understood. But no! So often I want to ask, 'Where is your curiosity?' If you've chosen to study drama then how come you don't know a thing about Brecht or even Shakespeare or the unities or even the simple difference between a proscenium arch and an apron stage? This is not heavy duty academic stuff but simply the kind of stuff that I'd expect anyone interested in the study of drama to know – or at least to want to know. Maybe this is just old-fartism on my part (although I'd take you outside and fight the fuck out of you to prove otherwise!) but I know, though, that I was someone who felt that language had (for complex cultural reasons) been denied me. Maybe that's what created within me my hunger for language. For me language was power but I'm not sure that the language that I and many of my class and generation hungered for is seen by the current generation as a language of power. I don't think that they feel that they would be empowered, respected and sexy in the way that we did by acquiring a certain kind of language, because it goes back to what I said about consumerism, the approval is the approval of everything to do with buying, of purchase.

JB: Would you like to be a student again?

WR: Love to. I am a student; I am a student of Fine Art. We were on a drawing weekend and I just walked into class one day and I said, 'This is great – being a student again,' and it is, it's brilliant to be actually taught and to not know remotely enough about the subject, and I know that every other student in the class knows so much more than me so I can learn from so many people. It's wonderful to be learning; of course I've never ceased to be a student, I have to say – I don't want to be too cheesy about it, but if one is as fortunate to be able to practise, to live the kind of life that I do, you have to perpetually be a student – what I mean is that it is very good to be in the formal situation where I go to a class and the teacher comes in and he is calling the shots, guiding me and putting me into situations where I have to dive off the top board and I don't know if there is any water in the pool, it's that kind of stuff. For years I have said that I would love – and I have even thought about trying to arrange it for myself as a sixtieth birthday present, which is in the not too distant future – to do an Arvon course as a student – I would love to, I'd probably do a poetry course or crime fiction or something. I remember Sue Townsend did one [as a student] years and years ago and Roger McGough was teaching it and she called Roger in advance and said, 'Look, I don't want to turn up and you go mad,' because it could be difficult for the tutors with a fully working pro writer amongst the students. And, equally, that sort of thing could upset the other students as well. So you have to get it right. If I was to go on a course I'd probably pick something which might push me in a completely different direction – something about which I know nothing at all. And that's such a wide, wide field.

16

Subversive Dreamers: Liverpool Songwriting from the Beatles to the Zutons

Paul du Noyer

1

The Beatles were not the beginning of Liverpool music but they are an almost inescapable starting point. In fame and influence the group stands at the zenith of our narrative arc: in them we can trace everything that went before, and their imprint is seen on everything after.

Through the Beatles' writing we see a city's whole history distilled, its musical traditions alchemized. Never before, and seldom since, was an act so closely identified with its place of origin. In 1963 the Beatles' accent and presumed attitudes fed a universal conception of Liverpool as young, fresh, cheeky and optimistic. If the impression proved short-lived, there was at least an authentic connection between the group and its home city. This is not to stuff the butterfly back into its chrysalis – the Beatles were undeniably original, and developed in ways that nobody could have predicted. But our initial proviso remains: the Beatles were inheritors of Liverpool's musical tradition rather than its inventors.

John Lennon and Paul McCartney became songwriters because, in the feverish activity of Liverpool's beat scene, there was a shortage of American rock and soul songs for each group to cover. Few of their rivals aspired to be writers: in that time of Tin Pan Alley it was considered a specialist craft. (Ironically, the first Liverpool rock star Billy Fury, the Beatles' immediate predecessor, was a rare exception: he penned several songs, some under a self-effacing nom-de-plume, Wilbur Wilberforce. Sadly, none were deemed commercial, and all were consigned to the obscurity of LP 'fillers'.) When a stable of 'Mersey-beat' acts emerged in 1963 around the Beatles' manager Brian Epstein, they usually sought material from the standard American sources or else from Lennon and McCartney themselves.

For all the flair of their composing, little in the first four years of John and Paul's partnership was lyrically distinctive. Stern conventions still applied to popular songs for the young: it is amusing to contrast the orgasmic patterns of 'I Want to Hold Your Hand' – tension, crescendo and release – with its chaste physical agenda. A new dispensation swiftly followed: Lennon in particular was straining at the lyrical leash. Emboldened by success, the mid-period Beatles looked outwards for ideas – to Bob Dylan, to Indian raga, to chamber music. And yet, as we will see, they were simultaneously delving backward. To Liverpool.

John's first consciously autobiographical song (though earlier numbers, like 'I'm a Loser', were surely rooted in real feelings) was 1965's 'In My Life', whose initial draft was a litany of bus stops on his boyhood journey from Menlove Avenue to Liverpool's centre. In that draft, a mention of Penny Lane struck Paul as picturesque and prompted his own nostalgic meditation of that name. It was mooted that the group compose a whole album of Liverpool reminiscences; though the idea was forgotten, John responded with 'Strawberry Fields Forever', an evocation of childhood trances on the land behind his Woolton home. The pairing of these two Liverpool songs, on a 1967 single, was conceivably the Beatles' artistic peak.

It is worth noting how much their writing might have owed to three Merseyside mentors. There was the Cavern club's DJ Bob Wooler, a punning wordsmith of impressive prowess, whose intricate stage patter was essential to the group's appearances ('Welcome, Cave-dwellers, to the best of Cellars'). There was their manager Brian Epstein, a cultivated man who assuaged his private disappointments by initiating the Beatles into unsuspected worlds, from gay show business to high-brow theatre. And there was the witty Wirral journalist Derek Taylor, variously the band's press agent, ghost writer and sleeve-note specialist, as well the eventual sponsor of Liverpool luminaries George Melly and Deaf School.

From their *Revolver* LP of 1966 onwards, the Beatles were hailed as pioneers of psychedelia, yet their kaleidoscopic enhancements of reality pre-date their discovery of hallucinogens. A glance at Lennon's early poetry makes that plain. The casual word-play that gave us 'Eight Days a Week' and 'A Hard Day's Night' was entirely Liverpudlian: John evinced the Scouser's Celtic, absurdist, sideways-on approach to the English language – with the additional influence of his childhood exposure to Lewis Carroll, Edward Lear and 'The Goon Show'. (The widely noted echoes of James Joyce, though, were almost certainly accidental.) Once entirely free of pop conventions, and deeper into their solo careers, all four Beatles drew more deeply on their pre-celebrity lives, forever referencing Liverpool as their last genuine contact with 'ordinary' life and authentic community. As Woolton's shrewd surrealist jazzman, George Melly, said of their psychedelic movie *Yellow Submarine*: 'The departure for the Sea of Dreams is from the Liverpool Pier Head.'[1] It quickly became a commonplace of Beatle biographies that their music was shaped by the early availability of American records through the Liverpool docks. As a theory it was over-simplified by repetition, though it's undeniable that the transatlantic seaport was unusually accustomed to jazz, blues and country influences. (A nearby US airbase at Burtonwood was likewise significant.) More fundamentally, the group were products of a tough, humorous and cosmopolitan place, somewhere at the Anglo-Celtic crossroads and steeped in the need for ad hoc entertainment. To be from Liverpool, even before the Beatles and mass media begat a certain self-consciousness about the city's identity, was to be at one remove from standard English reality.

Folk song, for example, survived as living art form here. In the months before his death in New York in 1980, John Lennon was still making home recordings of 'Maggie May', the Liverpool sailors' ditty he had known all his life and included on the Beatles' *Let It Be* LP. Folk songs of the sea and the seaport, and celebrations of the city itself, are a long-standing characteristic of Liverpool; they've informed its cultural atmosphere, and no local songwriter has ever grown up in ignorance of this tradition. Elvis Costello, for example, honed his craft at Liverpool folk evenings: his father Ross McManus made a notable LP of maritime ballads, *The Leaving of Liverpool*. Its title track, in fact, gained great fame through covers by acts around the world including the Dubliners and the Seekers, and has reinforced a dramatic sense of Liverpool's dual role – both a home of exiles and a producer of exiles.

Another storm-tossed tale, 'Johnny Todd', took on new life when adapted for the ground-breaking TV series *Z Cars* (and subsequently adopted by Everton Football Club). Evergreen local acts the Spinners and Jackie and Bridie kept Liverpool's folk songs in the population's repertoire, deepening the Liverpudlians' sense of place, and of their

---

1   George Melly, *Revolt into Style* (London: Penguin, 1970), p. 80.

town as a locale of special emotional freight. More remarkably, even as other towns ceased to generate new folk music, Liverpool inspired a batch of freshly minted examples: Pete McGovern's 'In My Liverpool Home', its rhythm like the rise and fall of a ship's prow, acquired extra verses every year in a bardic or griot fashion; Cilla Black took Stan Kelly's 'Liverpool Lullaby' to worldwide notice; the Scaffold, playing out the final years of their career under the aegis of Derek Taylor, signed off with an elegiac reading of Dominic Behan's 'Liverpool Lou'.

In common with country and western – which, while not indigenous, was so widely played in Liverpool as to be the city's alternative folk form – late-twentieth-century folk song was customarily carried by acoustic guitars. Democratic and accessible, the instrument's ubiquity was one more reason why the city took so swiftly to skiffle, the folk-blues-rock'n'roll hybrid which in turn became the basis of Merseybeat. The acoustic guitar also offers the quickest route to pop songwriting.

In fact, if we look to explain the lack of black musicians in that burgeoning 1960s' scene, one factor would surely be their exclusion from this jangling, strumming Celtic-and-country mainstream; at Afro-Caribbean gatherings, vocal harmonizing was the more valued skill, and dancing to imported R&B records was preferred over locally generated live imitations. The Beatles and other white acts were certainly familiar with Liverpool's black music, though: one of the scene's early sponsors was calypso artist Lord Woodbine; Brian Epstein himself managed Toxteth harmonizers the Chants, whilst the Beatles actually backed them live (though never, alas, on record).

2

For all that psychedelia bore a certain similarity to Liverpudlians' particular mind-set, the style found almost no resonance in the city. With the Beatles now seen as figureheads of the emerging global counter-culture, irrevocably sundered from their homely roots, few of their Merseybeat peers followed the template set by *Sgt. Pepper*; most, like Gerry Marsden and Cilla Black, repudiated rock's new direction and steered instead towards conventional family entertainment. The less successful returned to the beer-and-chips circuit of the region's working-class clubs. In 1967's 'Summer of Love', and for many years after, hippy's sun-soaked acid trappings were anathema to the grittier folk of our damp, sooty Northern port. A marvellous exception, though, was Jimmy Campbell.

Campbell emerged from the Kirbys, a standard beat group of the Beatles aftermath and formed the rather trippier 23rd Turnoff (although, prosaically, their hazy name was taken from the motorway junction leading to Liverpool). He wrote for them a plangent song, 'Michael Angelo', that has endured as a cult classic in the psychedelic genre. More importantly, like Lennon and McCartney, the acid diversion served to free Campbell's songwriting from the old conventions, without unravelling his pop discipline. He continued for several years to fashion albums of melancholy beauty: some chronicled the Liverpool scene that he returned to after rejection at the hands of the London music business; most were infused with sadness (note, for example, the opening and emblematic words of his *Half Baked* LP: 'Could've made it easily, why I didn't I really don't know'). Protracted ill health has curtailed Campbell's recent career, but his reputation will grow.

The generalization holds, though, that rock culture's watershed years of 1966 and 1967 saw most Liverpool musicians define themselves as entertainers rather than artists – a cautious course that would, in time, deny them the fabulous dividends won by their more adventurous Southern counterparts, such as Pink Floyd and Eric Clapton. Beyond the mainstream of commercial pop, however, Liverpool was nurturing a new scene – its leading lights were indeed called the Liverpool Scene – that lacked nothing in curiosity and daring. Clustering uphill from the orthodox night clubs, centred instead upon the Liverpool 8 nexus of university, art college and ethnically diverse Toxteth, this bohemian enclave was self-consciously artistic and avant garde. Even so, it drew its life force from the great city surrounding it, and never abandoned a mission to entertain and amuse.

Adrian Henri, the art teacher and focal point of the jazz-leaning Liverpool Scene, was already prominent in pop art and becoming nationally recognized as one of 'the Liverpool poets'. With the back-up of talented players, including Mike Hart, Andy Roberts and Mike Evans, he carved a third career with his band, who veered from poetry to satire to blues-rock pastiche. Rather more commercial were their friends from the Hope Hall venue, the Scaffold. Formed by Henri's fellow poet Roger McGough, John Gorman and photographer Mike McGear (brother to Paul McCartney), they sacrificed some of their early pungency in the cause of cheering up the nation – hence the pop hits, such as 'Lily the Pink' and 'Thank U Very Much', artfully bridging that gap between fringe surrealism and mass taste.

The point about both bands is that they might, in another time and place, have pursued their muse down more traditional avenues but felt, emerging in 1960s' Liverpool, that pop and rock music were proper and natural outlets too. Henri, like Roxy Music's Bryan Ferry, had studied under pop artist Richard Hamilton at King's College, Newcastle; they, like Peter Blake and Ian Dury, were among the first to move with ease between the worlds of rock and art. Other local artists, such as the acerbic Catholic/communist sculptor Arthur Dooley and the Irish-born portrait painter Sam Walsh, were quickly identified with this suddenly famous pop-and-football town. (Indeed, Dooley's madonna-with-cherubs tribute to Liverpool and the Beatles was hung over the Cavern's entrance, while a full-face image of McCartney remains one of Walsh's best-known works.) John Willett observed in *Art in a City* (London: Methuen, 1967): 'The artist who used to say evasively to his Southern friends 'Oh, I'm from Cheshire' now finds it more creditable to admit he is a Liverpool man.'

The special sub-culture of Liverpool 8, a district unique in its mix of academic respectability and student mischief, architectural grandeur and rude poverty, Anglo-Irish, Chinese and Afro-Caribbean bloodlines, always made it a place apart. But Liverpool is perhaps too small for town and gown to avoid fruitful intimacy. By the mid-1970s there arose a new group of art students who would ignite a musical revival across the city. Deaf School, named after their chosen rehearsal space, were an unwieldy cabaret rock act who included some considerable talents and, in total, offered the best live shows to be found in those times. Since the collapse of the Merseybeat boom there had been a dearth of distinctive Liverpool bands.

Deaf School's ramshackle shows, comical and hectic, offered personality and idiosyncrasy, and became the nucleus of the new live scene that developed in Eric's, the venue that opened in Mathew Street across from the site of the recently demolished Cavern. Deaf School were signed to Warner Brothers by their great champion Derek Taylor; unhappily for them, their gaudy good humour was soon rendered passé by the abrupt arrival of punk rock, stymieing their progress. But in Liverpool, where punk was welcomed and yet not allowed to usurp the entire aesthetic, Deaf School's fan-base spawned the city's next generation of acts. It was not their songwriting (largely parodic and camp) that inspired, so much as their commitment to pop as entertainment, with a dash of Dada absurdism.

The latter component was strikingly present in Big In Japan, virtually an Eric's house band. Several of its members were destined for fame, including Holly Johnson (with Frankie Goes to Hollywood), Ian Broudie (with the Lightning Seeds) and Bill Drummond (with the KLF). So rudimentary was their writing that the group might more aptly be called performance art, but they set the city's course in 1977: neither opposing nor imitating London punk, instead creating a specifically Liverpudlian alternative. Interestingly, despite the relative absence of acid in this period, Eric's most famous alumni, Echo and the Bunnymen and the Teardrop Explodes, were hailed as harbingers of a 'new psychedelia'.

Big in Japan's Bill Drummond, a Scot with a theatrical background, managed both acts and infused them with some of his own grandiose vision. (Each was initially signed to Drummond's heroically self-mythologizing label Zoo; like its Manchester counterpart Factory it was among the first provincial independent companies and briefly set the national agenda.) The Bunnymen's singer/lyricist Ian McCulloch and the Teardrops' Julian Cope were already ambitious in their scope; inflamed by mutual rivalry they concocted a baroque mystique in their music. McCulloch is a brooding Scouse romantic who deploys words for their colour more than their meaning; at best ('Killing Moon' and its 'sky all hung with jewels') he is stirring, at worst he is vague to a frustrating degree. (The group's guitarist and composer Will Sergeant is also key to the city's style: at once an archivist and an explorer.) Cope, like Drummond and Eric's professorial co-owner, the late Roger Eagle, was among those random outsiders who were drawn to Liverpool (in his case to a suburban teacher-training college) and formed a quasi-mystical attachment to the place. In his eventual solo career, Cope became quite literally psychedelic in his art, but the Teardrop Explodes stand as celebrants of Liverpool's quixotic weirdness. Their brief 1981 season of 'Club Zoo' nights requisitioned a grim city centre warehouse for random cabaret happenings from such acts as the Ravishing Beauties.

If Liverpool's punk generation developed along distinctively different lines, another factor was the influence of gay sub-culture. The city's gay venues offered a kind of sanctuary for such new wave exquisites as Jayne Casey, as well as for boys with a dress code different to the standard Liverpool male. The scene itself went on to present British pop with two quite startling entities: Frankie Goes to Hollywood and Pete Burns's Dead or Alive. Both bands were to benefit from slick production makeovers (by Trevor Horn and Stock/Aitken/Waterman respectively) yet retained their roots in Liverpool's dance-driven gay underground.

And in their lyrics they showed the feral hedonism that still amazes any observer of the town centre's pleasure zones, straight or gay.

While the Merseybeat era produced very few Liverpool songwriters beyond Lennon and McCartney, the Eric's generation gave rise to dozens. Pete Wylie of Wah! Heat promoted himself as 'the poet–ruffian' of ringing, declamatory rock. Andy McCluskey of Orchestral Manoeuvres in the Dark (subsequently OMD) took a path less travelled in Liverpool by eschewing guitars in favour of the synthesizer, but his zippy electronic hits were as tuneful as anything since the Beatles (and one song, 'Stanlow', is a masterly evocation of the Mersey's refineries at twilight). Henry Priestman, formerly of the Yachts and It's Immaterial, found his perfect medium in the Christians, combining his songcraft with the Christian brothers' peerless vocals. Like OMD, the Christians became dependable hit-makers of the 1980s and the Liverpool of that time is contrastingly well-represented in their pugnacious 'Forgotten Town' and bucolic 'Greenbank Drive'.

An interesting maverick here is Elvis Costello. London-born to Merseyside parents, he began writing while a teenager in Liverpool. His musical breadth is so encyclopaedic as to defy summary, but the fundamentals acquired in his childhood are quintessentially Scouse: a reverence for the Beatles, a scholarly interest in folk, country and Irish music and a taste for the old show tunes purveyed by his musician father. Gems in his considerable catalogue must include 'New Amsterdam', with its waltzing dockside reveries ('thinking about the old days of Liverpool and Rotherhithe') and, co-written with Deaf School's Clive Langer, the incisive Falkland War critique 'Shipbuilding', one of several Costello songs to evoke Birkenhead.

In parallel to the Deaf School/Eric's resurgence there existed another band whose national success restored Liverpool's musical reputation in the 1970s. Formed around the Amoo brothers, Eddie and Chris, the Real Thing were a Toxteth act whose harmony vocal style achieved the broad success denied to Eddie's old band the Chants. Their renowned soul-pop singles, such as 'Can't Get by without You', were generally supplied by outsiders but the group themselves were responsible for the socially conscious material on 1977's *Four from Eight* album: numbers including 'Stanhope Street' and 'Children of the Ghetto' were explicitly informed by their experiences of growing up black in Liverpool 8.

3

The Real Thing's interrogation of their city finds fewer echoes in Liverpool songwriting than people expect. By the early 1980s, when media reports and Alan Bleasdale's *Boys from the Blackstuff* had shaped a national view of Liverpool as the exemplar of post-industrial desolation, there was much perplexity among music commentators. Why were the city's guitarists not storming barricades? Where was the musical wing of Militant? Why so muted, so elliptical, its response to the depredations of Mrs Thatcher's government? These years would see the town produce a string of winsomely escapist bands who specialized in strange names and occasionally even stranger hairstyles: A Flock of Seagulls, the Lotus Eaters, China Crisis, the Icicle Works …

Back in the 1960s Bob Dylan's folk-protest style was seldom imitated in Liverpool, though the Liverpool Scene's Mike Hart was a notable exception, writing several polemics, such as 'The Shelter Song', proposing that the cathedrals be converted into vast refuges for the homeless. Twenty years later there was scant local evidence of anarcho-punk, nor the London proletarian cult of Oi, nor even of the country's largest sub-genre, heavy metal – which, although largely apolitical, at least sounded angry. On closer inspection, it's true, the Liverpudlians' habitual attachment to melody might conceal a darker outlook, a fine instance being the deceptively insouciant 'Wonderful Life' by Colin Vearncombe of Black. One could point to various songs that have struck a dissenting local note: Pete Wylie's 'Story of the Blues', Cook da Books' 'Piggy in the Middle Eight', Smaller's 'In My Livable Hole', Jegsy Dodd's 'Who Killed New Brighton?' or indeed Shack's 'Who Killed Clayton Square?'

It remains the case, though, that social commentary is not an especially dominant strain in the city's music. Perhaps it sits awkwardly with a certain native predilection for creative vagueness. So much Liverpool music explores an inner space, a dreamscape – quite unlike the observational streak that has run through classic London pop, from the Kinks and Squeeze to the Streets and Dizzee Rascal. Even the Beatles' 'Penny Lane', though praised for its reportorial concision, essentially describes a state of reverie; so do McCartney's sepia-toned memories in his contribution to Lennon's 'A Day in the Life'.

By the late 1980s Liverpool's young writers were even further adrift from British trends, rejecting the synthetic modernism of chart pop in favour of the arcane and the archaic. A dope-enhanced appreciation of

Pink Floyd, Frank Zappa and Captain Beefheart – none of which, like the drug itself, commanded much support the first time around in Liverpool's working-class communities – became the characteristic influence. Blues and primitive rock'n'roll were likewise rediscovered. An atavistic preference for the jangling guitars of Merseybeat opposed the high-production sheen of the era. Tunes were at a premium. So, too, was a strangely torpid mysticism. Later pundits came to call this amalgam 'Cosmic Scally', but in 1989 it was personified by one group, the La's.

The La's chief writer, Lee Mavers, helped devise at least two neo-Merseybeat classics in 'Timeless Melody' and 'There She Goes'; his bassist John Power carried the approach forward with his next group, Cast. The La's, and Mavers in particular, were ill at ease in London's music industry and the group fell apart, only to enjoy a posthumous reputation as prophets of Britpop, secured by the endorsement of Noel Gallagher from Oasis. Like their Liverpool contemporaries Rain and the Real People, The La's return to pre-psychedelic song values, albeit subdued with a smoky quiescence of mind ('I am the voyager of the ocean grey,' goes 'Liberty Ship'; 'I wayfarer see fairway'), would become widely influential.

Mavers resides, in rock legend, as a mysterious Lost Boy: the pop crafts-man whose melodies sparkle in the gloom of a depressed city. Arguably, though, his achievements are surpassed by Michael Head of Shack (formerly of the Pale Fountains). Head's songs, which have never won the widespread favour so regularly predicted for them, are immaculate examples of Liverpool's tuneful yearning, even when set in the drug-plagued estates of its grimmest districts. 'Streets of Kenny' (referring to Kensington, north-east of the city centre) documents an addict in search of his contacts, yet with a graceful swooping tune that pitches it as near to McCartney as to Lou Reed's 'Waiting for the Man'. Shack, too, rein-troduced a sea-shanty feel that subsequent local acts fell upon with relish.

Shack also championed West Coast psychedelic figurehead Arthur Lee of Love, backing him in Liverpool on a memorable live album. The marked affinity of so many local musicians with US acts has been a recur-rent phenomenon; from the fast adoption of rock and R&B in the 1950s (in a city already steeped in country, with a significant jazz following, too) to the Eric's generation's taste for the cult imports, such as Television and Patti Smith, to the 'retro-scally' hunters of vinyl bargain bins. There is something strikingly omnivorous in this appetite for American music, entirely transcending that country's internal divisions of race, region and cultural category.

Romantic as the semi-obscurity of Mavers and Head may seem, it is the business of pop to be popular, and Ian Broudie of the Lightning Seeds is certainly that. Remarkably for a graduate of the defiantly unlistenable Big in Japan, Broudie is perhaps the most radio-friendly musician of recent times. He served a studio apprenticeship producing both Echo and the Bunnymen and Teardrop Explodes. His mentoring of the city's talent would continue in his overseeing of twenty-first-century breakthrough acts the Coral and the Zutons. In between, he has translated his boyhood Beatle worship into the sophisticated production values of modern pop, writing supremely tuneful, often dream-like pop hits, such as 'Pure', 'Lucky You' and 'Sugar Coated Iceberg'. His collaboration with Ian McNabb, 'Feeling Lazy', rivals 'Penny Lane' for its sunny, slanted realism ('Mr Johnson's car gets the weekend shine … and Lisa in the garden, singing to the washing line'). In the tradition of Gerry Marsden, Broudie would compound his Liverpool typicality by writing the English football anthem, 'Three Lions'.

During the 1990s' supremacy of dance music, Liverpool's Cream club served to further the city's reputation for nightlife, though its staple diet was obviously in contrast to the city's normal regime of melodic guitar songs. A group who occupied the middle ground, however, were the Farm. Consciously distant from the 'arty' aspects of the Eric's performers, the Farm found an affinity with Liverpool's scally youth cult (especially in its love of football) and the dance scene that developed from club nights at the State and elsewhere; their writing team of Peter Hooton and Steve Grimes were also more willing than most to add a political edge.

Britain's most celebrated girl group at the turn of the century, Atomic Kitten, were not songwriters (in fact their material was partly the work of their founder, OMD's Andy McCluskey), although they wonderfully epitomised the Liverpool girl at large. Cilla aside, the more successful local acts have almost always been male, and female writers are hard to locate – one is tempted to include the Liverpool-born Kathryn Williams, though her musical story more justly belongs to her adopted home of Newcastle. Increasingly, no doubt, there will be Scousers-by-association, educated at the Liverpool Institute for Performing Arts (which claimed its first chart-topping graduate in the 2006 success story, Sandi Thom).

In the twenty-first century the city's offering has once again been dominated by melodic guitar bands, notably the Coral and the Zutons, both signed to the local Deltasonic label and each described, at least by outside commentators, as in the 'cosmic scally' mould. Both bands do exhibit an attachment to various retro styles, but their eclecticism goes much further than any of their predecessors: garage-punk, psychedelia and blues are prominent, with dashes of more unlikely influences: sea-shanties, polka, mariachi ... In fact, the gleeful indiscipline of their music recalls Deaf School as much as the La's. The Coral's main writer, James Skelly, tempers the Treasure Island exotica with sincerely romantic lyrics, often touching in their emotional directness, and reassuringly Merseyside in their dreamy evocations of stars, the sky and the universe. The Zutons' Dave McCabe, like his band, has a more urgently urban edge: typical themes concern the psychic turbulence of fractured romance and pressurized modern life – one song, 'Dirty Dancing', captures a clubland bloodbath on a 'night in the City of Culture'.

4

'You have to be a comedian to live here' and 'Look at the place: if you didn't laugh you'd cry' are two of the city's more venerable clichés. A militant whimsy defines the local comic tradition – a whimsy that might be called surreal, though its practitioners would scorn that term as pretentious. Deep in the Beatles' folk memory were such men as Arthur Askey (indeed, McCartney famously inherited his old school desk at the Liverpool Institute) who in 1938 commanded a radio audience of twenty million: his signature piece, 'The Bee Song', had the little man flapping invisible wings and hymning his love for pollen. Tommy Handley (pictured on the *Sgt. Pepper* sleeve) and Deryck Guyler of the *ITMA* wireless show foreshadowed the Goons. And who would dispute the ineffable strangeness of Ken Dodd's imaginary universe of Diddy-men?

Here was humour that was neither earthy nor blunt – those supposed Northern traits – but spacey and oblique. Its pop culture inheritors range from Anfield's Alexei Sayle (he made an early LP called *The Fish People Tapes*) and Birkenhead's Half Man Half Biscuit – the latter band an enduring resource for fans of indie satire and subversive juxtapositions ('The Trumpton Riots', 'Joy Division Oven Gloves'). Tommy Scott's band of the Britpop era, Space, specialized in a mordant hilarity, rewarded by hits like 'The Ballad of Tom Jones' (with Cerys Matthews) and 'Neighbourhood'.

As evident as humour is communality. In a town where no male exchange may omit the ship's term 'mate', honouring the comradeship of deck and dock, solidarity is perhaps the most-respected virtue. The late-period Beatles evoked their old community, even as their internal unity was dissolving: the charabanc all-togetherness of 'The Magical Mystery Tour', the terrace-like singalong of 'Hey Jude'; even Lennon, the willing artistic partner of avant gardist Yoko Ono, still took pride in crafting simple mass-anthems: 'Give Peace a Chance', 'Instant Karma!', 'Imagine'.

Gerry Marsden, of the Pacemakers, merits inclusion here – in part for a string of under-rated pop hits that ranked his band second only to the Beatles in Merseybeat success, but also as the architect of a signature Scouse style that remains ubiquitous. His 'Ferry Cross the Mersey' might almost have become the town's most dearly loved song – were it not surpassed by his interpretation of the Rodgers and Hammerstein show song 'You'll Never Walk Alone' (from the musical *Carousel*). The immediate adoption of 'You'll Never Walk Alone' by the Kop's choristers of 1963 was an inspired act of community branding. Not coincidentally, the song's emergence at the Liverpool football ground sound-tracked the team's Shankly-driven transformation into a world-class club side.

Later examples of that same anthemic impulse are found in Pete Wylie's epic 'Heart as Big as Liverpool' and, in a lower key, Ian McNabb's 'Liverpool Girl' ('The laughter from her golden throat / Can be heard from the Irish boat'). If the city's songwriters are dreamers, they are capturing a communal dream; theirs is not the art of the atomized individual. While most art and literature are essentially private experiences, music is shared with an audience; the performing arts, football included, are Liverpool's very heartbeat. 'You'll Never Walk Alone' would speak to the fans' collectivist ethos, to civic patriotism and – on every emotionally pungent occasion, from Shankly's funeral to ceremonies for the Hillsborough fatalities – to the deepest bonds of human fellow-feeling. Unconsciously, perhaps, it is the song that all Liverpool writers are trying to emulate.

In their varied ways the Liverpool writers display a passion for entertainment and musical accessibility, yet with a lyrical vision that is defiantly idiosyncratic. Forever at one remove from mere realism, they represent a population that was in a sense psychedelic before the term was even invented – a city of subversive dreamers.

17

Putting Down Roots:
An Interview with Levi Tafari

Dave Ward

Levi Tafari was born in Liverpool in 1960 to parents of Jamaican origin. He has published four collections of poetry: Duboetry *(the Windows Project, 1987),* Liverpool Experience *(Michael Schwinn, 1989),* Rhyme Don't Pay *(Headland, 1993) and* From the Page to the Stage *(Headland, 2006). His plays have been performed at the Unity Theatre and the Playhouse in Liverpool, as well as at the Blackheath Theatre in Stafford. He has also worked on educational projects, running creative writing workshops in schools, colleges, universities, youth centres, prisons and libraries. His musical projects include working with the Ghanaian drum and dance ensemble Delado, the Liverpool Philharmonic Orchestra, and with his own reggae fusion band Ministry of Love. He has also played with Urban Strawberry Lunch and Griot Workshop and has recently worked with jazz musician Dennis Rollins. Levi was talking to Dave Ward at the Windows Project office on Bold Street, Liverpool, in February 2006.*

LT: I was born and raised in Liverpool. My parents came from the island of Jamaica, so that had a huge influence on me. My Mum worked in Crawfords, the biscuit factory. My dad did joinery – he worked in Courthaulds, up in Aintree. My parents, particularly my Mum, were immersed in the oral tradition. When Mum used to be in the kitchen, cooking, she used to come out with little rhymes, stories, proverbs and riddles from Jamaica.

When I grew up in Liverpool, in the sixties and seventies, there was a large Jamaican population. There used to be sound systems and they would play the latest tunes.[1] And coming out of Jamaica in the seven-

---

1 The sound systems evolved to include large customized speaker boxes and twin turntables used by deejays at Caribbean style entertainment venues, such as parties, big halls and outdoor venues.

ties were deejays, people like Big Youth and I-Roy – and they used to pick up the mic and they would put this poetry together based on a popular rhythm. Then when the reggae poets came along, they started taking a reggae rhythm, not a specific rhythm, but they would just develop the poetry around a reggae feel. So rather than take a popular song that was out there like the deejays used to do, the Jamaican reggae poets – or Dub poets as they became known – would highlight the rhythm to words that they created. So all this was going on when I was a black youth growing up in the seventies and there were skinheads chasing us and attacking us in Toxteth. The police didn't help – and in fact the police seemed to be on the skinheads' side – so it was like we were being persecuted. We were being oppressed and ghettoized.

My Dad was quite political in his thoughts. I wouldn't say that he was very active in terms of being part of any black political party, but he used to have his ideas. He used to have a Marcus Garvey mentality in his chain of thought. This all had an influence on me. Growing up in Liverpool – because of the area, Liverpool's history and the way black people were being treated – I wanted to say something.

One day I came to realize that words have power. I used to do a little bit of deejaying. When we were at school, at Arundel Comprehensive, I remember a few of us went out and got into trouble. There used to be a Catholic girls' school down the road. Some of our girls used to go down there and they attacked the other girls and stole their hats. A gang of people got in trouble and the whole school was on a curfew as a result of that. This would have been about 1972. What happened was, when we had this curfew, kids were getting into trouble because they couldn't leave the school premises, so we needed to do something. Me and a couple of guys got together and we suggested that we should bring some tunes in at lunchtime and run a disco. So they agreed to it because it would ease the problem that was taking place. We had an abandoned dining room there then, which we cleaned up. We borrowed an old gramophone from the music department and we started bringing tunes in – James Brown, Jackson Five and Tamla Motown stuff.

It had a huge impact and slowly we introduced little bits of reggae and some of us used to do what was called 'toasting'. Rap hadn't hit – rap didn't come along till '79, '80. We used to have competitions to see who could out-toast the other – who could come up with the best lyrics and the best rhymes. I was quite good at it, so I used to do that – then that spilled over into social life outside the school. There were two sound systems. There was Kwamina HiFi and Crasher HiFi. It was like Everton and Liverpool – they would compete against each other, but both were from Toxteth. But then there were other sound systems in other cities like Manchester, Birmingham and London. Different sound systems would travel from the other end of the country to play against each other.

All of this was going on in the seventies in community centres like the Caribbean Centre or the Methodist Centre, even the Blackie (Great Georges Project). In other places like Manchester it would be in their Caribbean Centre and there was a place called the Nile. Some night-clubs would have sound systems where they'd been more long established. We used to listen to Jamaican deejays in clubs like the Time Piece and the Babalou and the Pun. Eric's used to have an Open Mic. Eric's was a great one because they used to have the live deejays straight from Jamaica – so people like Dillinger came over and Tappa Zukie. They would play with groups like the Boomtown Rats. They would have a lot of punks there. There would be a punk band and a reggae band. They were both empathetic to each other in terms of musical taste, whereas the mainstream shunned and looked down upon reggae. So reggae and punk got together. Bob Marley even did a song 'Punky Reggae Party'.

I went to Granby Street Primary, infants and juniors and then moved on to Arundel Comp. I really wanted to go to Paddington Comp. because there was safety in numbers, because during the seventies when I was at school there were a lot of skinheads. We did keep together as black people and the majority of black kids went to Paddington Comp. My wife Carol went to Paddington. But my Mum said it's a bad school, it's got a bad reputation, so I went to Arundel. But we were large in numbers there as well.

DW: Has Liverpool as a city influenced your writing in any way – did it when you started and does it now?

LT: Liverpool's had a huge impact on the way I write – or the things that I've written about – and still does to some extent. Liverpool's a political place. People here have taken politics seriously. It's got a rich oral tradition in terms of the Irish influence. It's got the oldest black community in Europe and the oldest Chinese community. And all of these communities have had a rich oral tradition. And the music scene, the thing with the Beatles, the poets themselves – Brian Patten, Roger McGough and the late Adrian Henri – have had an influence on the city, and it has had some impact on me.

When I first started writing I was told to join the Liverpool 8 writers' workshop. David Evans, a South African writer and novelist who was in exile here, was one of the leaders. There was also Ken Chevans, a Jamaican writer and poet, and Olive Rogers – they were the three workshop leaders. You couldn't have asked for three more different people. When I went to the workshop they told me I was a good writer. They inspired and encouraged me – so their influence also had an impact.

Liverpool with its sea port and its influences from different parts of the world – that has had a huge impact. Liverpool is multicultural and multiracial – although to me it doesn't really embrace that the way it should or could. I think there is a lot of racism here. The black community is still looked down upon and vilified to some extent. It's been difficult to shake '81 off – and I think that the reason why the riots happened in 1981 is because of the way that the black community was being treated at the time.

So all of those elements have had an influence on my writing or provoked me into writing. I feel whether it's positive or negative that it's definitely had an impact on my writing. The way I write and the style I write has influences from Jamaica, the Caribbean, and that side of my culture – but I don't divorce myself from the other sides, because I always say that I'm tri-cultural: I have an African root with a Jamaican heritage and a British experience. So those three elements are important.

DW: You mentioned music before and I know you've fronted your own band. Can you tell us something about that?

LT: I've been heavily involved in music because it was the Jamaican deejays who blended their brand of poetry with music which inspired people like the Last Poets: Jalal and Sulaman were working with jazz and so I've always been into music – Bob Marley in particular; and when the chance came to work with musicians I seized the opportunity.

The first band that I fronted was called the Singers and Players of Instruments because of the line from one of the Psalms which says that 'the singers and players of instruments shall be there and they will be included among those who are redeemed'. I see my tongue as being an instrument. I've even written a poem called 'The Tongue' which says that the tongue was the first instrument, before the drum. The band included Muhammad Khalil, a good friend and fellow poet. Milky was the guitarist, Jay was the bass player and Muhammad also used to do a bit of drumming. We formed about 1981 or '82. We went out and did a few gigs and built up a good reputation, then Muhammad and myself merged with Western Promise to form a new group called the Ministry of Love, which used a kind of rock/punk influence with our reggae and soul background. Muhammad came from an African-American tradition which dealt with soul and funk and mine was more reggae, ska and Jamaican. So we fused all those elements together.

I was singing and doing bits of poetry. What was interesting was that the music was specifically geared towards the poetry, so rather than getting a rhythm and trying to make our poetry fit the rhythm, the musicians listened to the melodies in the poetry and developed the music around it. Our poetry works verse/chorus/verse/chorus so it was almost like a song – it was easy to lend itself to music. It was hugely popular – we did stuff on TV, we toured, we played places like the Rock Garden in London, which was a big music venue. We played the Royal Court and Empire Theatre in Liverpool. At the time Liverpool was a hotbed for lots of musicians – A&R people were coming and signing bands. Echo and the Bunnymen were doing their thing and the Christians. The Flying Picket was another venue which would host and accommodate music, so we had plenty of gigs. We were gigging three or four times a week sometimes and going to London and doing stuff, and because my work as a poet was getting popular it meant the band was doing more and we were getting more. If a TV programme was doing a feature on me then they would want to include different aspects of my work – so they would feature the band, they would feature the poetry, they would feature workshops. A couple of the workshops I did for the Windows Project were filmed by Channel Four.

Out of that experience I worked with Chris Potter. We did workshops where we would take in percussive instruments and play. I also worked with Jennifer John for a while and that was a good experience because Jennifer was classically trained, so it was an opportunity to work in a different environment. We were doing clubs in London. We did the new variety circuit and we did the poetry circuit as well through Apples and Snakes, which was a good experience. We had a set up called Black and Blue. It was the idea of black people feeling the blues. We did a version of 'Strange Fruit' by Billie Holliday. We wrote bits of poetry to go with the verses – in the same way as a rapper would work with a R&B artist, but we were doing this back in the early eighties.

That led to working with the Royal Liverpool Philharmonic Orchestra. The Philharmonic were saying that not enough local people were visiting the Philharmonic Hall so Muhammad and I devised a Saturday Matinee show and called it the Hot House – and we worked with a hundred-piece orchestra. Each one of the national BBC radio stations from One through to Five ran a feature on it, including the Johnnie Walker Show on Radio Five and Janice Long on Radio One. The first season was based on dance – we had traditional Irish dance, Bhangra dance, contemporary and jazz. We had a Ghanaian group come and perform. It was so successful that we got a second season which was on the human voice – gospel music, choir music, choral singing. We also did a Christmas show. Ian McMillan was invited and he worked with schools to devise poems for the performance. We did one show a month for six months each season, involving a wide range of musical experiences.

DW: Do you think working with music and musicians has influenced the way that you approach performance as a poet?

LT: Working with music gives you a different perspective, including stage presence and confidence. I prefer working with live musicians as opposed to pre-recorded music, because if the technology breaks down then it makes it difficult. In terms of my writing it's made me more rhythmic. It's made me hear things differently as well and deal with melodies in a more intricate way.

My poetry has enabled me to meet people like Dr Maya Angelou and the Last Poets. I've also worked with Nina Edge on a piece called 'Trophies of Empire', looking at when Columbus set sail and said he discovered America – the whole thing of Columbus not discovering anything really. We did a series of installations which came out of the experience of poetry that was written by myself and Muhammad Khalil and Bisakha Sarker danced to that. Poetry has that ability to adapt to different situations. And I would say that my kind of poetry, even more so because it's more performance based, lends itself well to music, and it can be used in different types of venues – in the classroom, in the theatre, in a nightclub, in a concert arena.

DW: I know you travel widely throughout the world with the British Council and other agencies. Can you tell us about that?

LT: Through the British Council, I get sent to countries where there are British Council offices so I've done quite a lot of work in places like Portugal, Singapore, Jordan and Germany. Some of the tours have been quite high profile because in places like Singapore and Jordan I've done spots on television. If you get yourself in the newspaper then people recognize you in the streets. Just the experience of working in a different country where they have different ideas and they see poetry through different spectacles – the fact that they can acknowledge and relate to my poetry – is for me fantastic.

DW: Is poetry perceived in a different way in different countries?

LT: Some nations treat poets with more importance than others. Here, when you tell people you're a poet, straight away they start rhyming – 'You're a poet and you don't know it.' People who haven't seen me for a long time still approach me and say, 'Are you still doing that poetry, Levi?' The emphasis is on that – it's almost as if you've been messing about with it – you're not a proper poet . Whereas in other countries, when you introduce yourself or people find out that you're a poet, then people embrace you or show you great respect.

In places like the Czech Republic or Germany, where they take literature seriously, people see you in a different light. They see you as more than just someone who puts words together in rhymes. They also see you as a counsellor. I find in the Middle East, when I've worked there, they also see you as a spiritual person like a shaman, someone who deals with spiritual matters or who has a 'third eye'. It's not just an occupation, they see it as part of your life, both social and cultural.

There's a poetry society in the Czech Republic in Prague which meets once a month – they are musicians and poets but they have other jobs – but they are really respected. Even the ex-President of the Czech Republic is a poet. I did a performance with him at their National Poetry Festival along with Ahmed Baraka, who was a poetical hero of mine as a youth.

DW: When you're touring are people particularly interested that you come from Liverpool?

LT: Yes, because they know that Liverpool has a history with the three 'Liverpool Poets' as well as the Beatles. Whenever I say I'm from Liverpool no-one will ask the question, 'Where is that?' because everyone knows Liverpool and I think they know Liverpool's got a rich oral tradition.

I think the British Council want to show the diversity of Britain's culture – so Benjamin Zephaniah and myself have done a lot of work through them. And I think also it's not just the case that we get a lot of work – we deliver what is asked of us, otherwise they wouldn't ask us back!

I've also been doing work through the British Armed Forces, working in the schools in Germany and Cyprus. I'm not into war and I wouldn't like any of my children to be soldiers or in any of the forces really, but

I don't work with the Army per se, I work with the children of service people. It's great in the sense that although their parents are British, a lot of them are born overseas and have never been to Britain so it's good for them to see a black writer – a black person who is not a footballer or a singer – to see a black person involved in creative writing, who is doing something creative in that way.

I can express my style of poetry and explain it to them in a technical way, in an academic way that makes them understand not only the writing but the cultural and social history that goes behind the writing. So they don't just stereotype and think when they see me turning up with dreadlocks wearing a red, yellow and green hat, 'Here's a man who listens to reggae and smokes weed and lazes around all day!'

DW: I know you're a practising Rastafarian. Does that influence your writing as well as your way of life?

LT: Being a Rastafarian has given me a spiritual dimension as well as a political dimension, and it's made me understand the social make-up of society because of the way we think as Rastafarians. We don't see our way of life as a religion, though it can be categorized as that – but we're not dogmatic. We don't try to win religious converts like some other religions. It's something that you ease yourself into or you embrace. It calls you – you don't have to convert people. 'Many are called but a few are chosen.'

DW: I know that Rastafarianism particularly led to a journey to Ethiopia.

LT: I went to Ethiopia on a pilgrimage as a Rastafarian. Ethiopia is our spiritual home. Fortunately for me the BBC followed me and made a documentary of my pilgrimage. It's something that I always wanted to do, and I probably would have done it just on my own without the BBC, but then they got in touch and asked me if I would go to Ethiopia on a pilgrimage – and I just said yes!

What was interesting about the trip was it was my first time going to the African continent. To go to Ethiopia as a first trip was extra-special. We contacted the various organizations out there like the Ethiopian World Federation, the Twelve Tribes of Israel, the Boboshanti. I met a few Ethiopian Rastafarians who have embraced the faith out there.

That particular year it was the celebration of the centenary of the victory at the Battle of Adowa. The Ethiopians celebrate the event every year. There was a re-enactment of the battle and all the leaders of the African nations were invited. They were present at the ceremony and we filmed at the ceremony and I got to meet some of them. The only leader that wasn't there was Nelson Mandela, who was busy on other engagements. But it was a fantastic occasion, a great atmosphere. They wear white robes, but the place was awash with red, yellow and green, because that's the colours of Ethiopia.

The different faiths united: the Ethiopian Orthodox Church, the Ethiopian Coptic Church, and also the Islamic faith. So everybody was there as part of this celebration. It was a joyous occasion – it was uplifting. The Rastafarians were celebrating. The Rastafarians were invited from Jamaica by way of Ire FM – Mutabaruka, Yousef Green and Tony Rebel were there – so for me it was a great experience to go to Ethiopia, and to be able to give the world an insight into the relationship between Rastafari and Ethiopia.

When I was in Jordan I was performing at Lawrence of Arabia's house, which is now an arts centre, along with Brian Patten. At the end of the performance a family approached me, which I then learnt was Ethiopian. They had seen the film and they commended me on how good it was, and they commended me on my honesty as well. They praised the film's accuracy – in the fact that Ethiopia is a great nation, it's one of the oldest civilizations. The oldest bones to date have been found there. The oldest church is in Ethiopia, built into the side of a mountain. They profess to have the Ark of the Covenant, and we believe that it is there.

So there is all of this greatness – but there's a lot of poverty there as well and it has had its tribulations in terms of a coup and the drought in the early eighties when Band Aid got together to raise money. All of that makes Ethiopia what it is and it was great to be able to go there and see it for myself. As I said, it was my first trip to the African continent and I've always written about Africa in a romantic way – to actually go there and feel it and taste it was a different experience.

DW: I know you've recently been gravely ill. Has the experience of your hospital treatment influenced your way of thinking or your view of your own writing?

LT: I have recently been in hospital with a condition known as myasthenia gravis, which led to me getting a condition called colitis. Both are auto-immune conditions and will be with me for the rest of life, unless they find a cure. I have also got deep vein thrombosis (DVT), which with all the travelling I do anyway, I've had before. And then I have a condition called polycythenia, which is a thickening of the blood – too many red blood cells, which causes the DVT. So they're all inter-linked.

I came close to death, and that does make you reassess life and see things in a different way. I was two hours away from intensive care, which could have gone either way. I collapsed outside the hospital when I was going to get a test to see if I was myasthenia gravis positive.

It's made me think about life and my writing, and while I was in hospital I had a revelation that I should write about health issues. They're at the forefront of society at the moment because there are so many people that are ill. And I would say that it's our society and our lifestyle that is making us ill. This includes diabetes and heart attacks, rheumatism and various neurological conditions. Since I've been diagnosed with myasthenia gravis, which is a neurological condition, I've come across a number of other conditions which are to do with the nervous system – and people that I know that I didn't even realize were suffering from these conditions have revealed themselves to me.

Our society is plagued at the moment with obesity. Obesity to me is self-inflicted. We live in a society which deals in excess and we have this idea of 'buy one get one free'. We use cheap labour overseas so we can get cheap products. We have access to more than we need. I would say people are becoming ill, myself included – I'm a part of this society, and I indulge occasionally.

My faith and the fact that I'm a writer has made me more of a balanced person and made me see things in a different way. So my dietary needs are not what average or regular people want. I don't eat burgers and stuff like that or go to chicken joints and eat fried chicken. I don't have McDonalds or Kentuckys. I try and eat a natural diet. I like soups. I used to be a chef anyway – so it's made me see things in a different way – the way what we eat is linked to the Earth – and how we treat the Earth, how we grow these things.

I have written a couple of things, but not as much as I would have liked to, because I'm convalescing with this illness. I've got so many things wrong with me and I'm taking so much medication and I have to go to hospital on a regular basis and I've been to see an eye specialist recently who said that there could have been cancer at the back of my eyes, which they kept quiet – but now I've been given the all-clear. My DVT's sort of cleared up now and the myasthenia's under control.

I would like to set up a project where I could go into hospitals, because when I was in hospital, once I had started to get better, I found being a writer and a storyteller, that I was able to converse easily with some of the other patients in my ward. What's interesting is that men who were from a different cultural background, a different generation, related to me as a person and I could relate to them – some of them had never come across a Rastafarian before.

I was in a neurological centre and there were guys there from different parts of the country, from Wales, from Leeds, a couple of Scousers and people from different places. I found I started reciting poetry because they asked what I did. It seemed to be therapeutic to them.

The nurses said I had another condition known as PMA – Positive Mental Attitude. They were saying that each day they were coming and telling me, 'Levi, you've got this wrong with you now,' and, 'We've just discovered you've got a blood clot' – and they couldn't believe that I hadn't cracked up or gone into a deep state of depression.

Staying positive has helped me to get better and continue my work as a writer. The idea of being a writer and having a spiritual foundation, and having family support and support from other writers, it's all helped. And the fact that people are still enquiring about me as a writer, and everyone's wishing me well so that I continue what I'm doing, has all helped. So by reciting a few poems in the hospital, I've just seen the effect it's had on the nursing staff and patients and made me want to do a project.

Writing has been positive in my recovery. Even when I left hospital, I'd written a poem for the staff to thank them for getting me better. It had such an impact that a couple of the male nurses – it brought tears to their eyes. And if people don't believe me, they can ask my wife Carol who was there. When I performed it to the staff, you could see they really felt what I was saying. It's great to communicate in that way.

DW: How do you see your writing and performance work developing in the future?

LT: I would like to continue to write poetry. I would like to get into more script writing, and ideally it would be great to do some screen work, in the same way as Jimmy McGovern and Willy Russell. But I know it's not easy, it is quite difficult, and I'm not saying that as a cop out. I have done script-writing. I've had about three or four plays performed. I've had stuff at the Everyman, the Playhouse and the Unity theatres in Liverpool and the Blackheath Theatre in Stafford. I've also devised a few pieces that have gone out on the road – one being *Sacred Moves* with Bisakha Sarker – I wrote the poetry for that. It looks at people from the colonies, from the empire, who came to Britain and made a contribution: from the Caribbean, from West Africa, from China and Asia. So it would be nice to write more pieces in that sense.

There are certain things you can say in poetry that can be said better by way of drama – and also the other way round. I would like to pursue that side.

I would like to get back to working with music. I've done stuff recently with Dennis Rollins, who's a jazz musician who wrote a piece on the griot and the oral tradition, and when he heard my poetry he said it would fit perfectly to his show – so we're talking about that at the moment. I worked with Dennis in 2004. We set up a project which was well received in his home town of Doncaster and we linked it with six different schools. We got the students to write the poetry which we then set to music. Dennis is a jazz musician who's worked with people like Courtney Pine. He's really good, he's classically trained and he can improvise, he composes. So it was great working with him. He isn't an egotist either – he's a really nice guy, we got on really well. I can see us working together in the future, so I'd like to pursue that.

Also my education work is important. I like to feel that I'm not just giving something back but also showing students who might want to do it, that might think it's difficult or there's a big mystery around it, that there is no mystery – the mystery is in you and you need to bring it out.

The mystery's not around us. There's poetry around us, but what brings that poetry out is in you. So it's almost like – I remember a kung fu movie where they were seeking enlightenment and this guy went through all this hardship and everything to find the book of enlightenment, and when he found the book and he opened it, inside the book was a mirror. The book told him – life's mystery is you. So that's how I see things. I see that poetry is inside all of us and it will take something to trigger it, to bring it out. And with me, it was living in Liverpool and living in Toxteth in particular at a time when I was growing up as a youth in the seventies. That's what sparked it off. Maybe if I'd grown up in Winsford I wouldn't have been a poet, or found poetry inside me. If I'd had a privileged background ... I don't know. I think that the combination of all those things – of living in Liverpool, Liverpool being the city that it is – a creative city, a productive city, in terms of arts, in terms of industry.

My poetry has taken me far and wide, which was an ambition of mine as a youth, to travel. Which was why I became a chef, because I figured that if I ever went anywhere and decided to set down roots, then I'd always be able to get work, because people have always got to eat. But it's ironic that it wasn't through my catering that I started travelling, it was through poetry – which is something that I had no idea that I was going to do when I got the urge to want to travel. But I think that again it was living in Liverpool, Liverpool being a sea port, and maybe going on the ferries, going across the water, gave me that need to travel.

And then again, some of the racism and other schisms that I had to face when I was growing up made me want to move away from the area – but as you can see, all these years later – I'm still here!

18

'Out of Transformations':
Liverpool Poetry in the Twenty-first Century

Peter Barry

It's some time in the 1960s, and I'm 'in town', as always on a Saturday morning, in and out of bookshops, the Bluecoat, the Museum, the William Brown Library, and the like. I'm in my teens, and enjoying the bustle of the place. But around one o'clock, when the bookshops close, I'm glad to make for the Pier Head, getting that airy, opening-out feeling as the river is glimpsed from the top of Water Street, always with a cargo ship at anchor in mid-stream – Blue Funnel, Harrison's, Pacific Steam, or whatever – the superstructure glaring white in the sunshine, and the familiar blue line of the Welsh hills beyond. There is constant move-ment on the river – tugs, ferries, and the miscellaneous small craft that do chores for the 'MD&HB'. All that bustle seemed the epitome of a city whose job wasn't to make things, but to move them from one side of the world to the other.

That Liverpool scene, as many of its older citizens say, is now trans-formed, and so is the 'Liverpool Scene' of poetry and performance celebrated in the 1960s era by Edward Lucie-Smith.[1] The change of cultural scene is no surprise, of course, for the city itself is now being transformed yet again, and a corresponding transformation of its poetry is only to be expected. Like so many other UK cities, Liverpool has long been de-industrialized, and many inner-city parts of it have been 'rural-ized', for there are trees, suburban gardens, and grassy embankments on Scotland Road, and green hills round Everton Valley, producing a rather confusing mixed visual message, at least to my exile's eye. Above all, the city's core business has changed, with the docks tidied away down-

---

1 Edward Lucie-Smith (ed.), *The Liverpool Scene* (London: Rapp & Whiting/Andre Deutsch, 1967).

stream, leaving a place that is tourist-centred, geared to the requirements of massive 'visitor attractions', and dominated by the leisure arts, by sports and entertainment, and by the education industry, with three universities as well as various other forms of further and higher education.

'Intermedia' poetry

So the phrase 'Out of transformations' in my title (taken from a poem by Matt Simpson) is intended to suggest both the major changes of recent years in the Liverpool context of Liverpool poetry, and the many innovations in scope and technique which have been a notable feature of that poetry. The poetic presence of contemporary Liverpool is a broad spectrum of groupings, affiliations, and quirky individuals (a spectrum I will try to tidy up at the end into three broad 'spheres'), but in looking for some linking theme or orientation I would pick out, firstly, what might be called 'intermedia poetry'.[2] I am reviving this slightly dated term and using it to denote poetry which works in tandem with other arts, such as music, art, photography, genre fiction, or film. It is, in other words, poetry operating in a kind of extended 'ekphrastic' mode which seems to me particularly characteristic of what has been taking place in the city in the past few years.[3]

I will cite three examples of 'intermedia' work, the first an instance of what I initially took to be 'straight' ekphrasis (the kind in which a poem 'simply' describes a picture). The poem is 'We Meet at Last', and it occurs in Matt Simpson's collection *Cutting the Clouds Towards*.[4] Like many 'Liverpool' poets, Simpson does service abroad, and before leaving the UK to undertake a period as writer in residence in Tasmania, he had come across a book called *My Home in Tasmania*, the journal of the nineteenth-century writer and artist, Louisa Anne Meredith, who had

2 The term is of Canadian provenance and 1990s' vintage, and originally denoted texts which incorporated word and image in patterned or quasi-pictorial form. It fell out of use because this kind of activity was somewhat superseded by 'hypermedia' techniques.

3 'Ekphrastic' poetry is the kind which is (in the broadest sense) 'about' a picture or photograph, sometimes in an oblique or indirect way. 'Intermedia' poetry, in the way I am using the word here, is a more general term for work which exists in specific conjunction with other art objects – whether it be music, performance, art, or other forms of literature.

4 Liverpool: Liverpool University Press, 1998.

emigrated there from Birmingham. Simpson had read the journal and written a sequence of poems relating to Meredith before visiting Tasmania. The poem 'We Meet at Last' (consisting of seventeen brief couplets) is written in response to a photograph of her which formed the frontispiece of her book, and which (most unusually for an ekphrastic poem) is reprinted in Simpson's collection on the page facing the poem. The poem begins with an apparently simple description:

> This is what
> you look like then?
>
> An obvious
> charmer still,
>
> hand on shoulder
> fingering curls.

But the poem has already shifted out of its apparently simple ekphrasis when it uses the word 'still'; this word ought to have a simple 'fixing' effect, setting Meredith within her own time and place, with 'still' meaning 'at the time the photograph was taken', implying the thought 'even though you were then middle-aged'. But the connoted secondary meaning is 'even now', indicating her posthumous effect on the writer, and highlighting the romantic aura of the photograph, which is designed to look like a painting, with that 'soft-focus / pre-Raphaelite look / the men all like'. The speaker-poet himself, of course, is one of the men who like this look, so that the poem knowingly sets itself up as a description of a long-anticipated romantic encounter ('We meet at last'). The poet in the poem *seems* to be speaking to the woman herself, addressing her as if she were actually in front of him, but are these really *speakable* words? The phrase 'An obvious / charmer still' might be *thought* at such a moment, but surely not *said*, for that word 'still' registers the fact that she is now getting on a bit, and the phrase 'an obvious charmer' is not without its ironic edge. So the words in the poem must be envisaged as being performed 'musingly' or 'inwardly', rather than spoken, so that even this most apparently simple ekphrastic situation quickly develops complicating overtones.

The 'intermedia' element here, then, is a certain ekphrastic 'openness' and ambivalence: the poet is speaking 'with' the woman in the picture, but not 'to' her exactly, just as in his earlier work he was so often speaking 'with' his dead father, but not 'to' him, and to say 'of' him would make the writing seem much less intensely engaged than it actually is. In fact, as this implies, *Cutting the Clouds Towards* is not a complete break away from Simpson's earlier work, for it constantly overlaps and juxtaposes past and present, father and son, speaker and persona. The uneasy relationship between the tough Bootle sailor/docker father and the academic son – who never went to sea, but went to grammar school, then Cambridge, then into a career as a lecturer – is the bedrock of the earlier work which made Simpson's name, most fully represented in *An Elegy for the Galosherman*.[5] Thus, in going to Tasmania for a writer-in-residence post, the poet is repeating a frequent voyage of his sailor father, and in becoming involved in a romantic 'retro-attachment' he is echoing what he suspects happened to his father in the same part of the world.

There are also some excellent supplementary 'after-poems' on this father/son theme in Simpson's newer collection *In Deep*,[6] including 'Casting Off', 'Out There', and 'A Last Photograph of My Father'. The archetypal father–son conflict Simpson so acutely details is also about the fraught relationship between the old Liverpool of ships, docks, and warehouses and the new city of culture, entertainment, and education. I sometimes wonder what the nineteenth-century docks engineer and architect Jesse Hartley – the stern Victorian father-figure of the old Liverpool – would think of the city now, a place as busy as ever, but where probably not too much goes on that he would recognize as a proper day's work. Hartley's massive 'Cyclopean' masonry and louring, beetle-browed dockside clock towers can over-awe the imagination of Liverpool school-children. Indeed, the brutal scale of Hartley's works remains overwhelming even to the adult imagination.[7] So the abrasive and never-settled dialogue between generations in Simpson's work is part of that mutually uncomprehending relationship between the city of then and the city of now. But in *In Deep* Simpson moves the dialogue forward to his own adult life, re-visiting the scenes of an Anglo-German marriage between partners who, as children, had been on opposite sides in the Second World War, and who now seem to negotiate across a

---

5   Newcastle upon Tyne: Bloodaxe Books, 1990.
6   Beeston: Shoestring Press, 2006.
7   I note an element of this in Paul Farley's most recent book: in the poem 'I Ran All the Way Home' he says 'I remember dark green seawater sloshing against Roman numerals and dock steps'.

scarred, no-man's-land terrain. In the title poem, for instance, the speaker is swimming lengths in a pool, a space which is savoured like a truce-zone that is 'out of the noise of battle':

> Keeping my head down, I hear your voice,
> but not the words you speak,
> bouncing from blue-glazed tiles.
>
> It's not so much that I'm not listening.
> Just not hearing. In deep. Not up to but over
> my ears, searching the bottom for quietness
>
> and trying to keep steady, alternating lengths
> of breaststroke, crawl.

Down in the depths, he contemplates the mosaic emblem on the pool floor – two dolphins (reproduced on the cover of the book, ekphrastic-fashion, again) which have a way 'like saucy lovers of touching one another' – and then he reluctantly emerges, and 'Goggles off and heavier with each step, / I wade out to shower, asking what you said'. For much of this book, Liverpool has been left behind (a run of titles goes 'Twin Beds in Venice', 'Abroad Again without You', and 'Voices from an Island', the last being a short sequence based on *The Tempest*), but the final poem, 'The River on a Black Day', stages the *nostos*, or return of the wanderer. The setting is Liverpool's Landing Stage, as the Mersey becomes the Styx, across which the souls of the dead are ferried. The speaker contemplates the wild November riverscape, 'fists of wind / slamming in from a blurred North Wales', and imagines his own ashes 'poured in slow grey sift/ over a ferryboat's side'. 'Will you be there to see me off', he asks, 'searching moodily into the clay-brown river?' Her ashes, he speculates, will end up on her beloved grandfather's grave in the cemetery in Berlin, while his are distributed across the oceans:

> You in the heart of fought-over Europe,
> me wafting about in the Gulf Stream,
> under the old-salt gaze of seagulls, finally, fatally adrift.

So the son imagines himself finally at sea, placating the 'old-salt gaze' of the sea-gulls which are so strongly associated with the father in much of his earlier work. Simpson, then, continues to extend the explicit political reach of his concerns and now writes in a manner which can be both more unguarded and more multi-faceted than before.

A more strictly 'intermedia' work by a Liverpool poet which juxtaposes a book world and the world of contemporary reality is Deryn Rees-Jones's *Quiver*,[8] in which the juxtaposed book is a hypothetical crime narrative or film noir, which the protagonists seem to have strayed into, and which overlaps ambiguously with present-day Liverpool, the narrative viewpoint being 'anchored' in the perceiving persona of Fay Thomas, a 'poet with writer's block'. She becomes a murder suspect when, while running 'one morning in a local cemetery, she finds the body of Mara (her husband's former lover)', who has been 'pierced with an arrow like a fallen bird'. Subsequently she is questioned by the police, sees Mara in the street and goes to a rendezvous with her, tracks the movements of her geneticist husband, and at the climax of the events, she and the husband dine in Liverpool's Chinatown as the start of the Year of the Horse is celebrated. An attempt is made on their lives, just as the police had predicted, and the solution of the mystery is revealed. But the story has a feminist running motif, and mythic archetypes are juxtaposed with the present-day action. For instance, the Actaeon myth is featured, with the hounds that pursue him named after heroines of the feminist tradition. The irony is played up, as poor Actaeon is torn to pieces for the crime of peeping at Artemis in the bath. The comic-epic moment, with its Tam O'Shanter-style pursuit (in which Actaeon doesn't have Tam's luck), dramatizes some of the contradictions within Artemis, who is goddess of both 'childbirth and chastity', a masculinist rather than a feminist brief, one might have thought. The hallucinatory or fictive overlay of the action is multi-layered: for instance, in the poem 'White Nights' (p. 58), the insomniac protagonist is interrogated about the number of Raymond Chandler novels she can name, and in 'Good Cop, Bad Cop' (p. 28) the pair 'must practise their clichés till they know them by heart / say their lines … as they play their part'. The city is present throughout, but in a hyped-up, self-consciously noirish way, not a place, really, but a place-in-a-film, even when its streets are named, as in 'Liverpool Blues' (p. 27). The doubling motif (of father and son) seen in Simpson is strong in *Quiver* too, as in the pairing of Fay Thomas and her best friend Erica, who is also pregnant, a bringer of cheering 'tea in willow pattern cups', with 'pregnant belly eight months heavy'

8 Bridgend: Seren, 2004.

and 'hair a corona of auburn curls'. She is part of a Good Muse/Bad Muse pairing in which she is the more benign Muse counterpart to the dangerous and threatening Mara figure who spreads *angst* and division. This 'doubling' idea echoes the many other examples of the pairing of partial opposites, a motif in which notions of identity, in the context of a post-colonial Liverpool are explored (the two dragons, for instance, where West and East collide).

Adrian Henri's *Lowlands Away*[9] is 'intermedia' in a more literal sense than the first two examples, since it is a poetic sequence which has a precise personal and biographical 'deep context', a multi-layered inter-textual relationship with incorporated texts of various kinds, and what might be called a musical 'co-text', since *Lowlands Away* is the libretto for a modern oratorio of the same title. The oratorio is the result of a visit made by the composer Richard Gordon-Smith to his relatives in Maldon, Essex, in 1990, when he was shown the last letter written to the family by his great-grandfather, Captain George Gentry, in 1895. The letter was a real-life 'message in a bottle', cast into the waves when the Thames and Medway barge *Cynthia*, which he owned and captained, was lost with all hands in the North Sea in that year. Poignantly, *Cynthia*'s cargo on that trip was a consignment of empty mineral-water bottles, which were being taken back to the Apollinaris bottling plant on the Rhine. The composer says that the phrase 'farewell to all we love' from the letter haunted him for months: 'As the copper-plate writing of the beginning of the letter gives way to a more desperate hand, I could almost see the water lapping round the writer's boots and hear the howling gale' (sleeve notes). The main thematic material of the music is based on *Cynthia*'s registration number – 21361 – as applied to a major scale. Thirteen short written pieces were provided for *Lowlands Away*, six having been selected from various sources by the composer, and the remaining seven composed by Henri.

One striking fact about the material is the extent to which the poet

---

9 *Lowlands Away* is an oratorio with music by Richard Gordon-Smith and words by Adrian Henri, first performed, by the RLPO, in 1996. A CD recording was released by RLPO Choir and Orchestra/ RLPO *Live* RLCD 303, printing the full text in the sleeve notes. Substantial selections from the work were included in Peter Robinson (ed.), *Liverpool Accents: Seven Poets and a City* (Liverpool: Liverpool University Press, 1996), pp. 39–45, but the order, selection and presentation of the material is somewhat different. A book version of *Lowlands Away*, with eight pastel images by the poet, was published by the Old School Press (Hinton Charterhouse, nr Bath) in 2000.

seems to minimize the presence of his own words in the final libretto. In the preface to his section of the Liverpool anthology *Seven Poets and a City*,[10] he writes that in the eighties, because of writing poems for children and writing for the theatre, he began to practise dramatic monologues, which he describes as 'one's own voice using a borrowed voice',[11] which I see as yet another version of the 'doubling' motif already noted in Simpson and Rees-Jones. He describes a trajectory in which there is a gradual movement away from 'own voice', through a 'borrowed voice', a process which must end in the use of 'other voices' (though this last phrase isn't used by Henri). A connection might be seen here with the work of Carol Ann Duffy, a long-standing friend of Henri's in her early career period and a student at Liverpool University in the 1970s, for she too makes extensive use of the 'voiced' poem in which an oblique or 'angled' persona engages in a form of dramatic monologue. It's a movement, perhaps, from 'individualism' to 'collectivism', a progression which is particularly important in Liverpool poetry, and it is based on an emerging notion of the poet as one who channels the voices and experiences of others, so that this sequence expresses 'the lives and tragedies of Liverpool's mariners over the centuries', even though the location of this particular tragedy is elsewhere. One indication of this 'collectivist' stance is the act of self-effacement, whereby the words of others take precedence over the poet's own words. Thus, three of the seven items composed by Henri are really 'found poems', since they are mainly just alphabetical listings of the names of Thames and Medway barges, arranged into four-line stanzas, each having three lines of names, followed by a refrain line, on the pattern:

> Aidie Ailsa Agnes Mary
> Abergavenny Alice Ash
> Asphodel Atlantic Atlas
> Beyond the bay where breakers splash

Even the remaining poems are not entirely 'own voice', since they contain extensive elements of allusion, parody, or quotation, incorporating such items as traditional shanty elements, echoes from *The Waste*

---

10 The seven author statements in this volume are a valuable resource for students of Liverpool writing.
11 Robinson, *Seven Poets and a City*, p. 37.

Land, and lines from Tennyson. Thus, the poet isn't so much *professing* a theory of impersonality as *enacting* one, for the poet acts as the composer's verbal assistant, and Henri comments in *Seven Poets and a City* that '"Write me a storm" is one of the strangest requests of my career' (p. 36). Indeed, the libretto taken as a whole is a joint composition/compilation, for the composer trespasses on the librettist's territory by selecting the version of the ballad 'Lowlands Away' which would be used, as well as the three scriptural texts and the children's rhyme.

When Gerard Manley Hopkins (himself a reluctant 'Liverpool Poet' for a couple of years), told his Rector in 1875 how affected he had been by reading the account of the wreck of the immigrant ship *Deutschland,* the Rector said that he 'wished someone would write a poem on the subject', as if this were the natural response to such an event. In 'Lowlands Away' the poet uses the words of the last message sent by the victims of the shipwreck. In this sense, 'intermedia' becomes its own literal meaning, implying things mediated or intercepted, rather than direct and one-dimensional, and this connects with a deep-lying sense of Liverpool as always wilfully and determinedly 'off-centre', always, in some sense 'elsewhere', an off-shore island that happens to be attached to the mainland, but doesn't really belong there. (As a child I thought the signs that said 'No litter in Lancs, thanks' were about somewhere else, and wondered what they were doing in Liverpool.) There seems, at any rate, an affinity between this 'elsewhere' attitude and the impulse to produce poetry which isn't unambiguously 'placeable' as poetry – or rather, yes, it's poetry, but not as we know it. In the same way, Liverpool has paintings and sculptures which aren't in the gallery, but are outside on the pavement (like John King's 'Case History' outside the LIPA building on Hope Street, where the sculpted piles of luggage seem to epitomise this same need to keep moving, moving, that is, both into, and out of, the city.

Elsewhere, in fact, is the title of an important collection by another Liverpool poet, Michael Murphy.[12] His epigraph from Walter Benjamin neatly embodies the notion of leaving Liverpool, migrating there, and returning there which is prominent in so many of these writers: 'You have to have approached a place from all four cardinal points if you want to take it in, and what's more, you have also to have left it from all these

---

12 Beeston: Shoestring Press, 2004.

points.' The volume includes pieces like 'The Leaving of Liverpool' and 'Bootle Odyssey' (which is dedicated to Matt Simpson), but also poems which engage with the wider poetic tradition, such as the iconic 'Night Feed', which boldly sets up an implicit interface with Eavan Boland's well-known poem of the same title and about the same subject. The poem intervenes in Boland's interventions on the role of the woman poet, re-claiming a poetic topic which has arguably been the territory of women's poetry in the (Liverpool-)Irish tradition at least since Yeats's 'A Prayer for My Daughter'. Further, the father/baby poem tradition arguably goes back at least to Coleridge's 'Frost at Midnight', but Coleridge uses the occasion mainly to write about himself, as, indeed, does Yeats, whose poem is in implicit dialogue with Coleridge's, just as Murphy's is with Boland's. But Boland and Murphy both stay in the held moment, avoiding the 'back projection' and 'forward projection' which are the main substance of both the Coleridge and Yeats pieces. Both, too, have the moment of the child's eyes opening, and both set the peace within the room in the context of a surrounding suburb and its wildlife – this is Murphy:

> I whisper her name. She opens her eyes
> to starlight on the outskirts of a town
> where black hills kneel and a sclerotic owl
> brings an answer to the fieldmouse's prayer. (p. 47)

It is a poem in 'Kristevan' mode, seeing poetry as a vast network of inter-textuality (as envisaged by the French theorist Julia Kristeva) in which poem speaks to poem across generations and traditions.

Paul Farley

Paul Farley is one of the 'quirky individuals' among Liverpool poets whose work has achieved wide acclaim since the appearance of his first book, *The Boy from the Chemist Is Here to See You*, in 1998. His collection *The Ice Age*[13] opens with 'From a Weekend First' in which the poet, seated in the buffet car of a train speeding south, raises a glass to 'my homeland scattering by', looking, in that quintessential Liverpool way, at what seems another country – 'this is *England*', he has to remind

13 London: Picador, 2004.

himself. As the glasses set for dinner in the empty dining car 'are tinkling at a bend', he drinks his pinot noir 'on my expenses', and ponders his reflection in the glass as the landscape darkens, conscious of the fact that 'the miles of feint, the months of Sunday school, / the gallons of free milk, all led to here'. Like Simpson's, this is the trajectory out of the working class 'elsewhere within', and the train motif is familiar in (for instance) the work of the 'Hull' poets (another 'off-shore' or 'elsewhere' city), particularly in the writing of Sean O'Brien, who made it a major feature of his collection *Ghost Train*.[14] The poem 'Special Train' sets the keynote of that book, as the speaker rides in 'authentic discomfort', in 'carriages that smelled of when everyone smoked'. 'Weekend First' likewise sets the keynote of Farley's book, conveying that light-headed sense of dislocation which is a characteristic sensation of the grammar school boy or girl projected by education into another world, another country. But the country of the home town past has inevitably become unreal too, and there are poems about painful re-visits, such as 'The Landing Stage', in which the revenant brings a wheelchair-bound relative quelled by Alzheimer's to this spot, to see if familiar sounds and smells will revive her dormant spirit:

> I'm hoping the river's moods and play of light
> might kindle a sentence, or raise you from the deep
> and empty stare that gives nothing back.

Since 'the deepest strata are slowest to fade', he speculates that she is wandering somewhere in her own distant past, 'in that job straight out of school', for instance. The returned exile is 'talking into the wind' unheeded, but saying what? Well, what he says seems to concern the unstoppable force of de-industrialization, rolling through all things and obliterating lives and places like a Wordsworthian force of nature – the grey river of her childhood, with 'its tons of cadmium and mercury' (if you fell into the Mersey, according to childhood lore, they rushed you straight to hospital to have your stomach pumped) is now reverting to its own distant childhood, so that 'salmon are jumping the Howley Weir above Warrington'. Likewise, in 'An Erratic', the glacial boulder from Cumberland which was placed outside Wavertree District Library in 1908 becomes another painful image of dislocation. The boulder was

14 Oxford: Oxford University Press, 1995.

always referred to by Liverpool children as a 'meteorite', but its imagined magnetic properties are long dimmed, and now it stands grimly for 'scruple and endurance'.

In 'Thorns', the major poem in the collection, another natural object, namely, the thorn bush, represents similar qualities. This is a much longer poem (twenty eight-line stanzas), presumably receiving its originating impulse from Wordsworth's 'The Thorn', one of the less successful poems of *Lyrical Ballads,* which has twenty-three stanzas, and uses the thorn bush in its remote Lakeland setting as an emblem of suffering, endurance, and concealment. Farley's poem begins with the high-up overview that he is fond of – here, it is the viewpoint of a climber in the Lake District, looking round at a thousand feet up and catching sight of a thorn bush – 'the solitary black mass of a thorn / growing out of grey rock'. The remainder of the poem is about the meaning of the bush, or rather about its *significance* to a very specific perceiving sensibility, one whose eye is inexorably drawn to it, and whose 'ear was led' there by 'the song-flight / of a shrike on its way to the nest'. The poem then begins to knot into hard-edged thickets like the bush itself, on which this critic may well end up impaled like something in the shrike's larder. As I read it, it voices the trauma of urban dislocation, which is the great repressed trauma of the post-war British experience, virtually unrepresented in post-war literature, mainly because it only happened to working-class people. Decanted from the central districts of the city, like Farley's family in 1971, and posted 'twenty [bus] stops to "that midden"' [that is, Halewood] they were supposed to be grateful for gardens, bathrooms and central heating in the fake rusticity of the outer-city estates, where streets were named anything but streets ('the Groves and Brows and Folds') and lined with 'caged saplings', and with the thorn bushes that for Farley epitomise these places – as he says:

> I look back on that time as into a thornbush:
> never some easy flashback,
> more a tangle to be handled with due care.

Following one of the branches 'that twist and snarl' brings him to 'my grandfather', a First World War veteran decanted to the outskirts with the family in old age, and still caught on the 'millions of kilometres of wire' that lined the Western Front. A 'teenage Volunteer' catching 'the first whiff of phosgene', he 'pisses on a handkerchief and covers his face', and then the grandfather's image dissolves for several stanzas in which the speaker's own childhood is recalled, till it re-emerges, in the following stark verse:

> All his soft tissues eaten away.
> I wanted to point the finger, to blame someone,
> to turn this bush into a voodoo doll
> reversed out; so I could impale Lubetkin
> and Luftwaffe; the faceless councillors
> and aldermen who gave the nod one day
> decades ago; all those I thought accountable
> dangling in an aquatint by Goya.

The grandfather here becomes the archetypal victim of systematic urban displacement, and those accountable for what we should call the Urban Clearances of the 1960s are held bitterly to account, including idealist modernist pioneers like the architect Berthold Lubetkin, with their white dreams of monumental social housing projects, all sculptural stairways and under-floor heating. Also arraigned are the Luftwaffe bomber pilots who began the process of demolition, and the gullible city councillors who were swept along by the post-war appetite for a fresh urban start. And he might have added our present-day urban hate figures – architects, such as the Smithsons, Alison and Peter, who translated the white dreams into the nightmare of 'streets in the sky', creating notorious disasters like Poplar's Robin Hood Gardens estate (the very name a queasy conflation of rusticity, 'heritage', and populism).

When the grandfather's face dissolves, the meditation on the thorn bush reverts to the speaker's own childhood – 'I helped build such a zareba / myself once' (a zareba being an enclosure of bushes or stakes protecting a campsite or village in north-east Africa). The den was designed to 'keep out the shite-hawks' of other local estates, and the bush now spikes pages from that childhood world (Ed McBain, Sven Hassell, *The Joy of Sex*, etc.). The thorn bush embodies the hard-edged toughness of working class life ('the grudging *alright's* between shift workers / below my window, the barking of great-great-dogs'), but then the bush begins to speak, with 'a voice I'm sure was my own', and it is the self that might have been, '*you if you'd stayed / back there until the bulldozers moved in*'. This is something like the confrontation between himself and his skinhead alter ego which takes place in Tony Harrison's *V*, and what the earlier self says, of course, is what the later self has always known, that he's still there inside us, that other one, '*the prickly pear, the spiky fucker*'. Perhaps all ex-grammar school kids from Liverpool know that, however much we cultivate a taste for pinot noir and poetry readings, we will occasionally hear our own voices, at committee meetings and suchlike, suddenly going into 'whingeing Scouser' mode and developing that intonation which, says Alan Bennett, 'gives even the most formal exchange a built-in air of grievance'.[15]

Farley registers the fraught business of class transition and the human cost of large-scale urban demolition, which is the archetypal conflict, again, between the old Liverpool and the new. Now, in the middle of the first decade of the twenty-first century, the construction cranes are once more visible across the city's skyline. It is urban renewal time again – leisure complexes, covered shopping plazas, entertainment facilities, and the kind of buildings which make 'statements'. Again, there will be a price to pay, for every site cleared clears away somebody's childhood or youth or favourite adult haunts, removing a piece from an urban jigsaw which for them will never fit together properly again. Are we repeating old mistakes? The Thames in London, and the Solent in Southampton are hardly visible now from anywhere in those cities because of the crowding riverside presence of prestige offices and residential apartment blocks. That exhilarating 'opening out' feeling which the sight of a stretch of water gives is now only for the privileged, for those who live or work in the riverside offices, or for diners in the expensive restaurants and wine bars. The airless shopping citadels with their ear-battering noise levels are patrolled in the day-time by 'Security' and locked at night, leaving a dead lump in the heart of the city which requires a detour of several blocks for anyone eccentric enough to have strayed out of the designated leisure zones. Collectively, they drag the city centre off-centre, imposing somebody's corporate plan on everybody. The greatness of a poem like Farley's 'Thorns' is that it *ex*presses what we mostly *sup*press about all this most of the time.

Farley's third collection, *Tramp in Flames*,[16] further consolidated his reputation. Explicit Liverpool material includes 'Liverpool Disappears for a Billionth of a Second' (an elegy for his friend the Irish-American poet Michael Donaghy who died in 2004), and the poem 'Brutalist', which renews the attack on the decanting of people to outer-city estates

15 Quoted by Katie Wales in *Northern English* (Cambridge: Cambridge University Press, 2006), p. 119.
16 London: Picador, 2006.

– 'Try living in one' it begins – the 'cellarless, unatticked / place' where all the old furniture looks out of place. As in the earlier books, there are tightly focused poems about objects from the remembered past, full of that unique intensity of nostalgia which has been one of Farley's trademarks since the prize-winning poem 'Laws of Gravity' in his first book. Here, in 'Automatic Doors', for instance, it is the revolving doors of the Walker Art Gallery, 'a glass and darkwood turbine' where 'We'd spin for hours / or so it seemed'. Today's light-sensor doors, the doors of 'a new era of doors', just don't match up. They jump nervously out of the way as we approach, and we feel ourselves displaced into 'an era of never even having to lift a finger'. The ambitious longer poems are here too, such as 'Civic', which has twenty-one seven-line stanzas evoking the distant soul of the city (Manchester, in this case) from the pine trees around the reservoir ('a great glassy sheet, / dark trees and hillsides held upside down / in starlight'), and meditating on the uneasy balance of nature and culture. Another example of a longer poem is 'Requiem for a Friend', also in memory of Donaghy, a rather troubled, uneasy piece, unsure of its ultimate destination, though it does achieve at the end a sense of balance between the living and the dead, like a re-enactment of the Simpsonian generational struggle. In a sense, the conflicts within the family are shifted into a kind of 'anxiety of influence' in which poets stake out room for themselves in the face of the brooding power of strong predecessors. The book ends with another of the long poems, 'I Ran All the Way Home', which has seven pages in a long-line, litany format with each item beginning 'I remember', each obsessively pared down and resolutely 'unpoetic' – 'I remember being scared of bottle rockets and having my hair washed', and 'I remember the medicine cabinet and the meter cupboard / and the bin shed and the airing cupboard'. Again, destination is a potential problem with this kind of poem – should the memories be chronological and cumulative, and if so, where should they end? Farley solves the problem by ending with the decisive break into a new life:

> I remember my first night in London. It was a shared room
> in a hostel in Knightsbridge, and somebody had carved
> *I stumbled into town* into the headboard.

So the writing begins with the poet stumbling into another town, the metropolis, rather than the 'elsewhere' of Liverpool, a moment which is like a *reprise* of the scenario of 'Not Fade Away' in Farley's first book,

The Boy from the Chemist Is Here to See You, where the plane crash survivor walks from 'a cornfield deep in drifts' to 'the outskirts of a town / that felt, with all its ploughed streets and neon, / like stepping from a page'.

'Other' voices, 'parallel' lives

Though the poet Sean O'Brien – another of Farley's 'strong predecessors' – has recently become a pretty ferocious critic of 'radical' or 'experimental' poetries, his essay collection *Deregulated Muse*[17] proclaimed a newly democratized or 'deregulated' poetry world characterized by its 'disavowal of a single presiding Oxbridge-London centre of taste and judgement' (p. 20). O'Brien's publishers described this account of contemporary UK poetry as 'the most inclusive book of its kind', and it was the culmination of a series of books in the mid-1990s which saw a fresh 'dialogue' or state of 'new relations' between the 'experiential' mainstream of poetry and the 'experimental' margins. In 'experiential' poetry a stable 'I' relates or represents personal experience and reflection in a more-or-less direct and unproblematical way: in 'experimental' poetry, by contrast, such stability is replaced by shifting, multiple perspectives, by experiments in modes of perception and representation, and by varieties of 'play' with linguistic and poetic forms. Many commentators see increasing cross-over between the two modes since at least the 1990s.[18] Though they are undoubtedly to varying degrees 'deregulated', Simpson and Farley could be seen as predominantly 'experiential' poets, but the predominantly 'experimental' mode is also strong on Merseyside, even if (in classic 'deregulated' fashion) the names from one camp will often occur in the venues, journals and reading series that supposedly belong to the other.

One distinctive area, however, is that covered by the 'Neon Highway' umbrella. *Neon Highway* is a poetry journal edited by Anne Lenkiewicz which was set up in 2002, and is now on-line only, at

---

17 Newcastle upon Tyne: Bloodaxe Books, 1998.

18 See Ian Gregson's *Contemporary Poetry and Postmodernism: Dialogue and Estrangement* (London: Macmillan, 1996), and David Kennedy's *New Relations: The Refashioning of British Poetry, 1980–1994* (Bridgend: Seren, 1996). I 'buy' the dialogue/new relations/deregulation thesis in my *Contemporary British Poetry and the City* (Manchester: Manchester University Press, 2000). The best account I know of the 'experiential'/'experimental' divide in UK poetry is the article 'The Two Poetries' by Ken Edwards in *Angelaki*, 3.1 (April 2000), pp. 25–36.

http://www.neonhighway.co.uk/, with a linked poetry readings series under the same title which has been running since 2003. *Neon Highway* is a link to the avant garde or 'parallel tradition' of British poetry – radical, experimental, alternative – which has affiliative links to the so-called 'British Poetry Revival' of the 1960s and '70s. The BPR, in turn, was essentially a continuation of the tradition of modernist experimentation which originated in the 1920s and '30s, with strong American influences, such as early Eliot, Pound, and William Carlos Williams, and later the Beats and the New York Poets of the 1950s and '60s, and the 'Language Poets' of the seventies and eighties. *Neon Highway* has featured poetry, interviews, and readings by key figures from this UK 'parallel tradition' of poetry, such as Maggie O'Sullivan, Allen Fisher, Lawrence Upton, Ken Edwards, Bill Griffiths, and Steve Sneyd. The existence of *Neon Highway* on Merseyside keys the region in to a distinctive sphere of contemporary poetry activity, formerly in open conflict with the 'centre'.[19] The best available account of this 'other' tradition is Robert Sheppard's *The Poetry of Saying*,[20] Sheppard being a Professor of Creative Writing at Edge Hill University in Ormskirk, from where *Neon Highway* originated.

A very different grouping, at least superficially, is the Dead Good Poets Society (DPGS), currently based at the Everyman Bistro (details at http://www.deadgoodpoetssociety.co.uk/evening.html), where it provides 'open floor' sessions in the Everyman's famous 'third room' on the first Wednesday of the month, and 'Guest Poet' nights on the third Wednesday. In fact, there is considerable overlap between *Neon Highway* and the DGPS in terms of personnel, and my impression is that the two poles are more 'deregulated' in Liverpool than elsewhere, perhaps typi-

---

19 For an account of the high period of conflict between 'mainstream' and 'margins' see my *Poetry Wars: British Poetry of the 1970s and the Battle of Earls Court* (Cambridge: Salt, 2006). For examples of this 'Other' poetry see such anthologies as Ric Caddel and Peter Quartermain (eds), *Other British and Irish Poetry Since 1970* (Wesleyan University Press, 1999), and Nicholas Johnson (ed.), *Foil: An Anthology – Poetry, 1985–2000, Defining New Poetry and Performance Writing from England Scotland and Wales, 1985–2000* (Etruscan Books, 2000). For a descriptive account of such work see Peter Middleton, 'Poetry after 1970', in Laura Marcus and Peter Nicholls (eds), *The Cambridge History of Twentieth Century Literature* (Cambridge: Cambridge University Press, 2004), and chap. 6, '"The British Poetry Revival" – Some Characteristics', in my *Poetry Wars*.

20 *The Poetry of Saying: British Poetry and Its Discontents, 1950–2000* (Liverpool: Liverpool University Press, 2006).

fying the 'overlap' theory again. The DGPS started in 1989 when Liverpool was still in its grim 1980s period and bad news seemed to be its daily bread (Toxteth, Heysel, Hillsborough, and the rest). The aims were towards a new spirit of city-wide inclusiveness, involving the Asian, Afro-Caribbean, and Chinese communities, centred on performance and participation. Poets and writers who first became prominent during this period include Levi Tafari, a writer who increasingly works in several different media – jazz and performance, drama, film-making, and documentary, having started in the 1980s in that period of post-Toxteth Council-funded initiatives. His most recent collection is *From the Page to the Stage*.[21] The spirit of this kind of work was evident in the spring 2006 'Poetry in the City' festival, in which the emphasis was very much on the collective rather than the individualistic aspects of the poetry, for, as the publicity material memorably said:

> This festival does not celebrate the poet as an individual but the individual poet as part of a community, as part of a city, as part of Liverpool ... Poets in Liverpool do not wander lonely as clouds – they are too busy ... performing in bars, reading in theatres, running workshops, producing magazines, collaborating with other artists, musicians, dancers, talking to each other, talking to people who are bored by poetry, talking to people who are in love with poetry, helping those writing a poem for the first time or the thousandth time, helping others explore their senses, their ideas, their emotions as well as finding words for their own experience – and finding language that is strong enough for the task.

In the twenty-first century, arts funding and sponsorship are closely geared to this 'collaborative' approach – poetry has 'clients' and meets identified 'needs' and 'aspirations', helping to further desirable ends like social integration, personal development, and inclusiveness. Further, the work in question isn't restricted to places of entertainment like bars and theatres, but is just as likely to be found in schools, youth centres, libraries, and even prisons. The emphasis on Liverpool experience might at first seem parochial, but the key figures on this scene often have major standing both nationally and internationally, such as Tafari, again, who works extensively abroad as well as in the UK, using the persona of the 'urban griot', the 'griot' (pronounced 'gree-oh') being a West African

21 Oxford: Headland, 2006.

term for a community's 'traditional consciousness raiser, storyteller, newscaster, and political agitator'.[22]

Another important figure long associated with the DGPS is Jean Sprackland, now resident in Southport, her most recent collection being *Hard Water*.[23] Like Rees-Jones and Farley, she was one of the twenty poets promoted as the 'Next Generation' in 2004. Her five-part sequence 'No Man's Land (Poems for the Central Reservation of the East Lancashire Road)' ends this collection of pieces which are often bizarre and surrealist in tone and content. Who, for instance, in the first of the East Lancs poems, is the man who walks the central reservation?

> Every day I walk this tightrope of tarmac,
> blown toppling in the wake of juggernauts.
> I walk it to learn the line of the road,
> to keep my place on it.

Back home in the evening, the dinner his wife serves him tastes of diesel, his head is full of 'the endless falling cadence of the traffic' and 'The flannel's black when I wash my face at night'. Why does he do it? Is he a kind of redemptive Ancient Mariner figure *des nos jours* who somehow expiates our sins as he walks the line? He (if it is still him speaking) seems to protest in the second piece about environmental waste and pollution ('You can buy a roll of fifty black sacks for a pound. / They hang flapping in trees and no one bothers to free them'), and the last poem of the sequence (which I will quote entire) seems acutely aware of the fragility of the global ecosystem, and furthermore seems to have despaired of our ability or inclination to do anything about it:

> A butterfly shrugs in Sefton Park
>
> and a tsunami
> drowns every lighthouse
> from Kirkby to Castelfield.

22 Information from the British Council's 'Meet the Author Kit' on Levi Tafari at http://www.teachingenglish.org.uk/download/britlit/levi/levi.shtml. For downloadable video files demonstrating Tafari's unique reading style go to http://jech.bmj.com/misc/poems.shtml. This site has a series of eight poems on environmental health themes, with video and audio performances made at Windsor Street School, Liverpool.
23 London: Jonathan Cape, 2003.

> Again and again
> The dark wave arches and shatters.
> What help now
> on this treacherous spit?

> A wrecker's moon rises.

Sprackland's East Lancs Road piece is a poem whose words relate to a series of pictures and have a strong political edge, whereas the work of Mandy Coe, while just as hard-edged politically, consists in one case of pictures without any words at all. *Red Shoes* (Good Stuff Press, 1997) tells a tale of prejudice and social discrimination, but it does so without using any words, taking the form of a series of full-page graphic images which show the wearers of minority red shoes discriminated against by the majority, whose shoes are black. It draws on the highly politicized tradition of the graphic novel, or *bande dessinée,* and the sequence of the images can be viewed at http://www.graphicwitness.org/contemp/mandy.htmLink. It is a truly remarkable resource, perhaps rather unnecessarily glossed and explained on the cover blurb:

> Living within a Black Shoe World and denied their own language, Red Shoe people *speak in pictures.* Meeting in secret, their tales of discrimination and cultural division unfold in a language common to us all.

Coe's work as a whole testifies to the enormous advantages to a poet of regular contact with audiences via workshops in schools and local communities, but her work is by no means confined to this 'performance' sphere, her collections including *Pinning the Tail on the Donkey,*[24] and more recently *The Weight of Cows.*[25] Shoestring is run John Lucas, and is fast becoming one of the most prolific of the small press poetry publishers – presses like Bloodaxe, Carcanet, Salt, Shearsman, Shoestring, and Seren publish the vast majority of new poetry in the UK, but most of these are probably not familiar names even to people who occasionally buy poetry books (which is, of course, a tiny proportion even of the book-buying public, let alone of the public at large).

24 Liverpool: Spike, 2001.
25 Beeston: Shoestring Press, 2004.

Presses with regional affiliations, like the Brodie Press, sometimes move regions when founder members do so, as was the case with this one, founded by undergraduates at Liverpool University in 2002, and since re-located to Bristol, and now aiming to support readings and events in the two cities. A significant book published by Brodie in 2006 was Peter Robinson's *There Are Avenues*, which is set in suburban south Liverpool, and which he started writing in 1984, began publishing in 1991 (the earliest part in *English* in 1991), and completed in 2004. Like several of those considered here, Robinson is both a poet and academic; he was based for many years in Kyoto in Japan, and is now returned to the UK to a post at Reading University. Robinson's 'territory', then, is suburban Liverpool, evoked at times with McCartney-like nostalgia, not 'blue suburban skies', but:

> Ah yes, but there are avenues;
> and not far now, above us,
> see the mackerel cloud-forms
> moving across a full moon's disc
> luminously marbling
> like end-papers an inky sky.

This is not the world of the inner-urban dockside terraces, and the family background hinted at is the 'quarrels and silences' of the vicarage, rather than full-scale rows and generational conflict. The sequence is shot through with reticence, about the friendships and courtships which are obliquely glimpsed, and about the 'angry words' said long ago which are now 'petrified' and beyond un-saying. Like others whose work has been considered here, it's about the place the poet is 'from', but no longer quite 'of'. The life-long chain of return visits follow a familiar pattern, arriving on the train via the 'cutting walls of moss and fronds' into Lime Street Station, then being met 'at the barrier' – a barrier which remains in place throughout – and then, while being driven 'home', noting 'a derelict warehouse', 'a gap-toothed or toothless horizon, / a fresh sense of what's gone'. The tone is sombre – what is left are the 'ornate pubs rounding off their street corners' (usually with the streets they once rounded off long ago demolished). There is much 'emptied dockland', many 'deserted grain stores', and (worse) the 'maritime folk museum' of the Albert Dock, and the pretend Art Deco hotel which used to be an airport. The meaning of these experiences is hard to pinpoint, and the root sensation of return is honestly conveyed, which is a sense of ultimate bafflement, of something which is nearby, but always just out of range:

> But like so many childhood scabs,
> those meanings just evaporate
> here in the silence of now –
> this posthumous sensation, this late
> feeling I should have foreseen;
> and, yes, it's like the slabs
> that glint through privets, shrubs, and trees
> had petrified our angry words,
> translated, buried them
> in such overcrowded ground.

Coming back implies seeking answers, forgiveness, reconciliation, a perceived teleology, or even just acceptance and understanding, but the strength of this difficult and stoical book lies in its admission that none of these things seem to be there waiting. Somehow, between then and now, they slip beyond us.

Yet another important figure with great breadth of activity is the poet, short-story writer and performer Dinesh Allirajah, one of the founders of the North West writing group 'Asian Voices, Asian Lives' whose story collection *A Manner of Speaking* is published by Spike Books. Allirajah is one of the writers linked with the Windows Project, a charitable trust whose brief is to 'diffuse the knowledge and appreciation of language as a creative medium, thus improving the facility in that language … for those who have need by reason of their youth, age, infirmity or social or economic circumstances'. The project, based at 96 Bold Street in Liverpool, also publishes the magazine *Smoke*, and mounts an intensive programme of workshops and play schemes – an amazing twelve hundred, it is claimed, in 2003 – for people with mental or physical difficulties and in areas regarded as educationally deprived. The pieces in *A Manner of Speaking* challenge generic boundaries – like those suitcases on the pavement – acting as narrative prose-poems, as we might call them, exploiting the rhythms and idioms of the 'performing' voice, that is, the voice of the person telling a joke, or a story in the pub, or at a dinner party. The narrative detours and back-tracks which occur in such situations, and the little ironic, self-deprecating touches and self-corrections, are worked into the flow, so skilfully that they work 'performatively', as it might be called, on the page. They are sharp out-takes of demotic actuality, urban narratives somewhat in the tradition of the Ronnie Corbett joke-style, in which the detours and asides proliferate in a baroque manner, displacing the ostensible 'joke' and becoming the 'real' joke. This can be seen, for instance, in 'The Frank Sinatra Joke':

> As it is, I can't say when I started liking Frank. It may have started in Lisbon, when I was 15 (a very good year for Falklands War and Keith Burkinshaw) and I bought a cassette of his Greatest Hits. His Greatest Hits – and get a load of this – Volume Two. I bought a whole second volume – me, from a 2-minute-43-second culture in which the greatest bands' genuine hits couldn't fill an EP!

Here, the 'voice' performs the telling, but the print on the page also acts 'performatively': thus the capitalization in 'Greatest Hits' and 'Volume Two' is entirely ironic and (so to speak) 'deflationary', and has nothing to do with the print convention of capitalizing titles: '15' and '43' (rather than 'fifteen' and 'forty-three') reinforce a sense of informality, and the omission of the 'the' before 'Falklands War' commodifies that conflict, turning it into a background element in a childhood, and pairing it with football manager Keith Burkinshaw. The pairing at first seems arbitrary, but Burkinshaw was the Spurs manager who brought the Argentinian World Cup stars 'Ossie' Ardiles and 'Ricky' Villa to Spurs in the late 1970s, providing that team with a mini golden age and successive FA Cup wins in 1981 and 1982. The handling of the material allows 'meta-fictive' comment on the construction of the story itself, as the speaker continues, 'Perhaps it started [liking Frank] when I was – bear with me, it'll help the flow if I say I was 21 … but I reckon I would still have been 20.' Here the reader is entrusted with the task of suspending disbelief and accepting an age of twenty-one for narrative purposes, while also knowing that the age in actuality was twenty, thus highlighting the gap between the world-in-the-telling and the world in actuality.

Allirajah's work increases my overall sense of the predominant nature of poetry in Liverpool, which is that the three great 'spheres' of poetry, while they are distinct areas, are also, in this city, constantly cross-fertilizing and intermeshing. By the three 'spheres' I mean, firstly, what might be called the 'fine-art' version of poetry, published in high-prestige national presses, written about by critics in academic books and journals, and quite often these days produced by poets who are teaching on creative writing programmes in universities. In the past, these creative writing posts (where they existed at all) were short-term and part-time, but today they are established faculty positions, increasingly mirroring the situation in the United States, where creative writing has long been taught on MFA (Master of Fine Arts) programmes. The second sphere is the world of performance poetry operating in bars, clubs, and theatres, often linked with jazz, dub, rap, or reggae, a world of 'open floor' nights, 'poetry slams', and local poetry workshops, often with their spin-off magazines. This is a world of flourishing and inventive freelance performers, not a career for most of its practitioners, but an absorbing free-time activity. And thirdly, there is the sphere of poetry, writing, and performance which is linked to local council projects, charitable trusts, and to work in libraries, schools, play-schemes, and prisons. This will be career-oriented, providing the main income of its practitioners, but probably on a self-employed basis, and involving work at venues all over the region, troubadour fashion, almost, by people strongly committed, not just to writing poetry, but also to progressive social policy and ideals. To repeat, what is distinctive about the Liverpool situation is the extent to which the three spheres seem to draw upon each other, and the way many individuals have a presence in at least two of the three. Indeed, perhaps the best work arises out of the transformations which occur when all three spheres are in contact of some kind with each other.

Overall, the distinctive feature of Liverpool poetry has always been its emphasis on the oral, an emphasis which includes a certain knowing edge that comes from an awareness of (and of the audience's awareness of) the subtle feints and shifts which are part of the act of telling. This element is as marked today in the work of writers as different as Farley and Allirajah as it is in the work of Henri, Patten and McGough. Archibald MacLeish's '*Ars Poetica*' (the art of poetry) ends with the famous pronouncement 'A poet should not mean / But be', which it reaches via a series of such proclamations ('A poem should be motionless in time / As the moon climbs', and so on), all of which envisage a poem as a kind of contemplative, art-for-art's-sake icon standing somewhere over and above life as most of us actually experience it. That ideal is about as far away from the spirit of Liverpool poetry as it is possible to get.